# ORGANIZATIONAL CHANGE AND DEVELOPMENT IN MANAGEMENT CONTROL SYSTEMS: PROCESS INNOVATION FOR INTERNAL AUDITING AND MANAGEMENT ACCOUNTING

# STUDIES IN MANAGERIAL AND FINANCIAL ACCOUNTING

Series Editor: Marc J. Epstein

STUDIES IN MANAGERIAL AND FINANCIAL ACCOUNTING
VOLUME 10

# ORGANIZATIONAL CHANGE AND DEVELOPMENT IN MANAGEMENT CONTROL SYSTEMS: PROCESS INNOVATION FOR INTERNAL AUDITING AND MANAGEMENT ACCOUNTING

BY

**SELESHI SISAYE**

*Duquesne University*

2001

JAI
An Imprint of Elsevier Science

Amsterdam – London – New York – Oxford – Paris – Shannon – Tokyo

ELSEVIER SCIENCE Ltd
The Boulevard, Langford Lane
Kidlington, Oxford OX5 1GB, UK

First edition 2001

Library of Congress Cataloging in Publication Data
A catalog record from the Library of Congress has been applied for.

British Library Cataloguing in Publication Data
A catalogue record from the British Library has been applied for.

ISBN: 0-7623-0745-5

⊛ The paper used in this publication meets the requirements of ANSI/NISO Z39.48-1992 (Permanence of Paper).
Printed in The Netherlands.

# CONTENTS

# LIST OF TABLES AND FIGURE

## TABLES

**FIGURE**

# INTRODUCTION

The book, *Organizational Change and Development in Management Control Systems: Process Innovation for Internal Auditing and Management Accounting*, addresses process innovation, an area that has recently attracted research in behavioral managerial accounting. Organizational change and development entails a wide range of areas including innovation, diffusion, organizational learning, population ecology, contingency theory, and organizational growth and productivity. Measuring quality and improved organizational performance have now become two of the most important objectives in management accounting reports. Yet, the extents to which process innovation strategies of total quality management (TQM) and reengineering have been integrated into accounting research have been limited.

This book contributes to that integration by drawing from the sociological theories of process innovation, diffusion, organizational change and development. First, the book applies systems analysis to describe organizational change, development, transformation, population ecology and transactions and their relationships to management accounting and control research. Second, it broadens the scope of topics covered by quality and process innovation in both teaching and research of managerial and cost accounting courses at undergraduate and graduate levels. This book covers several organizational change and development topics, including leadership, acquisition and diversification growth strategies, organization design, collaboration and organizational management, ethics and quality education. These topics are examined within the context of management accounting and control systems.

It should be noted here that the terms 'management accounting' and 'accounting control' are used interchangeably. In general, accounting control systems function for internal use to assist managers in the day-to-day internal administrative control operations of the organization. Similarly, the phrases 'reengineering', 'process reengineering' and 'business process reengineering' (BPR) are also used interchangeably. They describe radical innovation strategies in organizational restructuring, design and implementation.

Accordingly, the book is divided into four parts containing eleven chapters and five appendices. Parts I and II – Chapters 1 through 6, discuss the sociological theories of organizational change and development. Part III –

Chapters 7 through 11, describes process innovation change strategies of TQM and reengineering within the context of internal auditing and management accounting and control systems. Part IV contains five appendices, which elaborate on specific issues of organizational growth and development. These issues include acquisition, diversification, collaboration, accounting ethics and quality education, quality costs, and the implications of reengineering on the design of internal auditing and accounting control systems.

A brief description of the contents covered in the chapters and appendices is provided below. Part I has three chapters. It outlines the adaptation and selection theories of organizations and accounting systems. Chapter 1 reviews the adaptation – stability, crisis, leadership and institutions- and contingency theories of organization management. Adaptation change provides the underlying rationale for some organizations to selectively adopt process innovation. Chapter 2 discusses population ecology and organizational selection as strategies for innovative change. Chapter 3 applies systems analysis to discuss changes within the broader context of the external environment, the contingency factors of organizational change and development strategies affecting management control systems.

Part II is divided into three chapters, which present in detail the adaptive systems approach to process innovation changes in accounting control systems. Chapter 4 discusses two adaptive systems approaches of organizational structures – mechanistic and organic – which provide the context for different types of organizational changes. Also, two types of organizational change: gradual-incremental and revolutionary-radical are introduced in Chapter 4. Chapter 5 suggests that successful organizations, regardless whether they adopt incremental and/or radical organizational innovation strategies are always in the process of continually practicing organizational learning principles of first-order (convergence) and second-order (double-loop and reorientation), which achieve planned organizational outcomes. Chapter 6 further elaborates on the relationship between culture and leadership characteristics – trait, functional and situational – and organizational development (OD) intervention strategies. It presents OD as an incremental process innovation change strategy. The OD approach has been applied to study the TQM innovation strategy in Part III.

Part III, which addresses process innovation and reengineering in internal auditing, and management accounting and control systems, has five chapters. Chapter 7 provides an overview of the innovation, adoption, diffusion and organizational change – incremental and radical – strategies as they apply to accounting and internal auditing systems. While Chapter 8 discusses TQM as an incremental innovation change, Chapter 9 reviews process reengineering as a radical innovative change strategy. Chapter 10 further elaborates on the differences between TQM and reengineering for process innovation changes in internal auditing and accounting control systems. Chapter 11 presents two types of incremental change strategies – technical and administrative innovations. The chapter discusses internal auditing and accounting control as part of the administrative structure in organizations, and analyzes process innovation changes in accounting control systems within the context of administrative innovations.

Part IV has five appendices, which discuss in detail several issues that are central to both organizational change and development and process innovation strategies. Appendix 1 presents two types of external oriented organizational growth and development strategies, diversification and absorption, as alternatives to internal growth strategies through process innovation. Appendix 2, prepared by Eileen S. Stommes, applies systems theory to advance the importance of collaboration in facilitating change in the management of scarce resources shared by several divisions or agencies. Collaboration corroborates TQM's strategy of gradual-incremental change in management of organization activities. Appendix 3 applies the incremental and radical-consequential approaches to accounting ethics and quality education that influence organizational process innovation. Ethics and quality education are inherent in process innovation and shape the future direction and success of an organization's innovative changes. When innovative changes disrupt existing organizational order, ethics and quality education can be used as building bridges to restore order and maintain/improve organizational performance. Appendix 4 documents several cases where TQM incremental strategy has positively changed the method of accounting for production and quality costs while bringing about performance improvement. In contrast, Appendix 5 uses the radical-reengineering strategy to outline a five step approach for the design and implementation of internal auditing and accounting control systems. Appendices 4 and 5 provide evidence that organizations can simultaneously implement the incremental (TQM) and radical (reengineering) process innovation strategies to achieve planned organizational change and development to accomplish targeted performance objectives.

The book has been structured to present organizational change and development strategies for process innovation changes in internal auditing, and in management accounting and control systems. Examples and cases are provided to demonstrate that both TQM and reengineering approaches can be instrumental for ensuring consistency in changing internal auditing and accounting control systems with management innovation strategies and planned organizational performance objectives.

As such, the book's contribution lies primarily in the field of behavioral managerial accounting research. Sociological approaches have recently gained attention in accounting research. Historically, sociological theories have valued the importance of multidisciplinary approaches in the study of organization change and development. This book has expanded on that tradition by applying sociological theories of organization change and development – population ecology, organization selection and transactions, systems analysis, contingency theory and diffusion of innovations, to study changes in management accounting and internal auditing systems. TQM and process reengineering are presented as specific process innovation approaches, which can bring about either incremental or radical organizational change and development in management control systems, particularly in internal auditing and accounting control systems.

The study of process innovation, organizational change, TQM and process reengineering are of interest to faculty and students who teach and conduct research in behavioral accounting and organization management. Innovation and change are primary preconditions for organizational change and develop-ment. As the population ecology and selection framework suggests, those organizations that do not value change either decline or decease. Internal auditing and management accounting play significant roles in organizational change and transformation. Thus, it is imperative for accounting researchers to examine internal auditing and management accounting systems within the broader context of organizational change and development.

Accordingly, the book can serve as a reference source for faculty and students involved in management accounting education and research in graduate programs. The book is also of interest to managers and practitioners in business organizations who want to appreciate the importance of sociological approaches in process innovation changes for internal auditing and management accounting and control systems.

Writing this book was both challenging and rewarding. I have been able to integrate sociological theories of process innovation strategies and social diffusion theory to analyze the quality movement and its impact on management accounting systems. This book gave me an opportunity to expand and integrate my research on TQM and process reengineering and devote time to write an in-depth analysis on the subject. For the last eight years, I have researched the area of quality control/management and organizational change and development. Throughout this book, I have enriched both the breadth and the depth of analysis by adding new materials and recent developments in organizational change and process innovations from the current literature.

I updated, revised and rewrote several of my publications and incorporated them into the following chapters and appendices. Sisaye (1998c) has been integrated in Chapters 1 and 3; Sisaye (1998a) in Chapters 1 and Appendix 1; Sisaye & Bodnar (1996 and 1995) in Chapters 8, 9 and Appendix 5; Sisaye (1999, 1998(b) and 1996) in Chapters 9, 10 and 11; and Sisaye (1997a) in Appendix 3. Eileen S. Stommes prepared Appendix 2 on 'Collaboration and Organizational Management Systems Approach to Inter-Divisional Collaboration'.

## ACKNOWLEDGMENTS

This book project could not have been started and completed without the support and encouragement of Marc J. Epstein, Editor of *Studies in Financial and Managerial Accounting* Series for JAI Press. This is the second project that I have had the pleasure to work with Marc. I am indebted to Marc for his continued assistance over the years and for making it possible to successfully complete the book project on time. I would also like to thank Susan Oppenheim and the editorial and publications staff of JAI Press, for their assistance and cooperation in the preparation and publication of the book.

I would like to acknowledge the support and cooperation of the administrative and editorial staff of the following publishers who authorized copyright permission of my articles to be used in this book. They are: Elsevier Science Inc. for two articles published in *International Journal of Applied Quality Management*, Vol. 2, No. 2, 1999, pp. 279–293; and Vol. 1, No.2, 1998, pp. 117–127; JAI Press for an article published in *Research on Accounting Ethics*, Vol. 3, 1997, pp. 233–244; American Accounting Association for an article in *Behavioral Research in Accounting*, Vol. 10, Supplement 1998, pp. 11–26; MCB University Press for an article in *Leadership & Organization Development Journal*, Vol. 19, Numbers 4 and 5, pp. 231–255; and the RIA Group of Warren, Gorham & Lamont for three articles, one published in *Internal Auditing*, Vol. 11, No. 4, 1996, pp. 37–47; and two articles (co-authored with George Bodnar) in *Internal Auditing*, Vol. 11, No. 3, 1996, pp. 16–25; and Vol. 10, No. 1, 1995, pp. 19–31.

Duquesne University has supported my scholarship and research publications over the last fifteen years. I was granted sabbatical leave during the Fall Semester of 1999 and awarded a course reduction during the Spring 2000 semester to work on this book. I would like to thank Drs. John Murray, President and Michael Weber, Academic Vice President and Provost of Duquesne for their support in my scholarship endeavors. The A. J. Palumbo School of Business and the John F. Donahue Graduate School of Business

Administration have continuously supported my research. The Accounting Division Coordinators, Ken Paige and Sharon Green, have both supported my research and extended technical and financial assistance to ensure its completion.

A number of other individuals have also supported my book project. I would like to express my appreciation to my colleagues at Duquesne and other institutions. I have benefited particularly from my association and research collaboration with Eileen S. Stommes and George Bodnar. For the last twenty years, I have worked and collaborated with Eileen on systems theory and organizational sociological research. With George Bodnar, I have published two articles on TQM and reengineering, which have been incorporated into this book.

I am grateful to my graduate research assistant, David Nelson for his contribution in all phases of library research. I owe special thanks to David for his diligent work on the book for over a year. He assisted in several phases of the project including database research, typing of manuscripts, proofreading, preparation of indices and references, as well as editorial assistance. It is because of his hard work and interest in the subject matter that I was able to complete the book on time. Carissa A. Revak, my student aide, provided expert secretarial assistance. She typed most of the tables, references and several of the chapters. I would like to thank all those, too numerous to enumerate here, who have offered their encouragement and support over the years.

Last, but not least, I would like to thank my family, and dedicate this book to my daughters: Sarah Laura and Anne Elizabeth Sisaye for their love and support. They shared with me both the good and bad times and willingly accepted the separation that this work entailed.

Seleshi Sisaye
Accounting Faculty,
Duquesne University
Pittsburgh, Pennsylvania

# PART I

# ADAPTATION AND CONTINGENCY ANALYSIS OF ORGANIZATIONAL MANAGEMENT AND ACOUNTING SYSTEMS

# OVERVIEW

Part I is divided into three chapters, which presents the sociological theories of adaptation and selection for organizations and management control systems. Chapter 1 deals with adaptation studies of organizational change. While there are several approaches to adaptation studies, not all adaptation studies specifically address organizational change and development and process innovation. The sociological adaptation theories of organizational change and development include institutional theory, contingency theory, and organizational transaction analysis. These theories advance the view that process innovations are central in organizational change and development strategies for internal auditing and management accounting control systems.

Chapter 2 further elaborates on the organizational selection-population ecology approach to the study of innovations. Under the organizational ecology umbrella, organizational transactions, resource dependence, and boundary spanning will be discussed. Organizational ecology, which emphasizes competition and survival within a given population of organizations, examines the effect of environment and market forces on organizational adaptation and innovation. The ecological approach utilizes a systems approach to examine the impact of internal and external environmental constraints on organizational adaptation and change.

Chapter 3 extends the ecological approach to study organizations as social systems. Systems theory studies the organization life cycle and organizational developmental stages to explain the relationship between process innovation and changes in accounting and internal control systems. It suggests that the organization's life cycle and developmental stages influence the degree to which organizations adopt process innovations.

In sociological research, adaptation and selection theories of organization entail either inductive or deductive research. Whether the focus of the theory is inductive, i.e. institutional and contingency theories, or deductive, organizational ecology approaches, both theories allow for comparative, historical, empirical, and quantitative research. However, most organizational change studies emphasize research establishing and testing causal relationships. While causal relations are difficult to establish in historical and case-oriented research, the historical approach enables researchers to examine the effect of environmental change on individuals, groups and organizations overtime (Noves 1980: 70–71).

A longitudinal study of organizational change and development is presented to understand an organization's founding history, past and present conditions which predict future process innovation behavior. Transformation and process changes, leadership styles, and environmental factors can all have an impact on the direction and type of change strategies. Parts II and III elaborate on organizational adaptation and transformation theories by examining total quality management (TQM) and process reengineering as incremental and radical innovation strategies for internal auditing and management accounting systems.

General sociological theory suggests the importance of utilizing theory to "produce causal relations revealed by their empirical research" (Kiser & Hechter, 1991: 24). This book's objective is to present both historical and case studies that are inductive and descriptive, and theory-based deductive research. The appendices in Part IV contain cases and specific applications, which expands on the organizational change and development theories discussed in Parts I, II and III. The adaptive and selection theories discussed in these appendices enable the utilization of both inductive and deductive approaches to the study of process innovation strategies in organizations. Appendix 1 discusses acquisitive and diversified organizational growth. Appendix 2 outlines systems approach to collaboration. Appendix 3 applies incremental and consequential approaches to the study of accounting ethics and quality education. Appendix 4 uses TQM as an incremental innovation strategy to evaluate changes in cost accounting systems. Appendix 5 incorporates process reengineering as a radical innovation approach in the design of internal auditing and accounting control systems. Appendices 4 and 5 demonstrate that planned intervention programs such as TQM and process reengineering can be successful if incorporated as part of overall corporate strategic planning.

Barnett and Caroll (1995) further suggest that the role of management in planned action and process innovation programs, such as TQM and reengineering, should be examined within the framework of organizational change models. A program "should be assessed in terms of both its organizational content and process relative to existing structure. For a group of such companies, TQM programs may differ, and these differences could be measured and used in assessing consequences" (p. 231). To set the context for the study of TQM and reengineering as process innovation strategies, Part I of the book discusses both adaptation and selection theories of social organization and change. Part II builds upon Part I by applying adaptive systems approaches – mechanistic vs. organic structural innovations, cultural change, leadership styles, organizational learning, development and transformation, to understand the many factors that influence process innovation changes. Part III then discusses TQM and reengineering approaches in internal auditing, and management accounting and control systems.

# 1. ADAPTATION AND CONTINGENCY ANALYSIS OF ORGANIZATIONAL MANAGEMENT AND ACCOUNTING CONTROL SYSTEMS

## INTRODUCTION

Organizations are continually changing and developing. Organizational change and development deals with those environmental, technological and ecological factors that affect process innovations in organizations. These issues have been of paramount research interest among social science and organization management researchers. Social science and organizational researchers have applied contingency analysis, systems theory, population ecology, organizational selection, and diffusion of innovations to describe the process of change and development in organizations. Sociological research has also focused on those internal and external processes that necessitate process innovation changes in organizations. The main research contribution of this book lies in studying process innovation strategies as internal process changes for management control systems, particularly internal auditing and management accounting systems.

Part I of the book reviews sociological adaptation and selection theories of organizational change and development. It discusses population ecology, selection, adaptation- stability, crisis, death and growth, leadership styles, and institutional and contingency theories to describe the relationship between organization change and process innovation in management control systems. Chapter 1 focuses on adaptation and environmental changes that contribute to both internal and external processes of organizational change and development in management control systems.

# ENVIRONMENTAL CHANGES AND ORGANIZATIONAL ADAPTATION

Environmental changes affect organizational systems, structure, strategy, functions, procedures, and day-to-day activities. The impact of environmental changes on current performance of the organization depends whether these changes are minor or significant. Whether the environmental impact is minimal or significant, organizations are primarily concerned with maintaining stability and continuity. During periods of stability, when the impact of environmental changes are minimal, organizations are less likely to change. They are able to implement incremental procedural changes that will sustain current operations of the organization with or without changing, and sustaining existing performance. On the other hand, when there are significant changes that contribute to low performance, current structures are unable to meet these changes. This requires a fundamental change in the organization's structure, strategy, and human resources. Whether the changes are minimal or significant, the adaptation process shows differences in organizational approaches and responses to environmental change.

> Damanpour and Evan (1984) suggest that: The organization-adapting function requires that as the environment changes, the structure or processes of the organization undergo change to meet the new environmental conditions. Innovative organizations tend to do more. They not only adapt to the environmental changes, but also use their resources and skills to create new environmental conditions, e.g. by introducing new products or services never offered previously. Innovations are means of providing these internal or external changes and are, therefore, a means of maintaining or improving organizational performance. The social and technical systems of an organization need to function in balance if the organization as a whole is to operate effectively (p. 395).

The question of sustaining and/or improving current performance becomes of paramount importance for organizations that face environmental changes and uncertainty. The mix between strategy and structure influences the ability of the organization to adapt to environmental changes. According to Lant and Mezias (1992), "organizations with an adaptive strategy search for information that reveals the relationship between organizational characteristics and performance. That is, they determine which mix of organizational characteristics is associated with the highest performance and adopt those characteristics" (p. 55). In other words, performance is dependent upon whether or not there exists a close relationship between current environmental changes and the ability of the organization to handle and process these changes (Lawrence & Lorsch, 1969).

Adaptive organizations thus develop networks of relationships that are open, dynamic, and capable of learning and handling situations that are of "ambiguity and uncertainty" (Bate, 1990: 100). Organizations develop networks and exchange ideas among them. They can foster cultural change to modify or alter network and organizational relationships that tend to be innovative.

Process innovation change is the main core competence in organizations, particularly in those organizations, for example, technology firms, characterized by a high competitive environment. The success of an organization depends on the ability of the organization to sustain and maintain continuous change. To remain competitive, organizations are continuously changing and reinventing themselves with new products and services.

Barnett and Carroll (1995) discussed two approaches to organizational change – the adaptation and the selection mechanism of organizational changes, which they referred to as the organizational ecology approach. Chapter 1 discusses the adaptation and Chapter 2 the organizational selection change approaches. However, not all organization models identified by Barnett and Carroll (1995) will be utilized in this book.

According to Barnett and Caroll (1995), the adaptive organizational change process "assumes that change in the world of organizations occurs mainly through the adaptive responses of existing individual organizations to prior changes in technology, environment or whatever" (pp. 217–218). Barnett and Carroll classify contingency theory, resource dependence theory, and institutional theory in the adaptive change process framework. The adaptation theory pays particular attention to the impact of external environmental factors and market conditions on organizational change and development. The analysis of the external environment and its impact on organizational change becomes the main focus of study for the institutional and contingency theories of social organizations.

## THE INSTITUTIONAL APPROACH TO ORGANIZATIONAL CHANGE

Bake, Faulkner and Fisher (1998) advance the view that markets and organizations go through at least three stages (see also Fligstein, 1987) when they get institutionalized. These stages are emergence, stability, and crisis. Emergence is when the social structures, roles, and relationships are fluid and the rules of interaction and exchange are not yet fully developed and understood. Organizational members learn and internalize these behaviors. During this period, founding leaders have substantial influence in shaping the future growth and direction of the organization (Boeker, 1989b).

In the second stage of stability, the social acts and behaviors performed by organization members tend to be recurring, persistent over time, and have a lasting impact on their actions.[1] These behaviors are transmitted across organization members. Control guidelines are developed and enforced to guide actors' behaviors, authority, management hierarchy, communication, and reporting systems.

The third stage, crisis involves a period of unrest and instability. During this period, there will be intense competition due to new entrants, exits of low performing firms and government intervention. Crisis necessitates the need for organizational change and transformation (Baker et al., 1998; Fligstein, 1987). It is in the crisis stage that process innovation becomes important for organizations to implement change. Stage two-stability, and stage three-crisis, are relevant for the understanding of process innovation changes.

## Stability

The functional view of sociology defines social organizations as rational purposive social systems (Blau & Scott, 1962; Perrow, 1986; Parsons, 1951; Scott, 1987). Its emphasis on stability and continuity has provided the foundation for the classical organization and traditional management account-ing concern on authority, accountability, and contractual relationships between supervisors and subordinates (Caplan, 1966; Birnberg, 1998). Stability and rational decision-making constitute the main contributions from the functional view of social organizations.

The functional approach described stability as the ultimate objective of organizations since it facilitated the utilization of the rational choice model for the design of management control systems, resource allocation decisions, and the provision of services to enable the socioeconomic system to function effectively.[2] Behavioral accounting research has applied the classical-functional approach to explain managers' use of formal control systems for incentives and performance evaluation, and to influence the behavior of subordinates consistent with management goals (Burns & DeCoster, 1969; Fayol, 1949; Merchant, 1985; Sisaye, 1997b, 1998c; Stedry, 1960; Fannenbaum, 1968).

Recent studies in cognitive and social psychology have extended the classical approach to examine the effect of individual and work group informal interactions on group and organizational performance. The personal and inter-personal attributes of manager (Deluga & Perry, 1994; Yukl & Tracey, 1992); leadership quality and leader-follower exchange relationships (Phillips & Bedian, 1994); and the type of control-related techniques used by supervisors to influence subordinate behavior (Lamude & Scudder, 1993) were related to individual and work group productivity. These studies support the view that control systems achieve congruence between employees' behavior and management goals.

The classical organizational control system theory has adopted the functional view of organizations, which focuses on the roles of formal organizational systems in promoting stability and continuity within the various components of organizational systems (Blau & Scott, 1962; Perrow, 1986; Taylor, 1947; Weber, 1947). Because formal structures contained inter-related and dependent sets of formal and less formal positions, these structures exhibited persistent social and management relationships.

The functional view of organizations provided the underlying principles for the traditional management accounting framework. This approach assumed that organizational members are self interested and motivated to work hard to achieve personal goals. The objective of control systems is to maximize firm profitability by institutionalizing economic rewards through contractual relationships (Ramakrishnan & Thakor, 1991). Accounting information systems take on functional roles because they facilitate the flow of information in the organization and guide employee behavior to be consistent with management goals. Management secures subordinate accountability through incentives, and controls behavior by offering economic rewards (Baiman, 1982, 1990). Corporate management has become technocratic rather than bureaucratic, relying on accounting information systems to evaluate performance and control behavior. Management control systems reinforce goal congruence, corporate values and beliefs through reward-incentive systems (Sisaye, 1995). This view has dominated most research in management control systems and corporate strategy (Langfield-Smith, 1997).

Industrial organization theory, which advanced the functional approach in sociology, has shaped most control research. Research on strategic business planning units, market portfolios and industry and competitive analysis applied industrial organization and microeconomic analysis to search for universal models in control systems (Porter, 1980, 1981, 1985, 1987; Williamson, 1975, 1987). Industrial organization theory in strategic management research focused on empirical findings to support the principle of universalistic approaches in management control, and to describe the optimal control system to maximize organizational efficiency and effectiveness. In economics, industrial organization is more concerned with understanding the structure and behavior of the industries (goods and service producers) of an economy (Stigler, 1968). Those studies represent modification to the classical theory of management in the 1960s (Birnberg, 1998). However, they did not receive much attention in accounting literature until the mid-1970s.

The functional view advanced the importance of the corporation as a dominant institution where human behavior and character "is molded through an external inculcation of supporting values and beliefs" (Dugger, 1988: 101). To become part of the corporate culture[3] that supports improved organizational performance, employees internalize these external values. The approach incorporates the recognition that external environmental contingencies influence the extent to which institutions themselves can control the behavior and performance of employees.

When organizations are institutionalized, they develop their own identity, norms, and values, which in turn provide direction, stability and solidarity to group members (Selznick, 1957). Organizational norms and values shape members' behaviors. They demonstrate loyalty and commitment by observing and abiding by them in all aspects of organizational life. Institutionalization becomes an effective process through which a planned change can be incorporated into the organization culture. "If organizational norms and values are supportive of the change, it will achieve a high level of institutionalization; if norms and values are not supportive, then the change is not likely to occur" (Buller & McEvoy, 1989: 34). When changes are introduced as planned intervention strategies, they are institutionalized. The results are observable changes on employees' behaviors, cognition, and values.

When there is homogenization among members, there is a high degree of social interaction that facilitates information sharing. There is an emphasis on stability due to the increased importance of personal ties among members. Employees develop loyalty, trust, and commitment, as their relationships with the external environment remain relatively stable. In these circumstances, the concern for the organization is on how to manage the existing relationships among employees, organizations, and the environment.[4]

Institutional stability achieved through conformity or compliance to existing norms affects social interaction, relationships, and exchange transactions. While continuity is essential to stabilize social relations, other factors such as market forces and competition may affect the continuity of the relationship. The nature of the exchange relationship depends on "... social embeddedness [which is] the formation of two types of social networks (personal ties and inter-organizational ties) that cross-organizational boundaries and promote conformity of organizational practice" (Baker et al., 1998: 159). While individual ties are based on personal attachments, inter-organizational ties involve structural attachments.[5]

In an undifferentiated social system, personal ties are important. There is balanced interaction, as the probability of access to the same information is equally available. Increased access to new information necessitates the likelihood for social differentiation and the creation of new social structures (Mark, 1998). As the number of new social structures increase, unequal access to information arises unless individuals form or belong to groups who share similar interests. Networks develop to minimize the disparity in information and resource flows.[6] Networks support the dissemination of innovation information among members.

When organizations grow over time they tend to become more complex. This complexity creates the need for the organization to be divided into sub-units or departments (Boeker, 1989a). Homogenization cannot be sustained within the organization. Grattet, Jenness and Curry (1998) suggest that in addition to homogenization, institutionalization ". . . can also produce differentiation of cultural forms and practices. Once the basic practices became institutionalized, subsequent adopters exercise liberty and expand the domain of the cultural form (e.g. the law), thus creating distinctive permutations . . . Homogenization best characterizes higher levels of abstraction; differentiation occurs at less abstract levels. Differentiation of content occurs only when the general construct is institutionalized" (p. 303). Differentiation thus allows the freedom to expand the domain of innovation.

Population growth and technological changes that improve productivity, advance specialization, and promote functional differentiation increase social differentiation. When technological advances increase functional differentiation, they create administrative and distributive needs. Society develops subsystems to meet those needs. Improvement in information and transportation technology allows interaction and communication, thereby reducing the effect of geographical distance on spatial and social differentiation (Mark, 1998). Specialization and differentiation increase the size and the complexity of the organization, and eventually change the unitary (U-form)-functional organization to the multiple (M-form)-divisional structures. The internal structures of divisionalized organizations are highly differentiated, bureaucratized, formalized, and less democratic. Managers seek to solidify their power by controlling the decision-making process for resource allocation decisions. They develop several levels of hierarchy to solidify their control over employees, consumers, and suppliers (Sisaye, 1998d).

Teece (1996) noted the drawbacks associated with the bureaucratic features of functional organizations which exhibited several levels of management hierarchy. Accordingly, "decision-making processes in hierarchical organizations almost always involve bureaucratic structures" (p. 200). There are formal procedures for budget preparations and approval, committee structures, reporting systems, and budget appropriations. Politics become important as committees "tend toward balancing and compromise in their decisions. These structures may inhibit innovations as each group attempts to appeal to its constituents. Funding decisions are based to these constituents than to the merits of the programs under review" (p. 201).

The question of politics and organizational performance is of importance to management researchers. Eisenhardt and Bourgeois III (1988) argued that politics lead to poor performance because "it is time-consuming to engage in politics" (p. 761). Politics take away time from management and diverts their attention from work and responsibilities. Eisenhardt and Bourgeois III (1988) suggest that management teams of high performance firms avoided politics while those of low performance firms used politics in strategic decision-making (pp. 760–761). They found that "where power was relatively decentralized . . . . the [management] team maintained a collaborative viewpoint. In effect, [they] found cooperative behavior focusing on group, rather than individual, goals" (p. 753). The best performing firms are those that are decentralized, less subject to political power, and share information among themselves (p. 764). Divisionalized structures that allow autonomy in decision-making tend to be prevalent in high performing firms.

While divisionalized structures are arranged to counter the coordination problems created by organizational size and manage businesses to pursue profit maximization, the corporate bureaucracy, according to Galbraith (1967), have been transformed into 'technostructures'. Corporate management became technocratic rather than bureaucratic, relying on accounting information systems to evaluate performance and control behavior. Management control systems have reinforced goal congruence through reward incentive systems, including coercion.

The corporation has thus become a dominant institution where human behavior and character "is molded through an external inculcation of supporting values and beliefs" (Dugger, 1988: 101). Employees who internalize these external values accept them as part of the corporate culture which support improved organization performance. As Dugger (1988) argued, the multiple-divisionalized form of organizational structure "has to do with the organization and control of people. The technological revolution is in organization and information rather than in production and distribution . . . the invention and spread of the new M-form lifted the limit on size; computer technology and communication advances helped lift the old size constraints as well" (p. 85). Management institutionalized several accounting standards including budget targets, profits goals, and performance evaluation systems to control management behavior, and develop commonly shared corporate culture and values among employees (Sisaye, 1997b, 1998d).

## Leadership and Organizational Change

Much of the literature on organizational management emphasizes the role of institutional leaders in organizational change and development, as well as the formulation and implementation of corporate policies and strategies. For example, Van de Ven (1986) suggests that "within the organization, institutional leadership is critical in creating a cultural context that fosters innovation, and in establishing organizational strategy, structure and systems that facilitate innovation" (p. 601). It is apparent that process innovations can be implemented effectively when they are institutionalized and integrated into the current organizational practice. According to Van de Ven (1986), "innovations must not only adapt to existing organizational and structural arrangements, but they also transform the structure and practices of these environments. The strategic problem for institutional leaders is one of creating an infrastructure that is conducive to innovation and organizational learning" (p. 605).

The leadership pattern displayed by managers is said to determine the accomplishment of corporate goals and objectives. Leadership behavior plays a central role in the cultural and political transformation processes of a firm by continuously changing the core values of employees, organizational structures, and contextual variables, and the contents of the business strategies followed by the firm (Pettigrew, 1987). "How these general managers formulate strategies and policies, and how they use strategy and policy as instruments of influence and power, will to a large extent determine whether the organization enjoys a long and useful life or whether it disintegrates in a shorter span of time" (Summer, 1980: 3).

Values, aspirations, and preferences of top management are important factors that influence the choice of strategy (Christensen, Andrews & Bower (1982): 359–365). Process innovation as a strategic decision will be affected by the personal values of the leader as well as the organizational political process that shape the power exercised by the leader.

The political subsystem of an organization "is composed of the sources, locations, and flow of power among organization members" (Cobb & Margulies, 1981: 50). French and Raven (1962: 602–613) have identified several sources of organizational power depending upon whether power is based on formal authority (i.e. the official organization position) or on the personal qualities of the leader. Sources of position power are based on reward, coercion, and legitimate power, whereas personal power refers to expert and reference power.

Table 1.1 presents the characteristics associated with leadership types: 'traditional' vs. 'modern' leaders. Traditional/bureaucratic leaders tend to rely primarily on positional power while, in contrast, modem/democratic leaders utilize personal as well as positional power, depending on the decision-making situation.

Managers use both positional and personal power to influence the behavior of employees to accomplish organizational goals and objectives. Leaders also

***Table 1.1.*** Characteristics of Leadership

| Dimensions | Modern Democratic | Traditional Bureaucratic |
| --- | --- | --- |
| Basis for leadership | A combination of legitimate and expertise power | Formal legitimate |
| Basis of power | Internal legitimate power is elected, accepted, use of both personal and positional power | External (positional power) |
| Degree of control | Managers have internal control | Strong external control through the use of budgets, variance reports and management meetings |
| Leadership behavior | Egalitarian, collegial influenced through professional norms and codes of behavior | Tendency towards charismatic and authoritarian leadership |
| Group formation | Both formal and informal groups | Emphasis on formal groups, e.g. management committees |
| Communication channels | Reliance on effective and informal communication processes that facilitate information decision-making and feedback | Emphasis on formal communication through the hierarchy channels, a less effective flow, method of decision making under conditions of uncertainty |
| Expertise power | General/specialized | Specialized (task specific) |
| Reference power | Identification | Introjection |
| Reward power | Job Context/ Job Content | Job Context Hygiene factors/dissatisfiers |
| Locus of control | Internal | External |
| Leadership style | Theory Y Consideration for Employees and tasks | Theory X Consideration for tasks. |
| Motivation factors/ Hierarchy of needs | Higher order needs (esteem, self-actualization, need for achievement) | Lower order needs (physiological, safety and social concerns, need for affiliation and power) |

use power to reduce environmental uncertainty by mobilizing organizational resources in support of their programs (Farrell & Peterson, 1982: 404).

Institutional leaders can be either charismatic-transformational or transactional-problem solving. For strategic reasons, institutional leaders can be effective if they are transformational leaders who recognize strategic problems, rather than concentrate on details of planning and problem solving. Institutional leaders thus focus on the recognition of limitations and choices surrounding innovations rather than end results. Institutional leaders can provide vision and guidance to innovation programs. They can idealize, guide, and formalize them as part of the organization's mission and strategy, ensuring they are successfully implemented.

It has been argued that leadership is effective and has the most impact at early stages of organizational growth (Selznick, 1957: 16). Strong leadership is especially critical at early stages of organizational growth since it provides direction and ensures institutionalization of organizational norms, values, and regulations.

Most executive leaders prefer to adopt incremental, gradual changes even in periods characterized by relatively sudden environmental changes. Leaders' ability for reorientation and adaptation of strategies to meet changing competitive market conditions is reflected in the performance of organizations. As organizations evolve through periods of convergence, leadership attributes are critical factors for differentiating between innovative and status quo oriented leaders. Within the context of process innovation, innovation leaders are referred to as 'modern' leaders, who are able to foster organizational renewal/ transformation changes. On the other hand, status-quo oriented leaders are referred to as 'traditional' leaders, who are unable to adapt to changes and eventually contribute to the decline of the organization (Tushman, Newman & Romanelli 1986).[7]

The distinctive management attributes of institutional leadership determines the type of growth strategies an organization will implement. As Table 1.2 indicates, patterns of leadership behavior can foster internal growth through innovation, research, and development or they can promote external growth through mergers and acquisitions. External growth through acquisitions can involve the purchase and absorption of companies in related businesses or it can involve the acquisition of unrelated businesses for the dual purpose of diversification and growth. However, diversification if uncontrolled, can become a purely political growth strategy, solely based on financial risk reduction, organizational fit, and management philosophy/cultural fit. Politically oriented growth strategies that are closely related to a leader's sources of power within the organization and are strongly influenced by the leader's desire

***Table 1.2.***   Leadership Style and Acquisition Decisions.

|                  | Approaches to Acquisition Decisions | |
| ---------------- | --------------- | ------------------- |
| Leadership Style | Political       | Rational            |
| Traditional      | Diversification Strategy | ?          |
| Modern           | ?               | Absorption Strategy |

to satisfy personal ambitions and meet the needs of intra-organization coalition may contribute to organizational disorder, stress, or crisis. Appendix 1 elaborates diversification as an externally oriented acquisitive organizational growth strategy influenced by rational as well as political factors.

## *Crisis*

When organizations grow from functional to divisional structures, there are increases in functional specialization, and organizational differentiation. These changes call for more management hierarchy and interdependency among units/divisions. Volatile changes in the environment affect the choice of organizational growth and development strategies as the needs for organizations to develop a higher degree of product/market environment interrelationships, and concentration in selected industries. Organizations characterized by a lack of product-market mix and lower average industry performance are less capable of adapting to environmental change. They are also unable to provide information and technological capability to support the innovation process. This results in the third stage, which is referred to as crisis.

Crisis calls for organization coalition groups to suspend politics sometimes for specific innovation programs that might contribute to overhaul the entire organization's program and policies. Prasad and Rubenstein (1992) examined organizational politics at the general-organizational and project specific-department in relation to technological innovation. While the general is related to the overall political environment of organization, the project organization politics is specific to the project where the innovation started. They noted that if organizational politics are not curtailed, the success of innovation programs in response to crisis is very limited. They argued that, "for example, the super-ordinate goal of beating the competition or coping with a major crisis may cause the various coalitions to put aside their interests temporarily in order to ensure survival of the firm. However, such crises are the exceptions rather than the rules" (p. 5). Even in such circumstances, there is room for certain interest groups to politically use the innovation project.

When the external environment is characterized by continual changes in technology and services, markets may become unstable, as competition increases from domestic and international firms. To compete effectively, it becomes economically advantageous for organizations to concentrate their resources in one or few industries. Organizations rely on absorption growth strategies, which are based on research and development to create improved or new products for targeted markets. To concentrate resources in selected markets, they divest marginal, unprofitable, and unrelated businesses.

Under such dynamic environmental conditions, innovative firms are likely to purchase firms whose products are related or interdependent. Growth decisions focus on absorption or concentration strategies. Rational economic motivations are predominant among such acquiring firms. Organizations attempt, through acquisition, to protect their primary business interest by working to achieve a level of monopoly power over marketing and distribution facilities. They focus on improving their strategic competitive position by upgrading product quality, controlling pricing decisions, and obtaining synergistic effects (Fray, Gaylin & Down, 1984: 46–56; Bing, 1980; Kierulff, 1981; Parson, 1984: 32–34). Related acquisitions thus become major strategic decisions that help firms reduce environmental uncertainty or directly influence their competitive environment. When an organization purposefully expands its resources by going outside the organization, such acquisitions are considered to have external political dimensions.

The power-dependence model assumes that organizations attempt to secure control of resources to minimize the threat of environmental uncertainty. At least two choices are available for organizations to reduce uncertainty (Sisaye, 1995). First, they can secure monopolistic power through absorption of companies in similar industries or markets. Second, companies can diversify into unrelated industries or markets to minimize political risks, product/market interdependencies and cyclical downturns in the economy. Some organizations choose and implement a growth strategy that centers on diversified acquisition of profitable companies. Such an acquisition strategy is based on a balanced policy of geographical and product differentiation. It may involve the use of a friendly take over strategy where top management of the acquired firms joins the new management team. The co-optation process is in line with a 'concertive control' system, whereby management attempts to centrally control the administrative management systems through high level coordination, consensus, and limited autonomy as a means of minimizing pitfalls associated with bureaucratic control systems (Barker, 1993).[8]

There are unanticipated problems associated with organizational growth strategies. When an organization is involved in any purposeful action, but most particularly when that action is a new undertaking, the organization will most probably face unanticipated problems (Merton, 1936). If an organization grows primarily by acquiring smaller firms, the bigger firms are less able to adapt to the unforeseen demands of technological innovative changes (Davidson, 1991).

Growth through diversification occurs more rapidly than internal growth achieved through research and development. Internal growth is a gradual process and occurs as an organization evolves new problem solving capabilities and develops new or improved products to serve its markets. An organization can minimize unanticipated problems associated with growth, when that growth is internally generated. It is possible to minimize the occurrence of unanticipated problems if organizational staff members associated with implementing planned changes are in a position of modifying the change processes before they disrupt organizational operations.

On the other hand, when growth is exogenously introduced, an organization may face new situations not previously encountered. Under these conditions, there is an increased potential for unanticipated problems, as the organization has not yet developed the necessary problem solving mechanisms. When an organization acquires diversified companies as part of its growth strategy, it is bringing business organizations into new areas in which they have little or no experience. A high-growth politically motivated diversification program focused on a risk reduction strategy may not be able to evolve in a timely manner, and develop adequate problem solving mechanisms to ensure smooth and profitable business operations. The growth strategy will generate a variety of unanticipated problems, including the acquisition of unprofitable firms, ineffective management of acquired firms, and potential conflict with government regulatory agencies.

Miller (1992) suggested that leaders of outstanding companies sometimes are responsible for their company's problems. He argued that success could result in overconfidence, carelessness, and other characteristics that might affect the leadership, culture, and structure of the organization. He defined the common causes of decline as focusing, venturing, inventing, and decoupling attributes. Miller's suggestions for successful organizations to avoid problems include: "(1) building thematic, cohesive configurations, (2) encouraging managers to reflect broadly and deeply about the company's direction, (3) scanning and monitoring performance assiduously, and (4) temporarily decoupling renewal activities from established operations" (1992: 24–35).

Volatile changes in the environment generate crisis and create the need for organizations to develop a growth and innovation strategy of concentration and absorption in related markets and products. The rational choice model assumes that modern/democratic leaders make choices to maximize their interests and thereby the interest of the organization as a whole. Given a set of alternatives, the rational decision maker will select the strategy that maximizes organizational objectives and benefits, while minimizing costs. The alternative selected is assumed to be independent of organized interest groups or dominant coalitions within the organization. A rational leader is expected to implement changes that are consistent with improving organizational performance. The patterns, in which process innovation changes are introduced, determine the success of the organization.

Damanpour and Evan (1984) have noted the effect of environmental factors on an organization's innovation strategies. They proposed that "environmental change or uncertainty stimulate[s] changes in the strategy and/or structure of an organization, which in turn leads to the implementation of innovations. A balanced implementation of administrative and technical innovations would help maintain the equilibrium between the social and technical systems, which in turn would lead to high performance. On the other hand, a discrepancy in the rate of adoption of innovations in the social and technical systems would retard the rate of improvement of performance" (pp. 406–407).

The institutional approach emphasizes the role of leadership in the organization's growth and developmental stages of emergence, stability, and crisis. During these three stages, an organization experiences changes in its function, structures, systems, strategies and policies. Following the functional framework, the institutional approach examined those aspects of the social system that are adaptable and amenable to change, and the role of leadership in the organization's transformation. It also noted the impact of external factors on the organization's developmental process. The institutional approach studies the impact of external environmental factors on organizational performance (Perrow, 1986; Selznick, 1957). This led to the development of the contingency view of organization. The contingency view studies those unique characteristics of the organization that adapt to environmental changes (Thompson, 1967). The contingency approach examined those particular social relationships that define a given system, where changes occur within the system, and what types of changes characterize the system. To set the social context of a given organization, the contingency approach defined the test of significance, as the functional relevance for the maintenance of social systems.

Institutional approaches in functional sociology emphasized the role of the leader in the evolution and gradual adaptation of organizational systems to environment changes. This approach recognized the importance of 'dysfunction' and the ability of organizational systems to change through a gradual, orderly, and consensual, not conflictual process. While environmental changes generate discontinuity and dysfunction in social systems, the institutional approach emphasized the ability of social systems to adapt to change (Perrow, 1986; Scott, 1987).

Social actions and structures were characterized by dominant characteristics, which shape regular relations of autonomy and dependence in social interactions. These social systems are continually shifting and adapting as leadership resources, skills, roles, positions, and structures change over time (Giddens, 1987). Contingency theory extended the functional view by providing a causal explanation of how some systems persist by adapting to innovation changes, while others disintegrate. Accounting and control studies expanded the scope of the contingency approach by studying change and adaptation in control systems (Fisher, 1995; Otley, 1980).

## CONTINGENCY THEORY AND THE STUDY OF COMPLEX ORGANIZATIONS

Contingency theory has its roots in the open systems framework. The approach views organizations as being made up of several inter-related social systems. Institutional theory in organizational sociology advanced the importance of contingency theory and the study of organizations in relation to their environment (Thompson, 1967; Lawrence & Lorsch, 1969; Aldrich, 1979; Scott, 1987). Systems theory and its impact on the study of organizations as interdependent systems, the definition of functions and formal positions as part of a particular social system and analysis of a structure in relation to its environment highlighted the importance of contingency theory in organizational sociological research.

Contingency theory focused on organizations as open social systems with unique characteristics. It shifted the research focus of the classical theory's search for universal organizational principles to the development of contingency guidelines, which apply to a specific organizational environment. The external environment now included technology and markets, as well as social, demographic, economic, political/governmental, and socio-cultural systems (Thompson, 1967; Lawrence & Lorsch, 1969; Otley, 1980; Fisher, 1995). Contingency research examines organizations in relation to the external environment in which they operate (Donaldson, 1987; Lawrence & Lorsch, 1969). Contingency research in the external environment includes major subsystems such as technology, markets, social, demographic, economic, political/governmental, and socio-cultural systems (Thompson, 1967; Litschert & Bonham, 1978).

Since the external environments of organizations often become dynamic and hostile, organizations can survive in the long run only if they adapt to such changes. However, this adaptive change process is seldom a smooth and continuous process. Rather, it shifts between periods of refinement or convergence and those of discontinuity or upheaval (Tushman, Newman & Romanelli, 1986).

Within the contingency model, "strategy emerges as a mediating variable which defines the relationship between the organization and its environment" (Litschert & Bonham, 1978: 213). Strategy has become a process through which a firm utilizes its resources or competencies to maximize environmental opportunities, while minimizing potential threats raised by the environment (Porter, 1987).

The analysis of current and future environmental trends has thus become the principal starting point for the strategic planning process (Steiner, Miner & Gray, 1982). To a large extent, the success of strategic planning depends on the 'fit' between the external environment and internal resources of the organization (Child & Smith, 1987; Grant & King, 1982). The effectiveness of such efforts continues to be of concern to practitioners and researchers (Hitt & Ireland, 1986; Grant, 1988).

Based on industry type and environmental uncertainty, contingency theory can provide organizations with an understanding of the "situational nature of strategic management." In addition to providing managers with "if-then perspective models," it can also develop 'if-then' decision-making guidelines tailored to a specific organization (Ginter & White, 1982: 254). Appendix 1 applies the contingency approach, which suggests that strategies developed for a particular firm, may not be applicable to another firm facing similar conditions. It suggests that there is a need to develop differential strategic plans for each firm according to its environmental (e.g. dynamic or stable) conditions and types of businesses it operates, particularly when an organization chooses to implement an externally oriented growth strategy. In addition, the contingency framework has also received a great deal of research in accounting literature as researchers approached changes in accounting systems as being influenced by external environmental factors and externally oriented change strategy.

# CONTINGENCY THEORY AND ACCOUNTING CONTROL RESEARCH

Within the contingency framework, corporate strategy and control systems were studied as mediating factor, between the organizations and their environment. Strategy is a process by which a firm utilizes its resources or competencies to maximize its environmental opportunities and minimize potential threats raised by the environment (Porter, 1987). Management control and accounting systems not only support competitive strategies, but also enhance the effectiveness of those strategies (Cunningham, 1992; Simons, 1995). Managers may show preference toward either rational or political behavior or may choose to apply both approaches in strategic decisions (Dean & Sharfman, 1993).

Analysis of current and future environmental trends became important in strategic control research. Contingency theory largely drew from the ecological approach of organizations. This approach analyzes how the environment and technology shape strategy, and affect the distribution of power, influence and control in organizations (Pfeffer & Salancik, 1978). Boeker (1989b) extended the ecological approach to study relationships among functional areas and subordinate power, strategies adopted by organizations, and the "environmental imprinting at founding," i.e. the prevailing environmental conditions when an organization was founded (p. 389).

Contingency theory greatly expanded the scope of strategic and management control research by emphasizing the 'fit' between external environmental factors and internal resources of the organization (Grant, 1988). Contingency research analyzes the components of the organization, structure, and cultural settings (Baligh, 1994) and the firm's ability to innovate and adapt to these changes (Child, 1970; Grant, 1988). Environmental scanning was used to test the effectiveness of contingency variables in strategic decisions (Yasaiardekani & Nystrom, 1996). Contingency theory's use of situational analysis on firms and industry types and environmental uncertainties provided research with an "if then" perspective to develop an "if then" decision framework tailored to a specific organization and its control systems. This approach led to the proliferation of case studies coupled with survey and field research methodologies on management control systems (Fisher, 1995; Merchant & Simons, 1986).

Fisher (1998) advances the contingency approach by reviewing contingency theory, management control systems, and firm outcomes. He suggests that the assumptions utilized within contingency theory have been too narrow. The theory focuses not only on the unique, situational characteristics of control systems, but also the environment in which some control systems have a better fit. On the other hand, critiques of contingency research suggest that while the research has generated several contingency studies, it has not yet developed a comprehensive contingency theory of accounting (Chapman, 1997). However, Fisher (1998) points out that contingency approaches have enabled researchers to develop generalizations about control systems relative to business and organizational settings. By studying contingency factors in different business settings, Fisher concludes that some generalizations about control systems could be made about specific business settings. Accordingly, he identifies five contingent control variables: uncertainty; technology and interdependence; industry, firm and unit variable; competitive strategy; and mission and observability factors. These factors can be either endogenous or exogenous to the organization, and can affect organizational outcomes, performance measurement, resource allocation, and rewards distribution.

Fisher classifies contingent control research into four levels of analysis (from simple to more complex levels) depending on the complexity of the contingent, control, and outcome variables used in the study. He then goes on to suggest potential research areas in contingency control research. Some of these included: casual relationships of multiple variables; study of control systems in relation to other organizational aspects; human resources policies and cultural systems; non-financial factors such as cycle time, lead time, frequency of orders, and production performance factors; and financial (budgeting and standard cost systems) factors. He calls for change and new directions in contingency control research that would move from financial to operational and production control factors critical to organizational performance.

For example, given current changes in the manufacturing environment, contingency approaches could be applied to explain variations in organizational process adoption strategies, relating to just-in-time and activity-based costing methods for improving cost accounting systems. Chapter 3 applies contingency analysis, derived from social systems theory to study process innovation strategies in accounting and control systems.

The sociological adaptation theories – institutional, contingency, and transactional analysis discussed in Chapter 1 have documented that environmental, technological and ecological factors contribute to both internal and external process changes in organizations. As organizations evolve from simple functional to divisional, and then to complex forms, these changes have been accompanied by process innovation in management control systems. Management accounting and internal auditing systems change in response to organizational quality and productivity needs, competitive strategies and environmental pressures for continuous change. Process innovation strategies in internal auditing and management accounting systems have now become central to both organizational development and changes in management control systems.

Chapter 2 expands organizational adaptation studies by applying organizational ecology to organizational change and development. In contrast to adaptation theory, the organizational ecology approach stresses the importance of competition and survival within a given population of organizations over time.

# NOTES

1. In economics and industrial organization theory, the stability stage involves the development of hierarchy of firms in a given market or industry. When explaining the structure of the economy, the institutional approach suggests that "economic activity is defined in terms of industries or broader sector such as manufacturing and services. The relative size of these industries and sectors are measured by indicators such as manufacturing and services" (Seal, 1990: 267). The approach recognized that relative size and number of firms in the industry and the locus of control be examined when looking at structural aspects of the economy. It looks at the process of economic activity as a basis for analyzing "competition, institutions, and production" (Seal, 1990: 267). In economics, industrial organization is more concerned with understanding the structure and behavior of the industries (goods and service producers) in an economy (Stigler, 1968).

2. Rational choice decisions are expected to be intentional and consequential. They operate on the principles of optimization for the objective good of the organization. Accordingly, the management principles involve planning, organizing, communicating, controlling, and coordinating (Morgan, 1986). If conflicts arise in the organization, they are resolved on how seriously they affect organizational goals and the number of people involved in the conflict. In resolving the conflict, "the rationality tactics consist of using reason, logic, and compromise in attempting to influence" (Brass & Burkhadt, 1993; 447). It assumes congruity of interests between the individual and organization, even though societal goals might not be easily quantifiable. While the function may or may not be exclusively rational in neo-classical economic terms, structural-functional approach (SF) includes non-economic rational organizational and cultural issues essential to the maintenance of the social system.

Williamson (1987) noted that early study of organizations focused on the function of the organization. "Purposive organization was emphasized, but the limits of human actors in bounded rationality respects and the importance of informal organization were predominantly featured" (p. 551). Bounded rationality has been defined as an intended rational behavior. It refers to humans limited ability to formulate and solve complex problems as well as in processing and transmitting information (Simon, 1957). These studies also noted the problems associated with complex organizations such as centralization, uncertainty, and problem solving. Williamson (1987) summarized them as follows: "Hierarchical organizations and associated controls are traced to the limited capacities of human actors to cope with the complexity and uncertainty with which they are confronted." While the organization handled problems, these "organizational efforts are often myopic, and demands for control can and often do give rise to dysfunctional outcomes." In these studies, "core technologies, domains (or boundaries) of organized action, and the powers and limits of market and hierarchical modes are all recognized" (p. 551).

In the early literature of organizations in the 1970s, Williamson noted there was an emphasis that "the study of organizations was a comparative institutional undertaking in which alternative governance structure – both within and between firms and markets – required explicit attention." While transaction cost was recognized, it did not receive attention due to the trade-offs involved between economizing production costs and factors that affect production such as "conflicts that lead to delays, breakdowns, and other malfunctions." (p. 552).

3. The SF approach considers organizational culture when attempting to describe the decision-making processes (Kilmann, 1984). Organizational cultures change are more likely to occur as organizations grow over time or their environment changes. Culture plays a central role in the formation of social structure and the distribution of power and resources in society (Sewell, 1992). Organizations incorporate certain beliefs, myths, knowledge, values, norms, perspectives, and attitudes that provide structures of resources for guiding the participation of members in organizational activities. When these ideologies are consistent and can be easily understood by members, they can be used to empower members, mobilize resources, and identify appropriate implementation actions. They help focus the selection of alternative choices, a rational choice process, which considers all possible actions before selecting the best alternative.

4. Beckett-Camarata, Camarata and Barker (1998) have stated the importance of relationship management as follows. For them, "relationships between the organization and its employees, from the new internal/external customer perspective, would need to be conceptualized and managed as long-term organizational investments and recognized as the means with which to build core competencies and to take advantage of the opportunities embedded within such relationships. Such competencies, once built, could not be readily replicated by competitors. They would offer the firm long-term strategic advantages in the market place. Opportunities enmeshed in a complex, uncertain, and emerging marketplace could not be tapped by competitors who are not a part of the trusting, committed, supportive, and enthusiastically, managed network of social exchange and equity based intra- and interfirm relationships" (p. 79).

5. Market forces, competition, mergers, and acquisitions might contribute for the dissolution of social relationships, including structural ties. Baker et al. (1998) suggested that mergers and acquisitions pose a threat to structural attachment. They indicated that "when companies merge, agencies may be dropped due to supplier redundancy (duplication of capabilities), conflicts of interest, or simply the power of the dominant party in the merger to break the structural attachments of the other party. The effect of mergers and acquisitions on dissolution should depend on whether the client is the *acquirer* or the target (the acquired company). Mergers usually involve the union of unequal parties; the target falls under the management and control of the acquirer. The acquirer is more likely to keep its agencies and drop the target's because it wants to integrate the target's products and services into its own advertising strategy, or because the acquirer wishes to preserve its structural attachments to its own agencies" (p. 161. italics in original). They stressed that when there are client-agency tie, "the departure of a top executive [management] *lowers*-the hazard of dissolution of client-

agency ties, while the arrival of a new executive has no effect. Individual attachments established with an in-house agency significantly lower the risk of dissolution of a tie with such an agency . . ." (p. 167. italics in original).

6. Networks support reciprocal relationships that sustain open, long-term and sustainable relationships. In reciprocity, the members know each other and attach value and importance to the exchange process. Plattner (1983) advances the view that in reciprocity, "the terms of any particular commercial exchange (the value exchanged) have meaning far beyond the money-for-goods domain, since the current trade-making up for a past imbalance or looking forward to a future one" (p. 849).

Not all networks exhibit reciprocal relationships. Where there is centrality in networks, there is a lack of open and supportive relationships since centrality provides access or control to valuable information and resources. Baker et al. (1998) recognized the importance of centrality in networks. They stated that "an agency that occupies a central position in the network of economic exchange is more valuable to its clients than an agency in a peripheral position, because the central agency gets better, faster, and more information about market conditions, new marketing ideas, competitors' actions, consumer trends, and so on. Access to information provides power" (p. 158).

7. Lant and Mezias (1992) proposed that organizations identify key leaders and try to imitate their characteristics. They search for information on their leaders, industry strategy, and legitimize themselves by imitating them. They pointed out that "size functions as the proxy for the designation of which firms [are] industry leaders. Firms search and identify the largest organization in the population and adopt the characteristics of [these] industry leaders." (p.55).

8. Tracy (1993) assumes that in every organization, department, unit or division, there is a decider – i.e.; a leader, who makes decisions, and set[s] purposive goals for the organization. In a larger organization, there are many layers and levels of leaderships (management hierarchy), where each leader has a defined responsibility. When there are many leaders, conflict arises due to differences in goals and divided loyalty to the organization. Managers attempt to use their power and influence to resolve conflicts among units/divisions (p. 227).

# 2. SELECTION AND ORGANIZATIONAL INNOVATION CHANGES

## INTRODUCTION

Chapter 1 applied the adaptation framework to explain differences in organizational approaches and responses to environmental changes. Organizations can adopt an incremental change strategy during periods of stability and a radical change strategy during periods of crisis and environmental volatility. Chapter 2 presents the organization selection view, which advocates the importance of competition and survival within a given population of organizations.

The selection approach to organizational change "assumes that individual organizations cannot change easily and quickly; it also assumes that when they do change, great risks are entailed. By this view, when technologies and environments change, some existing organizations fail, while some new organizations also appear. The selective replacement of old forms of organization by the new forms constitute the main way this mechanism accounts for change in the world of organization" (Barnett & Carroll, 1995: 218). The selection process goes through periods of evolution and ecological adaptation. In this chapter, both the organizational ecology and evolutionary theory are examined. Many studies have suggested that these approaches have significant relevance to the study of process innovation and change (Aldrich, 1979; Hannan & Freeman, 1984).

Chapter 2 discusses the population and organizational ecology approaches to process innovation. Within the context of ecological theory, the effects of organizational transactions, power dependence and boundary spanning on innovation changes are also examined.

27

# ECOLOGY AND ORGANIZATIONAL CHANGE

Broadly speaking, the ecological approach considers the environment or physical habitat, level of technology (including culture), social organization and population characteristics (for the theoretical background see Duncan, 1961) in a given society. It examines the effect environment and market forces have on organizational adaptation processes. It has shifted the nature of organizational studies from that of a purely cultural explanation to that incorporating the environment as an interactive factor in cultural practices of organizational systems. Ecological approach has thus enabled researchers to examine the impact of social and spatial groups, location, geology, level of technology, and patterns of land use in the development of organization density and population. It recognizes that there are internal and external environmental constraints on organizational adaptation and change.

The ecological approach explains changes within a population of organizations, similar to that of the institutional approach. More importantly, the ecology framework suggests that environmental shifts lead to the development of new policies and procedures to address these issues at the institutional level. Any substantial shifts in the environment call for changes in strategies and policies to maintain organizational stability and functional adaptation. Thus, ecology places the environment as an important factor in the organizational adaptation and selection process.

According to Frisbie, Krivo, Kaufman, Clarke and Myers (1984), the ecological approach comprises four dimensions: population, organization, environment and technology. Of these four factors, technology has the most impact in human population adaptation to change.

*Technology*

Technology plays an important role in the study of class relations, forces of production, division of labor and societal change evolutions/transformation. In human ecological theory, technology forms the basis for organizational competition, survival, resistance and change. According to Frisbie et al. (1984), technology is based on formulations "which recognizes three ecosystem flows – energy, materials, and information – as basic to the survival and adaptation of populations" (p. 751).

Technology is the main factor that accounts for most theories of societal evolution, including the radical and incremental approaches to social change. Technology not only increases the ability of organizations and society to adopt to change; it also improves their competitive advantage. The possession of advanced technology increases the competitive advantage in populations of organizations. If technology is consolidated, it not only expands the technology gap, but also contributes to the decline and mortality of organizations, which are inferior. Spatial and geographical location affect the distribution and dispersion of technological development among societies, regions, and populations of organizations.

## Population

The underlying framework in population ecology is that there is a natural selection to organizations in the adaptation process. The approach focuses on those environmental characteristics that select organizational forms, which are best suited and adapted to the ecosystem. Organizations are examined in reference to time and space, which explain their survival, growth and decline. According to Marple, "as populations interact to provide organization for sustenance necessary for the group's survival, particular patterns of population distribution over space emerge and remain temporarily persistent, although change in the structure of these patterns must be seen. Organizations of human population use technology to deal with changing environmental conditions (both physical and social) which enable them to survive. Human ecologists propose that organizations (defined as a collectivity) constantly attempt to bring themselves into an equilibrium with their environments" (1982: 107–108).

## Organizational Ecology

Organizational ecology "focuses on the demography of organizational populations (births and deaths of organizations)" (Baker, Faulkner & Fisher, 1998: 173). The approach describes the "relationship between population density and rates of founding, failure and growth"[1] (Barron, 1999: 424). The founding rate refers to "the rate at which new organizations are founded,"[2] the failure rate deals with "the rate at which existing organizations leave the population," and the growth rate addresses "the rate at which they grow or decline"[3] (Barron 1999: 424). The growth rate explains changes in organizational population – growth and decline over time. Organization growth is faster at earlier periods and then slows down gradually. Similarly, the likelihood for organization dissolution increases earlier rather than later. Organizational birth, growth and failure (decline) are caused by factors that are endogenous and exogenous to the organization (Carroll, 1984).

The impact of external environmental factors: stable or unstable environment varies according to the age of the organization and complexity of its structures.

In stable environments, older organizations have advantages over newer organizations since they have developed repetitive and fixed routines of handling their activities. On the other hand, in dynamic-unstable environments, newer organizations are able to adapt easier than mature organizations "as old established procedures [of mature organizations] may no longer accomplish what they were initially intended to do" (Marple, 1982: 109).

As organizations grow, gaining legitimacy is important. Organizations attempt to gain visibility and environmental impact through mergers, acquisitions or corporate interlocking with other organizations (Aldrich, 1979). The size and age of organizations may accelerate or impede process and technological innovations.

As organizations grow over time, they develop inertia. The structural inertia of organization change assumes that organizations become rigid and resistant to change (inertia) over time, as they develop well-established and accepted rules, procedures, functions and structures to conduct their activities. When a change is required because of crisis, market conditions, or resource shortages, those inertia are amenable for change and can be overhauled by new rules, regulations and structures (Hannan & Freeman, 1984).

When there is inertia, innovation programs can be successfully implemented only when new structures, strategies and systems are in place. However, changes tend to disrupt existing functions and relationships during the early stage, which affects performance. Over time as organization members learn and participate in the change program, there is less disruption and the organization is able to improve its current performance. Nevertheless, in a competitive environment, a change program may not necessarily contribute to retention if competition is so intense that the organization is unable to cope with the change. Competition may be a factor that is detrimental to organization failure along with inertia (Hannan & Freeman, 1984).

Competition[4] is a destabilizing force in organizations. It increases the likelihood for dissolution if there are too many small firms in the market, minimal or no barriers for entry and exit, firms are undifferentiated and products are homogenous (Porter, 1980, 1985; Stigler, 1968). While price[5] is the main form of competition in many merchandising and manufacturing firms, it is less important in service organizations such as auditing firms.[6]

In addition to competition, power and institutional factors impact organizational continuity and dissolution (Baker et al., 1998). Unequal power and exchange relationships increase the likelihood for organization dissolution. In any exchange relationship, power dictates the terms of exchange.[7] It creates dependency relationships if one party has possession of resources or commodity valued by the other party (Pfeffer, 1981, 1992). On the other hand, institutional forces create the pressure for conformity and reduce the risk for dissolution.

Baker et al. (1998) argued that competition, power and institutional forces shape organizational dissolution and continuity (meaning uninterrupted long-term market relationships). They suggested that while competition destabilizes market relationships[8] and contributes to dissolution, institutional forces create stability. The balance among competition, power and institutional forces is necessary if market-ties are expected to be stable and show continuity (pp. 153–154).

Organizational continuity and dissolution can occur if there is a change in one or more domains of the organization. According to Thompson (1967), organizational domain refers to the organization's stakeholders, including the technology used by the organization, the product and/or services rendered, and the clients – stockholders, employees and others – it serves. When the organization changes one or more of its domains, it involves changes in the organization's mission and strategy.

Diversification – whether related or unrelated – changes some components or aspects of organizational domain, which results in changes in organizational forms. Changes that have fewer impacts on organizational domain are easier to undertake, less threatening to organizational survival and performance (Haveman, 1992). Many organizations undertake related diversification of existing products and markets compared to unrelated diversification of new products, markets and customers. The effect from related diversification on organizational domain is lower. When compared to unrelated diversification, related diversification results in better organizational performance and adaptation (Rumelt, 1974, 1982). Increases in organizational death and failure are more likely to be associated with unrelated, rather than related diversification (Barnet & Carroll, 1995).

Haveman's (1992) study of Savings and Loan Associations in California corroborates Rumelt's (1982) findings. The study revealed that "under conditions of dramatic environmental change, change in an organization's core features (products offered, clients served, and technologies employed) will prove beneficial to financial performance and survival chances. Moreover, the direction of change affects financial performance, but not survival chances. If organizations build on their original domain, financial performance is enhanced; if changes bear no relation to the competencies developed through experience in the original domain, financial performance is hurt" (p. 72).

The resource-based approach to organizational domain puts emphasis on organizations to capitalize on their existing competencies, particularly if it involves the innovation of new products and/or services. If innovation change focuses on the original domain of what the firm does best, it utilizes past knowledge, experience and technology into the future endeavors of new products and services. The resources outlay and the costs incurred for such innovations can be managed and controlled to improve future performance. The ecological approach to organizational adaptation utilizes the selection process, whereby organizational resources are allocated in change programs where original domain existed and competencies are well developed. The change process can contribute to organizational evolution of survival or decline depending on the number of organizations within a given population.

## ORGANIZATIONAL EVOLUTION AND ECOLOGICAL STAGES OF ORGANIZATIONAL CHANGE

The evolutionary theory describes a series of sequential stages (life cycles) of evolution in organizational development and societal changes over time. Carroll (1984) suggested the developmental approach assumptions in evolutionary theory included an idea that "organizations change structurally over time and that the form of change is shaped by structural pressures and constraints" (p. 73). The approach assumes that survival depends upon the organization's ability for adaptability and resources sustenance as it interacts with the external environment. According to Carroll (1984), ecological theories emphasized that "environmental conditions constrain the organization and shape organizational structure; however, external constraints such as size and technology also affect its structure" (p. 73). Organizations are considered to be "highly adaptive and structural changes occur in response to internal and external simulations" (p. 73). In other words, there is a selection process in organizational adaptation.     Carroll (1984) provided a review of literature on the evolutionary theory of organizational change, and suggested that Aldrich's (1979) work on organization and environment contributed too much of the empirical research in evolutionary theory of organizations. He stated that "Aldrich (1979) linked the selection approach to the general literature on organizational theory and fleshed out the evolutionary logic of population ecology. . . . he characterized evolution as a three-stage process consisting of variation, selection and retention. Organizational variation is an essential precondition of selection" which could give rise to various organizational forms (p. 74). On the other hand, "the second stage, selection posits a mechanism for the elimination of certain types of organizations. Elimination can occur through any type of organizational mortality: dissolution, absorption by merger, or radical transformation. The mechanism of elimination is usually an environmental condition . . ." Lastly, "the final stage is retention. In formal organizations, retention is not (as in biological organisms) a generation problem – formal organizations can in theory be immortal. Instead, retention is a structural problem. Organizations with advantageous traits must not lose them through incremental change" (p. 74). While the retention stage makes the organizations more adaptive, "inertia now plays a more central role in organizational evolution by providing the basis for selection" (p. 74).

According to Amburgery, Kelly and Barnett (1993), the organizational inertia and change processes can be characterized as involving both adaptive and disruptive processes. While organizations show inertia and reluctance to change, they are more likely to serve as forces for initiating change over time. Organizational changes may contribute to failures for some organizational populations, by increasing mortality failures. For other populations, the change may be accompanied by other additional changes. The impact of these changes depends on the life cycle of the organization – the immediate effects tend to be significant at early stages and decline at later stages.

Tushman and O'Reilly III (1996) found the organizational ecology[9] approach relevant to explain organizational learning and change processes in ambidextrous organizations.[10] They defined ambidextrous organizations as capable of implementing both incremental and revolutionary innovation changes.[11] These two types of innovation strategies are discussed in detail in Chapter 4. They extended the ecological approach to study the change processes in these organizations. They found the population ecology adaptation and fitness approach in the evolutionary theory of variation, selection and retention (Aldrich, 1979) to be applicable to study organizational change and development. The organizational ecology approach is useful because it suggests that "populations of organizations are subject to ecological pressures in which they evolve through periods of incremental adaptation punctuated by discontinuities. Variations in organizational strategy and form are more or less suitable for different environmental conditions. These organizations and managers who are most able to adapt to a given market or competitive environment will prosper. Over time, the fittest survive – until there is a major discontinuity. At that point, managers of firms are faced with the challenges of reconstructing their organizations to adjust to the new environment. Managers who try to adapt to discontinuities through incremental adjustment are unlikely to succeed" (pp. 12–13).

According to the evolutionary theory, all organizations are assumed to go through three stages: variation, selection and retention over time. Organizational life cycles[12] involve both incremental and radical changes that occur through longer periods of time. External environmental changes including technologies, markets, government regulations, competitive forces and inter-national conditions bring sudden changes that require discontinuities. Radical changes from one stage to another are the result of discontinuous changes, which result in organizational transformation.

## THE TRANSACTION COST APPROACH: EXTENSION OF THE FUNCTIONAL AND POPULATION ECOLOGY OF ORGANIZATIONS

Williamson (1987) introduced the transaction cost economic analysis to the study of organizations and change. He provided an alternative view of the organization based on economic choice and cost efficiency. The transaction cost approach assumes that there are differences among organizations "because transactions differ so greatly and efficiency is realized only if governance structures are tailored to the specific needs of each type of transaction" (p. 568). Transaction then becomes the unit of analysis. He noted that transaction costs are critical because they constitute "the crucial importance of organizations for economizing on such costs. This brings organization theory to the fore, since choice of an appropriate governance structure is preeminently an organization theory issue" (p. 568).

Williamson (1987) suggested the transaction cost approach has similarity to the population ecology model of Hannan and Freeman (1977), Aldrich (1979) and Carroll (1984), because of its concern about an organization's ability to adapt to environmental changes. In order to answer the question of which organizations have better characteristics to fit and adapt, the transaction cost approach addresses "both product and capital market competition are the sources of natural selection pressures" (Williamson, 1987: 568).

Transaction costs extended the population ecology approach to examine organizational adaptation and inertia processes. It assumed organizations with better transaction costs could adapt and survive while others with poor transaction costs fail or disintegrate. For Williamson (1987), the transaction cost approach is based on the principle that organizations with "governance structures that have better transaction cost economizing properties will eventually displace those that have worse, ceteris paribus. The *cetera*, however, are not always *paria*, where the governance implications of transaction costs analysis will be incompletely realized in non-commercial enterprises in which transaction cost economizing entails the sacrifice of other valued objectives (of which power will often be one); the study of these tradeoffs is an important topic on the future research agenda" (p. 574. italics in original).

This proposition assumes organizations that are functional-purposive operate under the population ecology principle of natural selection forces.[13] In essence, Williamson (1987) applied the transaction cost approach to explain both the functional and population ecology theories of organizations. Organizations as systems, are not only functional and selective in their adaptation processes, but also pay attention to transaction costs associated with technology, production and distribution processes. Transaction cost analysis becomes important in the adaptation and monitoring task processes as well as in planning and management of organizational systems.

Van de Ven (1986) extended the transaction costs approach to study innovation processes in organizations. He viewed the "management of the innovation process ... as managing increasing bundles of transactions over time. Transactions are 'deals' or exchanges which tie people together within an institutional framework." Transactions more often go through "trial-and-error cycles of renegotiations, recommitment, and re-administration of transactions will occur" (p. 597). Transactions usually occur among people who "know, trust, and with whom they have had successful experiences. As a consequence, what may start as an interim solution to an immediate problem often proliferates over time into a web of complex and interdependent transactions among the parties involved" (p. 598).

Van de Ven (1986) made a connection between transactions and organizational structures and systems. He formulated that "transactions are the micro elements of macro organizational arrangements. Just as the development of an innovation might be viewed as a bundle of proliferating transactions over time, so also is there proliferation of functions and roles to manage this complex and interdependent bundle of transactions in the institution that houses the innovation" (1986: 598). Hence, organizational systems having interdependent functions are preoccupied with the management of transaction costs.

Chapter 2 reviews the population and organizational ecology approaches to describe selection processes taking place in organizational change and development. When organizations selectively replace old forms, new forms represent the method by which changes take place among populations of organizations. The ecology approach examines location, technology, geographical boundaries, and social and spatial arrangements of organizational development, and suggests that environmental changes contribute to the development of new organizational policies and procedures. Substantial shifts in strategies and policies require changes in internal auditing and management accounting control systems to maintain organizational stability and functional adaptation. The transaction approach expands the ecological approach to examine organizational adaptation and inertia. Organizations as systems are not only adaptive and functional but also incorporate transaction costs associated with technology, production and innovation. Therefore, transactions involving process innovations can occur even among organizations that are in direct competition with each other.

Open systems organizations have subsystems that are interdependent with one another and that are involved in managing transaction costs associated with technology, production, distribution, and delivery of products and services. Chapter 3 uses systems theory to examine organizational life cycles, and applies a contingency approach to explain the relationship between the functional approach to organizational change and process innovation in management control systems.

## NOTES

1. Barron (1999) elaborated further on the founding, growth and failure rates as follows. "The founding rate is a population-level process, while failure and growth rates are analyzed at the organizational level. Characteristics of individual organizations, such as size and age, can affect failure and growth rates, but not the founding rate. All three processes can be affected by characteristics of the population and its environment, but the size of such effects may not be the same for each of the rates" (p. 424).

2. Carroll states that organizational demographic studies of founding rates "examine patterns in organizational foundlings to time and attempt to relate variations in these patterns to the characteristics of the organization environment – e.g. resource abundance, organizational demography, political turbulence" (1984: 81).

3. Ecological researchers assume that organizational mortality or "failures are due to causes external to organizations." Research has shown that organizational death can be attributed to age (newness vs. mature), merger absorption or ownership transfer (Carroll 1984: 84).

4. Marple (1982) discussed the impact of competition on organization's adaptation, survival and structure as follows: "Survivorship is an outcome of the interplay among environmental arrangements, organizational structure, and technological introductions. The important underlying factor in the formation of organizational structure is competition. Competition is assumed to operate whenever the number of organizational units exceeds the resources necessary for the survival of that type of unit. Failure to obtain an adequate supply brings about a change in the interdependencies among these units, forcing some units to change structure (adapt) to meet some other necessity for system survival not competitive with those units who have maintained dominance over the resource supply" (p. 108).

5. According to Baker et al. (1998), "direct price competition is difficult to avoid in markets that approximate the ideal of perfect competition. In contrast, price is far less important in markets where: (1) products or services are complex, customized, unique, and difficult to compare; (2) quality is ambiguous and the link between quality and performance (outcomes) is loose and difficult to measure; and (3) market conditions are perfectly competitive. In such situations, so-called *non-price* forms of rivalry, such as quality or service are more important than price" (p. 154. italics in original).

6. Markets for most professional services tend to be differentiated on quality, customization and other non-price factors (Baker et al., 1998, 154). Differentiation among auditors and auditing firms are based on non-price factors such as status, reputation (the perceived quality of the audit) and service quality. Since most auditing fees are fixed to avoid pricing problems associated with professional services, price will not be the major (lead) factor for switching audit firms.

7. According to Baker et al. (1998), power creates dependency for resources and information. It shapes organizational relationships in several ways. They indicated that "clients can reduce their dependence, however, by using such tactics as dropping, continuing, adding and switching agencies. Over time, clients allocate and reallocate their businesses in ways that compel agencies to provide better quality, additional services, put better 'creatives' on an account, cut costs, and so on" (pp. 156–157).

8. Baker et al. (1998) research ". . . show that the mortality of market relationships is a function of the institutional rules of exchange created during the emergence of the market, which are supported, reinforced, violated, and transformed over the years by the interplay of competition, power and institutional forces" (p.173).

9. Tushman and O'Reilly III (1996) defined the three principles of population ecology "variation, selection, and retention" as follows. Organizations "promote variation through strong efforts to decentralize, to eliminate bureaucracy, to encourage individual autonomy and accountability, and to experiment and take risks. They promote wide variations in products, technologies, and markets" (p. 28). The selection process allows "'winners' in markets and technologies by staying close to their customers, by being quick to respond to market signals, and by having clear mechanisms to 'kill' products and projects" (p. 29). Finally, the retention process occurs when the market serves as "the ultimate arbitrer of the winners and losers" in deciding which of those organizations' "technologies, products, markets, and even senior managers" will be retained (p. 29).

10. According to Tushman and O'Reilly III (1996), ambidextrous organizations are those organizations that are capable of implementing both incremental and revolutionary innovation changes. In these organizations, "the real test of leadership, then, is to be able to compete successfully by both increasing the alignment or fit among strategy, structure, culture, and processes, while simultaneously preparing for the inevitable revolutions required by discontinuous environmental change. This requires organizational and management skills to compete in a mature market (where cost, efficiency and incremental innovation are key) *and* to develop new products and services (where radical innovation, speed, and flexibility are critical). A focus on either one of these skill sets is conceptually easy. Unfortunately, focusing on only one guarantees short-term success but long-term failure. Managers need to be able to do both at the same time, that is, they need to be ambidextrous. Juggling provides a metaphor. A juggler who is very good at manipulating a single ball is not interesting. It is only when the juggler can handle multiple balls at one time that his or her skill is respected" (p. 11. italics in original).

11. Tushman and O'Reilly III (1996) emphasized the importance of organizational evolution characterized by "periods of incremental change punctuated by discontinuous or revolutionary change. Long-term success is marked by increasing alignment among strategy, structure, people, and culture through incremental or evolutionary change punctuated by discontinuous or revolutionary change that requires the simultaneous shift in strategy, structure, people, and culture. These discontinuous changes are almost

always driven either by organizational performance problems or by major shifts in the organization's environment, such as technological or competitive skills" (1996: 11). In ambidextrous organizations, decentralization is needed for autonomy, but needs to be coupled with "individual accountability, information sharing, and strong financial control" (p. 26).

12. According to Barnett and Carroll (1995), the life-cycle theories of organizational change look at the internal factors that contributed to these changes. Most studies are cases which examine the historical growth and transformation of "a few large and successful organizations" (p. 220).

13. Williamson (1987) indicated that "transaction cost analysis supplements the usual preoccupation with technology and steady-state production (or distribution) expenses with an examination of the comparative costs of planning, adapting, and monitoring task completion under alternative governance structures" (pp. 552–553). He noted that transaction cost has two behavioral assumptions. These are "(1) the recognition that human agents are subject to bounded rationality and (2) the assumption that at least some agents are given to opportunism" (p. 553). Bounded rationality could lead to incomplete contracting in economic exchanges that are based on contracts (Simon, 1957).

# 3. ORGANIZATIONS AS SOCIAL SYSTEMS AND THEIR IMPLICATIONS FOR ACCOUNTING CONTROL SYSTEMS

## INTRODUCTION

The social systems theory of organizations has its basis in the functional view of organizations. Chapter 1 discussed the functional views of organizations and social change which demonstrate that other sociological theories of organizational change and process change, including the organizational ecology framework (Chapter 2) and systems theory (Chapter 3), have their foundations in the functional theory of organizational change. Chapter 3 examines organizations as social systems and traces the life cycles of organizational change and stages of development. The functional theory of sociology, which describes the importance of stability and change in organizational life cycles, constitutes the theoretical foundation for systems theory.

Bailey (1982) noted that systems theory is rooted in the functional assumptions of organizations. Accordingly, "systems theory owes a debt to functionalism for keeping the systems approach alive and for emphasizing the macro-sociological analysis of the society as a whole . . . Functionalism not only utilized the entire society as the unit of analysis but was also capable of encompassing a large number of components (such as institutions) or variables within its analytic framework" (pp. 509–510). Systems approach extends the structural-functional (SF) approach to study society and organizations as wholistic operations.

## FUNCTIONALISM AND SYSTEMS APPROACH TO ORGANIZATIONS

The SF approach has presented two major goal-directed systems or functions of organizations. These are organizations as tasks and social systems.

Researchers have focused on either or both views of organizations. The view of organizations as task, focus on the technical and productive orientation of the organization. Under the production view, the concern is on task accomplishment, where the primary consideration is on "economic efficiency and effectiveness" (Kabanoff, 1991: 419).

Morgan (1986) has advanced the technical/production-task orientation view of organization. He used the machine metaphor to depict the SF view of organizations. The metaphor assumes that organizations process operational characteristics comparable to machines. Like machines, they have mechanistic systems that operate efficiently. Their behavior is predictable. Organizations resemble like machines. Management can control them through budgets and standards. In other words, organizations are managed comparably to machines on a short-term basis where budgets and accounting performance indicators play important roles in measuring organizational performance.

On the other hand, the social system view of the organization has been concerned with the relational issues that affect maintenance of the organization system components. According to Kabanoff (1991), "the social system view has stressed those factors that are related to employee orientation and consideration, social environment and personal work relationships. In the systems view, the objective has become – to maintain and preserve the arrangement of roles or relationships created by the production subsystems. Its fundamental dynamic is the maintenance of cohesiveness, solidarity, or a sense of common fate among system members" (p. 419).

Accordingly, the systems view of SF centered on system maintenance to promote organizational goal achievement, stability, adaptability and survival. The goal of management is to ensure the organization is orderly and integrated, so that input-output relationships and labor productivity are maximized. In this environment, accounting systems and practices have technical roles to play in the appraisal, evaluation, and rewarding of employees (Sisaye, 1997b).

## SYSTEMS VIEW OF ORGANIZATIONS

### *Systems Analysis Definition*

Systems approach examines the relationship between organizations and their adaptation to the environment. Ludwig von Bertalanffy, the modern formulator of general systems theory, characterized the theory as a "general science of wholeness." He described that its subject matter as being "the formulation of principles that are valid for 'systems' in general, whatever the nature of their component elements and the relations of 'forces' between them" (1968: 37; 1975: 157). Systems theory concerns itself with "problems of relationships, of structure, and of interdependence rather than with the constant attributes of objects" (Katz & Kahn, 1969: 90; Buckley, 1967: 41; Churchman, 1979: 8). Systems are defined by internal processes as well as external processes, both of which link them to their environment.

As an analytical concept, systems theory can be approached in two distinct ways (Boulding, 1968: 5–10). The first approach selects general phenomena or processes found in many disciplines and attempts to construct theoretical models to describe these phenomena. An example is the study of activities in an individual atom, cell, plant, animal, man or nation in relation to its environment. The second approach arranges theoretical systems in a hierarchy of complexity, corresponding to the complexity of parts in various systems. Each hierarchical 'system' exhibits an increasingly complex internal structure and increasingly complex relationships with its environment. This book applies the second approach, namely the examination of a system as a set of interacting social organizational elements, rather than as an overarching synthesis of similar processes across broad disciplinary boundaries (Sisaye & Stommes, 1985).

## Characteristics of Open Systems

The systems approach considers several processes and conditions as character-istics defining features of any system. All open systems can be said to have certain common characteristics, all of which can be described as systems maintaining processes (Katz & Kahn, 1969: 92–100). All systems import energy from their environment, transform that energy through some work activity and export a product into the environment. The energy importation, transformation and exportation occur through recurrent cyclical processes, thereby creating a structure series of events.

All open systems tend toward a steady state, or dynamic equilibrium. Accordingly, the parts of the system and the relations between those parts, balance energy imported from the environment with energy being used to export system products.[1] Although the system may not remain identical over time, it will be similar: the basic principle is preservation of the system's character. In adapting to its environment, the system copes with external forces by acquiring control over them, thus allowing for system expansion.

Open systems move toward greater differentiation of internal structures/ functions. A final characteristic of open systems is equi-finality, or the principle whereby a system can reach the same final state from differing initial conditions and by different paths of development (von Bertalanffy, 1969: 75–77). Systems are characterized by wholeness, organized complexibility, internal and external interdependence; their component parts include structure, process, outputs, conditions of health and/or 'sickness', hierarchical order, control, growth and differentiation (Krone 1980: 14; von Bertalanffy 1975: 47). Their functions include system maintenance, policy-making, planning, goal setting, memory, control, learning, feedback, and self-integration (Krone 1980: 14).

### Systems Analysis: 'Hard' and 'Soft'

Systems analysis involves both 'hard' and 'soft' systems thinking. 'Hard' systems thinking involves programs that are introduced to improve organizational performance. On the other hand, 'soft' systems address the total system objectives.

'Hard' systems analysis deals with planned intervention strategies, for example, organization development (discussed in Chapter 5), which are designed to improve organizational performance. Intervention is a goal-directed strategy which takes as its starting point the definition of the goal to be achieved as a result of intervention (Checkland, 1981: 149). Yet the systems analyst called upon to implement change in a given system of human activity may be able to describe several versions of the system to be improved and may in fact define a variety of system boundaries before beginning to outline appropriate objectives (Checkland, 1981: 165, 190).

Because of the difficulty inherent in setting social system boundaries, system analysis in the social sciences remains at an exceedingly elementary theoretical level (Boulding, 1968: 9). If effective systems analysis is to have "economically rational models and tools," several problems, including a "high level of political content requiring consensus building, problems with high social implications, problems of policy implementation requiring the establishment of new institutions and problems where values must be balanced with utility and price for selection," and treated with special care by the analyst (Krone, 1980: 20).

Churchman (1968) outlined five system considerations of open systems approach as practiced by 'soft' systems analysis. The first system consideration is that of total system objectives and performance measures within the whole system. A second system consideration is the systems' environment or fixed constraints. A third consideration is the systems' resources. A fourth consideration is the examination of system components, including activities, goals, and measures of performance. The fifth consideration is the management of the system (pp. 29–30).

The 'soft' systems approach, by describing a situation where there is perceived to be a problem in one or more of the above five considerations, gathers data on process/structures not included in the goal-directed intervention strategy. The resultant 'soft' systems approach increasingly used by the social and behavioral sciences recognizes the need for a wholistic approach (Allen, 1978: 17; Churchman, 1968: 196–198, and 1979: 8, 29–31). It draws on its understanding of how a whole system functions to analyze system components (Ackoff & Emery, 1972: 5).

Systems analysis, therefore, remains an art requiring extra-rational expertise as well as a science involving rational expertise. Systems analysis combines formal models while accepting certain vagueness about the 'reality' of the system it describes (Cavallo, 1982: 5). The application of systems analysis for the study of organizational change and process innovation, while involving both 'hard' and 'soft' systems thinking, remains largely an art, even though formal models are applied to provide scientific rationale for systems analysis.

## Organizations as Open Systems

The open systems approach views organizations as being made up of several systems that are interdependent of one another. If there is a change in one or more parts of the system, it affects the entire system. Organizations are dynamic and always in a continuous movement to attain a state of equilibrium or balance. Organizations as open systems will take inputs and transforms them into outputs. The transformation process requires organizations to adapt to environmental changes for survival and improved organizational performance (Katz & Kahn, 1978). They strive to maintain a balance between the organization and the larger environment.[2]

The systems approach focuses on organizational transformation processes. According to Nadler (1981), the systems model looks at organizations as comprising four major components (subsystems). These include: "the tasks (work to be done in the organization), individuals (who perform the work in the organization), formal organizational arrangements (processes that motivate people to work or achieve organizational goals)," and a set of informal organizational arrangements that deal with "communication, power, influence, values, and norms" (p. 193).[3] The model assumes the four parts are inter-related with one another. They have functional relationships that promote congruence and system maintenance among organizations. Congruity ensures that there is a match between the individual skills and goals of the organization.

Functional importance matches rewards consistent with the skills of employees
and demands of the organization (Parsons, 1951). While systems theory puts
emphasis on stability, adaptation, and functional congruity, it also "recognizes
the fact that individuals, tasks, strategies, and environments may differ greatly
from organization to organization" (Nadler, 1981: 194). Organizations as
systems comprise individuals, groups/teams, structures, systems, and policies.
Over time, systems develop their domain and transform those domains into
institutions.

## TEAMS, INSTITUTIONS AND ORGANIZATIONAL DOMAINS: THE TRANSFORMATION OF ACCOUNTING CONTROL SYSTEMS

The domain of systems analysis includes individuals, groups, and organizations. These system components are of concern to managers along with the
study of communities, societies, and other environmental factors that affect the
organization (Tracy, 1993). Moreover, other factors including culture, inter-
departmental coordination, collaboration, and teamwork necessitate changes in
organizations, or facilitate organizational transformation into institutions.

System approach suggests that accounting control systems will be affected
by changes in organization systems, performance improvement requirements,
and environmental changes. These changes have shifted the nature of
accounting control systems from being based on individually budgetary goals
to team-based performance goals. These changes have altered the principal-
agent (management-subordinate) relationships, hierarchy of authority,
chain-of-command, and bureaucratic control. In some organizations, the shift
in accounting control has changed from the individual to the team (members of
the group). Recent literature in organizational management has paid attention
to team-based management for organizations that are innovative and under-
going organizational change and transformation.

Recent trends in management control research reveal an emphasis on the
study of organizational and macro sociological variables, which impact
accounting control systems. Contingency research and systems theory have
concentrated on a variety of sub-systems including the external environment,
organizational structures, and production technologies that involve the study of
formal work groups or teams. These factors explain the effective functioning of
control systems in certain environments. More recently, less formal aspects,
including power and coalition groups, types of exchange relationships, and
their substantive domains, have been studied within their operational
environments (Sisaye, 1998c). Interpretive studies have provided an alternative

explanation to the institutionalization of control systems and the role of accounting in the rationalization and legitimization of management and control systems (Dirsmith, 1998).

## *Teams and Organizational Systems Change*

The development of teams and work groups has changed the top-down hierarchical management control systems in industrial organizations. Barker argued that in team based management, organizations transform from a hierarchy to "a flat confederation of concertively controlled self-managing teams" (1993: 402). Self-managing teams eliminate unneeded supervisors, middle-level managerial positions, and change the management-labor authority relationships. They facilitate concertive control, because they use corporate vision and guidelines to formulate rules and regulations to maintain organizational stability through group behavior.

Concertive control is a team-based control system where control shifts from management to workers. Workers through consensus develop their own control systems and self-managing teams. Peer review and participatory control systems guide member performance and reward systems. Concertive control allows workers to develop a new set of core corporate values through negotiation. "This negotiated consensus creates and recreates a value-based discourse that workers use to infer 'proper' behavioral premises: ideas, norms, or rules that enable them to act in ways functional for the organization" (Barker, 1993: 411–412). Over time, concertive control further rationalizes the legitimacy of rules in organizations, and its institutionalization.

By granting teams autonomy and flexibility, corporate management empowers them to be responsible for completing their assignments, tasks, or jobs (Campion, Medsker & Higgs, 1993). Teams have changed traditional individual management control, contractual relationships, and incentive structures into collective control and responsibility systems, whereby teams are held accountable for their group performance. If individuals are committed to the group, willing to take risks in situations of social uncertainty and interdependence, and are expected to share information (feedback), groups are expected to improve organizational performance and resource allocation decisions (Sniezek, May & Sawyer, 1990). Teams have contributed for changes in organizational systems including structures and accounting control systems.

The importance of top management teams has received attention in improved strategic management decisions (Siegel & Hambrick, 1996). Commitment within the top management group promotes shared control and mutual responsibility and facilitates concertive control systems to monitor the behavior of group members. Concertive control can evolve into administrative innovation systems which can be used by production and service industries to introduce new approaches for resolving existing bureaucratic problems. Accounting as an administrative control tool, can play a central role in the design and implementation of concertive control systems for self-managed teams and groups.

Evans (1998) highlights the current importance of healthcare teams in cost management and their effect on changing operational processes. Team management has decentralized decision-making and enabled the effective use of physician profiles to compare use of hospital resources. Departmental teams compare results and develop alternative systems in situations where a physician's consumption of resources exceed the hospital average. While this approach can provide effective individual incentives, it also facilitates cooperation and mutual working relationships among team members. Evans (1998) noted that the relationships among changing organizational structures, teams, and employee commitment; satisfaction and retention affects organizational performance.

In line with Birnberg's (1998) and Evans' (1998) suggestions, current emphasis on groups and teams is likely to influence future directions and research methods in accounting control research. Groups and teams can be observed only in social interaction contexts in actual organizational settings. Anthropological and sociological research methods: participant observation, field studies, in-depth interviews, key informants, case studies, and archival sources of original documents, can be utilized to study group and team behavior in organizational settings. Birnberg (1998) emphasized the importance of macro sociological variables – groups and teams and their contribution – in understanding the effect of social and political factors in control research. Ethnographic work and archival analysis in anthropological field research methods [personal ties, friendships, social networks (Morrill 1991b)] allow researchers to obtain first hand information on individual and group relations, and to observe cooperative and conflict management customs that cannot be gathered through secondary sources.

## Organizational Domain Systems Change

Dirsmith (1998) suggested that accounting and control research could be extended to examine substantive domains of organization systems and processes in their natural settings. He discussed substantive domains within the context of professional bureaucracies – universities, hospitals, accounting firms

– and studying them within the context of their social and political environments.

Van den Ven and Poole (1995) maintain that substantive domain changes in organizations focus on the internal development of "a single organizational entity" as well as "the relationships between two or more entities" (p. 521). Power and conflict in organizations require a minimum of two entities with opposing views: "the dialectic theories require at least two entities to fill the roles of thesis and antithesis . . . to produce a synthesis" (p. 521). Dialectic as a process of change for accounting and control systems requires organizational transformation.

According to Porras and Silvers (1991), organizational transformation involves "promoting paradigmatic change that helps the organization better fit or create desirable future environments" (p. 54). Substantive changes in control systems of professional bureaucracies are necessitated by their political and environmental settings (Dirsmith 1998). In a political analysis of inter-organizational domains, Porras and Silvers suggest that ". . . powerful and legitimate stakeholders must participate in domain definition and action. Key environmental forces must also be successfully managed." Professional bureaucracies found in not-for-profit (NFP) organizations "are often loosely integrated, and interventions that create more bounded systems are more appropriate here" (p. 67). In this context, accounting and control systems can be used to legitimize the power and political exchange mechanisms in organizations.

Power struggles, coalition domination, subordination techniques and stake-holders' claims over organizational goals, result in the domination of certain strategies and control systems (Fligstein, 1987). Control systems thus become dependent and intertwined with the political configurations in organizations. Dirsmith (1998) suggests that control systems should be studied within the context of their substantive domains and operational environment. Abernethy and Chua (1996) have also suggested that the mix of control systems is contingent upon the organization's technical and institutional environment, and the strategic choices adopted by the dominant power group. They conducted a longitudinal field study of a large professional bureaucratic organization to show changes in control mix, their institutionalization over time, and the role of accounting in the rationalization of the control system.

In professional and NFP organizations, political factors and exchange mechanisms govern management control systems, budgeting, and resource allocation decisions. In contrast to industrial and manufacturing organizations, NFP organizations are characterized by a lack of established indicators of organizational performance, internal structural constraints on goals and strategies, the importance of political influence on strategies, and a tradition of inadequate management control systems (Anthony & Herzlinger, 1980: 31–60). The prevalence of these characteristics in NFP organizations may affect the adoption of process innovation strategies to bring about changes in accounting systems.

### Systems Theory and Process Innovation Change

Katz and Kahn (1978) emphasized that organizations as open systems are functionally goal oriented, systematic, structurally complex, responsive to environmental changes, and adapt through information linkages, networks and feedback. The feedback process may encourage organizations to innovate or as Thompson (1967) indicated, to adopt a non-standardized response that allows organizations to innovate new ideas, processes, products and services. Feedback plays an important role in organizational learning. In systems analysis, organizational learning involves the understanding of changes required by the external environment and the subsequent adoption of beliefs, behaviors, and values compatible and consistent in learning those changes (Stata, 1989: 67). Information systems including accounting, facilitate the organizational learning and systems change processes.

Young, Houghland, Jr. and Shepard (1981) discussed competition, growth, size, and departmentalization as critical factors related to open systems theory which affects organizational innovation. Growth is related to innovation, because the potential for growth increases the likelihood of innovation. They viewed competition as an environment in which most business organizations operate. Increased competition for markets, new products and services increase innovation among competing firms (p. 178. see also Porter, 1980). Size[4] influences the rate of innovation because it is associated with complexity and centralization, where increases in size may lead to decentralization and innovation (p. 179). Since size increases the availability of resources – financial, human and technology – organizations can afford to take risks.[5] Decentralization provides autonomy for each unit or department to pursue its own innovation programs.

Departmentalization increases organizational inputs, outputs, transformation processes and occupational specialization that stimulate innovation. It increases task complexity and expertise in specific functional areas. "Knowledge and identification, in turn, encourage individuals to develop innovative ideas on the department level" (Young, Houghland, Jr. & Shepard, 1981: 179). While increased departmentalization may speed up innovation processes within the department, it also contributes to increases in organizational complexity and bureaucratization, which would affect accounting control systems. In large, specialized organizations with differentiated departmentalization, complexity results in organizations' "inability to achieve a balance between corporate control and sub-organization autonomy, [which] is a central problem in the management of innovation" (Feldman, 1988: 60). Accounting systems, as part of the corporate control policies, are intertwined and implicated in the management of process innovation. The design and implementation of accounting systems change for management/corporate control depends on the degree of autonomy and departmentalization and scope of process change[6] undertaken within the organization.

Systems analysis makes it imperative that the current competitive environment creates crisis within organizations. The adaptation process requires organizations to change and renew their business conditions and control systems. The dialectic approach suggests that crisis, whether real or perceived, creates conditions for corporate renewal and innovative change in organizational control systems (Mezias & Glynn, 1993). Crisis can be used to motivate managers to improve or change existing control systems. In this book, the concern is to explain the process whereby managers use crisis to stimulate innovative organizational control responses.

To minimize the negative impact of crisis on performance, organizations implement technical and administrative innovations. For these innovations to be successful in improving organizational performance, a direct balance needs to be struck between technical and social systems. Damanpour and Evan (1984) elaborated on the interrelationships between these two subsystems in maintaining systems balance. They stated that "in the socio-technical systems framework, changes in one system are generally assumed to be followed by appropriate changes in the other system. However, because the technical system is generated and controlled by the social system, changes in the social system might be assumed to have a stronger impact on the changes in the technical system, rather than vice-versa" (p. 397). Nevertheless, the current lack of a new paradigm in management limits the ability of researchers to fully explain organizational change and development strategies (Pfeffer, 1993; Willmott, 1993). An integrated approach is needed, one that can examine the impacts of the external threats of government regulation and competitors, and the effects of the availability of organizational resources on performance and process innovation outcomes (Sisaye, 1999).

Process innovation changes in accounting address routine administrative practices, strategies or reporting systems that are generally less subject to objective measures of evaluation, rather than technical innovations. Resistance of organizational, personnel, and hierarchical structures slows the adoption process (Sisaye, 1999). Foucault (1983) and Giddens (1987) maintain that resistance may create conflict, instability and crisis in social systems, which in turn may push organizations to seek process innovation resolutions.

Chapter 3 described the systems approach, based on the SF assumptions of organization and society, as focusing on the interdependency of the organizational subsystems in promoting system maintenance. The functional goals of organizational systems are to sustain organizational achievement, stability, adaptability and survival. In accounting, the systems approach suggests that environmental change, systems interdependency, transaction costs, and performance improvement requirements will affect management control systems. These changes shifted accounting control systems from individual based budgetary goals to team based performance targets. Team based management controls have been used in production quality and cost control, and are advocated for the design and implementation of process innovation in internal auditing and management accounting systems such as activity-based costing (ABC).

The remaining chapters address organizational strategies in managing process innovation, including incremental and radical changes. To examine these subjects, Part II applies systems theory to study operating assumptions of management control systems and suggests that a planned organizational development intervention approach is the preferred strategy for bringing change to accounting control systems. Part III reviews the process innovation literature as a way to study accounting systems as administrative processes in organizations. Administrative innovations encompass the structure and management processes of organizations, including internal auditing and accounting control systems. Recent advances in computer information systems have speeded up change in administrative innovation, particularly in accounting, at a pace comparable to technical innovations in production and manufacturing systems. These developments highlighted the importance of accounting in management information systems.

Part III discusses why accounting systems as administrative structures, are not easily amenable to radical innovative changes commonly associated with technical innovation. Instead, changes to these structures require a phased innovation approach.

Part III addresses the effect of political barriers on the relative effectiveness of innovation adoption. It considers the lack of compatibility between social and political cultures of the organization. Part III further elaborates on the impact of the slow pace of change on the diffusion of innovation. The systems approach and contingency theory both recognize the effects of political and social barriers on organizational adaptation and innovation. In the next section,

Part II further elaborates on systems theory, adaptive change, organizational development (OD) and transformation to describe adaptive change processes in management accounting and control systems.

# NOTES

1. Hrebiniak and Joyce (1985) summarized the inherent characteristics of open systems as follows: "An open system tends toward a state of dynamic equilibrium with its environment through the continuous exchange of materials, data, and energy. Both the system and its environment can affect this process of exchange and transformation, suggesting their independence and importance of their interactive effects. More importantly, open systems are characterized by equi-finality, that is, the same outcomes can be achieved in multiple ways, with different resources, diverse transformation processes, and various methods of means" (p. 338. for details, see von Bertalanffy, 1968).

2. Nadler (1981) expanded systems theory into what he called a Congruence Model of Organizational Behavior, which is based on the general systems model. "The model is structured around input, transformation, and output. The major types of input to the system of organizational behavior are seen as the environment which presents constraints, demands, and opportunities; the resources available to the organization; and the *history* of the organization, including key events, decisions, crises, norms, etc., which influence current behavior. A fourth input, and perhaps the most crucial is the organization's *strategy* . . . The output of the system includes the patterns of activity and performance at different levels of analysis. Specifically, the output includes *organizational performance*, as well as *group performance*, and i*ndividual behavior and affect*, of course, contribute to organizational performance. The basic framework thus views the organization as the mechanism that takes input (strategy and resources in the context of history and environment) and transforms it into output (patterns of individual, group, and organizational behavior)" (pp. 192–193. italics in original).

3. Porras and Hoffer (1986) present an open systems view of organization which is similar to the classifications developed by Nadler (1981). For them, "organizations consist of various elements constituting the overall environment of each organization member. These 'system elements' can be clustered into four broad categories: (1) the organizing arrangements of a system, (2) the social factors of a system, (3) the technology of a system, and (4) the physical setting of a system ... These system elements, taken together, send organization members cues on how to behave on the job, which affect individuals' expectations about consequences of performing various behaviors and about their own abilities to behave in ways the organization desires. Environmental cues and constraints interact with the internal needs, desires, and abilities of individuals, who end up behaving in various ways in the work setting. The collective behavior of all organization members influences two primary outcomes: organization performance and individual development, which in turn influence each other . . ." (p. 479). External environmental factors such as technology and social factors affect individual/group behavior as well as organizational performance.

4. Young, Houghland, Jr. and Shepard (1981) elaborated that "open systems theory provides two reasons for predicting that size will have a direct influence on innovation. First, large organizations have already experienced success in importing energy (e.g.,

raw materials, production hardware, and human talents), and they are likely to possess the means for importing additional resources if necessary. For these reasons, large organizations are able to initiate changes, which would require large expenditures of energy. Second, the operations of larger organizations involve a relatively large segment of the external environment. An increase in external relationships is likely to be accompanied by further development of the sensory apparatus, which exists to monitor environmental communication. With this more elaborate environment, the organization's receptiveness to innovative ideas is likely to increase" (p. 179). The effect of size is relevant only when size is associated with excess (slack) instead of scarce availability of resources (p. 188).

5. Young, Houghland, Jr. and Shepard (1981) noted the negative effects of increases in size of the organization. They stated that "large organizations are found to be highly departmentalized. Thus, it appears almost inevitable that as organizations increase in size, existing departments will be divided and/or new departments added. But this result of increased size is likely to adversely affect innovation, for as departmentalization increases, other things equal, innovativeness declines slightly" (p. 189).

6. The scope of process changes in an organization can be either incremental or radical. The change scope affects the planning, training and implementation of the change program. Orlikowski (1993) recommended that "the training and incentives given to system developers should be tailored to the type of change attempted. Incremental change, which builds on existing skills, work practices, and norms, require programs and policies that reinforce the existing cognitive and social processes. Radical change, which departs from existing skills, work practices, and norms, require programs and policies that foster the acquisition of new cognitive and social processes. While radical change offers the opportunity to implement a new vision and create fundamental change, it also invites greater risk and difficulty" (p. 336). Radical change may disrupt the normal functioning of the organization leading to chaos, work slow down and possibly strike.

# PART II

# THE ADAPTIVE SYSTEMS APPROACH TO PROCESS INNOVATION CHANGES IN ACCOUNTING CONTROL SYSTEMS

# OVERVIEW

Part I discussed the institutional, population ecology, contingency and open system theories to explain organizational adaptation, change and development processes. The adaptive approach focuses on an organization's ability to adapt to changes in the external environment. This framework holds the view that organizations can successfully change, if they adopt process innovation strategies, incremental or radical, to bring about organizational change.

Part II applies these adaptive theories to further examine the organizational change and transformation processes necessitated by the volatility in external environments, markets and competitive forces. Contingency, institutional-leadership and systems theories explain the developmental changes, which require process innovations during an organizational life cycle.

Part II is divided into three chapters to detail the organizational change, development and transformation process. Chapter 4 outlines the nature of organizational change, characteristics of organizational structures and systems-mechanistic and organic, and the type of change – incremental and radical used to process innovation changes. Innovative organizations learn from past and present experiences to establish process innovation changes, which improve performance.

Chapter 5 suggests that successful organizations continuously practice organizational learning principles to achieve desired outcomes in the organizational transformation process. Organizational learning, whether incremental or transformational, is instrumental to the successful planning and implementation of process innovation, organizational change and development.

Chapter 6 examines organizational development (OD) intervention as an incremental adaptive systems strategy for organizational change. In this context, theories of individual change and leadership are supplemented, to explain the contexts in which OD intervention strategies might be successful. Incremental changes that focus on OD strategies require minimal structural: whether mechanistic or organic, modifications for implementation.

# 4. THE MECHANISTIC VS. ORGANIC APPROACHES TO ORGANIZATIONAL AND ACCOUNTING INNOVATIONS

## INTRODUCTION

Chapter 4 discusses the relationships between organizational structures – mechanistic and organic, and organizational change and development. Management of adaptation and innovation depends on the type of organizational structure: mechanistic structures support internal auditing and management accounting innovation. On the other hand, organic structures facilitate change in new product development and sales management.

In Chapter 4, incremental and radical organizational changes are compared. The organizational development (OD) intervention strategy is presented as incremental change, whereas organizational transformation (OT) is described as a radical change. While change is inevitable in organizations, the degree of change introduced into the organization varies according to the type of organizational change management strategy, whether it is incremental or radical.

## ADAPTATION AND STRUCTURAL CHANGES

The adaptation change framework suggests that environmental changes, crisis, competition, changes in leadership, strategic shifts in directions, and new technological developments create the preconditions for organizational change. To be successful, change has to be managed. Every organization has its own change agents or champions. To make changes happen in an organization, change agents have to demonstrate success or minor accomplishments as a result of the change programs. Otherwise, the prospects to overcome those individual, group and institutional barriers/resistance to change would be less likely.

According to Richardson and Denton (1996), "organizational change can take many forms. It may involve restructuring the company, moving to more employee involvement, downsizing, being involved in a merger or acquisition, modifying the corporate culture, or any combination of the above. Regardless of the specific change, there is always some ambiguity, doubt, anxiety, and fear associated with major changes" (p. 204). For management to overcome these barriers to change, communicating change and the choice of the change program becomes critical.

Fruytier (1996) suggested that intervention strategies designed to facilitate organizational change, such as organizational redesign, would encounter less resistance if they include broader employee participation. Participation encourages commitment and learning from the change process. By expanding the role of management as an agent of change and change sponsor, the role of consultants could be redirected to teachers and coaches in the design and management of the change process. In other words, "effective change management depends on recognizing complements among technology, practice and strategy. Interactions play a critical role in affecting outcomes, a role that leads to new analysis and theory" (Brynjolfsson, Renshaw & Alstyne, 1997: 37). These changes will be institutionalized over time if they are consistent, or are able to modify the organizational norms and values (Buller & McEvoy, 1989).

To understand organizational change, it is necessary to understand the form and nature of existing structural, political and economic systems. Before enacting change, it is essential to review the existing structures and control systems, so that there is a match between the form of the organization and proposed change strategy. Most process innovation studies starting from Burns and Stalker (1961) have identified two types of organizational structures that could affect the success of innovation programs.

## ORGANIZATIONAL STRUCTURES

Organizational structures deal with the organization of work activities, including both personnel and production systems. Structures can be simple – functional or complex – divisionalized. Management control, levels of hierarchy, decentralization, complexity of job tasks, degree of specialization of functions, and extent of departmentalization/divisionalization varies according to the size of the organization. These characteristics influence the type of structures – mechanistic or organic that will prevail in an organization. These structures in turn affect the degree to which an organization can adapt to changes in institutional environments.

Two types of organizations: modern vs. traditional are identified to describe the type of structures – mechanistic and organic associated with these organizations. Table 4.1 lists the characteristics of modern and traditional organizations using several dimensions: structures, processes and content of plans. Table 4.2 enumerates the output – mission, objectives, strategy, policies, resource statements and planning assumptions of these two types of organizations. To explain what type of structures prevail in these organizations, Table 4.3 outlines several dimensions describing the mechanistic structures that are associated with traditional hierarchical organizations, and the organic structures that prevail in modern institutional organizations.

### Organic Structures

Organic structures prevail in modern organizations. Organizations with mechanistic structures are flexible and adaptable to changes in their institutional environments. They have horizontal hierarchy with less differentiation and limited chain-of-command, minimal bureaucratic features and decentralized decision-making that facilitated the flow of information and dissemination of new innovative ideas and knowledge (Burns & Stalker, 1961). There is dispersal of power among divisions and less reliance on formal control systems to monitor performance.

In organic structures, formal control systems are substituted by teams-based management,[1] which Wilson (1981) referred to as a cognitive approach to control when teams have the autonomy and independence to establish and enforce their own performance goals. In most organizations, formal control is substituted with frequent use of personal/flexible feedback, interpersonal relationships, face-to-face contact and communication, cooperation, and easy coordination among divisions (Burns & Stalker, 1961).

### Mechanistic Structures

Mechanistic structures are commonly available in traditional hierarchical and bureaucratic organizations. They are less adaptable to environmental changes and minimally responsive to process innovations. Mechanistic organizations exhibit hierarchical differentiation with several levels in their chain-of-command, concentration of power by top management and centralized decision-making. There exists a highly developed planning and control system that specifies the importance of rules and roles in performance evaluation and

*Table 4.1.*  Characteristics of Modern vs. Traditional Organizations.

| Dimensions | Modern Organizations | Traditional Organizations |
|---|---|---|
| *Organizational Structure* | | |
| Organization Form | Divisional and/or matrix | Functional |
| Structures | Organic | Bureaucratic |
| Management Control Systems (MCS) | Well organized MCS that provides frequent budget reports on operating programs | Loosely organized MCS |
| Hierarchy | Clearly defined hierarchy that facilitate coordination and delegation of authority | Hierarchy is ambiguous, problems of coordination frequently encountered |
| *Organizational Process and Behavior* | | |
| Communication | Effective formal and informal communication processes that facilitate information flow, decision-making, and feedback | Emphasis on formal communication, a less effective method of decision-making under conditions of uncertainty |
| Group | Both formal and informal | Emphasis on formal groups |
| *Leadership* | | |
| Basis of Leadership | A combination of legitimate and expertise power | Formal legitimate |
| Degree of Control | Managers have internal control | Strong external control over internal administration by donors and other interested parties |
| Leadership Behavior | Egalitarian, collegial influenced by professional norms and codes of behavior | Tendency towards charismatic and authoritarian leadership |
| *Content of Plans* | | |
| Tests for Consistency of Plans | Strategies regularly evaluated and redefined according to the current situation facing the organization | Less systematic, done as the situation warrants |
| Resource Appraisal | Resources periodically evaluated according to environmental needs | Almost non-existent except crisis situations |

***Table 4.2.*** The Output of Modern vs. Traditional Organizations.

| Dimensions | Modern Organizations | Traditional Organizations |
| --- | --- | --- |
| *Mission* | | |
| Scope | Narrow | Broad |
| Definition | Clear | Vague |
| Purpose | Customer/client oriented | Organization determines mission, not the client |
| Orientation | External | Internal |
| *Objectives* | | |
| Measures | Both qualitative and quantitative | Qualitative |
| Evaluation | Accomplishment of objectives tied to performance measures of efficiency and effectiveness | Evaluation not necessarily tied to performance |
| *Strategy* | | |
| Statements | Expressed in product-market relationships | Broad and vaguely defined |
| Strategic Orientation | Feed forward | Feedback |
| Growth Strategies | A combination of growth/ expansion and/or retrenchment strategies requiring major changes in programs and resource allocation | Retrenchment |
| *Policies* | | |
| Statements | Broad at top and narrow at bottom | Narrow |
| Interpretation | General, allowing managers to exercise their discretion/ judgements | Specific |
| *Resource Statements* | | |
| Source of Revenue | Well defined | Several, cannot be determined precisely |
| Human Resources | Specialized and skilled with college and/or professional education. | Large semi-skilled |

*Table 4.2.*   Continued.

| Dimensions | Modern Organizations | Traditional Organizations |
|---|---|---|
| *Planning Assumptions* | | |
| Existence of Common Assumptions | Yes | Possible, but cannot be determined |
| Degree of Acceptance of Planning Assumptions | Internalized by members of the organization | Less internalized |
| Means of Communication | Both formal and informal | Primarily formal |

reward systems. The predominance of formal rule based relationships has created problems of coordination among departments and divisions (Burns & Stalker, 1961).

In mechanistic structures, the concentration of power at the top creates barriers for the flow of information and information sharing, circulation of knowledge and ideas, and the dissemination of innovation. Reliance on accounting control systems restricts the use of personal feedback and inter-personal relationships in management control systems. As a result, mechanistic organizations experience structural problems that affect the success of planned intervention-innovation programs.

Organizational structures are instrumental for change, particularly in innovation programs. While mechanistic structures support administrative innovation, organic structures facilitate technical innovation (Damanpour, 1987). However, success of administrative innovation is less likely in highly bureaucratized and rigid structures. While a formal control system encourages a structured administrative innovation, it does not continue to support the innovation without promoting changes in the hierarchical structures and chain-of-command. To set the context for analyzing innovation changes, the next section presents the relationship between organizational structures and change management.

## ADAPTATION AND CHANGE MANAGEMENT

The adaptation theory of change advocates a functional view of organizational change. Functionalism views change as a planned, goal oriented action to bring improvements in organizational performance. The change is expected to bring minor disruption, so that the organization continues to function in such a way where the future changes the expected results. The role of top management is stressed in the transition process ensuring planned targets are accomplished.

***Table 4.3.***   Characteristics of Organic vs. Mechanistic Organizational Structures.

| Dimensions | Organic Structure | Mechanistic Structures |
|---|---|---|
| Organizational Structures | Loose, decentralized and flexible structures | Centralized, orderly, and highly controlled inflexible structures |
| | Provide discretion in resolving conflict and ambiguity | Provide rules and regulations to resolving conflict and ambiguity |
| | Limited structures increase communication and fast response to environmental changes | Complex structures limit the ability to respond fast to environmental changes |
| Management Control Systems | Less reliance on budgetary goals by pursuing balanced strategies | Emphasis on budgetary goals for performance evaluation |
| Modes of Communication | Prevalence of less rules and regulations | Dominance of organization rules and regulation |
| | Lateral and horizontal communication | Vertical-top down communication |
| Degree of Autonomy | Loosely governed structures promote higher degree of autonomy | Centralized structures diminish autonomy and increase management hierarchy and administrative intensity |
| | Job descriptions are loose. Jobs that are less specified and flexible allow employees to engage in a variety of work settings that are stimulating, less repetitive and low boredom | Job descriptions are rigid. Specialize jobs and specificity of roles make the tasks rigid contributing to monotony and boredom |
| Change Orientation | Proactive to change | Reactive to change |
| | Look for the present and future | Emphasis on the past |
| | Responsive to innovation | Less responsive to innovation change |
| Approaches to Innovations | Specialization, autonomy, lateral communication, and network structure support the initiation of innovations | Hierarchy of authority, management control, and top-down decision-making, and communication enhances the implementation if innovations |
| Relationship to innovation | Support technical innovations-new technologies, products, and services | Support administrative innovations-new organizational structures, policies, strategies, and administrative procedures |

*Source*: Adapted from Burns and Stalker 1961: 568–569; Damanpour 1987: 685–687.

The planning and implementation of corporate change programs affect all aspects of the organization including control systems, organizational structures, hierarchical arrangements and power relations (Dunphy & Stace, 1993). The adaptive systems changes suggest there have to be congruity among all sub-systems in the organization. Because all parts of the system are integrated, if there is a lack of fit, a change in a sub-system creates imbalance or disrupts other systems (Nadler, 1981). Structural changes such as management control and reporting systems, if not managed properly create unintended dysfunc-tional consequences (for the theoretical argument, see Merton, 1936). Therefore, managing structural change requires what Nadler (1981) calls the "use of *multiple and consistent leverage points*" (italics in original). That is "structural change, task change, change in the social environment, as well as changes in individuals themselves are all needed to bring about significant and lasting changes in the patterns of organizational behavior" (p. 202).[2]

The change management process not only requires the alignment of resources and structures, but also securing the support of coalition groups.[3] Organizations as political subsystems, comprise various management power groups which could impede the success of change programs (Pfeffer, 1981, 1992). Their involvement and support shape the eventual success of planned intervention organizational change.

Systems approach advances the functional view that change is a purposive action, which involves the actions of individuals and groups working in an organization.[4] The utilitarian economic view argues that change is necessitated by individual need, satisfaction, motivation, utility and outcome. The social and political view, on the other hand, suggests that there is action for change at the organizational and institutional levels (Migdal, 1988). Research on organiza-tional action suggests that while organizations change over time, there is continuity of change. This continuity of change is where "threads of the past are woven into fabrics of the future" (March, 1996: 287).[5] In other words, the adaptation process maintains stability in the system by ensuring that those aspects of the social system that are functional are continually integrated and adapted to new changes in organizational systems and structures.

## CHARACTERISTICS OF CHANGE

Organizational change is initiated in response to changes in the external environment and/or in internal characteristics of the organization. The changes can be either incremental-gradual or radical-revolutionary, depending on the magnitude of the change. Table 4.4 compares the incremental and radical changes on several dimensions. While incremental change seeks solutions that

***Table 4.4.*** Approaches to Organization Change.

| Dimensions | Incremental Change | Radical Change |
|---|---|---|
| Ideology of Change | Gradual, piecemeal, consensus building, planned, and orderly change for stability and growth | Dramatic, coercive, and dictated by top management and/or outsiders (stakeholders). Discontinuity and environmental changes call for major structural changes |
| | Bottom-up orderly change, first-order change that does not affect the organization system components | Top-down disorderly change, second-order change that involves overhauling the organization rules and regulations |
| | A one-dimensional evolutionary change brought by consensus and collaboration | A multi-dimensional change that brings new order |
| Sources of Change | Internally initiated changes within the organization for improving current operations | Externally imposed changes such as industry reorganization or major technical breakthroughs |
| Relevance of the Approach | Applies when the organization is in fit with current and predicted future environment. To respond to these changes, continuous adjustments can be made in mission, strategy, structure, and internal process | Applies when the organization lacks the appropriate fit due to turbulence in environment changes. For the organization to survive, it needs to achieve discontinuous change process |
| Organizational/ Environmental Interface | Limited organizational/ environmental interface. Maintain existing operational functions/ systems through in-depth contact among networks, inter-functional teams, and computerized information systems | Broader organizational contact through communication feedback diversity and early warning techniques causing for an organization to leap resulting in discontinuous change |
| Aspects of Change | Slow-gradual focusing on transactional changes of structure, management practices and system task requirements such as policies and procedures | Comprehensive focusing on organizational transformation for new structures, leadership, and strategy |

*Table 4.4.*  Continued.

| Dimensions | Incremental Change | Radical Change |
|---|---|---|
| Knowledge Basis | Analytical depth in advances or improvements in current routine knowledge basis-extensions and replications, modify existing knowledge | Analytical breadth in different exploratory/confrontational methods, demands for the creation of new/original knowledge, pioneering new technological advances |
| Means of Affecting Organizational Changes | Participation encourages communication, acceptance of change and collaboration effort for the development of a commonly shared view of the change process and outcome | Managers can use directive or coercive (dictatorial) power to accomplish the goals of the organization. These changes are accomplished through major organizational restructuring |
| Organizational Changes | Low-positions defined, functions changed/improved | High restructuring calls for takeovers, mergers, diversification, and closures, termination of employees and changes in management process |
| Structural Implications | Realigning existing structures for system maintenance/stability. The focus is to improve operational systems that require highly specific information on a particular business or product line | New organizational structures for adaptation and creating new relationships between the organization and the environment |
| Organizational Strategy | Defender strategy focusing on production learning to defend a stale product-market position. Emphasis on internally oriented hold and maintain strategy | Prospector strategy focusing on innovation learning to develop viable new product market positions. Reliance on externally oriented turn around strategy |
| Organizational Learning | Single-loop learning dealing with associations based on repetition and routine tasks that support existing systems | Double-loop learning involving changes in the organizations activities leading to new invention, production, and evaluation which could challenge/disrupt current norms |
| Basic of Leadership | Institutional power-bureaucratic/technocratic | Personal power of the leader-charismatic/ inspirational |

***Table 4.4.*** Continued.

| Dimensions | Incremental Change | Radical Change |
|---|---|---|
| Leadership Style | Participatory-effective leader moves the organization in an orderly manner | Dictatorial/authoritarian-imposed chief executive, charismatic leader disrupts the existing order of the organization. Attempts to bring new order of the organization. Attempts to bring new order and relationship management |
| Technological Change | Minor improvements | Ground breaking |
| Innovation Objectives | Improve existing business services/products to strengthen a hold on the current market share. Focus on operational levels that require highly specific information on a particular business or product line | New business development strategies. Open new markets, for creating new relationships between the organization and the environment |
| | Project level innovation targeted to the performance of individual product innovations | Program level innovation focusing on the organization's ability to innovate and learn general innovation skills to new product development |
| Degree of Expertise | Expertise is high because they work on existing products and services | Technical inexperience makes innovations uncertain if the venture is in new products |
| Level of Uncertainty | Low-outcome can be determined | High-outcome is unknown |
| Chances for Risk-Taking | Low-since the focus is on production volume and low cost base efficiencies | High-due to substantial investments in new products (that could fail) to maximize product performance |
| Relationship Management | Inter-functional teams, job rotation, and better communication/contact among teams | Boundary spanning, outside involvement and environmental contact |

*Source*: Adapted from Burke and Litwin 1992; Dunphy and Stace 1993; Green, Gavin, and Aiman-Smith 1995; McKee 1992.

help the organization adapt with minimal structural changes, radical change involves a complete transformation of the organization's mission, strategies and leadership.

## Incremental Change

An incremental change is a transactional change that is "within the purview of management" (Burke & Litwin, 1992: 531). The change process is gradual and is initiated in response to improvement in certain organizational activities. Incremental change impacts the organization's systems, structures, management practices and climate which requires changes in task requirements such as policies and procedures, matching individual skills and abilities with the job requirements, i.e. job-person match, and rewards (motivation-performance). This change may result in reassignment of personnel to different functional areas of the organization.

In manufacturing organizations, incremental change may contribute to changes in production schedule and quality improvement. These improvements do not alter management and production systems. The organizational systems remain intact and unchanged. Dunphy (1988), and Dunphy and Stace (1993) referred incremental change as a first order change that does not affect the organization systems components.

In incremental change, the degree of organizational change and structural implications are low. Structurally, the focus of change is limited to operational levels[6] that require highly specific information on a particular business or product line (Green, Garvin & Aiman-Smith, 1995; McKee, 1992). The result of these structural changes is to ensure continued system maintenance and stability.

## Radical Change

A radical change is a transformational change undertaken in response to changes in the external environment. A transformational change affects the organizational mission, strategy, leadership and culture (Burke & Litwin, 1992: 530–531).[7] It is a comprehensive change focusing on changing the organization through new organizational structures. It is a second order change that involves overhauling the organization rules and regulations (Dunphy, 1988; Dunphy & Stace, 1993). The organizational-environmental inter-facing is characterized by early warning techniques causing an organization to leap, resulting in discontinuous change (Green, Garvin & Aiman-Smith, 1995; McKee, 1992).[8] A radical change, thus involves reconfiguring the entire system and its components to create a totally new and different system. When compared to smaller organizations, larger and more complex organizations are capable of undertaking radical change programs that affect entire systems.[9]

In a study of information systems (IS) design, Orlikowski (1993) noted that "radical change implies a paradigm shift, which requires a reframing and renegotiations of the IS mission, role, and relationships in the organization" (p. 337).[10] In other words, the focus of radical change is on creating new relationships between the organization's subsystems, including IS and the environment. The paradigm shift (Kuhn 1970) in radical change contributes to a higher degree of new knowledge and thinking (Dewar & Dutton, 1986).

> Accordingly, radical change is 'frame breaking' in the sense that it requires changes in mental models of operation. Mental models involve goals and values, system boundaries, casual structure, and relevant time horizons. A transition matrix with more densely interfering relationships can therefore indicate a greater need for changing mental models (Brynjolfsson, Renshaw & Alstyne, 1997: 45).

Radical change promotes the creation of new knowledge and acquisition of new skills to explore new methods and approaches to meet demands of the external environment. The development of new paradigms advances the organizational change and transformation process.

To further elaborate on the differences between incremental and radical change strategies, Appendix 3 provides a comparison of the incremental and consequential approaches to ethics and quality education. The consequential approach applied to ethics education is conceptually similar to the radical theory of process innovation. Appendix 3 discusses in detail the intellectual and academic rationale behind the two approaches in college education. The appendix supplements this chapter by extending the incremental and radical approaches with specific examples: ethics and quality instruction in higher education.

## ORGANIZATIONAL DEVELOPMENT AND TRANSFORMATION

Both OD and OT deal with organizational change. The differences between the two approaches are in their strategies to bring about the desired changes. Organizational development follows the incremental change approach while organizational transformation follows the radical approach. Chapter 8 discusses total quality management (TQM) as an incremental-OD intervention strategy and Chapter 9 highlights reengineering as a radical-organizational transformation strategy for change. Table 4.5 compares OD and OT using several dimensions                                                      to demonstrate that both approaches advocate different, but complementary strategies for organizational change.

## *Organizational Development*

Organizational development (OD) has been defined by Porras and Silvers (1991) as a change program designed to create a "better fit between the organization's capabilities and its current environmental demands, or promoting changes that help the organization to better fit predicted future environments." "OD concentrates on work-setting changes that help an organization adapt to its external environments." It focuses on 'planned change' approaches that emphasize "change in individual employees' cognitions as well as behaviors" (p. 54).[11] Recently, the focus of OD has shifted from "individual and group processes to interventions focusing on structural arrangements and reward systems [i.e. a shift from SF (social factors) to OA (organizing arrangement) research"] (p. 73).

***Table 4.5.***   A Comparison of Organizational Development (OD) and Organizational Transformation (OT) Change Intervention Strategies.

| Dimensions | Organizational Development | Organizational Transformations |
|---|---|---|
| Organization Types | Low performing organizations that are likely to use participative/ collaborative style to gradually improve performance in the changing environment | High performance organizations that employ directive/coercive leadership style to take radical action to transform their organizations to survive and strive in the new conditions |
| Intended Environmental Impacts | Minimal due to incremental improvements | Large scale because of revolutionary changes |
| Change Management Strategy | Incremental involving improvements 'within already accepted framework'-fine tuning strategy | Discontinuous shifts in framework-revolutionary strategy |
| | First order change in improving/revising the organization's strategy | Second order change where there is rethinking the organization's mission |
| Styles of Change/Leadership | Participative/ collaborative leadership style to change-consultative approach | Directive/coercive leadership style to change-top-down approach |

*Source*: Adapted from Dunphy and Stace 1993.

The incremental approach of OD has been popular in continuous improvement programs of TQM, where bottom-up participation and the use of change leaders (quality circles) have been advocated for production and quality improvement programs. As Brynjolfsson, Renshaw and Alstyne (1997) noted, targeted changes in a single system can be counter-productive. "It may be that no single isolated change can improve a process, but that a coordinated change can" (p. 38). This approach calls for an OT strategy that requires simultaneous change in all organizational systems. Since all systems are inter-related, a change in one aspect of the system affects all other organizational systems.

### Organizational Transformation

Organizational transformation (OT) requires changes in organizational paradigm. Porras and Silvers (1991) view OT as "promoting paradigmatic change that helps the organization better fit or create desirable future environments." It focuses on organizational learning and "a new vision for the organization" (p. 54). The paradigm shift in OT affects the entire behavior, and thereby "creates new behavior, and gives individual employees a totally new way of viewing their work" (p. 58). Thus, OT intervention leads to both cognition change and commitment to radical change.

The transformation change process in organizations involves reciprocal exchange and dependence relationships among various components of the organization systems. The social exchange theory elaborated by Bacharach, Bamberger and Sonnenstuhl (1996) suggest that "to understand the organizational transformation process, it is necessary to consider the micro-political exchange processes within organizations as well as the macro-environmental changes that often trigger transformations" (p. 477). For exchange to occur among organizational subsystems, there has to be alignment in terms of mutual dependency and constituency in the means and ends of exchange (p. 478). Social exchange[12] and dependency, suggests that there have to be congruency and coherence among subsystems and organizational units. Congruence promotes stability and the alignment of resources to satisfy requirements for system maintenance necessitated by environmental changes.[13] The transformation process results in exchange transactions in either organizational content and/or process.

Barnett and Carroll (1995) indicated that OT involves either a change in content or process. When an organization changes it's content, the change has dramatically altered an element or all parts of the organizational structure including mission, strategy, authority structure and technology (see also Hannan & Freeman, 1984). A process change on the other hand, affects "the way the transformation occurs-the speed, the sequence of activities, the decision-making and communication system, [and] the resistance encountered" (p. 219).[14] It is within this context of OT process change, that the book approaches the question of administrative process innovation changes in accounting and internal auditing systems. Accounting as an administrative tool involves planning, budgeting, internal control and reporting systems, which impact managerial communication and decision-making in organizations. The culture of the organization shapes the accounting system and degree to which planned administrative innovative changes can be implemented.

Chapter 4 outlines the assumptions of systems theory for organizational change and development. Organizational structures – mechanistic and organic influence the types of organizational changes. While mechanistic structures enable administrative innovations in internal auditing and management accounting, organic structures support innovations in new product development and sales management. Most process innovation changes, such as TQM, follow the incremental change strategy. In accounting control and internal auditing, administrative innovations change are primarily incremental, involving procedural and operating changes. However, if a structural change is planned, radical changes involving process reengineering of accounting and internal auditing functions are suggested.

While organizations attempt to reduce the risks associated with any incremental or radical innovation, the organizational change and development process itself is a continuous process dependent on past knowledge, experience, and trial and error learning techniques. Chapter 5 further presents in detail organizational learning, transformation and performance issues. Two types of learning are discussed. Incremental learning is described as single-loop (convergence), while radical learning involves double-loop (reorientation). Chapter 5 argues that organizational learning, whether single or double-loop, is necessary for innovation and change. Organizational learning becomes critical when innovation requires transformation through cultural and leadership changes.

## NOTES

1. In team based management; there is openness and objectivity. Stata (1989) describes characteristics of openness as being involving team members making agendas and motives known to promote cooperation and trust. Objectivity, on the other hand, looks for searching fact-based solutions that are free of political and parochial interests (p. 70).
2. Nadler (1981) identifies five organizational arrangements for managing change. First, a transition manager and a team must be assigned to implement the change.

Second, resources should be available for the transition period. Third, a transition plan is put into effect with benchmarks, standards of control for performance, and assignment of specific responsibilities. Fourth, it may be necessary to develop a transition management structure, which will define special tasks, projects, assignment of people, and allocation of resources. Fifth, it is critical to develop a feedback mechanism to provide information to senior managers on the progress of the change implementation (pp. 203–204).

3. Change by definition means new ways of doing things, which could affect the status quo of those, who hold power in the organization. If the change affects existing management control systems and formal organizational arrangements, it will be resisted. It will increase political activity among those who are affected, so they will either block or attempt to influence the change process. To overcome individual and group resistance to change for successful implementation, it is necessary to secure the support and involvement of all power holders in the organization (Nadler, 1981; Pfeffer, 1981).

4. Wacker (1981) provided a cognitive view of organizational behavior, with a reference to individual's and group's understanding of organization goals and structures. The proposed argument was that "behavior in organizations is primarily a function of members *construed goals* rather than of their *fixed needs*" (p. 115. italics in original). That is, the observable organization structure rests upon employees' cognitive understanding of the organization chart, job description, and title. From this, employees develop a cognitive map of the organization structure. The cognition process thus allows organization members to articulate organization goals accordingly, and allows them to intervene and get involved in understanding organizational goals and being aware about them (Wacker, 1981: 115, 127).

5. March (1996) provided a short review of the development and continuity of research on organizational action. For him, theories of action are rooted in autonomous consequential action in early organization research, followed by autonomous rule-based research. Here "action is seen as resulting from a matching of rules to situations" (p. 282). He argued that "the importance of such ideas for theories of autonomous action was emphasized by students of organizational decision making who observed the ubiquity of standard operating procedures, professional rules, social norms, and rules of thumb in organizational action. Action, for example, the adoption of new technology or organizational form, was portrayed as driven not by estimation of its consequences for productivity but by an association with the demands of an identity or by an attempt to gain legitimacy. Theories of choice became theories of situation recognition, socialization, institutionalization, and initiation and developed stronger links with theories of cognitive processes, artificial intelligence, and diffusion than with theories of calculation" (pp. 282–283).

March (1996) also indicated that action is studied in ecological context, because action involves interactions and communications, whether the actors consist of other rational or political actors, in the form of cooperation, conflict, or adaptation. "For example, it is clear that certain 'magic numbers', such as performance measures or summary statistics often guide organizational action. Thus, the theory of action has come to emphasize theories of the politics and technology of numbers and the social construction of accounting" (p. 286. For details on action perspective of management, see Nohra & Berkley, 1994).

6. Incremental changes involve minor adjustments in operational systems, including information technology (Dewar & Dutton, 1986). At the operational level, there is an attempt to improve individual components of the system, without affecting the operation of the total system, i.e. leaving the total system in balance. Orlikowski (1993) examined incremental changes in information systems at the operational level. These changes involve either process or product variations. Process variations occur when "information system managers use computer-aided software engineering (CASE) tools to improve the existing process of systems development through increasing productivity or cutting costs." Product variations occur "where CASE tools are used to improve the product delivered to clients, without significantly altering its nature, ownership, or delivery arrangements" (p. 331).

7. Ramaprasad (1992) noted that while a radical-revolutionary change affects the system entirely, and requires organizations to reframe their mission and objectives, the change could also become orderly. The suggestion was that for a revolutionary change to be effective "first, the change need not be dramatic . . . Second, it does not need to have immediate, dramatic effects . . . Third, the change need not entail the total destruction of the existing system configuration . . . . Fourth, the change need not entail reconstruction of the system from the basic elements" (p. 389).

8. In industrial organizations, discontinuous change involves technological discontinuity, which results in restructuring or changes in industry leadership. Failure to undertake discontinuous change may contribute to a loss in industrial leadership for some companies. After reviewing several case histories of companies and industries, Tushman and O'Reilly III concluded there were at least three 'variants of error' that contributed to changes in technological discontinuity. "First is the decision not to invest in the new technology. The second is to invest, but picking the wrong technology. The third variant is cultural. Companies failed because of their inability to play two games at once: To be both effective defenders of what quickly became old technologies and effective attackers with new technologies" (p. 10. For more details, see Tushman & O'Reilly III, 1997).

9. Dewar and Dutton (1986) imply there is a relationship between the size of an organization and adoption of radical innovation. Larger size organizations have the resources-financial as well as human-to support radical innovations and sustain loses and expenses from such innovation. "Economies of scale may also operate, allowing larger organizations to take the financial risk entailed in radical changes of their technical processes. [They] found that radical innovations are somewhat less likely to be adopted by smaller firms. In the case of incremental innovations, large size has no adoption advantage" (p. 1432).

10. According to Orlikowski (1993) radical change in information systems (IS) involves either process or product reorientation. Process reorientation occurs when "managers implement CASE [Computer-aided software engineering] to substantially change how systems are developed through radically changing the process of systems development." Product reorientation happens when "managers use CASE tools to significantly change the nature of the product delivered to clients, including ownership and delivery arrangements" (p. 332).

11. Porras and Silvers (1991) list those organizational components associated with OD interventions. They include organizational arrangements (goals, strategies, formal structures, administrative systems); social factors (culture, roles, individual attributes, management style, individual and group interaction); technology (tools, expertise, job

design, technical systems and work flow design); and physical setting (space configuration, architectural design, physical ambiance and interior design) (p. 56).

12. Bacharach, Bamberger, and Sonnenstuhl (1996) identified three levels of hierarchical exchange: technical, managerial and institutional. "Thus, viewing organizations as a hierarchy of exchange, the transformation process may be illuminated by examining actors micro-political search for consistency in the logic of action across organizational levels" (p. 479).

13. Environmental threats that are dramatic initiate changes that require OT at institutional levels. Bacharach, Bamberger and Sonnenstuhl (1996) suggested that the process may be directed "in terms of the micropolitics of dissonance reduction" for consistency and "stability as the alignment of logic of actions across organizational levels" (p. 480). If the environmental change is external, for example, in the case of deregulation in the airline industry, the OT strategy is designed for organizational continuity. "To survive in this new competitive environment, top management abandoned its quality-oriented logic of action and adopted a cost-oriented logic of action" (p. 502). In other words, the OT strategy shifted from quality improvement to cost reduction and containment.

14. Barnett and Caroll (1995) suggested that there is less resistance (inertia) when a radical change strategy is introduced at the process level, rather than content level. They sited the experience of General Motors Corporation with Saturn. They stated that: "for instance, when an organization attempts to make a radical change in technological and marketing strategy by creating a new decentralized and semi-autonomous sub-unit (for example, General Motors and Saturn), the process effects should be less than when such a redirection entails reorienting an existing structure. Similarly, a major reorientation in an organization operated by consensual decision making may take a long time to decide. But its rationale is likely to be better understood and its implementation is less likely to meet resistance than the same change undertakes in an organization with hierarchical autocratic decision making. The general point is that, as with organizational content, differences in process may matter for the outcome of a change. Moreover, although content and process effects are clearly distinct, there may very well be interactions between the two" (p. 233).

# 5. ORGANIZATIONAL LEARNING, TRANSFORMATION AND PERFORMANCE ISSUES

## INTRODUCTION

Chapter 5 discussed two types of organizational learning: incremental or single-loop, and radical, or double-loop learning. Single loop learning involves first-order convergence learning, while double-loop constitutes second-order reorientation that includes learning new ideas, knowledge and cultural practices. When organizations utilize convergence learning techniques, they wish to maintain a satisfactory level of organizational performance. In contrast, if they adopt reorientation approaches, they plan to implement radical strategies, policies, administrative procedures and cultural systems to bring about dramatic improvements in organizational performance.

Organizational learning occurs when organizations use their knowledge and experience to improve organizational task performance. Learning involves knowing organizational rules, procedures, operating manuals, strategies, norms, behaviors, and in general, the culture that governs the organization. Learning enables organizations to strategically align themselves with changes in their institutional environments.

## ORGANIZATIONAL LEARNING TYPOLOGIES

Lant and Mezias (1992) suggested that organizational learning models "can contribute to our understanding of organizational change by offering an alternative explanation for patterns of stability, change, and organizational performance. This alternative explanation is focused on understanding organizational routines; in particular, the role of adaptive performance targets in mediating the probability of organizational change is stressed" (pp. 47–48). They proposed three basic components and assumptions of organizational learning models: First, organizations set their targeted level of performance goals and aspirations, and periodically monitor or compare their actual performance with the desired goals. Second, when performance is below desired goals, it creates the conditions for change. Third, the search for alternatives is a trial and error process, costly to the organization and happens under conditions of uncertainty and ambiguity (p. 48). They proposed that "in sum, an organizational learning model suggests that the impetus for organizational change and adaptation is triggered by performances below aspiration level, and the content of change depends on the outcomes of the organizational search process" (p. 48).

Argyris and Schon (1978) identified two types of learning that are associated with improving organizational performance: single-loop and double-loop learning. Single-loop learning occurs when an organization has "the ability to detect and correct deviations from a set of values and norms." On the other hand, double-loop learning "occurs when the organization also learns how to detect and correct errors in the operating norms themselves" (Van de Ven, 1986: 603). In other words, single-loop learning is limited to the correction of an error or a deviation in the organization's norms and procedures. Double-loop learning involves the institution of new norms and procedures to correct errors in existing norms. Single-loop learning is associated with incremental changes whereas double-loop learning is categorized with radical-transformational changes.

Lant and Mezias (1992) "propose [d] that the capabilities for both stability and change, and thus patterns of convergence and reorientation, can be described as outcomes of different types of learning" (p. 48). They identified and discussed two types of learning: first-order and second-order learning. They suggested "that routine processes of organizational learning can account for a pattern of convergence and reorientation" (p. 49). Incremental changes are associated with first-order learning and convergence, whereas transformational changes involve second-order learning and reorientation.

The organization's institutional environments affect the type of organizational learning: incremental or transformational. The organizational ecology approach recognizes the organizational learning process as organizations evolve, adapt, and change their technology, strategy, and structure to fit environmental changes and meet performance goals. To this effect, Tushman and O'Reilly III (1996) stated that "successful companies learn what works well and incorporate this into their operations. This is what organizational learning is about: using feedback from the market to continually refine the organization to get better and better at accomplishing this mission" (p. 18). Both incremental and transformational learning strategies are used to accomplish these objectives.

# ORGANIZATIONAL DEVELOPMENT AND INCREMENTAL LEARNING CHANGES

Organizational learning that promotes incremental changes focus on first-order learning. Table 5.1 lists that the characteristics of incremental changes are routine and involve minor adjustments to correct errors from existing rules and regulations. The incremental changes are done to maintain or restructure existing rules, regulations, and culture so that systems remain in balance (Lant & Mezias, 1992; Tushman & Romanelli, 1985).

Organizations are more likely to approach incremental changes as their preferred strategies if they consider their level of performance to be satisfactory or unsatisfactory in relation to their desired/targeted goals. Lant and Mezias (1992) indicated that "satisfactory performance will tend to result in reinforcement of the lessons drawn from the organization's past experiences; the status quo will be maintained and justified, resulting in first-order learning and convergence. By contrast, this tendency toward convergence will be mitigated when unsatisfactory performance calls existing routines and practices into question" (p. 49).

Incremental change approaches to learning are commonly associated with organizational development (OD) change strategy. Porras, Hargis, Patterson, Maxfield, Roberts and Bies (1982) uses the term social-learning theory to describe the learning approach in OD. The social-learning theory in OD is directed towards behavioral[1] and attitudinal changes of individuals and groups in the organization. They described earlier efforts of OD interventions that focused on improving interpersonal relationships through team building. The social-learning approach portrays that through team building, members can improve their feelings about each other, express emotions of their work accomplishments and promote long lasting personal relationships among members. The view was that OD "agents are concerned with producing permanent behavior change in the actual work setting" (p. 435). This is accomplished through job restructuring, changes in work environment and improvement of employees' personal skills and work qualifications, which enrich their jobs and make them independent.[2]

The social-learning theory of OD follows a contingency approach to organizational adaptation and change. Porras et al. (1982) described it as having "the potential for providing a means to determine the utility and situational appropriateness of various intervention approaches" (p. 436). It can be used to categorize OD techniques according to efficiency and outcome expectations. "Practitioners would then be able to make more rational decisions about the most effective interventions for achieving their goals" (p. 445).

In OD, rationality in decision-making is limited only to individual and cultural changes. But most corporate incremental changes that utilize rationality in decision-making focus on the economic performance of the

*Table 5.1.* Approaches to Organizational Learning.

| Dimensions | Incremental Changes | Transformational Changes |
|---|---|---|
| Types of Learning | First order learning A routine incremental learning whose objective is to maintain or restructure existing rules, regulations, culture, and relationships without fundamentally changing existing organizational culture | Second order learning An organization attempts to explore several new alternatives of technology, innovations, and rules to adapt to environmental changes. Adaptation may involve restructuring existing overall norms and behaviors instead of specific activities so that the organization develops new skills, culture, norms, and behavior |
| Occurrence of Learning | Single-loop learning "An ability to detect and correct deviations from a set of values and norms" | Double-loop learning "Occurs when the organization also learns how to detect and correct errors in the operating norms themselves" |
| Implementation Strategy | Learning focuses on how to better implement the incrementally revised strategy | Learning focuses on experimentation, development of new constructs, formulation of new goals, strategies, products, and mission |
| Learning Outcomes | Convergence learning whereby organizations make incremental changes in strategy, structure, and systems to remain competitive | Reorientation learning occurs when the organization realizes that the current system and theory is not working and needs to be changed through the creation of new structures, systems, strategy, paradigm, and cognitive framework |

*Source*: Adapted from Lant and Mezias 1992; Tushman and Romanelli 1985; and Van de Ven 1986.

organization. Marshall (1994) has stated the relationship between rationalization and changes in corporate control systems as follows: "rationalization for some firms was simply a means of reducing indirect costs and sustaining the viability of the firm in increasingly competitive markets. But it was usually also part of a broader attempt to improve the speed and flexibility of a company's response to business change. As part of the rationalization process the majority of firms sought to reduce internal bureaucracy, and by reducing the management hierarchy provide more 'hands on' management" (p. 44). Continuous improvement programs in quality management and product improvement are commonly identified with rational incremental change strategy.

It is assumed that successful organizations will use incremental change to manage and control short-term performance issues by controlling costs, making continuous improvement in products, services, and quality to achieve goal congruence and fit in the organization's strategy, structure, people, and technology. An incremental change rooted in first-order learning enables the organization to adapt to environmental changes without involving transformation.

Organizations, which attempt to maintain their competitiveness through incremental changes, may contribute to structural and cultural inertia. Tushman and O'Reilly III (1996) defined structural inertia as "a resistance to change rooted in the size, complexity, and interdependence in the organization's structures, systems, procedures, and processes" whereas cultural inertia "comes from age and success. As organizations get older, part of their learning is embedded in the shared expectations about how things are to be done. These are sometimes seen in the informal norms, values, social networks, and in myths, stories, and heroes that have evolved over time" (p. 18). In successful organizations, these norms and values become institutionalized and could possibly create a cultural inertia characterized by "organizational complacency and arrogance" (p. 18). Cultural inertia cannot be solved through incremental changes of strategy and structural changes. Inertia could create obstacles to revolutionary changes that require organizational transformation, without organizational learning programs that require second-order learning.

If an incremental change – first-order learning fails to result in organizational convergence consistent with a satisfactory level of organizational performance, it is possible that an "organization is more likely to undertake major changes in an effort to raise performance above aspiration level. Thus, the equivocal experience associated with failure may produce a level of organizational change consistent with reorientation. It is important to keep in mind, however, that aspiration levels adapt to performance, providing a moving target which implicates the dynamics of stability and change" (Lant & Mezias, 1992: 49–50).

## ORGANIZATIONAL TRANSFORMATION AND RADICAL LEARNING CHANGES

Table 5.1 describes transformational changes as involving second-order, double-loop learning. An organization's strategy is to alter and change existing rules and procedures with new goals, strategy, structure, and mission. An organization develops new cultures, norms, and behavior to adapt to changes and new requirements in the organization's institutional environments (Lant & Mezias, 1992; Van de Ven, 1986). An organization will adopt a transformational change strategy if its performance is below the industry average. The change is discontinuous and requires major leaps in the development of new products and services.

When an organization introduces discontinuous change involving major technological changes in the form of new products and/or services, second-order learning which introduces new patterns of communication and organization culture is required to assist in work coordination, programs integration, learning new technological skills, and information sharing and flow.

> During the reorientation period that follows change, an organization diverts a considerable portion of its resources from operating to restructuring ... The effort involved in developing a structure and system of activities de novo or in restructuring an existing organization lowers the efficiency of operations, which leads to poor performance in the short term and lower survival chances in the long term (Haveman, 1992: 51).

But once the reorientation and structural changes are over, "adjustments in organizational structures and activities will prove beneficial to short-run financial performance and long-run survival chances." When organizations 'undergo punctuational change' during periods of rapid environmental changes, they are likely to succeed as demonstrated in Haveman's (1992) study of the Savings and Loan Association in California (p. 71).

The ecological approach suggests that there are risks associated with transformational-discontinuous change strategy. Discontinuous change could affect existing organizational performance and survival. On the other hand, when there are fundamental and turbulent environmental changes that make existing organizational strategies and structures obsolete for population of organizations, some organizations attempt to retain themselves through reorientation by adapting to these changes (Haveman, 1992; Lant & Mezias, 1992; Tushman & Romanelli, 1985). While incremental changes enable some organizations to avoid death, those successful organizations that Tushman and O'Reilly III (1996) referred to as ambidextrous organizations, adopt both incremental and radical changes at the same time.

Organizational learning, whether incremental and/or transformational-radical, is a key factor for innovation[3] and change. Learning allows an organization to position itself strategically ahead of environmental changes. The success of organizational learning largely depends on leadership and management effort and action for innovative change. If an organization is successful in the planning and implementation of learning, the learning outcome should lead to institutionalization[4] of innovation (McKee, 1992: 233–241).

Chapter 5 discusses the incremental and radical learning strategies that organizations adopt to maintain a satisfactory level or improve current organizational performance. Incremental learning has been associated with single-loop (first-order) convergence learning, and radical learning with double-loop (second-order) reorientation learning.

Appendix 3 applies incremental and radical learning strategies to explain the institutional and consequential approaches to accounting ethics education. Appendix 3 provides examples and descriptions, which further explain the implications of incremental and radical organizational learning strategies in the convergence of institutional and reorientation of consequential approaches to accounting ethics and quality instructions in higher educational institutions.

In Chapter 6, the incremental and radical change approach to organizational learning is applied to study planned change intervention strategies. The OD approach is based on incremental change strategy to bring about changes in culture, leadership and organizational operating functions. In contrast, the organization transformation (OT) framework advances radical change that reorient strategies, policies and operating systems for dramatic improvements in organizational performance. Total quality management (TQM) follows the OD approach, while process reengineering adheres to the OT strategy of change and development. The OD and OT approaches to organizational change and development are presented in Chapter 6.

# NOTES

1. According to Porras et al. (1982), social-learning theory towards behavioral change is related to "three classes of personal expectations. First, individuals are not likely to engage in a given course of behavior if they do not expect it to lead to desired outcomes (outcome expectations). Further, individuals will have differing values for any particular outcome (valence). A highly valued outcome (high positive valence) provides a much stronger incentive to act than does one of low value. These three cognitive

process, in turn are influenced by information gained through experience in the environment" (p. 434).

2. The social-learning approach emphasizes individual and cultural change in concrete terms that have desired outcomes. The approach describes the specific tasks and capabilities associated with such intervention outcome. The strategy not only promotes long-lasting individual behavioral changes, but also provides techniques to measure the success of planned change intervention programs such as OD (Porras et al., 1982: 436).

3. According to McKee (1992), innovation includes, but is not limited to product innovation and development. "Product innovation learning is the increasing effectiveness of product development efforts as a result of practice and the refinement of innovation-related skills. Individual product innovations require organizational learning and, at a more general level, organizations can learn to institutionalize innovation" (p. 232).

4. "Institutionalizing innovation brings interpersonal contacts to a new level. The new product development team provides a structure for contact among functional areas that is focused on a particular project." Teams experience the "need to be shared and linked through periodic briefings," forums and seminars (McKee, 1992: 241).

# 6. CULTURE, LEADERSHIP, AND ORGANIZATIONAL DEVELOPMENT

## INTRODUCTION

Chapter 6 addresses the role of culture and leadership in organizational change and development. This chapter outlines cultural change strategies and the various theories of leadership: traits, behavioral and situational, associated with organizational change. It advances the situational-behavioral theory of leadership as the appropriate approach for the design and implementation of planned change in organizations.

In Chapter 5, organizational development (OD) was approached as a planned change intervention for the design and implementation of cultural change programs. The OD intervention strategy is viewed as an incremental approach in consonance with the functional systems view of organization and process innovation strategies. In Part III, Chapter 8, the OD approach is applied to study total quality management (TQM) and continuous improvement as a way to implement incremental change.

## CULTURE AND ORGANIZATIONAL CHANGE

Organizations have cultures. In studying culture, particular attention needs to be focused on the differences between various sub-units including individuals and groups in the organization. The cultural view assumes that organizations are made up of coalitions and groups, who hold contrasting views about the organization's activities (Meyerson & Martin, 1987).

### Culture – Definitions

Culture by definition encompasses a set of shared assumptions, values, beliefs, norms, and agreed upon behaviors. They constitute formal and informal practices that are understood and accepted by several members and groups in an organization.[1] "Drawn from anthropology, the concept of culture is meant to

85

describe the relatively enduring set of values and norms that underlie a social system" (Burke & Litwin, 1992: 526). Cultural behaviors tend to exhibit enduring patterns of persistence and continuity. According to Smith (1982), in a socio-cultural context, "continuity is . . . defined as a synthetic phenomenon with the property of appearing flexible and adaptive under some conditions and persistent and self-replicating under others" (p. 127). Continuity thus involves adopting and altering behaviors to adapt to dynamic changes in socio-cultural systems (p. 128).

Organizational culture consists of norms, values, beliefs, procedures and rules that are shared and bind members together.[2] "Organization culture is the essence of an organization's informal structure" (Teece, 1996: 205). Culture thus represents the subjective and non-rational values shared by organization members.[3] It becomes "an effective way of controlling and coordinating people without elaborate and rigid formal control systems" (Tushman & O'Reilly, 1996: 18–19). Culture can thus be "managed, controlled and intentionally changed" by managers (Alvesson, 1990: 37). If managed properly, culture becomes an important factor, which affects organizational performance.

## Cultural Change and Development in Organizations

Managers can use culture as a lever to influence the course of strategy formulation and implementation. Culture in essence becomes "the central focus of an organization's strategy for change" (Bate, 1990: 84). "The belief is that firms that have internal cultures supportive of their strategies are more likely to be successful" (Smirich, 1983: 346). The cultural perspective, views organizational change as encompassing "changes in patterns of behavior, values and meanings" where "changes in strategy, structure and leadership . . . are intimately connected to cultural change" (Meyerson & Martin, 1987: 624).

For organizations to remain competitive and successful, a planned cultural management program is essential. Lawson and Ventriss (1992) suggested a step-by-step guideline for the implementation of cultural change. They suggested three steps. The first steps dealt with the determination of the scope of the change. The second step is selecting appropriate methods to study the change process. Step three outlines a learning system of cultural change at the individual and organizational levels (pp. 214–215).[4] On the other hand, Bate (1990) suggests a three-stage approach in managing cultural programs. They are: initial orientation, cultural diagnosis, and creation of a new cultural vision to achieve the desired change (pp. 97–98).[5] Both authors noted cultural change involves a longitudinal plan to achieve the desired change. The strategies may involve either incremental and/or overall cultural changes.

Kanter (1983) advanced the view that an organizational culture that has less bureaucratic hierarchical structures and decision-making processes promotes employee involvement in organizational decisions, facilitates effective lateral and horizontal communication, creates positive climates,[6] and encourages egalitarian working environments which are conducive to innovation. Organizations that have clear goals, vision and resource coordination, and leaders who support collaboration, communication,[7] consultation and participation, facilitate the adoption and dissemination of innovation. The successful implementation of innovation programs such as business process redesign, requires an organizational culture where individual[8] and group behaviors are compatible and/or able to adjust to meet technological requirements (Baba & Falkenburg, 1996). It is imperative that "organizational learning, goal setting, and self-and-collective efficacious are central to the influence of organizational culture upon specific organizational performance" (Lawson & Ventriss, 1992: 205).

The literature on organizational culture reinforces the view that cultural changes and behaviors are learned over time as the organization adapts and changes its culture to fit requirements of the environment. Accordingly, "organizational culture allows an organization to address the ever changing problems of adaptation to the external environment and the internal integration of organizational resources, personnel, and policies to support external adaptation" (Lawson & Ventriss, 1992: 206). The adaptation framework suggests the study of organizational culture in relation to the environment and the wider societal culture are based on systems theory framework. The systems theory "is concerned with articulating patterns of contingent relationship among collection of variables that appear to figure in organizational survival." The systems approach examines those contextual environmental factors such as "structure, size, technology, and leadership patterns" that affect corporate culture (Smirich 1983: 344).

The adaptive systems framework emphasizes the role of leadership in cultural and organizational change, as well as in the management of process innovation programs. Leadership styles, qualities and behaviors largely influence the outcomes of innovation changes. Adaptation to change, is thus dependent on leadership quality and style in the organization.

# LEADERSHIP STYLES AND ORGANIZATIONAL CHANGE

The organizational behavior literature has advanced several theories of leadership. Hamilton (1988) discussed three approaches to leadership styles:

trait, functional and situational-behavioral. A brief review of these theories will be provided in this chapter to highlight the importance of leadership in organizational change.

## Trait Theory

The earliest approach in leadership attributes list those desirable trait characteristics that are common to all leaders. These traits are acquired through birth. Leaders possess certain characteristics that are not possessed by others (Hamilton 1988).

The shortcoming of the trait approach is that it focuses exclusively on personality characteristics of the leader. The trait theory can be equated to the universalistic view of organizations, where all leaders are expected to exhibit similar personality characteristics, irrespective of cultural, geographical and environmental differences.

## Functional Theory

The functional theory, which was advanced by Parsons (1951), replaced the trait theory. Functionalism stressed the instrumental role of leaders in maintaining the stability of social systems. Leaders exhibit rational and purposive behavior in directing organizational activities. In other words, leaders have a "functional role serving important purposes for the group" (Hamilton, 1988: 39).

Reisman (1986) further developed the functional theory by discussing the three types of roles that leaders play in organizations: facilitator, administrator and model. As facilitator, leaders help their followers identify issues, resolve conflicts, and encourage creativity and enthusiasm among workers to complete organizational tasks. As administrators, leaders have responsibility and accountability of their functions and organizational performance. They follow up rules and regulations in the conduct of their activities. Effective leaders develop participatory management, which involves employees in the decision-making process. As role models, they demonstrate values, beliefs, traditions and customs that followers emulate (see also Hamilton, 1988).

## Situational Theory

The situational theory is based on the contingency theory of social organization. This approach emerged to replace trait and functional theories of leadership. Situational theory advanced the view that "the nature of the task performed determines who will emerge as the leader." The situational-contingency interrelationships focused on "the interaction between a leader's behaviors and the characteristics of the specific situations in which they function" (Hamilton, 1988: 39).[9]

The situational-contingency theory was later advanced by behavioral-based studies of leadership. The behavioral approach focused on "a set of behaviors required of leaders, and these behaviors can be learned and executed" (Hamilton, 1988: 39).

## LEADERSHIP – CONTINGENCY/SITUATIONAL THEORY OF ORGANIZATIONAL CHANGE

Of these three theories of leadership, the situational approach is more appropriate to the role of leadership in organizational change. Both the contingency and systems theories, recognize the importance of external environmental institutional forces in affecting organizational performance and the ability of organizations to selectively adapt to these environmental changes. The situational/behavioral theory argues that leaders who can adapt and modify their functional roles and attributes accordingly, are able to successfully lead their organizations during periods of environmental uncertainty or crisis. It is those situational attributes of leadership that enable an organization to undertake organizational change programs to remain competitive.

These contingency/situational attributes call for leaders who can coach, communicate, provide a big picture of the organization, support the change and articulate how the change fits into the overall organization mission, plan and strategy. These leaders are expected to take ownership of the change program, be champions of change, encourage early adoption of change and risk-taking behaviors by establishing reward systems for early adoption, and providing needed resources.

## SITUATIONAL APPROACHES TO CULTURAL CHANGE

The situational-behavioral theory argues the adoption of new methods, including technological and administrative innovations, requires changes in attitudes, behaviors, beliefs and culture. The adoption of these new behaviors by leaders and followers, can be taught and learned through formal education and training, seminars, delegation to employees, reward systems and communication channels. It is essential for leaders to encourage team-work, employee involvement in the decision-making process, granting employees more responsibility and discretion to make managerial decisions involving products and services, structural intervention through job restructuring and enrichment, organizational design, changing tasks and reporting systems to promote change and progress in organizations.

If members of an organization show resistance to change, the contingency/ situational theory calls for leadership to institute cultural change intervention strategies that focus on specific goals and programs accepted by organizational members. Kanter (1983) suggests that organizations with clear goals, vision and resource coordination facilitate innovation.

# ORGANIZATIONAL DEVELOPMENT APPROACHES TO CHANGE

OD treats culture as an internal organizational variable. OD interventions focus on cultural subsystems to learn underlying values, beliefs, norms and rules prevalent in the organization (Smirich, 1983). This cultural learning will allow leaders/managers to devise intervention strategies that will make the organization adaptive and responsive to environmental changes.

*Organizational Development as an Incremental Change Strategy*

Organizations go through different developmental stages. These stages may range from one stage that involves the need to develop systematic organizational procedure to another developmental stage which requires the organization to adopt flexibility and creativity to handle competitive requirements and environmental changes (Howe, 1989). It is this later incremental and adaptability approach to planned change, that calls for an OD intervention strategy for the management of change programs.

The OD approach to change advocates a gradual and incremental adjustment of change over time. It emphasizes the importance of consensus, participation, acceptance and involvement of employees in the change process. According to Buller and McEvoy (1989), ". . . the initial adoption of a planned organizational change is a function of a number of individual, group, and organizational factors. These factors combine to determine the overall level of acceptance and commitment to the change by organization members" (p. 35). The institutionalization of these factors is supported through training, employee involvement, promotion and a combination of intrinsic as well as extrinsic rewards (p. 36). The objective of OD is to contribute to the personal development of organization members and improvement of organizational performance.

Porras and Hoffer (1986) advanced this view of OD by "propos[ing] a model of organizational change in which *on-the-job behaviors of organization members* act as the important mediating variables" (italics in original). They argued that a focus on organization member's behavior helps "to learn whether any behavior changes are common to successful change efforts, and if so, what those behavior changes are" (p. 478). Managers' and employees' acceptance of these desirable behavioral changes is considered functional for organizations to adapt and change.

### Functional Systems View of Organizational Development

The OD approach advocates a functional systems view of organizations and change, where changes in organizational subsystems trigger changes in individual behavior consistent with organizational goals. Porras and Hoffer (1986) considered the functional-congruence view of OD as being important for organizational change. For them, the argument is that "if behavior is influenced by characteristics of an organization's internal environment – that is, its system elements – then altering the system elements should lead to altered behavior on the job. This, they proposed, is the function of OD interventions." These interventions "send organization members new messages about which behaviors are desired and will be rewarded. The more the pattern of the new messages is consistent and related to behaviors contributing to the desired and goals of improved organization performance and personal development, the more likely organization members are to behave in the desired ways, and the more likely the desired outcomes are to be achieved" (p. 480).

The OD strategy when properly planned, not only improves supervisory skills, it also enhances organizational climate. Organizational climate, in turn, influences labor relations, "employees behavior and organizational perform-ance" (Porras et al., 1982: 443, 445). Organizations that employ OD consultants, search for experts who demonstrate congruity of behaviors with organizational goals. Congruency of behaviors, are those behaviors which are consistent with the OD agents' values, adaptable to change, open to new ideas, willing to learn from experience and adapt to organization culture and values. These skills, while necessary for change could be acquired through education and training (Hamilton 1988).[10]

In practice, OD strategies for change follow traditional principles of power, superior-subordinate relationships, conflict resolution, communication, goal setting, team building,[11] information sharing, and participation in the decision-making process (French & Bell, 1984). In promoting these changes, it is critical for change agents to examine the organization's power structure,[12] environment, history and economic aspects to impact planned change in the organization.

Bass (1983) suggest that a time frame of evaluating OD intervention strategies is more critical than the rigor or sophistication of the analysis. A time frame allows individuals to learn more about the acceptance and failure of new practices. Since it takes time to adopt new ideas and practices, the time frame provides a long-term analysis of the relationship between those improved attitudes and improved organizational outcomes/performance. A long-term evaluation of planned change programs, is effective in the institutionalization of OD into organization culture and process innovation strategies.

### Organizational Development and Process Innovation

In terms of institutionalization and institution building, there is the question of which process innovation strategy – administrative or technical – an organization should implement. According to Damanpour and Evan (1984), in terms of institution building, an administrative innovation that brings structural changes has more impact in organizational performance than one can expect from technical innovation alone. Administrative innovation supports and facilitates the adoption of technical innovations and improves the organization's ability for institutional problem solving. "Administrative innovations can change an organization's climate, communication, interdepartmental relations, personnel policies, and so on. In turn, they provide new opportunities for the initiation and adoption of innovations in the technical system" (p. 406).

In administrative innovation, the main concern has been on those hierarchical levels that link the organization to its broader environment. Once those institutional environmental issues are addressed, an organization is in a better position to adopt technical innovations.[13] In essence; an administrative innovation facilitates the organizational learning and transformation process.

In Chapter 6, the OD intervention strategy is described as incremental and gradual. The OD approach stresses the importance of leadership and change agents in the management of change programs. As such, OD stresses cultural change and education, which focuses on changing employee attitudes, behaviors, work habits and beliefs.

The OD approach to administrative innovation espouses changing employee job behavior and adopting administrative procedures to improve job characteristics. This approach includes changing job design and empowering employees through delegation of authority, participation in decision-making, reward allocation, and instituting broad vertical/horizontal communication and reporting systems. In Part III, Chapter 7, theories of innovation and diffusion are discussed. The OD approach, which follows the incremental approach, has contributed to the basic foundations and philosophies of many quality oriented process innovation approaches, including TQM.

# NOTES

1. Dietz and Burns (1992) elaborated on the definition of culture as follows. "Thus a culture can be thought of as a population of rules, and for each rule there is a frequency of occurrence determined by the number of members of the population who hold that rule . . . For [them], culture change is a change in the frequency distribution of rules in the population. Cultural diversity is the variance in rule frequency in the population. Sub-cultures are the cultures of subgroups, and their degree of cultural distinctions depends on the difference in rule frequency between the subgroups and the larger population" (p. 188).

Cultural diversity is related to the size of the organizational populations and systems. As systems size increases, cultural homogeneity decreases. "Large organizations have greater cultural diversity than do small organizations" (Mark, 1998: 322). In larger organizations, specialization, diversity of topics discussed on work-related issues, as well as opinions and political differences are higher. On the other hand, topics discussed in smaller organizations tend to concentrate on a few topics and are more likely to be homogenous (Mark, 1998: 322).

2. Feldman (1988) defined "organizational culture . . . as a set of meanings created within the organization but influenced by broader social and historical processes. Organizational members use these meanings-norms, roles, plans, ideals and ideas-to make sense out of the flow of actions and events they experience" (p. 57). Leadership, founding members and individual/group commitment to certain ideals can help create an organization culture that influence behavior, commitment, organizational decisions and attitudes towards innovations. Feldman (1988) used the interpretive concept of culture to examine the ways in which "organizational participants used their experience-stored in such things as ideals, ideas, memories, plans, and stories-to create a situation in which certain kinds of behavior were encouraged. The advantage to this approach is that it provides a description of important, shared categories that stimulate some activities and constrain others" (p. 59). The interpretive concept of culture assumes "the collective predisposition's organizational members create through their shared history, predisposition's that influence them to understand events, react to situations, and solve problems in certain ways" (p. 60).

Culture thus provides a framework for social activities of the organization, which in turn sets a limit on the productive and service activities. In this context, it is that "organizations are seen as social instruments that produce goods and services, and as a by-product, they also produce distinctive cultural artifacts such as rituals, legends and ceremonies." The focus on corporate culture is "on socio-cultural qualities that develop within organizations" (Smirich, 1983: 344).

The cultural model of organization culture envisioned by Smirich (1983) views organizations in terms of language meanings, which are associated with the mental functions of human behavior. Bate (1990) espoused that "language is the primary cultural form of any society or organization." Since language cannot be observed directly, Bate used speech to study organization language. Since "speech is performed language, therefore, by studying and comparing what people say, and looking for similarities in the meanings expressed, we should be able to draw inferences about the cultural form of language itself." Language or speech conveyed messages related to "perceptual information about issues and problems" (p. 90). The implication is that one can learn about management culture from the speech and language of employees.

3. The non-rational subjective view of culture has been advanced by Smirich (1983). "Despite the very real differences in research interest and purpose [of culture], whether one treats culture as a background factor, an organizational variable, or as metaphor for conceptualizing organization, the idea of culture focuses attention on the expressive, non-rational qualities of the experience of the organization. It legitimates attention to the subjective, interpretive aspects of organizational life. A cultural analysis moves us in the direction of questioning taken-for-granted assumptions, raising issues of context and meaning, and bringing to the surface underlying values" (p. 535). It addresses issues not inquired by the rational model of organizations.

According to Smirich (1983), a cultural model of organization views organizations in terms of language and meaning, that is associated with the mental functions of human behavior. "A cultural mode of analysis encourages us to recognize that both the practice of organizational inquiry and the practice of corporate management are cultural forms, products of a particular socio-historical context and embodying particular value commitments ... A cultural framework for analysis encourages us to see that an important role for both those who study and manage organizations is not to celebrate organization as a value, but to question the ends it serves" (p. 355).

4. Lawson and Ventriss (1992) proposed two cultural change guidelines that are based on public organizations, which might have relevance for business organizations. The guidelines included are first, the determination of the scope of change, where the change has to be specific in terms of the desired goals to be achieved. Second, they recommend selecting appropriate methods, e.g. survey questionnaire, in-depth interviews, observations and interactions to identify those cultural behaviors that need to be identified and changed. Action learning approaches through discussions, small group seminars and conferences, help to identify shared organizational culture, which can be changed and shaped. The guidelines focused on shaping the culture and learning system at the individual and organizational levels (pp. 214–215. Italics in original).

Lawson and Ventriss advocate for "the development of action plans that include specific organizational goals, performance measures, feedback learning mechanisms, incentives, and constant recalibration of the change program based upon program performance outcome measures" (1992: 215).

Accordingly, when cultural change emphasizes innovation and risk taking, members' commitment to achieve specific organizational goals increase. Members will have a positive view of the organization's ability to execute changes and their role in the realization of organizational goals (Lawson & Ventriss, 1992).

5. Based on a study of client-consultant reciprocity relationships, Bate (1990) suggested three stages in cultural change programs. In the first stage of "initial orientation," the requirement is "breaking out of vicious circles of thinking." This stage requires breaking the "closed loop" of thinking, and getting out of the old habit of inward looking that is "narrow and restricted" (p. 97). The second stage is "devising culture labels" where there is "diagnosis of present state" (p. 97). This stage requires interpreting language, discourse and communication, and being able to discuss these cultural changes among themselves. The third stage involves "reversing cultural

changes" through "visions of the desired state" (p. 98). The objective is to create bigger visions where employees reverse their images by adopting new values and norms (pp. 97–98).

6. Climate, by definition, is subjective and interpreted differently by organization members. According to Burke and Litwin (1992), organizational climate is "a psychological state strongly affected by organizational conditions (e.g. systems, structure, manager behavior, etc.). Climate is defined in terms of perceptions that individuals have on how their local work unit is managed and how effectively they and their day-to-day colleagues work together. The level of analysis, therefore, is the group, the work unit. Climate is much more in the foreground of organizational members' perceptions, whereas culture is more background and defined by beliefs and values. The level of analysis for culture is the organization. Climate is of course affected by culture, and people's perceptions define both, but at different levels" (pp. 526–527).

7. Richardson and Denton (1996) highlighted the importance of communicating clear, concise, accurate full disclosure, and repetitive information to avoid failure in any change program, including cultural change. Communicating clearly the desired change for the future helps avoid confusion, minimizes resistance, helps individuals know their expectations, targeted goals, and overall create a better understanding and support for the program. The modes of communication may include newsletters, memos, informal discussion groups, face-to-face discussions, or the use of mailboxes to solicit suggestions from employees and other stakeholders. Nadler (1981) stressed the need to identify those individuals and groups who have stakes in the change, and solicit their support and full involvement in the change program. In some cases, it is feasible to use an outside consultant to conduct diagnostic interviews, analyze the data, and provide the results to management (p. 207).

Various sources of communication channels allow all levels of management to be involved in the planning and implementation of change. Supervisors can facilitate as agents of change for effective communication links. They can also provide quick responses to problems on a timely basis, communicate to employees, and take action if needed to correct them. All aspects of the communication program are centered on the principle of communicating change and creating reward systems to motivate employees to support change. This in turn effectively enhances employees support and commitment for planned change.

Burke and Litwin (1992) extended the argument to say ". . . corporate culture (beliefs and values) determines the type of reward system an organization has . . . to change culture the reward system should be used (i.e. to reward the behaviors that would reflect the new values . . . ." That is, "culture change must be planned as well and aligned with strategy and leader behavior." When cultural change focuses on organizational mission, it affects the total system. "Changing structure, on the other hand, may or may not affect the total system. It depends on where in the organization a structural change might occur" (p. 529).

8. Early psychological study of individual behavior and personality change suggests that there is a hierarchy of individual needs. These needs have to be met at each level to minimize individuals' resistance to change. The most noted theory on this subject was that of Maslow's individual hierarchy of needs. Maslow (1954) argued for a unity of personality and hierarchy of needs for individuals. These needs are in a hierarchy, so that an individual is not going to seek the next higher level without satisfying the lower

need first. He suggested that there have to be a critical threshold in personality change when an individual moves to the next level in the hierarchy.

Compared to Maslow (1954) who studied total personality needs, McClelland (1961) examined the selective needs for individual change. He attempted to develop a theory of motivation behavior that rested on personality needs. His theory was referred to as 'the Need for Achievement' or N-achievement. He suggested that societies that have achieved high economic growth and development have inculcated in their young population the desire for high achievement motivation. In other words, socialization shapes an individual's attitude or desire for high n-achievement. His explanation of social change or economic development rested on the need of individuals or groups for high achievement.

Lerner (1958), on the other hand, provided general propositions and assumptions on individual change in outlook and motivation. His propositions are based on the assumption that first; individuals reach a critical psychological threshold that triggers fundamental changes in their personalities, outlook and motivations. He saw the process of change as systematic, where individual progress from one stage to another, until they reach the threshold, which triggers the change. Second, individual change is unidirectional. It progresses until it reaches the critical threshold. Third, individuals have a multiple personality, where there is the ability to adapt oneself to changes over time in life. Fourth, Lerner downplayed individual's experiences and society's tradition of values and beliefs as having no bearing or impact on the direction and content of change. Changes in social and political life occur only where there are sufficient mobile personalities [i.e. 'modern' as opposed to 'traditional'], who serve as agents of the change process. He suggested that changes come as an integrated package for individuals as they pass the threshold (see also Inkeles & Smith, 1974).

Researchers who have applied Lerner's (1958) theory of individual change, attempted to develop a social psychology theory of social change to explain individual change from traditional to acquiring modern personalities. They focused on examining the interaction between individuals and their immediate surroundings, particularly when the environment changes. Researchers attributed that schooling, employment and other environmental factors as shaping the attitudes and individual scores on overall modernity (OM) scales. They concluded that modern individuals have better psychic adjustments compared to traditional individuals (for details see Inkeles & Smith, 1974).

9. The situational theory of leadership is based on the premise that "leadership is a functional role serving important purposes for the group." It "holds that the nature of the tasks performed determines who will emerge as the leaders." It assumes that the situation selects the leader. The situational approach presents one dimension of the set of behavioral traits possessed by a leader (Hamilton, 1988: 39). While the situational theory focused on specific conditions under which specific characteristics or behaviors prevail to match functional requirements, it ignored personality traits that account for differences among individual leaders. It discounted the importance of traits in leadership qualities.

Hamilton (1988) summarized the shortcomings in both traits and situational theories. "The trait approach tends to ignore the situation in which leadership occurs, whereas the situational/behavioral approach tends to ignore the influence of innate or deeply conditioned individual differences ... The behavioral approach argues that a set of behaviors is clearly more important to one role than to another. Consequently, the degree to which the leader has learned the appropriate behaviors and can execute them in the particular job environment will determine the leader's effectiveness" (p. 39).

The behavioral approach stresses social similarity among leaders in an organization. Morrill (1991a) referred social similarity in economic, class and cultural background of managers as honor. Morrill (1991a) used honor as a basis for social similarity for grouping of managers. In this context, "honor not only allows individuals to maintain a sense of balance and efficacy within the volatility of American business, it also operates as an organizational culture control in terms of social similarity" (p. 609). Social similarity reduces tensions of uncertainty among executives. "Executives tend to hire people who are socially similar to themselves in terms of ethnicity, education, class background, and gender to fill top managerial posts, in order to assure some predictability and trust in their behavior" (pp. 609–610. see also Kanter, 1977).

10. Hamilton (1988) lists three categories of personality characteristics associated with effective OD consultants. The first factor is "openness and responsiveness to others" needs and concerns' (p. 40). Those listed characteristics and behaviors included are "adaptable, collaborative, discreet, flexible, open, reassuring, sensitive, trusting, affiliative, cooperative, empathetic, friendly, patient, respectful, tactful, warm (i.e. caring toward people" (pp. 41–42). The second factor calls for "comfort with ambiguity and the ability to make sense of it." Those attributes include "ambiguity, (i.e. tolerant of it), analytical, conceptual, imaginative, innovative, intelligent, insightful, intuitive, perceptive, timing (i.e. has a sense of it)" (p. 42). The third factor deals with "comfort with oneself in relation to others." The distinguishing characteristics include "confrontational, congruent, (i.e. one's behavior is congruent with one's espoused values, courageous, enthusiastic, honest, humorous, initiating, marginality (i.e. comfort with it), positive, risk taking, self-confident, spontaneous" (pp. 42–43).

11. In team building, the focus is to minimize individual decision making and share decision-making processes among team members. It is assumed that matrix structures promote the formation of teams and team decision-making processes. Matrix organizations reduce the tracing to individuals in the accountability of decision making. "Matrix systems promote the syndication of risk by entire executive corps as groups of high-level managers embedded in complex authority relations are responsible for decision making rather than individual managers. In such a structure, it is different to trace decisions to any one manager; most decisions must be traced to some group process within or between product teams or departments" (Morrill, 1991a: 612).

12. Bradshaw-Camball (1989) noted that the ". . . discussion of OD and power tend to assume that organizational reality is objective and can be quantified and measured, within the sources of power and major players identified and mapped" (p. 33). If OD consultants share the ideology of the power holders, it can be assumed that they can be used to reinforce their power by disseminating their views.

Bacharach, Bamberger and Sonnenstuhl (1996) presented a coalition view of organizations, as an alternative to the functional view of organizations and OD. The coalition view assumed that power is not objectively based. It is rather formed when groups in organizations develop mutual trust among themselves to act in their best interests. Coalitions allow the institutionalization of groups whose interests are aligned towards specific objectives, instead of overall organizational objectives (see Pfeffer, 1981, 1992). If there is managerial conflict among subordinates, it is likely that superiors can use it as a source of information to strengthen their power and control in the organization (Morrill, 1991a: 610). In contrast to the functional OD approach, the coalition view supports a change program that takes into consideration various stakeholders of the organization. A stakeholder analysis indicates the degree to which an organization can satisfy its diverse constituents: customers, employers, investors and government organization including regulatory agencies. It reveals the organization's willingness to change in response to its diverse constituencies.

13. Porras and Hoffer (1986) indicated that technological intervention, such as the introduction of new computer systems improve information access and flow. This then contributes to improved administrative systems such as team work, alterations in organizational structure, and changes in individual behavior through training which would promote open communication and collaboration (p. 481).

Teece (1996) provided on the other hand, systems definition of technological innovation and expanded the notion of interdependency among technological subsystems. Firm structures, both formal and informal; influence innovative activities in firms. "Innovation is characterized by technological inter-relatedness between various subsystems. Links to other technologies, to complementary assets, and to users must be maintained if innovation is to be successful. If recognizable organizational sub-units such as R&D, manufacturing, and marketing exist, they must be in close and continuous communication and engage in mutual adaptation if innovation in commercially relevant products and processes is to have a chance of succeeding" (p. 196).

# PART III

# PROCESS INNOVATION STRATEGIES IN INTERNAL AUDITING AND ACCOUNTING CONTROL SYSTEMS

# OVERVIEW

The 1990s brought significant development in organization management and accounting literature. Scholars and practitioners noted the need for organizations to embrace process innovation approaches to adapt to changes in their institutional environments. To be competitive, the current business environment requires organizations to be adaptive, innovative, and open to new paradigms, introduce better methods of managing people and organizations, and innovative internal control and auditing systems.

Part I presented the sociological theories of adaptation and selections: population ecology, institutional and contingency theories, organizational transactions and systems analysis – that have shaped research on organizational change and development, and process innovation. Part II applies these theories to examine the organizational change and transformation processes in management control systems. Two types of organizational structures, mechanistic and organic are described as well as two types of process innovation approaches, incremental and radical, and two types of organizational change intervention strategies, organizational development (OD) and organizational transformation (OT).

Parts I and II noted that there are limitations to the practicality and relevance on the functional forms of organizations and mechanistic structures, which are based on scientific management principles for the purpose of management planning and control. Even organizational division structures that are organic and organized along product lines or geographical territories, are less likely to improve quality and productivity goals, unless they are able to adapt to the current competitive business environment. Contingency management and systems analysis suggest that the current organizational structures and processes are capable of dealing with contemporary business problems, if they adopt process innovation as part of their strategic planning processes. In response to current environmental changes, many organizations have adopted incremental, gradual change approach exemplified by total quality management (TQM)) or implemented transformational, radical change strategy demonstrated by reengineering. Part III then discusses the role of process innovation and compares TQM and reengineering as approaches to bring about incremental, radical, technical and administrative process innovation changes in internal auditing, and management accounting and control systems.

Accordingly, Part III is divided into five chapters, which address process innovation strategies in management control systems. Chapter 7 introduces the innovation, adoption and diffusion process in organizations. TQM and reengineering are described as process innovation changes that are planned and implemented to bring about technical and administrative changes in organizations.

Chapter 8 discusses TQM as an adaptive innovation change in organizations. In this chapter, the systems approach is utilized to describe mechanistic and organic organizational types and their impact on innovative change.

Chapters 9 and 10 discuss TQM and reengineering. Chapter 9 describes reengineering and its evolution as an alternative to TQM. Chapter 10 compares TQM and reengineering as incremental versus radical innovation change approaches. Innovation strategies and their impact on organizational change and development are discussed within the context of the adaptive view of organizations.

The last chapter, Chapter 11, elaborates on the impact TQM and process reengineering have on the design and implementation of management control systems. Two types of process innovation strategies, technical and administrative process innovation are illustrated to describe changes currently occurring in accounting control and internal auditing systems.

# 7. INNOVATION, ADOPTION, DIFFUSION AND CHANGES IN ACCOUNTING SYSTEMS

## INTRODUCTION

Many organizations today have pursued innovation, adoption and diffusion as mechanisms for survival, growth and development. Organizations have incorporated innovation into their competitive strategy. However, the degree to which management plans for initiating the adoption of innovations have varied depending on their organization's life cycles and developmental stages: inception, growth, crisis, decline and maturity.

Chapter 7 presents several theories of innovation, adoption and diffusion. The chapter discusses two types of innovations, technical and administrative, which are prevalent in internal auditing, and management accounting and control systems. Also, the chapter elaborates on the behavioral strategies of convergence learning through communication and education, and reorientation learning through the adoption of new cultural practices for the diffusion of technical and administrative innovation. It is suggested that while organic organizational structures support technical innovations, mechanistic organizational structures facilitate the adoption of administrative innovations. Nevertheless, operating procedure constraints in mechanistic structures and unrealized tangible benefits from administrative improvements have contributed to administrative innovation lags. Administrative innovation lags in turn have been used to describe constraints and drawbacks inherent in internal auditing and management accounting systems.

## INNOVATION AND COMPETITIVE STRATEGY

The success of innovation depends on the link-fit between competitive strategy and innovation (Porter, 1980, 1985). While innovation involves both administrative and technical changes, many authors have examined innovation primarily as an improvement in manufacturing technological process innovation[1] and its role in an organization's competitive strategy (Schroeder, 1990). It is widely accepted that an organization can sustain competitive advantage through improved manufacturing technological processes in research and development, new products and processes. Technological innovations include developments in new technology, as well as knowledge and technical know-how. New technologies and innovations create opportunities, for example, the Internet and e-commerce, for smaller firms to compete effectively in markets dominated by large firms. They have increased the number of new entrants (as well as exits) into/out of the competitive market.[2]

The degree to which organizations and industries respond to investment opportunities in new technologies are influenced by several factors including: size of the market, demand for new products and services, number of firms in the industry, and the industry's life cycle (Gort & Will, 1986; Porter, 1980, 1985; Schroeder, 1990). It is assumed that in the early stages of development or industry life cycle, technological innovations and opportunities to environmental changes are higher than in later stages. At early stages, organizations are more responsive to continual innovation changes and refine them over time.

As adaptive systems, organizations learn from past experiences and continually improve their performance, management systems, organizational structures and strategies by making minor modifications and changes. They make the innovative process flexible, less costly to administer and easier for adoption to improve products and services. However, at later stages, when organizations reach their maturity of development, Gort and Will (1986) suggest that, over time there is "eventually, of course, the continued decline in technical opportunities and market saturation will lead to a decline in changes in technology" (p. 750).[3]

Even though firms in the same industry have comparable resources, technology and people, they respond differently to innovations and environmental changes. Some firms perceive innovations as a threat, while others capitalize the new opportunities for competition and entry into new markets and products. While innovation changes the rules of competition and the competitive strategies of firms, its effect on firms and organizations change over time. While innovation has a positive impact on some firms, it has a negative competitive impact on other firms. What forces drive the changing impact of innovation on competition include "an innovation's ongoing development, its gradual diffusion, and the emergence of complementary technologies" (Schroeder, 1990: 38). How these firms shift their competitive strategies to respond to innovation and environmental changes is as equally important as when they adopt the innovation – early or late in the innovation process. It needs to be noted that the strategic shifts shape the success of the innovation in improving performance.

After reviewing the innovation literature from rural sociology, anthropology and economics, Schroeder (1990) identified three dynamic patterns of innovation. "First, innovations do not emerge in their final form but continue to develop and improve. Second, innovations tend to develop in clusters that rely on each other for synergies to achieve full potential. Third, innovations are not adopted by all firms simultaneously" (p. 26). Therefore, successful process innovations are developed over time, dependent on organizational synergies and are not adopted by all firms in the same industry.

## *Innovation – Definition*

Innovation refers to an introduction of new ideas, products, technologies or programs in an organization (Burns & Stalker, 1961). New programs may include the introduction of quality improvement programs and changes in accounting and internal control systems. In cases of process innovations, organizations introduce new approaches and methods for handling organizational tasks and activities. These new procedures are introduced within existing organizational domains and boundaries. Organizations that plan process innovations may introduce either technical and/or administrative innovations. Van de Ven (1986) defined the process of innovation

> as the development and implementation of new ideas by people who over time engage in transactions with others within an institutional context. This definition is sufficiently general to apply to a wide variety of technical, product, process, and administrative kinds of innovations. From a managerial viewpoint, to understand the process of innovation is to understand the factors that facilitate and inhibit the development of innovations. These factors include ideas, people, transactions, and context over time (p. 591).[4]

Damanpour and Evan (1984) approached innovations within the context of reducing impacts of environmental uncertainty. They considered innovations as responses to "environmental changes or means of bringing about change in an organization" (p. 393). Innovations help organizations reduce the impact of environmental uncertainty. "Innovations at the organizational level may involve the implementation of a new technical idea or a new administrative idea. The time of its adoption in the related organizational population is expected to result in an organizational change that might affect the performance of that organization. Therefore, an idea is considered new in relation to the adopting organization, not in relation to its organizational population" (p. 393). They identified three innovation stages: initiation, development and implementation. They viewed innovations as "a means of creating changes to ensure adaptive behavior" for organizations (p. 405).[5]

Innovations can be either autonomous (stands alone) or systemic (integra-tive). Teece (1996) discussed these two types of innovations. "An autonomous innovation is one that can be introduced without modifying other components or items of equipment component or device in that sense 'stands alone'. A systemic innovation, on the other hand, requires significant readjustment to other parts of the system" (p. 205). In systemic innovation, there is integration of information flows. This minimizes the prevalence of institutional barriers to innovation. Moreover, "the more systemic the innovation, the greater the interdependence. Exposure to re-contracting hazards is likely to be frequent" (p. 216).[6]

Most technological innovations, including changes in manufacturing and production, are autonomous/stand alone changes that can be implemented directly in a department, division or unit. To the contrary, systemic innovations, such as accounting and internal control changes require coordination of resources – personnel, financial and material – as well as the sharing of information – technology and communication channels. According to Teece (1996), "innovations of this type require that the design of the subsystems be coordinated in order for the gains from the innovation to be realized. Since these innovations span current technology boundaries, a complex coordination problem [could arise]" (p. 217). Systemic innovation raises the question of whether or not an organization has the resources and capabilities for implementing such innovation strategies.

## Technological Innovation

Innovation is primarily described as the generation, development and implementation of new technology in organizations (Green, Gavin & Aiman-Smith, 1995: 203). Technological innovation involves the introduction of tool, physical equipment, or technique that affects work structures. It changes the methods in which products and services are produced and delivered (Damanpour, 1987: 677). It involves a continuous improvement process for quality of products and services and technological processes. Similarly, radical innovations are mainly defined within the context of technological innova-tions.

Technological innovation can be either incremental or radical. A radical-revolutionary change happens when combinations of the "dynamic of product, service, and process innovation, dominant designs, and substitution events, which together make up technology cycles" take place (Tushman & O'Reilly III, 1996: 15–16). Incremental changes usually follow after major/radical changes have occurred, and involve minor adjustments in product design and features, which happen in product life cycles. In process innovation, the basis of competition is incremental, where the focus is on "driving down costs, and adding features" (Tushman & O'Reilly III, 1996: 10).

Butler (1988) has noted the link between competitive strategy and technological innovation, which is, a strategy – technology relationships. Technology not only improves an organization's economic performance and competitive standing; it may entirely alter the structure of the industry. Innovation affects market relationships by breaking up monopoly and encouraging competition (Schroeder, 1990). Economic, social, political and other external environmental forces shape technological changes. Environmental factors including competition, government regulation, stages of technological development, market forces, and organizations' strategy for managing the innovation process affect performance (Butler, 1988: 18).

At the organizational level, structural factors such as specialization, functional differentiation, organization size and structure, age of plant, research and development intensity, type of industry and company (Erickson, 1994: 361) influence the innovation process. At the group and individual levels; culture, organization structure and systems, intrinsic characteristics to a job such as autonomy, freedom and satisfaction, contribute to the success of innovation programs (West & Farr, 1989: 21–23). In addition, individual characteristics associated with leaders' values, personalities and roles affect innovation outcomes (Damanpour, 1987).[7]

Innovation should not be limited to bringing technological change; it has to be able to demonstrate that it can contribute economic advantages to the adopter. Early adopters are able to win more customers, including their competitors' customers when compared to those who adopt later (Young, Houghland & Shepard, 1981: 180). However, profits from innovations are short-lived,[8] since innovation will attract new entrants and competitors. (Davelaar & Nijkamp, 1990: 183). According to Erickson (1994), technological change is important "in the long-term creation of income and wealth in the industrialized economies" (p. 354). Regional patterns of growth and decline and differential rates of growth are associated with technological change and economic development.

Technology has a direct effect on the complexity of organizational structures and their survival and adaptability – winners and losers – to environmental changes. Podolny and Stuart (1995) suggest, "that an organization's role in the process of technological change is meaningfully embedded in the socio-technical context into which its innovations are introduced and developed" (p. 1256). They proposed that the analytical study of "the process of technical change" involves the simultaneous examination, not the separate distinction "between the rate, direction, diffusion, and adoption of innovations . . . ." They argued for the avoidance of "conceptual separation of these areas." Their social constructive view of the role based ecology[9] of technological change focuses on innovation and uncertainty. It emphasizes that "technologies develop as they diffuse, and as they progress they become more attractive to potential adopters, affecting the pace at which the initial innovation is modified; thus, rate direction, diffusion, and adoption are intertwined" (p. 1256).[10]

While there are stand alone technological innovations, most innovations are systemic and interdependent. When innovation is viewed as involving interdependency among technologies, the benefits of those changes are clearly observable. "This occurs because, in the related set, each new innovation enhances the value of others. Each innovation is also going through a process of continual improvement, which enhances not only its own value but also those of related innovations" (Butler 1988: 21).

Technological changes affect the distribution of power and hierarchical relations in organizations. It impacts the administrative structure, including accounting and control systems. As such, technological changes create the precondition for administrative innovations. Technological changes that bring a shift in production functions, such as new investment in equipment/technical progress, result in administrative innovations in accounting systems.

Table 7.1 compares the differences between technical and administrative innovations. While technical innovation is limited to a particular task or activity, administrative innovation affects the entire social system, relationship and structure of the organization. Technical innovation is a bottom-up strategy while administrative innovation is a top-down strategy for managing change in organizations (Damanpour & Evan, 1984).

*Administrative Innovation*

Damanpour and Evan (1984) defined administrative innovation "as those that occur in the social system of an organization . . . an administrative innovation can be the implementation of a new way to recruit personnel, allocate resources, and structure tasks, authority and rewards. It comprises innovation in organizational structure and in the management of people" (p. 394). Administrative innovation stimulates changes in technological innovation which impacts production systems and work arrangements. It "has a clear social and applied component since it impacts directly upon others in the work group, organization, or wider society" (West & Farr, 1989: 16).

Administrative innovation is designed to improve internal control, accounting and auditing systems, organizational structures and systems, administrative processes, management systems, and departmental coordination. Damanpour (1987) listed changes in recruitment and personnel policies, structuring of organizational systems, changes in control and motivation systems including budget systems as examples of administrative innovation (p. 677). According to Daft (1978), the success of administrative innovation depends on organizational structural arrangements supporting the innovation. Structural arrangements refer to the level and ratio of management groups in the

***Table 7.1.***   Comparison of Administrative and Technical Innovations

| Dimensions | Administrative Innovation | Technical Innovation |
|---|---|---|
| Definitions | Occur in the social system of an organization including changing roles/ relationships among employees, improving organizational structure related to rules, procedures, allocation of resources, tasks, authority, and communication, as well as the implementation of new personnel polices for recruitment and promotion purposes | Focus on improving the technological performance/ activity of the organization such as a new product, equipment, service, or introduction of new elements in the organization production process |
| Attributes | Complex, hard to observe, and difficult to substantiate results | Observable, triable, and perceived to be economically advantageous, and help to improve organizational performance |
| Impact of Change | Administrative innovation encourages technical innovation. It has greater impact on the social system including the technical system, i.e. changes in the administrative-social system leads to changes in the technical system | The innovation is limited to the particular task or structure. It may not trickle into the other parts of the organizational social systems. |
| Origins of Change | It begins from the top of the hierarchy and trickles down to the bottom of the organization | It starts from the bottom – professional groups and goes to the top – management group |

*Source*: Adapted from Damanpour and Evan 1984.

organization hierarchy. The higher the number of management groups, the greater the management hierarchy and intensity within the organization.

Damanpour (1987) suggested that administrative intensity, which is related to high managerial ratio and increases in management hierarchy, facilitates the adoption of administrative innovation. Since administrative innovations start at the top of the management hierarchy, administrative intensity impacts the adoption process the most (p. 679). He noted that as the ratio of management group increases, the chances for integration and successful adoption are greater (p. 682).

Organizations with high management intensity and hierarchy support administrative innovations. Since administrative innovations are introduced at levels higher than the technical core in the hierarchy, they affect the organization at large when compared to a technical innovation that is limited to a single unit. A successful adoption of administrative innovation facilitates technological innovation (Damanpour, 1987: 685). Administrative intensity increases the capability of organizations "to resolve conflict and integrate units," thereby facilitating the adoption and diffusion of innovation (p. 686).

Mechanistic organizations have higher levels of administrative intensity than organic organizations. A centralized decision-making process and the concentration of power within top management, facilitates the adoption and diffusion of administrative innovation, including accounting and information systems. Changes in information systems, cause the organizations to modify/change the way they assign individuals to specific positions or work assignments to conduct organizations' business (Krovi, 1993). Information innovation serves as an agent of social, technological and economic development, due to its increased role in specialization and diversification functions in mechanistic organizations and society (Laszlo, 1992).

Swanson (1994) approached information systems (IS) innovation within the context of organizational innovation. Information Systems is considered a functional unit/department within the organization. This approach extended Daft's (1978) dual-core model of organizational innovation – administrative and technical, by adding a third core – an IS core. "The functional IS core, serve[s] to link the other two cores together." The IS core has a business impact through its products and services. Swanson identified "three basic types of IS innovations, termed Types I, II, and III" (p. 1076). Table 7.2 defines these three types of information innovation systems.

Changes in information technology directly affect accounting and internal control systems. These changes have created uncertainties among employees. The resistance to IS implementation is mainly behavioral, related to the threat of job security, lack of commitment, cross-departmental/divisional coordination, increases in job complexity and the requirements for a cost-effective comprehensive plan approach, to implement the new system (Krovi 1993). Employee concerns about performance and normative influences, affect the ability of the organization to adopt and implement organizational-wide innovations.[11]

# DIFFUSION OF INNOVATION

Michaelson (1993) applied Roger's (1971) two steps of innovation decision process to define diffusion. "Diffusion is the process by which an innovation (any new idea, activity or technology) spreads through a population. Before any person adopts any innovation, two things must occur. First, he or she must

*Table 7.2.*    Types of Innovation in Information Systems (IS)

| Dimensions | Type I | Type II | Type III |
|---|---|---|---|
| Definitions | Restricted to the functional IS core such as management and administrative support of IS work | Applies to IS products and services to the administrative core such as introduction of computerized accounting systems, payroll, and personnel record systems | Integrates IS products and services with core business technology such as introduction of material requirements planning (MRP), computer integrated manufacturing or automated materials handling |
| Impacts on Business and Overall Organizational Performance | Effect is limited to the IS task itself such as introduction of systems programming, software maintenance where the focus is on IS administration. The changes may support business innovation | Impact is limited to administrative processes and infrastructure beyond internal IS work processes | Impacts upon general business administration in terms of strategic and competitive advantages for early adopters, improved product services and differentiation as well as low cost production |

Adapted from Swanson, 1994: 1076–1079.

become aware of the innovation and second, there must be a decision to adopt" (pp. 217–218).[12]

Communication enables individuals to become aware of new technology and its availability to potential adopters. The pattern of communication – word of mouth, face-to-face and interpersonal contact, network links through personal or peer/professional organizational ties, mass media and publication sources – in the adoption process becomes critical in influencing the individual's decision to adopt. Individual – friendship ties, social relations, organizational character-istics-and the organization's external environment influence adoption decisions. For example, in the diffusion and dissemination of scientific knowledge, social networks[13] based on interpersonal sources of information encourage adoption decisions.

On the other hand, when implementing a complex technological innovation and know-how, the process is difficult and involves a great deal of time, learning,[14] and resources. Knowledge transfer is complex, and skills are acquired through trial and error, feedback and communication, and learning-by-doing before their benefits can be fully realized. The process involves modifications, reinvention, recognition of unanticipated consequences, and risks learned over time. Adoption decision entails a learning innovation approach that is accomplished through information[15] sharing and communica-tion.

In capital-intensive technology, cost reduction in diffusion declines as the number of adopting firms increases. The firms adopt the technology in sequence, so that it is spread across the industry over time. Since firms in a competitive environment are assumed to have access to information on the value of the innovation, the adoption of new technology becomes primarily a strategic decision (Reinganum, 1981). When diffusion becomes effective in these organizations, it helps to reduce gaps in organizational performance. In this context, accelerating intra-organizational diffusion with limited resources, becomes important to reach performance goals (Cool, Dierickz & Szulanski, 1997).

Attewell (1992) discussed four factors that affect individual's and/or firm's/ organization's adoption decisions. The first factor is firm size, where larger firms adopt innovations earlier than small firms. The second factor is profitability of innovation affecting early adopters. Thirdly, innovative champions act as the innovation leaders who persuade others to adopt. The last factor includes organizational and environmental attributes related to firm size, degree of centralization, availability of resources – slack or scarcity, degree of functional specialization/expertise, and centralization vs. decentralization of decision-making process (p. 2).

Social, contextual and work environmental factors; such as autonomy of work which is associated with role innovation, as well as interaction among group members who exhibit cohesiveness and homogeneity, tend to affect creativity and influence individual and group innovations (West & Farr, 1989: 19–20). Ecological differences including geographical boundaries, cultural/ social norms, rules, procedures, strategy and structure influence the ability of organizational systems to adopt innovations. Table 7.3 lists the character-

***Table 7.3.***    Innovation Behavior Characteristics.

| Dimensions | Champions | Non-Champions |
| --- | --- | --- |
| Leadership Attributes | Exhibit transformational and charismatic leadership behavior. Serve as informal, inspiring, and motivational leaders to encourage commitment among followers to pursue their goals | Portray attributes that are associated with doers and followers instead of initiators |
| Issues Identification | Identify their own issues | Follow issues identified by others |
| | Promote the issues | Accept the issues |
| Personality Characteristics | Willingness to take risks if the plan fails. Demonstrate creativity, originality, commitment, self-determination, entrepreneurial qualities, and high need for achievement | Resistance to take risks, accept responsibility for failures, and exhibit low need for achievement |
| Influence Tactics | Ability to use personal power, build coalition and share information. Effective in using several influence tactics – friendliness, communication, reward, and punishment – to convince followers to accept their ideas/plans | Are more inclined to follow than to lead. Reliance on organizational basis of power |
| Involvement in Innovations | Design and develop the innovation as well as involvement in implementation. Provide direction and information to achieve system  objectives | Less involvement in the design and development of the innovation technology |

*Source*: Adapted from Howell and Higgins 1990.

istics associated with innovative champions such as: leaders who are transformational and charismatic; able to identify issues; design and implement them; convince others to follow their initiatives; and willing to take risks.

## ECOLOGICAL AND SPATIAL ASPECTS OF DIFFUSION

There are ecological and spatial factors that affect the geographical adaptation of diffusion. Ecological factors are related to geographical settings such as space, land, building, water, spatial pattern, and other environmental factors that innovation changes require for adoption and diffusion. Such geographical adaptation demands of innovations limit the speed and acceptability of innovations (Ormrod, 1992: 258). According to Ormrod (1992), geographical and spatial factors have "three dimensions of diffusion adaptation effects . . . they include: (1) the environment testing and selection of innovation during transfer, (2) the possibility of modification of diffusing innovations or receiving environments to improve adaptive fit, and (3) the filtering of innovations based on adopter motivations and cognitions" (p. 259).[17]

The spatial process of diffusion recognizes variations in geographical differences among regions, which account for the hierarchical order in innovation diffusion. Hierarchy among regions creates contagious forces where innovation filters down from a central, in most cases larger metropolitan areas, to peripheral regions. As the diffusion spreads from central to surrounding areas, the technological changes are adopted and improved to fit spatial conditions. However, these technological changes focus more on incremental improvements and are largely demand driven (Davelaar & Nijkamp, 1990: 183–184).

## ADOPTION ISSUES RELATED WITH TECHNOLOGICAL INNOVATION

Overall technological changes affect production relations and economic organizations in society. It shapes organizational power and structures, individual goals, social order and distribution of resources. It alters existing political power structures in the organization if adopted by those that are not part of the coalition. In other words, there are risks and uncertainties associated with technological innovations, which could result in delays in adoption, resulting from power conflicts among coalition members. Such delays in adoption makes the result of the "technologically improved product" short-lived and obsolete (Butler, 1988: 20).

While risks and uncertainties explain delays in adoption, differences in early and late adoption may be attributed to factors related to cohesion and structural equivalence,[20] as well as timing differences in investment decisions. In a study of medical innovation, Burt (1987) discovered that physical proximity, friendliness and network relationships caused social contagion of diffusion of innovation. Structural equivalence indicated that in medical innovations, physicians adopted new inventions, for example, prescription drugs, when their peers in the medical hierarchy profession adopted these innovations.

Soete and Turner (1984) noted that the costs and resource outlays associated with innovations, are the principal reasons for delays in innovation investments. The economic approach,[21] which is based on the contribution of technological change to economic development, stresses return on investment and cost saving mechanisms when making investments in technological innovations. It is assumed that organizations make different decisions about investment choices: when to adopt, how to seek the most profitable investment technique, where to invest, how to find the costs of new investment, and obtain more information on time, costs, and alternatives. It may involve a rational decision to delay action until all the relevant information on other organizations' experiences is obtained (p. 615).

To this effect, Witt (1997) expressed the economic risks associated with early adoption decisions. "The agents who adopted the new technology or variant at an early stage would have to bear a negative total relative benefit resulting from the initial network diseconomies. In contrast, those who adopt at a time when the diseconomies have already turned into network economies would profit from the 'investments' of the early adopters" (p. 769).

While some organizations learn the success of technological innovation through trial and error, other organizations adopt and imitate only those successful innovations. The economic rationale behind this decision is that the adoption of innovation "will increase a firm's present value above the pre-innovation level" (Jensen 1983: 162).

# INNOVATIONS IN ORGANIC VS. MECHANISTIC-TYPE ORGANIZATIONS

The size, work structure and task complexity of an organization determines the form and orientation: organic vs. mechanistic (sometimes referred to as mechanical) of that organization. Organic organizations are usually small or medium in size. They have complex tasks which require specialists, and handle relatively small work. Mechanistic organizations, on the other hand, are large in size. They process non-complex, routine and repetitive large-scale tasks that do not require specialized technical experts to handle work assignments.[23]

In mechanistic organizations, there is formalization, differentiation and several layers of management hierarchy. When there are large-scale, non-complex tasks, many employees are required to handle these tasks. There is the need for vertical and horizontal hierarchical arrangements and differentiation to process the workflow. Differentiation minimizes frequency of contact and exchange of information flow. As these hierarchies separate workflow, face-to-face communication becomes difficult (Hull & Hage, 1982: 572). Formalization of work arrangements and control systems have undesirable negative effects on process innovation and innovation behavior. Such prevailing characteristics affect mechanistic organizations' orientation towards process innovation changes.

The organization management literature suggests that organic type organizations encourage process innovation. For example, Hull and Hage (1982) indicated that the relationship between the size of the organization and responsiveness to innovation is more applicable to high technology firms than to other types of organizations. They "argue[d] that the organic model is not the only appropriate model [for innovations]. For example, organizations having mixed structures for performing large scale and complex work can achieve a medium level of innovation" (p. 566). This suggests that large-scale organizations with decentralized structures, have attributes that support innovation.

In decentralized organizations, there are small-scale autonomous units that handle small complex tasks and large-scale divisions that process several simple tasks. Decentralization promotes autonomy in decision-making and empowers managers to make investment decisions that improve the performance of their divisions. This indicates that organization type is not the only factor that affects innovation. Divisional structures and arrangements influence the degree and success of innovations in organizations. These characteristics explain whether or not there is an innovation lag in organizations.

## Adoption and Innovation Lag

There are individual, group and organizational differences that contribute to innovation lag. While individual factors deal with personality, behavior and attitudinal constraints, organizational factors are more general and address institutional environmental factors that affect innovations. Organizational lag refers to the relative differences in the degree by which organizations adopt technical and/or administrative innovations (Damanpour & Evan, 1984: 394). In addition to organizational type, divisional structures, work arrangements, and individual group characteristics all influence innovation behavior and the degree to which innovation can impact organizational performance. Information and communication are considered critical in the dissemination of innovation and in the creation of adoption lag.

Rogers (1971), and Rogers and Shoemaker (1971) concluded that the flow of innovation information and technological know-how is important in the diffusion process of innovation. Particularly, they stressed the level of contact between the originators and adopters, the personality characteristics of early adopters, the nature of the flow of information, and the choice of communication channels as key factors which affect the degree and speed of the adoption process. They suggested that the best strategy to accelerate the diffusion process is through the identification and dissemination of innovation through influential early adopters (opinion leaders). Once they are identified, the next step is to provide them with the support they need to influence others (followers) to follow them and adopt the innovation. Table 7.3 lists the innovative behavior characteristics associated with opinion leaders (champions) and followers (non-champions).

Failure to target influential early adopters and lack of appropriate means of communication, could reduce the demand for innovation information and create an adoption lag.[24] In essence, what Rogers and Shoemaker (1971) are suggesting is comparable to the view of Grattet, Jenness and Curry (1998) who viewed "diffusion as a process involving the homogenization of cultural practices and policy forms" (p. 288). In other words, diffusion involves cultural assimilation and the sharing of norms and values within the population of the targeted organization.

## *Innovation and Organizational Learning*

The diffusion process can accomplish organizational change if supported by education, training and organizational learning. The diffusion of administrative and management innovation programs[25] include the transmission of new knowledge and methods. If the innovation process is planned for quality improvement programs including total quality management (TQM), it requires education, training, organizational learning, and a planned intervention strategy.

Stata (1989) viewed organizational learning as a competitive advantage for organizations to be adaptive to changes in their institutional environments. "Organizational learning entails new insights and modified behavior. [It] occurs through shared insights, knowledge, and mental models" (p. 64). The objective is to find new ways and methods to speed up organizational learning and improvement. "Quality improvement, or total quality control as it is often called, is a management methodology for achieving improvement and change" (Stata, 1989: 68).

Chapter 7 reveals a causal relationship between organizational structures and process innovation strategies. In other words, the success of process innovation depends on organizational type structures. It has been documented that organic structures are best suited for technical innovations, while mechanistic structures are appropriate for administrative innovations. However, administrative innovations face organizational constraints. Bureaucratic procedures in operating systems of mechanistic structures and difficulties in establishing cost-benefit linkages in administrative innovations have contributed to innovation lag. While internal auditing and accounting control systems as part of administrative operating systems have experienced innovation lag over the years, recent developments in information technology have contributed to incremental change in accounting, recording and reporting of production and quality costs in business and manufacturing organizations.

Chapter 8 uses the mechanistic vs. organic structure typologies to examine organizational development's (OD) intervention strategy for organizational change and development. It applies the systems approach to examine quality improvement programs, the most notable of which is TQM. TQM as an incremental change strategy is based on the principles of education, training and organizational learning to sustain continuous improvement and change in organizational performance. TQM entails teamwork, interdivisional cooperation, cultural change and institutional development in planning and implementing successful process innovation change.

## NOTES

1.  Schroeder (1990) has noted the importance of complementary innovation changes in benefiting the overall achievement that would not have been possible from one aspect of the change alone. A good example of a complementary innovation is an improvement in communication and transportation systems, which enhances the overall impact of a given technological change. To this effect, Schroeder (1990) commented that "the presence of complementary technologies moderates the effects of the primary technology. In some cases an innovation's full utility is only realized after the emergence of other innovations" (p. 27). Accordingly, a change in one aspect helps to disseminate the overall components of the technological changes. "The proportion of firms in an industry using an innovation also affects its competitive role" (p. 27). As the number of firms that adopt the innovation increases, it becomes less costly to use cost-saving technological innovation.

2.  Gort and Konakayama (1982) described the controlling force in the market for entry and exiting firms as "the accumulation and use of knowledge. Two sets of

variables are decisive. The first is technological change; the second is the accumulation of knowledge through experience of what has come to be called 'learning by doing'."

Technological change arises from two classes of new information: "(1) information that can be appropriated by its producers and, hence denied to others; and (2) information that is transferable among firms without legal barriers . . . Transferable technology arises largely from developments in the underlying sciences and represents information that, once again is external to the industry . . . Thus . . . the sources of technical change [are] associated with: (1) proprietary information that (a) is internal to the industry, and (b) is external to the industry; and (2) non-proprietary, . . . transferable, information" (p. 1113).

Knowledge that is not transferable ". . . operates as an obstacle to entry, increasing the advantage of existing firms relative to new firms. It also generates a rise in the failure rate (exit) for firms that do not possess the new technology. To the extent that technical change is derived from information that is transferable or external to the firms in the industry, its impact on entry can be predicted to be strongly positive" (p. 1113). During the course of a firm's product cycle, the importance of internal proprietary information increases. Firms use patent rights to protect proprietary information (p. 1115).

3. Gort and Will (1986) were aware of the impact of competition on investments in innovations at early stages and their effect on not generating the desired rate of return. For them, competition increased the potential number of investors, due to increases in new ideas. "On the other hand, the division of the total market among competitors may mean that an innovator will have to share the returns to his innovation with his competitors. This should have a negative impact on investment" (p. 756). That is, the effect of competition on innovation is not significantly different from that of single firms over time during the industry life cycle.

4. Van de Ven (1986) elaborated the four factors of ideas, people, transactions, and context in terms of their importance in the management of innovation. "First, there is *the human problem of managing attention* because people and their organizations are largely designed to focus on, harvest, and protect existing practices rather than pay attention in developing new ideas. The more successful an organization is the more difficult it is to trigger peoples' action thresholds to pay attention to new ideas, needs, and opportunities. Second, *the process problem is managing ideas into good currency* so that innovative ideas are implemented and institutionalized. While the invention or conception of innovative ideas may be an individual activity, innovation (inventing and implementing new ideas) is a collective achievement of pushing and riding those ideas into good currency . . . . Third, there is *the structural problem of managing part-whole relationships*, which emerges from the proliferation of ideas, people and transactions as an innovation develops over time. A common characteristic of the innovation process is that multiple functions, resources, and disciplines are needed to transform an innovative idea into a concrete reality – so much so that individuals involved in individual transactions lose sight of the whole innovation points to *the strategic problem of institutional leadership*. Innovations not only adapt to existing organizational and industrial arrangements, but they also transform the structure and practices of these environments. The strategic problem is one of creating an infrastructure that is conducive to innovation" (p. 591, italics in original).

5. In a later study, Damanpour (1987) expanded the notion of innovation and innovation theory. He suggested that "innovation does not occur when a new idea is generated, but rather when that new idea is put into use. An innovation is not considered

in use when the decision for its adoption is made, but rather when its actual utilization by organizational members has begun. Organizations adopt innovations in order to maintain or enhance their performance. Innovations cannot influence performance until they have been actually used" (p. 676).

Innovation is solely considered in terms of its newness and its impact on organizational change. "As the environment changes, organizations must also change to adapt to the new conditions. Innovation are a means of introducing change into the outputs, structure, or processes of an organization in order to facilitate the adaptation process" (p. 676).

West and Farr (1989) provided a comparative perspective of innovation to that of Damanpour (1987), in terms of innovation's role in bringing change to work settings. They viewed "innovation [as] the intentional introduction and application within a role, group or organization of ideas, processes, products or procedures, new to the relevant unit of adoption, designed to significantly benefit role performance, the group, the organization or the wider society" (quoted not in italics). Innovation is an "intentional attempt to derive anticipated benefits from some change" and that "the possible benefits could be personal growth, increased satisfaction, improved group cohesiveness, better interpersonal communication, as well as those productivity and economic measures are more usually assessed" (p. 16). Thus, innovation benefits individuals and groups, as well as societies.

6. Teece (1996) further elaborated on the differences between autonomous and systemic innovations. "Autonomous innovations do not depart from current industry standards in terms of improving products and services within existing systems. However, systemic innovation changes technological requirements and offers new opportunities, so the resulting configuration of both the innovation and its related technologies (which comprise a system of technology) are different" (p. 217).

7. Damanpour (1987) identified six organizational variables that affect innovation outcomes. They include specialization, functional differentiation, professionalism, size, slack and administrative intensity (which is used as an indicator of management ratio and the degree of management hierarchy in organizational structure) to be positively related to adoption of innovation. Functional differentiation, specialization and professionalism are associated more with technical innovation changes, than administrative innovation (p. 678). He defined functional differentiation in terms of the extent to which the organization is divided into units. The larger the units in an organization, the higher the number of professional supervisors needed to manage the organization. Functionally differentiated units are expected to have higher rates of technical innovation. Specialization is the extent of the skills and specialists found in the organization. The higher the tasks and jobs are specialized, the greater are the chances for adoption of technical innovations. Professionalism is the knowledge and expertise of organizational members through education and experience. Professionalism is related to positive attitudes towards technological adoption (p. 679).

Dewar and Dutton (1986) reported a relationship between specialization and innovation. They suggested that the higher the number of specialists in an organization (for example, as indicated by membership affiliation in professional and trade organizations; diversity, complexity and depth of knowledge; broader perspectives; and mix of areas of specialization), the more likely radical technological innovations would be implemented.

Damanpour (1987) associated size with the rate of adoption, where the larger the size of the organization, the greater the rate of both administrative and technical innovations. This happens because larger organizations have both the resources and personnel to support innovation (p. 680). Organizational slack increases adoption. Organizations with more slack resources have better chances of adoption and are able to sustain the risks associated with innovation.

8. Witt (1997) argues that profits from innovations, even in situations of 'lock-in', will not be long lasting. If innovations result in technological 'lock-in', there will be limited chances for disseminating innovation. Even in situations where the effects of increased returns from innovation may halt, innovation will not succeed in 'lock-in' hypothesis. There are competitors and rivals "who threaten the market dominance of a technology or a variant." Competitive pressure erodes market dominance, creating changes in market structure and disrupting the possibility of technological 'lock-in'. Even if there is a 'lock-in', it does not prevent other firms from entering and succeeding (p. 762).

Witt recognized the inherent weaknesses in the 'technological lock-in' and 'virgin market hypothesis'. The virgin market hypothesis portrayed a market situation "as one where a number of rival variants enter a virgin market and compete to gain an advantage in their disseminating" of innovations creating a technological lock-in to dominate the market. Witt suggested that, "there seems to be some counter factual elements in the modeling approach that produces an interpretation of the 'lock-in' phenomenon as an inescapable state of affairs." The alternative model which Witt proposed, challenged the virgin market assumption by suggesting "a situation where an incumbent technology is challenged by an innovation that has been chosen as the initial condition. Since under increasing returns, earlier diffusion processes would have been 'locked-in' to the incumbent technology, such an approach quite naturally demands another interpretation of the very notion of 'lock-in'. A newly introduced innovation could never have a chance of disseminating if irreversible 'lock-ins' were indeed to occur" (1997: 771).

Witt elaborated that "in situations where a new technology is introduced, it is possible for the new technology to successfully disseminate in markets [despite] existing network externalities. Because these externalities always favor existing and more widely used variants, all success conditions seem to come down to ... the same prerequisite – the capacity to pass a 'critical mass' threshold, or more precisely, to attract a critical number of potential adopters who then make an adoption decision. This condition may, in many cases, be considered a prerequisite for industrial change ... Innovating agents have developed certain strategies to take account of the critical mass phenomenon" (1997: 771).

9. Michaelson (1993) discussed the importance of roles and positions in networks and their effect on the innovation process. While roles are expected behaviors associated with a position, positions on the other hand, are relational and embedded within the organizational structure. Accordingly, "... an aggregation of individuals will be referred to as a *position*, and a representation of the associations among relations will be referred to as the *relation structure*" (p. 222. italics in original). Michaelson expanded that "all the proposed models of an individual's position in a network are formally defined in terms of his or her relations with others in that network. Models of positions most often are based on structural equivalence or less strict regular equivalences. To the degree that two individuals are involved in similar social relations with similar others, they are said to occupy similar positions .... The relation structure

of a social network, a more abstract idea, is a model of the interlock among relations in a network. A relation can be defined as a set of individuals or on a set of positions ... the relation structure is examined from the perspective of a subset of individuals or positions" (pp. 222–223).

10. Gort and Konkayama (1982) differentiated between technical change and diffusion in production, that is, adopters of technical change, whom they referred to as producers. They stated that "diffusion in *production* is defined as the increase in number of producers, or net entry, in the market for a new product. It is to be distinguished from the more familiar problem in the literature on technical change, namely, the diffusion among producers in the *use* of new products and, hence, of changes in production processes for 'old' products (or services)" (p. 1111. italics in original).

A concern for diffusion studies in production is related to the supply side factors that affect innovation. Attewell (1992) highlighted that studies, which focused on individual behavior, focus on the demand side of innovation and assume that all individuals have equal access to innovation information and opportunity for adoption. Individual innovativeness behavior has thus become the focus of study. Attewell noted that the emphasis on the demand side of innovation has underscored "the supply-side institutions of diffusion. Institutions that supply and actively market innovations affect the spread of innovations, and determine to some degree who adopts and when. Since supply-side institutions often focus their marketing and educational activities on certain types of firms, it is unlikely that each firm will have an equal opportunity to adopt" (p. 3).

11. Lewis and Seibold (1996) discussed three types of concerns: performance, normative and uncertainty that affect the adoption of innovation in organizations. They are relevant to accounting and IS innovations, since these innovations directly affect performance and the normative-coping ability of employees to respond to organiza- tional-wide innovations. They attributed both performance and normative concerns to individual preferences and awareness.

"An individual's performance concern is a heightened state of awareness of, or anxiety about, his or her ability to perform, performance-related knowledge, or performance evaluation. Each of several incentives may act to promote an individual's concentration on performance and appearance of performances" (p. 134). Individuals' motivation and their desire to improve performances influence adoption decisions. On the other hand, "a normative concern is a heightened state of awareness of, or anxiety concerning, one's congruency in beliefs, actions, and values with members of social groups with which he or she strongly identifies" (p. 135). There are social and environmental factors that impact individuals' development of values, beliefs, attitudes and behaviors towards innovations. These organizational and social normative behaviors influence employees' attitudes, and their willingness to accept them, and have them fit organization innovation requirements.

12. Chatterjee and Eliashberg (1990) differentiated between macro and micro levels of diffusion and adoption. The macro-level which is related to "the diffusion of an innovation in a population involves the adoption of the innovation by individuals in the relevant population. Adoption, in turn, involves a deliberate choice decision on the part of the individual, especially in the case of high involvement products (such as consumer durables). Heterogeneity in the population suggests systematic differences in adoption times across individuals" (p. 1057).

On the other hand, the micro-level of adoption and uncertainty, focuses on "an individual's perception of the innovation [which] determines his evaluation of the innovation which in turn determines his adoption decision. Perceptions of the innovation are initially uncertain: these perceptions change over time as the potential adopter receives additional information about the innovation. An individual's timing of adoption is thus determined by the dynamics of perceptions, given his preference structure. Aggregation across individuals, yields the penetration curve; the distribution of individual adoption times determines the rate and pattern of adoption" (p. 158).

Grattet, Jenness and Curry (1998) provided an alternative view of the diffusion process based on the institutionalization of government laws and policies, particularly the institutionalization of hate crime laws in the United States. For them, diffusion "as a process involve[s] the homogenization of cultural practices and policy forms" (p. 288). They identified six factors: "temporalization, regionalization, structural/ cultural similarity, homogenization, exclusivity, and domain expansion" (p. 289). Temporalization refers to innovation being a time (period) specific event. "Social actors operating in different locations at the same historical moment share similar institutional environments" (p. 289). Regionalization refers to whether or not the diffusion can be spatially or geographically concentrated, since physical proximity speeds up the diffusion process. Structural or cultural similarity facilitates the emulations or copying of innovations among actors. Homogenization happens when the context of innovations (for example, new laws or regulations) are comparably similar among regions/actors (p. 290).

Exclusivity happens when changes/new laws tend to be unique to a specific situation. When "there is a pattern of 'exclusivity' in which states become committed to their past legislative enactments and are less receptive to ascendant strategies that actually may have greater legitimacy within the system. In other words, states that pass novel laws early in a time period are not expected to adopt dominant forms or forms institutionalized later" (p. 290). In exclusivity, there is differentiation when a state adopts a "single legal remedy [to] satisfy the demands of key constituencies as well as the larger institutional environment. In other words, some of the observable differentiation in policy is attributable to states that adopted early forms of law which never became dominant" (p. 291). On the other hand, in domain expansion, responses to innovation vary. "Like exclusivity, domain expansion is a countervailing force to homogenization; it implies that states' responses diversify, rather than converge, over time" (p. 291). Similarly it narrows over time, as things get more complex and expansive.

13. Midgley, Morrison and Roberts (1992) studied the effect of network structures/ typologies, on the manner in which innovations diffuse in industrial organizations. They suggested that the process of establishing a new innovative specific network "takes longer than establishing a communication link among existing networks." This establishment creates innovation lags that "slow down the rate of diffusion" (p. 549).

Networks help to understand the formation of linkages and development of relationships, exchange of information and other economic resources among organizational members (Midgley, Morrison & Roberts, 1992: 550). The effect of networks is to allow early adopters to influence late adopters. However, the decision to adopt or modify innovation is largely influenced by the number of people who have already adopted within the network. For network effects to be effective and reciprocal, Rogers (1971) suggested that there is a need to have a critical mass (at least a 25% adoption rate) in innovation where innovation has spread large enough to be self-sustaining and have a continuing phenomenon (Cool, Dierickz & Szulanski, 1997).

14. According to Attewell, the success of complex technological transfer and/or diffusion depends on the outcome of "both individual and organizational learning. Individual learning involves the distillation of an individual's experiences regarding a technology into understandings that may be viewed as personal skills and knowledge. Organizational learning is built out of this individual learning of members of an organization, but is distinctive. The organization learns only in so far as individual insights and skills become embodied in organizational routines, practices, and beliefs that outlast the presence of the originating individual. These routines may reflect an amalgam of individual learning or skills, and need not correspond to any one individual's understanding" (1992: 6).

15. Ormrod (1992) noted that "explanation of diffusion outcomes and diffusion patterns have typically emphasized the differential effects of information movement and innovation availability" (p. 258). The content, description and methods of communication information affect the reception and acceptance as well as the attitudes of the target population. Accordingly, the outcome of the diffusion of innovation depends upon the evaluation of the purpose of innovation, its suitability and acceptance. "It is reasonable to assume that a positive motivation must exist for an innovation to be adopted" (p. 259).

16. According to Ormrod (1992), "the spatial pattern that emerges as an innovation diffuses will be shaped by two primary influences, that of information flow, which creates local knowledge and awareness of the innovation, and that of local selection, which tests the adoptedness of the innovation" (p. 259).

17. Ormrod (1992) elaborated further on the three dimensions of diffusion and adaptation effects. First, the testing and selection dimension considers several factors that support or inhibit diffusion including geographical patterns such as location and space as well as spatial arrangements (p. 259). The modification dimension alters the success of an innovation even in situations where the innovation had failed in the past. Modification as a dimension is achieved through systematic efforts that might involve "evaluating, testing and adapting" (p. 260). Cost factors are included in the decision for the modification process. In addition, "modification during diffusion can also occur through the selective filtering of complex innovations. In this situation, some parts of an innovation may be found useful and workable in the new environment while other parts may fail" (p. 261).

The third dimension – motivation and cognition address "behavioral dimensions of innovation diffusion involving evaluation and decision making by potential adopters" (Ormrod 1992: 261). Motivation plays a role in adoption, when subjects expose "themselves selectively to innovation ideas and communication that are consistent with their interests, attitudes and desires" (see also Rogers & Shoemaker, 1971).

18. Davelaar and Nijkamp (1990) provide specific examples from high tech firms to support the theory of the spatial aspects of technological innovations. Innovations in the new 'high tech' firms, focused at the beginning on improving/changing product quality characteristics. Later over time, the focus of the innovation changed to capital investments "towards improving the efficiency of the production process" (p. 184). Because of the need for greater interaction, the spatial aspects of innovation assumed that the "new high tech firms" will be "concentrated in centrally located regions, (or model areas of network" (p. 184). The large metropolitan areas provide networks,

communication, information sharing and exchange. Over time, push factors such as government regulation on environmental issues, pollution, wage factors, and unionization contribute to the spatial shift of technological transfer from large metropolitan areas to peripheral areas where these factors are less of a constraint (p. 183).

19. According to Lewis and Seibold (1996), "an uncertainty concern is a heightened state of awareness of, or anxiety regarding, one's own and others' information access and information use" (p. 135). Limited information processing ability creates conditions of uncertainty in innovation investment decisions. Daghfous and White (1994) expressed their concern with innovation information and its impact in management of uncertainties. For them, "the most critical element in the innovation is enterprise information . . . explicit consideration of how uncertainties may become resolved to precision, of how negligence may become displaced by knowledge, and of how risks, costs, and rewards may be adjusted by information are the heart of effective innovation management" (p. 280).

As such, information uncertainties hinder the diffusion of innovation. Soete and Turner (1984) found "both uncertainty and lack of information about the new technology and the often proprietary nature of the technology" to affect innovation diffusion (p. 612). After reviewing several studies published on technological innovation, Tushman and Nelson (1990) concluded that "technology and technological change are consistently seen as sources of uncertainty for organizations. Technological change ranges from competence enhancing, incremental, and compatible to competence destroying, discontinuous, and incompatible. The greater the degree of technological uncertainty, the higher the pressure becomes for learning or knowledge pressure facing the population of organization. These learning or competence requirements are reflected in new work roles, new work flows, and revised language used to describe the work itself" (p. 6).

20. Midgley, Morrison and Roberts (1992) explained that "the structural equivalence model stresses competition between people of similar status and roles within a social structure . . . . [It] emphasizes the strength of the relationship between each of the two people and a set of third parties. The reason for this emphasis on third parties is that competitors are unlikely to make inferences about each other from the comments of third parties . . . In competitive industries there may be strong norms restricting direct communication between competitors, particularly if the innovation provides a significant competitive advantage to the adopter" (p. 536).

Since "many innovations have wider relevance and cross industry boundaries; for example, personal computers, facsimile machines, photocopiers, cellular telephone, and so on . . . these innovations messages may not be confined to sources originating within the industry" (p. 536). Such a view provides support for the structural equivalence view of innovation perspective. However, it needs to be noted that interpersonal communication is less relevant in diffusion, particularly currently, when research and development (R&D), marketing managers and venture capitalists use other types of medium of communication – mass media and other channels to get the information to potential adopters easily and quickly.

When rational adopters attempt to maximize their behavior consistent with their preferences, risks, attributes and social status, they are also in a position to influence those individuals who occupy similar structural equivalent positions. These behaviors create competition among individuals to satisfy their desired goals.

21. According to Attewell (1992), economic studies that analyze the demand and supply side of the institution of innovations, concentrate on "price and profitability" and "ignore non-monetary barriers and facilitators to diffusion" (p. 4). The diffusion of innovation is viewed "in terms of knowledge *transfer* . . . where technological knowledge are being transferred from the originating institution to user organizations" (p. 5 italics in original). These studies approach "the movement of complex technological knowledge under a model of communication most appropriate for signaling" (p. 5).

22. Soethe and Turner (1984) listed several factors that influence adoption decisions. Some of the list included the importance of the contribution of the new innovation to firm profitability, risks/uncertainties from adoption of the new techniques, and availability of information on the likelihood of adoption of new technology (p. 616). They suggested that while a higher rate of return from technological investment is desirable for innovation adoption and diffusion, adoption is more likely to be slow due to uncertainty and other limiting factors, for example, lack of availability of information on a timely basis (p. 617).

23. Hull and Hage (1982) proposed that the kind of work an organization performs, explains the differences between organic vs. mechanical (mechanistic) organizational structures. "Two critical dimensions of work affect whether the organic or mechanical model is most appropriate: the scale of operations and the complexity of the task. Organic organizations are best for small-scale, complex work while mechanical organizations are best for large-scale, simple work . . . . Typically organic organizations produce outputs requiring the utilization of skilled personnel . . . In contrast, mechanical organizations are best suited for mass-production operations . . . Clearly, the mechanical type of organizations has the best opportunity for maximizing productivity while the organic type has the greatest potential for stimulating innovation" (p. 565).

24. Attewell provided an alternative perspective on the adoption lag between early and late adopters. The explanation was based on the assumption that what caused "non-adopters [to] lag behind early adopters [was that] the former have not yet been influenced about its desirability by better informed contacts. Diffusion is therefore limited by the timing and pattern of communication" (1992: 4).

Attewell criticized the early adoption studies of Rogers (1971) and Rogers and Shoemaker (1971) because they "failed to distinguish between two different types of communication (or information) involved in the diffusion process; signaling versus know-how or technical knowledge. Differentiating between these two leads to very different perspectives on technology diffusion. Signaling refers to communication about the existence and potential gains of a new innovation. Unless a potential adopter knows about an innovation, and is informed persuasively about the benefits of using it, the innovation is unlikely to be adopted" (1992: 4).

Attewell also suggested that "learning and/or communicating the technical knowledge required to use a complex innovation successfully places greater demands on potential users and on supply-side organizations than does signaling. The amount and detail of information is far greater in the former case. If obtaining technical knowledge is slower and more problematic, one may hypothesize that it plays a more important role in patterning the diffusion process of complex technologies than does signaling. It should therefore move to center stage in any theory of complex technology diffusion" (1992: 5).

25. Stata (1989) suggested that management innovation programs could be best understood if systems theory is applied to improve management thinking. The implication of this approach is that "the rate at which individuals and organizations learn may become the only sustainable competitive advantage, especially in knowledge-intensive industries" (p. 64).

Stata also recognized that organizational behavior and the organization's character-istics influence the learning process. More importantly, "the values and culture of an organization have a significant impact on the learning process and on how effectively a company can adapt and change. In particular, poor communication between people and between organizations can be a major block to learning and quality improvement" (p. 70).

# 8. TOTAL QUALITY MANAGEMENT AS AN INCREMENTAL ADAPTIVE INNOVATIVE SYSTEMS STRATEGY FOR INTERNAL AUDITING AND ACCOUNTING CONTROL SYSTEMS CHANGE

## INTRODUCTION

Chapters 1 through 7 described various approaches to management and organizational innovations over the years. New paradigms and approaches to organizational management ranging from functionalism, systems analysis, contingency approach, population ecology and organizational selection were discussed. Chapter 8 presents management concepts in quality control, statistical control, quality circles and total quality management (TQM), which have appeared since the 1980s in accounting and organization management literature.

In the 1990s, increased global competition and a changing institutional environment have contributed to the emergence and development of new management approaches in quality and productivity. The emphasis on quality has evolved from quality control (QC) in the production process to quality circles to quality management. As such, the concept of quality, formerly limited to QC, has been expanded to include all aspects of quality management, notably TQM in the production and distribution process.

Chapter 8 discusses: (1) the TQM framework as an incremental innovation strategy for managing change in organizations, and (2) describes those TQM attributes applicable to accounting systems. The chapter outlines the internal auditing and control function of accounting systems that supports an organization's quality goals. The systems approach is utilized as a framework to evaluate TQM and the effectiveness of its uses in internal auditing and accounting control systems. An organization development (OD) planned intervention strategy is applied to describe organization-wide steps necessary to design, plan and implement internal auditing and control systems consistent with TQM objectives.

TQM's approach to manufacturing productivity and its emphasis on improved production operations, with or without minimal quality costs, have required changes in all organization systems, whether they involve mechanistic or organic structures. These changes have affected the functional areas of management, including accounting and internal auditing. The application of TQM to accounting function has brought an emphasis on meeting the accounting information needs of customers/users. Accordingly, accounting has focused on facilitating the allocation of organizational resources to meet the desired organizational quality objectives.

Chapter 8 uses the organic systems approach to demonstrate that TQM use in management control shapes the internal auditing and control function of accounting to provide information on quality costs and quality control. Management control systems in organic organizations report costs associated with storage, delivery, service and warranties to improve manufacturing processes and marketing distribution systems to better meet customer demands. However, meeting these quality goals depends on whether the organization has established an effective operational linkage between TQM and its internal auditing and accounting control system. To set the context for this discussion, Chapter 8 first reviews the evolution of TQM in manufacturing organizations.

# TOTAL QUALITY MANAGEMENT: AN OVERVIEW OF ITS EVOLUTION

The concept of quality is not new and dates back to craft-based work during the industrial revolution, that was popularized in mass production through quality inspection and design based prevention. However, quality was not until recently, stressed as the ultimate goal of an organization. International competition, particularly from Japan, has instilled the importance of quality and productivity in American businesses as a way of succeeding nationally and internationally.

Though the term quality is as old as manufacturing itself, it was not until recently when Japanese firms set quality standards for the rest of the world to follow, that quality became an issue of major concern for United States firms. While quality control and quality management have been discussed in management literature since the 1950s, it is only in the 1990s that the subject has received prominence in both the management and accounting literature (see Deming, 1986; Drucker, 1990; Johnson, 1992a; Harrington with Harrington, 1995). The 1990s put quality in the forefront as providing a competitive advantage for U.S. firms against Japanese and European firms. As a result, U.S. companies started emphasizing quality control/management by putting quality at the top of their priority list for the future (Krajewski & Ritzman, 1990: 81). In today's world economy, total improvement management (Harrington with Harrington, 1995) and competition are among the most important factors in running a business. For almost every product or service offered, there is more than one organization trying to make a sale. And, with more and more companies moving towards the Just-in-time (JIT) production system, price is no longer the only factor a customer considers in buying a product or service. Quality has also become an important factor customers consider when buying a product or service.

Increasing global competition and the volatile nature of business external environmental factors (Porter, 1992) have alerted U.S. companies to incorporate quality and productivity goals into their strategic planning processes. These concerns have brought a paradigm shift from quality control to TQM, so that firms can compete effectively by allocating limited resources at their disposal to those products and/or services they do best and where they have competitive advantage over competitors. Total quality has thus been adopted as the underlying framework that guides the production and delivery of products and/or services customers need by continually improving the manufacturing processes, internal operating activities and functions of the organization (Christofi & Sisaye, 1992: Sisaye & Bodnar, 1995).

Johnson (1992a) has discussed the evolution of the TQM philosophy in the United States. In the 1950s and 1960s, quality was based on scientific management principles, focusing on product quality by improving specific functional areas such as production and marketing that have a direct link with the customer. In the 1970s, manufacturing organizations started utilizing statistical process control (SPC) to improve quality and reduce costs associated with quality inspection programs (Drucker 1990). SPC was intended to eventually "eliminate the need for a separate quality inspection department" (Young, 1992: 683). However, the use of SPC was limited to setting acceptable quality levels, where errors and defects were not tolerated (Young, 1992). SPC and other statistical techniques such as total quality control (TQC),[1] control charts and graphs helped identify trends in physical defects/quality and directed the attention of production managers to address quality problems (Turney, 1991: 191, 198).

The use of SPC has been applied to improve the efficiency of the accounting function. Walter, Higgins and Roth (1990) discussed the application of control charts to analyze, evaluate, control, correct and improve four accounting processes which include: internal auditing, customer billing, tax return preparation, and travel and entertainment expenses. Since control charts are cost effective when they are applied to "large-scale repetitive processes," many of the procedures used in internal auditing "to determine the extent to which company policies and procedures are being followed" are repetitive and amenable to control charts (p. 90). Walter et al. (1990) identified how several of the internal auditing processes such as payroll accounting, invoice payments and revenue collection can be monitored easily through control charts. Accordingly, control charts can be used to map the 'in-control' and 'out of control' processes, i.e. outliers that require investigation and immediate corrective action. While 'out of control' processes require the implementation of remedial action, the 'in control' processes can provide examples/methods for implementation of improved internal control systems (pp. 90–91). Firms who use control charts to improve internal control systems are more competitive and profitable than those firms who do not use control charts. Control charts enable firms to provide quality-auditing services to client organizations.

In the 1980s, quality focused on improving the production function of organizations. In addition to SPC and control charts, JIT emerged as a means to improve scheduling and delivery systems, and reduce the costs associated with purchasing and distribution systems.[2] In fact, the JIT system is based on and thrives from total quality. In order for a JIT system to work, every material must meet quality standards; every part arrives at the place and time promised. Quality is controlled at the source, with workers acting as their own inspectors and encouraged to stop the entire assembly line if a quality problem arises. The goal of JIT was later expanded to the marketing and accounting functions, to support quality production goals of organizations.

Garvin (1984) identified three categories that constitute product quality in organizations. They are: (a) the user-based, (b) the manufacturing-based, and (c) the product-based. The user-based quality definition suggests that quality "lies in the eyes of the beholder." This is of special importance to marketing people, since to them, higher quality means better performance, nicer features and other (sometime costly) improvements. Manufacturing-based quality appeals primarily to manufacturing people, since they usually relate quality improvements to cost reductions. Manufacturing people believe that quality means conforming to standards and specifications and "making it right the first time." The third approach (product-based), views quality as a precise and measurable variable with specific identifiable characteristics that are quantitative in nature (pp. 25–43). Accountants, for example, use this approach frequently to calculate product costs, and use them as a basis for allocating service-department-costs to products or operating departments.

However, SPC, control charts, and JIT definitions of quality are all structurally limited to bringing improvements in the operating activities and functions of the organization. They emphasize the importance of quantitative measures in bringing about improved methods of internal operations. However, they underscore process improvement strategies that promote employee involvement in decision-making processes, employee empowerment, formation of cooperative work teams, improved communication channels, and cultural changes that support the quality goals of the organization. Later, TQM programs added process improvement strategies which structural job related changes.

TQM expanded the efforts of quality improvement begun by SPC and JIT in the functional areas of production, widening the focus from accounting, marketing and distribution to overall organizational wide intervention strategies. This effort expanded and included the creation of cross-functional quality teams designed to facilitate process improvement strategies which improve the quality of products and productivity of employees.

## TOTAL QUALITY MANAGEMENT: EARLY DEFINITIONS AND APPROACHES

TQM has been identified as a technique used primarily in the manufacturing environment, because of its value added contributions to management through the elimination of waste and quality costs in the manufacturing process, thereby achieving high quality products. TQM in the manufacturing process involves three interrelated approaches. First, JIT is used for reducing costly lead-time and excess inventories. Second, TQC focuses on eliminating waste and sustaining a zero defect objective in the total manufacturing cycle through standardization and flexibility of design, process and materials. Third, total employee involvement (TEI) is concerned with employee participation, creativity and fostering a culture that encourages full involvement of both production workers and plant managers in the work process (Smith, 1990; Drucker, 1990; Bhimani & Bromwich, 1991). TQM is based on JIT,

TQC and TEI to satisfy the product needs and requirements of the organization's clients.

The concept of quality evolved from craft-based work during the industrial revolution. It was later popularized in mass production through quality inspection and design-based prevention. Thereafter, the concept of quality, instead of being limited to quality control expanded to quality management in all aspects of the production process (Reiman, 1991). Later, management realized the relationship between quality and improved financial performance, and focused on eliminating costs associated with quality control, i.e. quality costs.

The principle of TQM rests on eliminating quality costs.[3] The three key concepts or elements associated with TQM include:

(a) customer satisfaction through continuous product improvement, production of error-free products, i.e. design quality as well as prevention of defects, and rapid delivery of high quality products or services to ensure on-time customer requirements/commitments, motivation, training and full involvement of employees in the work place.
(b) the role of leadership to provide company-wide vision, shared values and corporate culture, which stress quality performance.
(c) the development of strategic planning systems that define a corporate mission and long-term goals and formulate policies that match the strength of an organization, with requirements of the external environment (Reiman, 1991; Murrin, 1991).

There are other elements of total quality requirements that companies have incorporated in their mission statements. Many organizations have included the concept of quality in everything they do in the business. The objective is to foster stockholder value, through improved financial performance. There is a concerted effort to win public and media approval by providing total quality products/services. Organizations attempt to present a favorable company image, by ensuring that appropriate business ethics guidelines are followed, which conform to professional standards of conduct. Eventually, such concerns for public and social affairs contribute to the well being of the community and business stockholders (Fooks, 1991).

While TQM is largely a qualitative concept centered on the notion of effectiveness, quantitative indicators such as the value/cost ratio, value/price ratio, and error-free performance are also used to measure total quality performance (Fooks, 1991). Value/cost ratio is defined as the relationship between quality improvement and reduction of quality control costs. Value/ price ratio specifies the relationship between costs of TQM and product pricing as evidenced in gross margin, cost of goods sold, sales ratio, and profit margin (net income to sales ratio). Error-free performance is usually measured by the decline in quality inspection and control costs.

The quantitative aspects of TQM focused on improving production, distribution and marketing efficiencies to meet customer needs effectively. This approach focused on efficiency methods of organizations to utilize limited human, financial, technological and information resources, including accounting systems, on those products and/or services they can best provide to achieve quality and gain price advantage over competitors.

TQM, which encompasses quality control and quality circles, was initiated primarily in the manufacturing environment. Because of its value-added contributions to management through elimination of waste and quality costs, organizations that adopted TQM achieved high quality products. TQM provides a systematic approach to organizing all planned activities of the organization and implementing them accordingly.

TQM focuses on eliminating quality costs associated with the production process. In doing so, TQM's objective is to maximize customer satisfaction through continuous product improvement, production of error-free products, and rapid delivery of high quality products or services to ensure on-time customer requirements.

The role of leadership is to provide vision, shared values and corporate culture that stresses quality and performance development of strategic planning systems, which define corporate mission and long-term goals. Innovative leaders formulate policies that match the strength of an organization, with the requirements of the external environment. The cumulative effect is to promote the identification of employees with the organization and commitment to achieve organizational goals. TQM thus emphasizes teamwork and employee training and development programs that motivate them to get fully involved in the work place.[4]

Nowadays, TQM has been incorporated into every aspect of the business. While customer satisfaction is the ultimate goal of TQM, there is an emphasis on fostering stockholders' wealth and earnings through improved financial performance.

TQM also strives to win public and media approval by providing total quality products/services and promoting business ethics, by conforming to professional standards of conduct and involvement in public and social affairs that contribute to the well being of the community and business stakeholders.

TQM has been accepted as a management philosophy by many organizations to help shape their policies and competitive strategies.

## TOTAL QUALITY MANAGEMENT: MANAGEMENT PHILOSOPHY

TQM is based on a philosophy of continuous improvement of the manufacturing and production, as well as the service operations of the organization to provide high quality products and/or services to customers/users. TQM suggests that the first step an organization needs to take is to develop a mission statement that defines the organization's purpose, market, product, competitors, technology and customers. The organization's strategic plan incorporates the principles of TQM, as a long-term strategy to concentrate resources and efforts in those activities that the organization does best and where it has a competitive advantage over its competitors. TQM thus takes a pro-active rather than a reactive approach to managing organizational activities. TQM becomes an organization-wide intervention strategy that utilizes process (people-oriented) improvement strategies "to empower workers and managers to solve problems scientifically with an eye to constantly improving customer satisfaction" (Johnson, 1992a: 6).

The management emphasis of TQM is primarily to create a cooperative working environment that allows full employee involvement (participation) in the organization decision-making process, including the formulation of mission statements, meeting production quality goals, and improving delivery systems. To achieve the ultimate objective of TQM, improving the overall performance of the organization, people work in groups/teams to identify, analyze and suggest changes and ways to solve those problems that affect performance. To fully realize the process improvement goals of TQM, the philosophy calls for cultural change that fully supports TQM by employees, as well as by all levels of management, including top leadership of the organization.

In general, the main attributes of TQM include: continuous quality improvement, total customer satisfaction, and performance leadership in meeting customer preferences for products and services. An active role of leadership in providing vision, commitment, shared values and organizational culture that emphasize quality performance ensures the institutionalization of TQM in the organization's mission and strategic plans (Reiman, 1991; Tenner & DeToro, 1992).[5]

The U.S. government has encouraged business and service organizations to implement TQM to improve their competitive performance nationally and internationally. The federal government passed the Malcolm Baldrige National

Quality Improvement Act of 1987 (Public Law, 100–107), which led to the establishment of a new public-private partnership (Department of Commerce, 1987). The award was established in 1988 to promote TQM. The award recognizes companies who have demonstrated excellence in quality management and quality achievement in manufacturing industries, service companies and small businesses. "The award criteria are designed to support dual, results-oriented goals: delivery of ever improving value to customers; and improvement of overall company operational performance" (Department of Commerce, 1993: 2).

The Malcolm Baldrige award criteria are built upon a set of core values and concepts. They focus on customer driven quality products and services. Leadership characteristics stress the importance of strategic quality planning, information planning and personnel policies, commitment to public responsibility, and corporate citizenship. The enhancement of human resource development and management is evaluated on the basis of continuous improvement, employee participation and development. Fast response to success in competitive markets is examined in terms of customer focus and satisfaction, strong emphasis on design management quality, development of long-range outlook, management-by-fact (i.e. quality and operational results), partnership development, corporate responsibility, and citizenship (Department of Commerce, 1987, 1993: 2–4. For details of the program, see Garvin, 1991).

The role of accounting and control systems, thus become central to the implementation of TQM philosophy by providing accurate, timely and objective reports to management on the organization's operating activities. Internal auditing and control can support TQM and management actions, by identifying and correcting errors that affect the production and delivery of quality products and/or services. In other words, companies can use accounting information systems to enhance their competitive advantage.

Porter (1992) calls for a change in accounting information if it is to facilitate competitive advantage. He suggests modification of accounting rules to provide both quantitative and qualitative information on investment and performance measures, quality of life in the work place, management-worker relationships, as well as customer relations. He suggests that a competitive drawback is created by neglecting accounting measures for intangible assets such as research and development, human resources development programs that are necessary for continuously improving products and services, and established long-term relationships with customers and suppliers (Porter, 1992). Therefore, the accounting function needs to be improved in order to play an important role in accomplishing TQM objectives. The accounting function, which comprises one of the major subsystems of TQM, will be addressed in the next section.

## TOTAL QUALITY MANAGEMENT: A SYSTEMS APPROACH

TQM can be viewed as a systems approach for planned intervention strategy to bring continuous improvements in all operational areas of the organization. Systems approach is concerned with "problems of relationships, of structure, and of interdependence" (Katz & Kahn, 1969: 90; Churchman, 1979: 8). Systems are defined by their link with internal and external environmental processes. The systems approach considers several processes and conditions as characteristic defining features of any system. Systems are characterized by wholeness and internal and external interdependence. Systems component parts include structure, process, and outputs; and their functions include system maintenance, policy making, planning, goal setting, control, feedback and self-integration (von Bertalanffy, 1975: 47; Krone, 1980: 14).

TQM as a systems approach is a proactive organizational development intervention strategy. Organizational development (OD) has been used by behavioral researchers to address organizational effectiveness, adaptability and responsiveness to changes in the environment-markets, technology, information, values, service, and problems of employee commitment to achieving organizational goals (French & Bell, 1978: 14–19). OD examines four components in the organization that must be congruent. First, people denote employees of the organization. Second, processes refer to behaviors, attitudes, inter-personal and inter-group interactions. Third, structures deal with formal mechanisms designed to organize behavior to accomplish organizational goals and satisfy member needs. Fourth, environment includes external conditions – market forces, competitors, social and cultural situation with which the organization operates (Beer, 1980: 4–5).

As an organizational development strategy, TQM takes an organization-wide focus to bring desired changes in people's behavior. TQM has a customer focus and appraises the organization's structures and processes to meet product and/ or service needs and expectations. As a systems approach, TQM advocates a continuous improvement strategic planning process in all functional areas of management including accounting, in order to match the strength of organizational resources and capabilities with opportunities and threats present in the external environment.

TQM as an incremental organizational intervention strategy can take two approaches: process or structure. Process intervention is targeted towards changing people's behavior, organizational communication styles and flow of information. On the other hand, structural intervention strategy is oriented towards changing the components of organizational systems, which include changes in organization/job design, reward systems, performance management systems, and accounting control and internal auditing systems (Beer, 1980: 133–135, 159; French & Bell, 1978: 74–80, 165–170).

As a process improvement strategy, the philosophy of TQM is "to empower workers and managers to solve problems scientifically with an eye to constantly improving customer satisfaction" (Johnson, 1992a: 6). The principles behind process intervention strategy are based on teamwork, which promotes non-hierarchical/status-oriented cooperation for total employee involvement in problem identification and solutions. TQM encourages the formation of inter-departmental and cross-functional management teams/ employees who work on specific problem areas in the organization. TQM attempts to institute quality throughout the organization, thereby minimizing departmental interests in favor of organization-wide objectives.

The TQM strategy is to empower employees by enabling bottom-up, rather than top-down approaches to solve organizational problems (Zamutto & O'Connor, 1992). The human resources management program is designed to bring cultural change through training programs, thereby motivating employees to get involved in all aspects of decision-making processes in the organization. The quality improvement process of TQM is based on the need for process and structural changes within the organization, and the desire to do better quality work when performing daily operating activities in the organization.

As a structural intervention strategy, TQM is designed to gradually bring about long-term changes in organizational components or sub-systems, which include production, marketing, human resources, finance and accounting. As a systems approach, TQM evaluates the inter-relationships of various organization sub-systems/functions to examine the total flow of jobs or operations to find better modes of operations, so as to improve the quality of products and services to achieve total customer satisfaction.

The next section applies this systems approach, to study the accounting control and internal auditing functions of organizations. The systems approach has been utilized to examine existing internal auditing systems, and outline the organizational development intervention strategies needed for the design and implementation of TQM-oriented accounting control and internal auditing systems.

# INTERNAL AUDITING AND ACCOUNTING CONTROL SYSTEMS: THE MECHANISTIC (TRADITIONAL) VS. ORGANIC (SYSTEMS) VIEW OF CONTROL

Systems view of organization, studies the internal auditing system in terms of its contributions to the effective functioning of the organization as a whole. Internal auditing comprises one of the several sub-systems of the organization including production, marketing and human resources.

Systems analysis employs a wholistic approach to study the inter-relationships of the internal auditing function with other sub-systems/ functional areas in the accomplishment of organizational goals. The systems approach focuses on exploring how the internal auditing system can contribute to achieving quality product and/or services and continuous improvement goals.

To understand the internal auditing and control systems, the traditional (mechanistic) and the systems (organic) view of organizations has been applied. While the mechanistic approach facilitates control-oriented design strategies by consolidating managerial decision-making through centralized hierarchical control, the organic approach promotes flexibility and adaptability of organization structures through decentralization (Zammuto & O'Connor, 1992). As discussed earlier, the systems approach will incorporate both the process and structural views to understand internal auditing systems.

## The Mechanistic View of Control

The traditional (mechanistic) view of control assumes that the role of accounting information systems is to facilitate the allocation of reward systems, so that the action of the individual is consistent with the existing hierarchical structures that have clearly defined super- and sub-ordinate relationships. The functional view of accounting, which is based on the principles of the mechanistic view of control, stresses the role of accounting numbers in controlling employee behaviors and actions, as well as operating activities of the organization. The traditional (mechanistic) perspective of accounting, concentrated on those centralized accounting and audit tasks dealing with operation and production activities that are routine, repetitive, and pro-grammable (Dirsmith & McAllister, 1982). It advanced the view that operational control information such as variance reports and budgets, came primarily from accounting information, i.e. flows from accounting to operations, and ignored feedback from customers and other sources. Thus, accounting is to provide information that will enable managers to achieve desired profitability and income objectives (Johnson, 1992a: 123–124).

The traditional (mechanistic) view of control ignored the inter-relationships of the accounting function with other departments/functions such as operations, in processing information to assist quality improvement processes. As such, the internal auditing function was limited to ensuring the accuracy and consistency of the accounting report, used to dictate management actions towards meeting short-term accounting profit targets. As a result, the internal auditing and reporting function has contributed to management action that is not consistent with continuous quality improvement and competitive excellence strategies (Johnson, 1992a: 119).

## The Organic View of Control

On the other hand, the organic systems view of organizations examines the accounting and internal auditing function in relation to other functions or departments. The accounting function is viewed as providing the necessary financial information to report the company's operating activities, rather than controlling management's behavior and company operations (Johnson, 1992a). Traditional and mechanistic cost accounting systems designed to allocate costs, determine product costing and measure short-term performance measures do not facilitate behavioral control systems that promote cooperation, team work and group-based incentive mechanisms (Young, 1992: 693–694). As such, the flow of information is not from accounting to operations, but from operations to the accounting department (Johnson, 1992a: 123).

In accordance with the systems view, the internal auditing function is amenable to behavior and social control functions (Anderson, 1991: 71). Internal auditing facilitates the review of information quality, which is generated to prepare financial reports to check the accuracy of cost information and income figures to be used for planning purposes. The systems view thus integrates the internal auditing function with the other functions of the department, such as operations, to achieve TQM goals. In other words, the internal auditing function becomes an integral part of the business and is "able to assist in evaluating the productivity/quality of other departments" (Lampe & Sutton, 1991: 64).

In general, the internal auditing function in an organic system is adaptive to changes in environment and provides the company with the information it needs for competitive excellence. Similarly, "cost management systems must measure the key indicators by which manufacturing performance is based, such as continuous improvement, quality costs, flexibility, customer satisfaction, value-added and non-value-added activities, product life cycle costs, and other measures of strategic success" (Young, 1992: 693). The internal auditing function can monitor the cost accounting system to ensure cost management systems provide information that supports TQM.

Lampe and Sutton (1991) suggested two ways in which internal auditing departments can facilitate TQM programs. These are: "(1) to better define, measure and monitor the output of the internal audit department as one segment of the total entity; and (2) to assist in the quality reviews of other departments and segments comprising the total entity" (p. 52). Lampe and Sutton (1991) also suggested measures of effectiveness, such as the contribution of the internal auditing function to the achievement of the organization's quality goals. 'Efficiency' is defined as "the degree to which the total amount of auditor and audited resources consumed during the audit process conforms to predetermined allocations" as measures of internal audit quality (p. 53). 'Internal audit quality' has been defined as "the degree to which the service performed conforms to predetermined characteristics that determine the value to designated users of the audit" (p. 54. see also Lampe & Sutton, 1992: 26–27).

Similarly, Anderson (1991) defined internal audit quality functions as "the degree to which the function carries out its responsibilities to management, the audit committee, and the organization as a whole" (p. 67). The systems view suggests that a cross-functional team of experts should be formed to ensure congruence of the internal auditing function with organizational TQM goals.

Table 8.1 presents a comparison of traditional-mechanistic and systems-organic views of organizations. The application of traditional-mechanistic approach to accounting systems is similar to Johnson's (1992a) classification of the conventional-traditional approach, and the systems-organic view is comparable to the new-quality goal of accounting systems. The table adapts Johnson's (1992a) Chapter 7 on 'Management Information to Competitive Excellence' and other writers to present the two views of internal auditing functions.

A number of articles have discussed internal audit quality, quality circles, and TQM as they relate to audit quality and audit review processes (for example, refer to Anderson, 1991; Cashell & Presutti, 1992; Lampe & Sutton, 1991 and 1992). This book follows the suggestions of these articles in advancing the importance of TQM principles in the internal auditing function.

***Table 8.1.*** A Comparison of the Traditional (Mechanistic) vs. the System (organic) View of Internal Auditing Systems.

| Dimensions | Traditional (Mechanistic) | Systems (Organic) |
|---|---|---|
| Approaches to Costing Systems | Conventional – product-costing systems | Target costing – upper cost limit based on what the customer is likely to pay – activity-based cost management system |
| Role of Accounting Information | Control performance, operations, and people's behavior | Planning and tracking the results of operations |
| | Manipulation of financial results to achieve accounting targets | Improved organizational performance |
| Flow of Information | From accounting to operations department | From operations to accounting department |
| Cost of Quality | Attempt to reduce unit cost per internal audit work performed even if it lowers quality of work | Produce error-free reports by minimizing or eliminating cost associated with prevention, inspection, and correction of errors |
| Cost-Saving Mechanisms | Reactive short-term measures such as downsizing through early retirement, termination, and elimination of some internal auditing jobs which will not affect the activities that cause the costs to rise | Pro-active long-term measures designed to understand costing systems by type of activities performed in the internal auditing department |
| Capital Budgeting Decisions | NPV rule – accept if the PV of cash inflows is greater than the PV of cash outflows | Decisions based on both process (people orientation) and output based factors to evaluate the contribution of capital project to improved product and/or service quality |
| Planned Change Intervention Strategies | Departmental/functional orientation designed primarily for the internal auditing function | Organizational wide intervention strategy where changes in internal auditing function are examined in terms of their fit to other functional/departmental changes in the organization |

*Table 8.1.*   Continued.

| Dimensions | Traditional (Mechanistic) | Systems (Organic) |
| --- | --- | --- |
| Management/Leadership Style | Top-down approach that promotes individual specialization and work in the given area | Bottom-up, encourage team/ group work and cross-functional work in a given area |
| Organizational Structure | Hierarchical and formal structures<br>Centralized structures with functional orientation | Less hierarchical, fewer formal structures<br>Decentralized structures across functional areas, departmental orientation |
| Management Control Systems | Push control where the focus is on individual or departmental achievement of accounting-based performance measures | Behavior control that emphasizes cooperative work and team/group based incentive mechanisms |
| Organizational Goals | Short-term profitability goals | Strategic process orientation for total customer satisfaction |

*Source*: Adapted from Johnson, 1992(a); Young, 1992; Zamutto & O'Connor, 1992.

# QUALITY INDICATORS FOR INTERNAL AUDITING AND ACCOUNTING SYSTEMS

TQM can assist in improving operations of the internal audit department. It can promote process-oriented human resource management approaches, which include employee training development programs. It can enhance the education of employees on the use of accounting information for decision-making purposes, and the role of the internal auditing function in the accomplishment of organizational quality goals. Involvement and empowerment of employees to make decisions are achieved through the formation of cross-functional cooperative work teams, which encourage active interaction and communication among members when working on specific projects/programs in the internal auditing department.

Structurally, TQM calls for changes in organizational structures that allow decentralization. Less hierarchical departments encourage delegation of authority. Job design facilitates job rotation, enrichment, task simplification, work flexibility, reduction of cost and time required to complete an internal audit task, and the establishment of quality-based standards against which the performance and output of the internal auditing department can be evaluated and improved.

Lampe and Sutton (1992) noted that TQM or quality approaches to internal auditing involve "the development of a set of 'benchmarks' against which current measures can be compared to determine strengths/weaknesses in the audit and to measure degrees of change in quality between audits" (p. 26). In other words, TQM can assist setting up acceptable quality measures of audit performance, by both supervisors and subordinates. Since both management and employees work cooperatively in teams to identify and classify those service activities that affect audit quality, TQM processes institute self-correction devices to address audit service quality problems/errors when they arise. In addition, TQM encourages employees to continuously improve audit service quality.

The internal auditing function of an organization is a staff function, which ensures that the quality of accounting information reported/provided to line managers is objective, accurate, timely, consistent and representative for decision-making purposes. As a staff function, the internal auditing department provides service to other units and/or departments of the organization. Lampe and Sutton (1991) suggested the use of outcome and process measures of quality to evaluate the performance of the internal audit function. They have defined "outcome measures [to] concentrate on the increased value perceived by users of the audit report" and "process measures [to] concentrate on work performed by the auditor and how well it conforms with guidelines and objectives" (p. 56).

Cronin and Taylor (1992) indicated that quality in service organizations/departments is evaluated in relation to performance, while Turney (1991) relates service quality to activities rendered or provided to users. Since activities incur costs, auditing which entails checking and verifying accounting information according to accepted management guidelines, utilizes resources such as salaries, equipment, and financial and informational resources consumed to support the auditing function. According to Turney (1991), costs will be assigned to the auditing activity based on a number of criteria that measure the resources consumed such as labor hours, supplies used, space utilized to do the work (pp. 51–53). As such, activity based cost management systems help to identify and correct audit errors before their occurrence, thereby enhancing the internal efficiency of audit operations (Cashell & Presutti, 1992).

The demand for internal auditing services will be highly influenced by the weight assigned to cost objects, based on the amount of resources consumed by auditing activity drivers. Activity based cost management allows cost reduction by identifying and eliminating those non-value-added costs that influence the demand for auditing service activity. The primary performance indicator of audit service quality is the frequency of errors reported. If the audit service were in line with the TQM objectives of the organization, one would expect a minimum or zero error reported in the auditing function. This is likely to decrease the cost per unit of the internal audit service, thereby increasing the demand for such service in the organization.

Table 8.2 provides quality checklist indicators that can be used to evaluate the internal audit function performance. These quality checklists are adapted from *AICPA Auditing and Accounting Manual, AICPA Statement on Quality Control 1 – System of Quality Control for a CPA firm, Quality Standards Committee of the AICPA,* and publications from *CPA Journals* (refer to Goldstein, 1987; Loscalzo, 1988; Manusco, 1990). The checklists broadly outline those elements of quality control such as independence, human resource management, internal structures and operational activities associated with internal auditing functions.

However, quality service as a goal of the internal auditing function will not be achieved unless the organization designs and implements a system-wide based planned intervention strategy program. The following section presents an OD approach for the design and implementation of TQM principles in the internal auditing function, as part of an organizational-wide planned change intervention program.

# PLANNED INTERVENTION STRATEGIES TO IMPROVE THE SERVICE QUALITY OF INTERNAL AUDITING SYSTEMS: AN ORGANIZATIONAL DEVELOPMENT APPROACH

Organizations introduce planned change programs such as TQM to bring about new methods of operating activities. However, unanticipated problems of implementation are likely to prevail if these change programs do not involve all members of the organization; including the accounting and internal auditing staff, and are not supported and implemented by management as part of overall organizational change strategies. Several authors have identified some of the problems management has ignored in the design and implementation of accounting systems.

***Table 8.2.*** Quality Checklist for Internal Auditing Function.

### Structural Issues

*Internal Structures*

- Does the organizational structure facilitate delegation, autonomy and independence of the internal audit function?
- Does the job design and structures of the internal auditing function allow flexibility, initiative and independence?
- Are both formal and informal means of communication frequently used among internal audit staffs and between the internal auditing and other departments within the organization?
- Does the organization utilize cross-functional teams to study or investigate specific work inefficiencies for improvement in the internal audit department?
- Is the importance of the internal auditing department related to its size as measured by number of personnel, and size of budget allocation?

*Operational Activities*

Reports

- How often are reports prepared?
- Type of reports, e.g. sales, budgets, expenses prepared?
- Frequency of reports completed on time and submitted late including complaints received for late reports?
- Number of reports prepared to meet specific departmental requests?
- The extent of problem identification, definition, analysis, and frequency of errors in the report?
- What is the cost involved in both personnel and time to correct these errors?
- Are the reports both useful and user-friendly?
- Are the reports understandably relevant, accurate, timely, and up to date?

*Current Assets and Liabilities Management*

- What is the length of time required to process payroll, travel requests, customer bills, and purchase vouchers?
- How often are internal audits performed on cash management and other liquid assets?
- What is the average collection period and the types of action taken to reduce number of collection days and uncollectable accounts?
- How often are mistakes incurred when recording cash receipts/register, customer checks and payments to suppliers and vendors, processing travel requests and payroll?

### Process Issues

*Independence*

- Do internal auditors enjoy independence from upper level and departmental/functional management while performing internal auditing and accounting functions?
- Does the organization prescribe to professional organizations such as AICPA, IMA, IAA internal code of ethics governing the behavior and action of internal auditors while conducting their jobs/activities?

**Table 8.2.**   Continued.

Process Issues – Continued

*Independence – Continued*

- Has the organization developed its own internal code of ethics governing the professional conduct of its employees, including internal auditors?
- What reward/sanction system does the organization utilize to insure that its internal audit employees are independent and have conducted their functions according to predetermined professional standards?
- Are staff members encouraged to join professional organizations such as AICPA, IMA, IIA and AAA, to attend their seminars/conferences and read their publications to stay current in the field and acquire the professional expertise needed to exhibit independence and compliance to procedures when performing internal audit functions?
- Do staff members have access to libraries and/or consulting services for referral on accounting and internal auditing issues that require significant research?

*Human Resource Management*

- Did the organization develop qualification guidelines specifying education, course work, technical skills, and experience required of the internal auditing staff positions?
- Does the recruitment and selection policy ensure that individuals who possess the appropriate qualifications required to fill each position fill all positions?
- Is quality performance recognized and rewarded through quality awards such as merit bonus, certificates, plaques, and posters for employee of the month?
- Are there internal guidelines that ensure that when making transfer and promotion decisions, there is a match between personnel background and the required qualifications for those positions?
- Does the organization facilitate professional growth and development through on-the-job training, course work, short-term training, attendance at seminars and conferences to meet state and professional association licensing and continuing education requirements?
- What is the average length of time needed to complete training programs and how often do staff receive training and career development programs?
- Does the supervisor and the subordinate discuss the nature of audit work to be performed in a given time period and thereby agree on the procedures to be used to ascertain if the job has been done according to accepted guidelines?
- How often do supervisors and subordinates meet to discuss projects and specific assignments?
- Does the organization utilize specific guidelines that include questionnaires, checklists and other formalized methods to assess the quality of audit work performed?
- Are individuals given the power and responsibility to review a report, conduct a study or develop checklists to monitor and improve the daily activities of the audit work team?
- What is the level of job satisfaction as measured by employee turnover, length of tenure, absenteeism, and tardiness?

*Sources*: Adapted from Goldstein 1987; Loscalzo 1987; and Mancuso 1990.

Johnson (1992a) pointed out that for TQM programs to be effective, organizations have to be willing to change their focus from short-term goals such as cutting production costs, increasing the efficient utilization of resources, and reinforcement of top-down hierarchical control systems. Otherwise, TQM programs are not likely to bring long-term solutions that will make the organization competitive and responsive to customer needs (pp. 7–8).

Barfield and Young (1988) have discussed the lack of accounting and internal control departmental staff involvement in the design and implementation of JIT and TQC systems. Since these systems were designed by manufacturing engineers to bring production efficiencies, improvements in cost management systems were later introduced in response to information needs of production departments. However, the indicators were not adequately developed to measure productivity performance.

Johnson and Kaplan (1987) have found that existing cost management systems are inadequate to support JIT and TQC programs. They reported that the information provided for product costing was limited only to the production control function of the organization (see also Kaplan, 1989).

In other words, planned intervention strategies that are designed to bring long-term process and structural changes are not likely to be successful, unless they are systems oriented programs focusing on overall organizational changes, instead of improvements focusing on specific departmental or functional changes. In addition, the success of these change programs depends on the total support and commitment of top management, as well as organization members at lower levels.

A systems approach examines the adequacy of organizational resources, management commitment to meet organization objectives, and fulfilling member needs. Organizations are viewed in terms of open systems, which are comprised of structural components. Each system component functions and adapts to changes within the total system (Beer, 1980; French & Bell, 1978). As an open system, the organization responds to its environment by adapting internal processes/structures to meet system objectives, thereby maintaining its character as a system (Krone, 1980). As a specific application of systems analysis, process and structural intervention strategies are used to analyze systems and implement planned change programs. If internal auditing and control systems are expected to improve overall organizational service and productivity consistent with TQM objectives, it is advocated that a systems-based intervention strategy that involves both structural and process changes in the internal auditing and control functions be put in place.

## Structural Intervention Strategies

Structural intervention strategies focus on the modification of organizational structures through organizational design. This approach requires changes in levels of hierarchy and decentralization of decision-making, job design, realignment of organizational divisions/departments or functions, and institutionalization of reward performance management systems designed to improve an organization's operating activities (Beer, 1980). Structural changes in the internal auditing function specifically address the nature of work activities and mode of internal auditing operations.

Table 8.2 provides a checklist of the internal auditing function. Structural change addresses those factors listed under internal structures, and operational activities that involve safeguarding the organizational resources by continuously monitoring current assets and liabilities, and verifying accounting reporting systems. Since structural intervention strategies institute internal auditing structural changes as part of the overall system-wide organizational change strategy, the internal auditing function will support TQM objectives and other planned change programs, by developing and reporting accurate accounting indicators that can be used to evaluate organizational performance.

Decentralization allows the internal auditing department staff to participate actively in the planning and implementation of programs that will affect their department and jobs. Their full involvement and empowerment to make changes will bring continuous improvement in the quality of work performed in the internal auditing department. The cumulative effect of this change is in the development of an effective internal control system for the management of current assets and liabilities and the preparation of error-free, timely, reliable and relevant reports for management decision-making.

Structural barriers that impede people from participating in planned changes need to be removed before introduction of process changes in an organization. That is, long-term oriented changes in the internal auditing function cannot be fully realized unless structural changes are followed by process changes.

## Process Intervention Strategies

Process intervention strategies are designed to initiate attitude and behavioral changes among organizational employees. Process changes involve new behavior patterns that foster interpersonal and inter-group interaction, and create improved formal and informal communication linkages within work groups/teams and among individuals at all organizational levels. Process changes enable employees to participate in the achievement of internal auditing department and organizational-wide objectives.

Table 8.2 lists the process issues associated with the internal auditing function. Process intervention strategies designed to change the behavior of the internal audit staff and instill new attitudes to support TQM programs, need to at a minimum address those issues related to independence and human resource management. Since TQM is designed to provide employees with full involvement and empowerment in all aspects and phases of planned organization changes, it requires the re-examination of trouble spots by employee teams (a bottom-up rather than top-down strategy) (Zamutto & O'Connor, 1992). It advocates cooperative team work that draws from all functional areas to solve specific problems. Improved interaction and communication among individuals and team members enables them to work more effectively on a given problem.

The internal auditing function will improve, if process changes bring about new behavior among the staff that encourages independence and initiative in carrying out auditing responsibilities. The implementation of human resource management programs that recognize quality work, reward employees and promote team work through group incentive mechanisms, will produce long-term quality programs directed towards continual improvement of internal control and auditing systems.


# INCREMENTAL PROCESS INNOVATION CHANGES: STRUCTURAL AND PROCESS IMPLEMENTATION STRATEGIES IN ACCOUNTING CONTROL AND INTERNAL AUDITING SYSTEMS


A planned systems-based intervention strategy designed to bring structural and process changes in the internal auditing systems requires a gradually phased, incremental, step-by-step implementation strategy. If total quality is to be successfully implemented in the internal auditing and accounting control systems, it needs to be implemented as part of a systems-wide strategy in all functional areas of management. In other words, the intervention strategy becomes part of the overall corporate strategy supported and initiated by management, with full employee involvement in all phases of the implementation process (Christofi & Sisaye, 1992; Sisaye & Bodnar, 1995).

Planned intervention strategies advocate the use of a change agent or facilitator for the effective implementation of planned change programs. Organizations can recruit senior managers or experts who enjoy the respect and confidence of employees, to serve as change agents for specific improvement programs. Change agents can publicize and help secure the support of employees for the new programs. Improvements in the existing internal auditing systems are likely to create uncertainties that might positively or negatively affect some employees through attrition, consolidation of functions and restructuring of jobs by introducing new equipment. This makes it necessary that change agents explain and educate employees about the new program's objectives, and solicit their support and active involvement in the design and implementation processes.

If quality is a primary goal of internal auditing systems, the accounting systems should strive for continuous improvement in the quality of information that is collected, analyzed and reported. This requires a planned implementation strategy that involves a gradual, incremental, step-by-step or staged approach for the institutionalization of total quality principles in internal auditing systems.

Rosander (1989) suggests five steps for implementing the quality improvement process: (a) problem identification, (b) problem analysis, (c) planning, (d) data collection, (e) data interpretation, (f) action, and (g) appraisal (p. 143). Other authors, for example, Manusco (1990);[6] Smith (1990); Turney (1991); and Woods (1989) also recommended similar staged intervention strategies for the implementation of new accounting systems. Smith (1990) suggested six stages of TQM intervention strategies: (a) problem identification, (b) ranking, (c) analysis, (d) innovation, (e) solution, and (f) evaluation to implement quality improvements. He recommended total employee involvement in all aspects of the design and implementation process.

Turney (1991) discussed the importance of gathering the necessary information through interviews, questionnaires, on-site visits, as well as meetings, when designing and implementing new accounting systems (pp. 241–245). Woods (1989) called for setting up an executive steering committee composed of top management personnel, who serve as change agents to institute total quality concepts in all functional areas of management including accounting.

The formation of cross-functional teams who have the expertise in internal auditing and accounting, and the involvement of the internal auditing department staff in all phases of the implementation processes, ensures the institutionalization of total quality internal auditing objectives in new systems. TQM programs encourage team members and auditing employees to search for continuous improvement in accounting systems (Christofi & Sisaye, 1992). Appendix 4 provides short descriptions of cases, to show the relationship between TQM and cost management and the effect on accounting for production and quality costs.

Chapter 8 argues that the ultimate objective of a planned systems-based intervention strategy is to bring about both structural and process change into the accounting and internal auditing system. To do so, TQM programs need to be implemented in a gradual, staged, step-by-step approach, whereby OD agents are used to solicit employees' support and motivation, to actively participate in the design and implementation of new or improved internal auditing and accounting control systems.[7]

Chapter 8 outlines a systems-based OD approach to planned intervention strategy, which is appropriate, if structural and process changes in internal control and auditing systems are needed. This piecemeal approach is intended to create a staged, step-by-step implementation strategy to achieve purposeful, continuous quality improvement changes in internal auditing functions.

The implications of the Chapter 8 discussion are that systems-based organization-wide change strategy is a pre-requisite for any planned change intervention, which aims to achieve desired quality changes in internal accounting control and auditing systems. Any improvements in internal auditing systems, therefore, need to be designed and implemented as part of an organization-wide planned change intervention strategy. The desired structural and process changes in internal auditing systems can be successfully achieved, only if these changes are part of an overall organizational strategy, actively supported by organizational management and enjoying the full participation of employees in all phases of design and implementation. However, despite the emphasis on planned change and development efforts, the TQM approach has demonstrated mixed results. Management began to consider the limitations associated with TQM's approach in OD gradual intervention strategy, which has been less effective in creating significant improvement in organizational performance.

In the mid 1990s, management researchers and consultants began seeking new paradigms to bring about changes in organizational structures and operating systems. Thus, reengineering came to the forefront to overcome management shortcomings associated with TQM programs. Management's desire to establish linkages between the costs and benefits of change necessitated a paradigm shift from TQM to reengineering. Chapter 9 presents the management philosophy of reengineering and its structural and behavioral strategies for the management of process innovation in organizations.

# NOTES

1. Total quality control (TQC) focused on zero defects and statistical process control (SPC). Basadur and Robinson (1993) elaborated TQC and SPC as quality tools that shape the strategic management approaches of organizations, which emphasize cost saving strategies in their production decisions. They stressed, "zero defects is the concept that no defects at all in the products and services delivered to customers is a reachable goal and should be pursued relentlessly. SPC is a convenient catchall phrase for a family of specific statistical tools, such as control charts. Pareto analysis, process flow diagrams, and fishbone diagrams apply statistics to control work processes (especially, but not confined to, manufacturing) in organizations. Identifying and reducing variation in a system continuously improve the quality of products and services. These statistics are kept by the workers themselves, and the primary responsibility for good quality work is thereby placed with the people doing the work, not with these rational tools to quality problems that require team effort across system, quality circles are used in which workers are organized into small problem-solving groups" (p. 123).

2. Flynn, Sakakibara and Schroeder's (1995) study of Japanese manufacturing firms demonstrated that there is a relationship and synergy between JIT practices (lot size reduction, set up time reduction, inventory size reduction and JIT scheduling) and TQM practices (statistical process control, product design, and customer flows) in improving organizational performance. While JIT focuses on the elimination of waste, TQM concentrates on improving the quality of products and services to satisfy customers. To be effective, both JIT and TQM practices interacted with common infrastructure practices: "information feedback, plant environment, management support, supplier relationship, and workforce management" to achieve quality performance objectives (p. 1354).

In addition, "common infrastructure practices were found to form a strong foundation for both JIT performance and quality performance ... TQM practices interacted with common infrastructure practices and JIT practices to reduce cycle time. As JIT strives to produce in lots of one with minimum inventory, TQM practices help to provide the levels of quality that allow production to proceed with minimum safety stock inventory while remaining in schedule. In addition, TQM practices facilitate cycle time reductions through reducing the time required for rework of defective items and production of non-value-added scrap items" (p. 1354).

Moreover, Flynn, Sakakibara and Schroeder (1995) found that "JIT practices interacted with common infrastructure practices and TQM practices by exposing opportunities for process improvement and reducing the potential for spoilage and damage through the reduction of inventories" (p. 1354). However, they noted the limitations and tradeoffs of TQM and/or JIT by suggesting "management needs to carefully assess an organization's culture and strive to match elements of TQM and JIT to it" (pp. 1354–1355).

3. Quality, time (service), and cost are three important areas in which companies compete in the market place. Quality provides information for strategic decision-making. By compiling information not provided by traditional cost systems, accountants can highlight the cost of poor-quality products for potential cost reduction, without actually affecting the quality of the product or service as perceived by

customers (non-value-added costs) (Horngren & Foster, 1991). The quality of a product or service is its conformance with a pre-specified (and often pre-announced) standard. One way to measure quality, according to Crosby Associates Inc. (1988), is through the calculation of how much it costs when things are wrong. They called this measurement the Price of Non-Conformance (PONC). PONC is composed of costs associated with reprocessing, expediting, unplanned service, computer reruns, excess inventory, complaint handling, downtime, rework, returns, and discounts. In short, PONC is the cost of wasted time, effort, and material.

With a quality-measurement program in place, management will be able to decide whether and where corrective action is needed, how well it has done, and how much it will cost the firm if it does not improve. A cost-quality program collects product-quality-related costs incurred in the different business functions of an organization, and reports them in a comprehensive reporting format.

Morse, Roth and Rosten (1987), and Horngren and Foster (1991) view quality costs as costs incurred as a result of the existence of poor quality and they classify them into these four categories: (a) Prevention costs which are incurred to prevent poor quality costs from being produced. This is accomplished through quality training development of control mechanisms, as well as planning and designing for quality management. (b) Appraisal costs which result from activities undertaken to prevent poor quality products from being produced, and may be accomplished through inspection and continued testing of products as well as quality audits. (c) Internal failure costs arise from producing products that do not meet quality standards. These costs arise when products fail to meet internal quality standards, and are incurred for repair, rework, retest, re-inspect, and other related costs. (d) External failure costs arise when low quality is delivered to customers and are incurred to meet warranty replacement, recalls or returns and allowances, and product lawsuits or liabilities.

By pooling costs across different business functions, the magnitude of total quality related costs could be determined. The items included in a cost of quality program come from all major business functions. Any individual in a single business function would probably not be able to observe the magnitude of total quality costs, unless they are summarized in a comprehensive system. Most existing accounting systems, while reporting a subset of the cost items (rework etc), are not designed to focus comprehensively on cost of quality for the organization as a whole. The cost of quality report can be used to examine interdependencies across the four categories of quality-related costs. Business functions are interrelated by having an impact on customer service and satisfaction. By understanding and promoting these interdependencies, management accounting can help a company eliminate non-value-added costs, without affecting product or service quality. Traditional cost accounting systems do not isolate costs of poor-quality products, and since these costs are not visible, they are not included in the performance evaluation/reward system. An increasingly important role of the management accounting system is to compile these costs and make their total magnitude visible to upper management (Horngren & Foster, 1991).

4. Sterman, Repenning and Kofman (1997) pointed out that there are at least three components of good quality programs: training of employees, team work and setting up a realistic achievable objective to be accomplished within a specified time period (p. 504). "TQM initiatives require management support in the form of training, assistance, rewards, and release time from normal responsibilities" (p. 509). The success of TQM depends on the commitment of organizational members. Commitment

in turn, is affected by several factors including the role of the leaders, results of quality programs, management support and job security.

Accordingly, "the introduction of TQM stimulates a few initial improvement efforts. If support resources are adequate and job stability is high, early results of the improvement effort will encourage others to participate, leading to still greater results. Commitment will grow rapidly and defects will fall. However, if participating in TQM takes too much time away from people's primary responsibilities, or if the productivity gains created by improvement lead to reorganization or layoffs, the effects of inadequate support and low morale can overwhelm the effect of results and cause commitment to fall. Thus the feedbacks from the diffusion of commitment to the rest of the organization are critical" (pp. 509–510).

5. To successfully implement TQM, "an effective organization must be skilled in three distinct types of change-making activity. The three different levels of change skills that are important in organizations (in order of increasing difficulty) are flexibility (quick and positive reaction to sudden disruptions to routine processes), efficiency improvement (proactively making continuous improvements to current routine processes, products, and services), and adaptability (deliberately seizing new changes in the environment of the organization to create new products, services, and processes that did not exist before)" (Basadur & Robinson, 1993: 136).

6. Manusco (1990) outlined a similar set of five steps for the design and implementation of quality control systems appropriate for internal auditing systems. They include: (a) collection of the required information and assembling of subject expertise, (b) evaluation of existing systems to assess what changes may be required to improve them, (c) preparation of manuals, reference guides and employee training programs and staff meetings to implement required revisions to existing policies and procedures, (d) revision and analysis of operating results of the improved system, and (e) modification of the system based on feedback received and the institutionalization of the final revised systems (pp. 97–98).

7. There are several pitfalls that are associated with TQM and quality improvement programs. Some of these pitfalls are associated with poor implementation; lack of integration with the organization's strategy and policy; weak leadership and support for quality programs; lack of training; resistance by organizational members; threat of employee lay-offs; and/or displacement by quality programs; and impact of reorganization on job security, turnover, staff reduction, and turn over. When TQM was adopted by some organizations, it was largely used as a slogan and rhetoric to elicit support of employees and empower them. TQM was used to dress up strategies and policies that have not either changed or worked in the past. It never fully achieved the support and cooperation of those individuals and or groups who were involved in TQM projects.

While quality improvement programs contributed to lower product costs, product defects, manufacturing cycle-times; increases in quality products were not followed by improved financial performance. Increases in productivity and lower costs of production contributed to excess capacity, which affected price and profit margins. The structural effect of cost reduction strategies resulted in financial distress and below average industry performance.

Sterman et al. (1997) noted that in many organizations, improvements in quality programs benefit customers in both quality products and low prices, but sometimes fail to be translated into market advantage and increased profits. As quality improved, prices declined as a result of increased competition. Increases in market competition offered several substitutable goods and services, which reduced prices and profits. Investors' confidence decreased, when earnings eventually dropped, which resulted in lower stock prices and firm valuation (pp. 513–514). Decline in short-term financial performance could lead to threats of take over, thereby affecting support and commitment to TQM (p. 516).

# 9. REENGINEERING AND STRUCTURAL INNOVATION CHANGES

## INTRODUCTION

During the mid-1990s, many business organizations started to question the total quality management (TQM) goals of continuous improvement in manufacturing processes. Organizations that implemented TQM programs operated under the motto that "successful companies compete on quality, but not on costs," significantly reduced manufacturing cycle and product/service delivery time, defect rates, inspection costs and machine set up times. Nevertheless, they found that TQM programs were too expensive, required too much time and resources, and lacked continuity when leadership/management changed or introduced cost-cutting measures to downsize personnel and programs.

The mid-1990s highlighted reengineering as an alternative approach to overcome the pitfalls and problems associated with TQM. Many organizations adopted reengineering and began to examine their approaches to quality. Chapter 9 discusses reengineering as a process innovation instrumental in initiating structural and behavioral changes in organizations. It discusses the underlying framework of reengineering to study and evaluate accounting and internal control. Chapter 9 applies a systems view of process reengineering to study accounting and internal control process innovation.

To provide a contextual framework, Chapter 9 first discusses background for changes in TQM approaches and the quality movement. It then reviews emerging approaches in organization management literature that brought about changes in TQM and advocated process reengineering, particularly as these issues apply to accounting control and internal auditing systems.

# BACKGROUND REASONS: TOTAL QUALITY
# MANAGEMENT AND THE QUALITY MOVEMENT

The debate in the 1990s focused on whether or not a continuous improvement program of incremental changes along the lines suggested by TQM, are contributing to long-lasting improved business performance.[1] TQM emphasis in piece-meal approach to continuous change lasted for only a few years. It left organizations without a vision to tackle/handle unanticipated problems and future changes in both the internal and external environment. If organizations have to remain viable and competitive in the long run, a departure from the current TQM business outlook and perspective is needed.

In other words, the conventional rules and ways of thinking where changes can come in one functional area or operation and transmit in an incremental or a gradual step-by-step process to other areas over time has been questioned. Scholars and practitioners have called for a new paradigm shift that involves "new ways of doing business." They advocated for a new "vision of what you intend to be, not build forward from the bedrock of the status quo" where your business has been currently operating. This approach "requires companies to build resource capabilities and customer satisfaction" (Johnson, 1993: 9). The new paradigm shift brought a new thinking and approach to business performance, which resulted in radical process innovation changes. There has been a change from the old ways of thinking by new methods of learning, which required organizations to adopt reengineering and process innovative change strategies in both the technical-manufacturing and administrative-accounting systems.

The debate over the viability of TQM, reengineering, process innovation and other quality programs still continues in accounting and internal control literature (Adamec, 1994: 3–13; Bodnar, 1994: 59–63; Sisaye, 1996, 1998b; Sisaye & Bodnar, 1996). The high cost of quality associated with TQM programs was echoed in popular publications in *Newsweek*, September 7, 1992; and *Business Week*, August 8, 1994.

The cover story of *Business Week*, August 8, 1994, addressed the drawbacks and limitations of 'Quality: How to Make it Pay' associated with TQM programs. The article pointed out that the major problem in TQM and quality improvement programs was that it focused on mechanical/mechanistic incremental improvements in manufacturing processes and product quality. These quality improvement programs became very costly to organizations and do not have meaning, unless customers are willing to pay for the cost of these programs. Thus, many organizations started "rethinking (their) quality goals" in terms of "return on quality" (p. 55). The relationship between cost and return on quality was accompanied by a paradigm shift in management philosophy from TQM to process reengineering.

Reengineering as a process innovation approach has recently brought paradigm shifts from continuous improvement, to a radical change requiring a complete business transformation (Davenport, 1993a: 171). The recent developments in quality thinking gave rise to new innovative process change approaches in both technical and administrative innovative changes. The next section presents the emerging organizational and structural issues associated with process reengineering.

## EMERGING ISSUES IN ORGANIZATIONAL STRUCTURES AND PROCESSES

The organization management literature in the 1990s has brought to the forefront the realization that today's business environment, requires radical changes in existing organizational structures. The conventional method of structuring organizations by functions, product lines, or geographical territories has been found inadequate to address the current competitive needs and challenges of business organizations. The argument stressed that existing organizational structures and processes are based on old and outdated paradigms, which hindered business innovations programs for superior performance.

Prominent management scholars and practitioners noted that the present information/knowledge society required a radical organizational surgery comparable in magnitude to those change transformations, which occurred from the agrarian to the industrial revolution. Radically different kinds of organizations are needed due to "the inability of old institutions, old functions, and core competencies to adapt and cope with new problems" (Mitroff, Mason & Pearson, 1994: 11). In essence, while there is an agreement that the old methods of organization design have to be replaced by new ones, there is no consensus as to the type and form of the new organizational design and structure.[2]

Others have argued that a radical surgery does not necessarily require a complete change and turnaround in organizational design (Delano 1994).[3] Clancy (1994a) approached the need for radical organizational structures and new paradigms, within the context of reengineering and reinventing some existing functions and structures (73–78). Clancy (1994a) suggested reengineering is the first step in implementing what Mitroff, Mason and Pearson (1994) envisioned in their radical surgery of organizations (11–22). In other words, reinventing and replacing current practices with new vision and strategy, work process, technology and infrastructure, and trained people would enable existing organizations to improve their performance and satisfy customers' service needs, without fundamental and radical surgery which require new organizational structural designs. Similarly, Clancy suggested the need for applied management research questions to study the relationships between business process reengineering, and organizational structures and systems in managing the virtual corporation in an information age society (1994b: 8–10).

Chapter 9 extends Clancy (1994a, 1994b) and Delano's (1994) conception of reengineering and its relationship to organizational structural changes. That is, reengineering is one form of business process innovation change. As a process innovation change, reengineering involves behavioral process changes/orientations of people/employees' learning; accepting new paradigms, cultural values and norms; and participating in the change processes. These dramatic changes are likely to create enthusiasm, hope, fear and uncertainty among employees, and might even contribute to unanticipated consequences that could disrupt the organization's normal operations and work flows.

Reengineering as a business process innovation approach is designed to bring improved business performance in the functional areas of management – production, marketing, human resources, and finance/accounting that includes internal control. A process innovation approach to organizational administrative change including accounting and internal control requires both behavioral and structural changes, as well as cultural and paradigm shifts.

### Behavioral Change Strategies

Behavioral change strategies involve the adoption of new attitudes and values by individuals and groups. Attitudinal changes are learned over time and are brought about by cultural training programs. These educational programs involve workforce training, teaching of new cultural work behavior such as team and cooperative work, and empowerment of workers to make changes. Top management provides leadership, vision, inspiration, support and commitment to innovation programs. Management ensures that change agents/facilitators are in the right place to implement change programs.

There is an open line of communication to all organization members to solicit their support and commitment for planned programs. Organization members form functional teams that span and cut-across traditional boundaries to gather information, define/develop benchmarks and implement change programs (Davenport, 1993a: 175–183).

## Structural Change Strategies

On the other hand, structural change entails changes in organizations' divisions/departments and functions, job design and organization of work processes and performance evaluation systems (Zamutto & O'Connor, 1992). Technological innovations such as reengineering have made significant structural changes in manufacturing processes, among others, in inventory and production scheduling management, delivery techniques and product design and quality improvements (Hammer, 1990).

Reengineering work has resulted in downsizing and restructuring of organizations. According to Tomasko, management needs to follow an intelligent resizing that aims not on job elimination, employee termination and replacement programs, but focusing on organization design issues that address "how should work and work processes best be configured" (1993: 22). With the advent of new information technology, the implications of resizing and work processes configurations are substantial for accounting and internal control, particularly with those functions dealing with the management of current assets and liabilities that are repetitive and routine. Thus, the information technology revolution has brought a paradigm shift in the way in which the internal control function is viewed.

## Cultural and Paradigm Shifts

The third aspect of process innovation requires cultural and paradigm shifts. In the last fifty years, there have been major changes in management literature. Two of the major changes have been from scientific to contingency management and from quality control to TQM. These changes primarily constituted a reformulation of the old method of thinking and conducting business.[4]

The real cultural and paradigm departures from the old way to a new radical thinking, started with the publication of reengineering (Hammer, 1990) and process innovation (Davenport, 1993a, b, 1994). According to Davenport, cultural and paradigm shifts involve fundamental changes of thinking about work, organization values and infusion of new cultural behaviors to change existing and outdated assumptions (1993a: 175). Kuhn (1970) stated that a paradigm shift occurs when there is a major departure from the existing accepted state of theoretical thinking, analysis and modes of operations. Similarly, in accounting and internal control, a paradigm shift requires cultural changes to the way in which organizations use control systems to evaluate performance and profitability. Johnson (1993) has noted the implications of paradigm shifts to accounting and internal control.

Johnson expressed that "the old paradigm assumes implicitly that customers most want what your cost systems [report] is the most profitable to sell. But there may be no connection between customer satisfaction and accounting estimates of product quality." On the other hand, the new paradigm thinking suggests that, "it is achieved by *profitability making what customers most want and by organizing work to adapt flexibly as those wants change*" (1993: 11. italics in original). According to Johnson, the new paradigm shifts involve a radical departure from "top-down, remote control management-by-the-numbers" performance evaluation systems. The goal is for management to use organizations to build human competencies; cooperative team work relationships, bottom-up empowerment, and make great people through the creation and design of jobs that fulfill the intrinsic needs of individuals (1993: 12. See also Johnson, 1992a). These changes have significant implications on the traditional management control – principal-agent – power relationships of organizations.[5]

## THE RATIONALE FOR RADICAL CHANGES IN THE CONVENTIONAL/TRADITIONAL PARADIGM OF ACCOUNTING AND INTERNAL CONTROL SYSTEMS

A process view of control requires a radical departure from the traditional economic model of management accounting assumption that agents are self-interested and motivated to work by economic rewards. The traditional paradigm advanced the view that the role of accounting is to control management's behavior and business operations through short-term performance measures of accounting numbers, manufacturing process controls, compensation and related performance measurement systems (Johnson, 1992a; Ross, 1990). It assumed "a direct relationship between the level of internal control and the existence of formal control mechanisms. [Accordingly] audits confirm the existence of formal controls and the degree of compliance with them. Audit recommendations tend to promote the use of formal mechanisms . . . which tend to be authoritarian and rely on a hierarchy of enforcement" (Maskosz & McCuaig, 1990: 44–45).

Garvin (1986) compared the impact control systems have on management's perception of commitment, to quality goals in the United States and Japan. He argued that formal control systems that are based on standards and tight evaluation systems have a lesser role to play in eliciting management's commitment to the importance of quality. On the other hand, Japanese companies have been successful in influencing employees' behavior through "statements of company philosophy and values" rather than formal control systems. The presence of shared values has been reinforced through the use of clan control, instead of the bureaucratic control system that is commonly used in the United States (657–658). He suggested that the notion of quality as a process could not be copied as it is. Rather, quality has to be more adaptive to existing control systems, if the control system cannot be changed to support process quality innovative changes.

Kaplan (1991) has pointed out the shortcomings in management accounting and control systems, by tracing back its roots to the scientific management movement period of 1880–1915. Kaplan (1991) also discussed the problems associated with budgets and standards and its use in controlling management behavior and divisional performance through the reward system (see also Semich, 1989). Kaplan (1991) suggested that instead of meeting historically determined standard goals, the focus should be changed to quality improvements which meet customers' requirements (pp. 205–208).

Similarly, Turney and Anderson (1989) have suggested that the role of accounting information is to support continuous improvement, by providing information "on all aspects of manufacturing including cost, quality and delivery" (p. 43). Conner, Jr. (1992) has extended this view to internal control and auditing, by suggesting that a continuous improvement program requires a reevaluation of internal control and auditing reporting systems and its use for control and evaluation purposes.[6]

The new manufacturing environment thus required that the role of internal control is to help develop techniques that will realign accounting methods with performance evaluation systems. In such a way, supervisors and employees could cooperatively work together and use information to achieve organizational goals.

Process innovation and reengineering have thus brought major cultural and paradigm shifts to organizations and management in the 1990s. While process innovation was widely used in the 1970s and 1980s in social sciences literature to study planned intervention and cultural change programs (see Rogers and Shoemaker, 1971), it is only since the early 1990s that it has received attention in business management literature. The next section examines the characteristics of the process innovation approach and its implications to accounting and internal control functions.

## PROCESS INNOVATION CHANGE CHARACTERISTICS

Process innovation change has its roots in the quality movement. However, it was not until the early 1990s that it received attention in business management literature. Davenport (1993a) discussed the importance of process innovation strategy for bringing about multi-faceted, radical (not incremental) changes in business organizations' performance. He viewed process innovation as "the adoption of a process view of the business with the application of innovation to key processes." This approach, which would enable organizations to "achieve major reductions in process cost or time, or major improvements in quality, flexibility, service levels, or other business objectives" (p. 1). Reengineering which focuses on specific radical design processes such as accounting and internal control is one aspect of process innovation. The process innovation view looks at the inter-relationship and inter-dependence of functional areas of management. It facilitates the adoption of a company/ organization wide view of structured, well-designed and implemented cross-functional team solutions.

Most process innovation changes have been targeted at manufacturing and engineering processes. Technological innovation processes have been success-ful in radically changing production and on-time delivery schedules, quality improvement of products and inventory management. According to Davenport, "marketing, selling and administrative processes receive very little investment" (1993a: 6).

Even though accounting and internal control as part of the administrative process, have fallen behind technical innovative changes such as manufacturing processes, recently there have been major developments within accounting and internal control/auditing professions as a result of the quality movement. Several accounting techniques such as process or activity value analysis and activity-based costing have been introduced. However, these approaches have been targeted to bring about incremental improvements in the way accountants calculate overhead costs and account for product costing (Sisaye, 1998b).

Even with these changes, the roles of internal auditors have been primarily limited to the implementation of activity-based costing systems in the organization (see Conner, 1992; Peters, 1992; and Turney & Anderson, 1989). These accounting changes constitute part of a TQM strategy designed to accelerate continuous improvements in the internal operations of the existing internal control work processes. They are not as comprehensive and broadly defined as process innovation and reengineering to achieve radical business improvements (Davenport, 1993a: 25, 141–145).

A systems view of process innovation, suggests that a balanced and appropriate mix is necessary between technical and administrative innovations focusing on the relationship between product inputs (material, labor, capital) and outputs (products, customers, stakeholders). The approach provides a system (company-wide), rather than a functional (departmental) view of business. Accordingly, innovation entails a radical level of change. It requires a long time horizon, a broad cross-functional scope and a combination of both cultural (behavioral) and structural (organizational) changes. Process innovation uses information technology as the primary enabler of change. Innovation is likely to succeed if there is a top-down strategic vision and orientation to change involving the full participation, involvement and acceptance of the change process by employees at all organizational levels. The outcome depends upon the organization's ability to incorporate customers' perspectives on the product design and output processes (Davenport, 1993a: 10–18). Reengineering has thus emerged as a process innovation approach for internal audit and control work design processes, through the use of computers and other advanced technological methods of information and data management.

# A PROCESS INNOVATION VIEW OF ACCOUNTING AND INTERNAL CONTROL

A process view of innovation focuses on radical transformation of the accounting process as a precondition to bring improved business performance. It examines the cross-link and inter-dependence of the accounting function to various organizational activities/functions. A process view requires that work process changes in internal control be linked/tied to overall improvements in organizational performance. That is, the conventional view of accounting and internal control as a specialized area or department in the organization whose sole function is for the safeguarding and custody of the organization's resources has to be replaced by a radical view of internal auditing and control.

The radical view entails a paradigm shift from the conventional view of internal control. This approach is not limited to bringing incremental changes that are in the form of continuous improvement into the existing mode of operations. Rather, it is intended to radically change the accounting process consistent with the philosophy of business process innovation and reengineering.

A quality movement, process innovation and reengineering have required a paradigm shift in the definition of accounting and internal control. The process view has called for a broader view of internal control, including all control processes that management uses to intervene to achieve organizational objectives. This requires the use of both formal and informal controls that are based on group norms (accepted behaviors), and a change from a centralized to a decentralized flexible control system that can be adapted to the work process requirements. In other words, the old thinking that formal management control techniques help achieve behavioral congruence through the reward system is replaced by new thinking/assumption about management, principal-agent relationships and the role of accounting in the organization.

Maskosz and McCuaig (1990) have raised a number of issues that are relevant for the process view of internal control. First, they argued that the definition of internal control used in bigger firms has been limited in terms of rules and procedures, related to the safeguarding functions of audit control systems. Rather, control is viewed as a philosophy that is consistently changing and covering all processes that are needed to accomplish corporate objectives. These processes, among others, involve organization controls, system development and change controls, authorization and reporting controls, accounting systems controls, safeguarding controls, management supervisory controls and documentation controls (pp. 44–47).

Second, they suggested that independence needed to be substituted by a control self-assessment process. That is, independence, which has been prized by internal controllers and auditors for a long time has been based on the traditional/conventional view of auditing, which emphasizes isolation including rejecting joint work with the other functional areas of management. They argued that such a view of independence is no longer appropriate in the current competitive environment. They referred to new thinking as "control self-assessment process involves employees in a collaborative relationship with auditors" (p. 49). When internal controllers and auditors work cooperatively and jointly with other managers to identify and solve problems and correct errors, they can avoid the adversarial relationships embodied in the philosophy of auditors' independence. A paradigm shift is a step in the right direction to change the conventional 'independence-isolation' view of internal control to 'control self-assessment-collaborative relationships' between internal controllers, auditors, and other functional managers of the organization. This paradigm shift calls for the application of reengineering to the internal control function.

## REENGINEERING AS A PROCESS INNOVATION STRATEGY

Reengineering as a process innovation strategy has necessitated a paradigm shift from continuous improvement of old operation methods to the reinvention of new ones. Reengineering required a "breakthrough thinking inspired by the potential of information technologies to re-create the company" (Tomasko, 1993: 20). Organizations have used reengineering to design business processes to achieve substantial improvements in critical performance measurement indicators of cost, quality and service (Hammer & Champy, 1993: 32).

Reengineering has contributed to substantial improvements to organizational productivity and performance (Dutta & Manzoni, 1999). Organizations have realigned business functions to obtain competitive advantage over others, and to facilitate relationship management (Spadaford, 1992/93).

Reengineering specifically focused on the inter-dependency and coordinating activities of the functional areas of management such as production, marketing, and human resources. The objective is to establish sound business relationships between quality programs and accounting indicators of performance such as returns on quality. It supports changes from an existing organizational mechanistic system to an organic company-wide management system. This shift is necessary to overcome barriers of communication and cooperative work relationships, created by fragmented and specialized organizational structures.

Reengineering entailed a contingency approach for change management, where the framework can be adapted to fit particular business process tasks such as internal auditing. In other words, reengineering is a dynamic adaptive (i.e. flexible not a static/fixed) approach that can be modified/customized to bring long-term radical changes to certain organizational business processes. Appendix 5 applies five reengineering and process innovation steps to describe those suggested changes in accounting control and internal auditing functions.

Adamec (1994) noted that there are certain limitations in the application of process reengineering to internal control and auditing, since internal auditing projects are short-term oriented projects designed to bring incremental, instead of radical changes in the audit control functions (p. 4). In spite of these limitations, reengineering can be applied to examine the total business environment of the organization, to determine whether process change requires the redesigning of both technical and administrative aspects of the internal control and audit processes.

The adaptive-radical approach necessitates a paradigm shift from a functional (conventional) view of internal auditing to that of a business process (reengineering) view, which utilizes an organic system-wide approach to the study of internal auditing processes. An organic view looks at auditing as being instrumental for the implementation of innovative changes in organizational control systems. A systems approach uses an organization-wide analysis to understand the link between internal auditing and other sub-systems or functional areas of management. It describes how change improvements in internal control are unavoidably linked or intertwined (i.e. affect and/or are affected by) with other functions of the organization including production, marketing and human resources.

Chapter 9 advances the view that many organizations that adopted reengineering changed their approach to organizational structures and their definition of quality. Reengineering enabled organizations to consider the multiple aspects of quality programs that involved change both in technical-manufacturing procedures and administrative-accounting processes. Reengineering an organization's quality goals included accounting bench-marks/yardsticks to measure the financial returns of quality improvement programs, a measure that managers and stockholders require when evaluating business performance. Reengineering revolutionized accounting method-ologies so that measuring the success of quality programs was as important as improvements in product quality and service delivery.

Chapter 10 further elaborates how reengineering approaches can bring about radical-transformational changes in accounting and internal auditing systems. Reengineering is contrasted with TQM to highlight their differing approaches to change in accounting control and internal auditing systems. Chapter 10 shows the effect incremental and radical change strategies have on admin-istrative and technological innovation developments in management accounting and control systems.

## NOTES

1. For example, Wilson (1991) has noted the problems associated with the quality movement by using a baseball analogy: "the road to quality is best achieved by bunting, not by hitting home runs. The point [he emphasized] is that you have to be in for the long haul" (p. 73). He also stressed that quality should not be viewed exclusively as a manufacturing problem where the focus is on purposive approaches such as statistical process control, just-in-time and simultaneous engineering to prevent defects, reduce inspection costs and improve product quality. Instead, quality should be viewed as a process that "pervades the whole enterprise" (p. 73).

2. Mitroff, Mason and Pearson (1994) "propose[d] that organizations [should] be structured around five new organizational entities: (1) a Knowledge/Learning Center, (2) a Recovery/Development Center, (3) a World Service/Spiritual Center, (4) a World Class Operations Center, and (5) a Leadership Institute" (p. 11). They believed that their alternative design would enable organizations to be in the forefront in constant innovation and continuous redesign programs to meet and exceed the requirements and challenges of their competitors, satisfy their customers and handle the problems generated by the volatile and turbulent environment (11–21. See also Davenport, 1994: 93–95).

3. Delano (1994), based on his experience with Eastman Kodak, suggested that a "radical change should come from, and reside in, the core of the business – the parts of the organization where people are engaged in inventing, making and selling the product" (96).

4. For example, one of the major obstacles to the TQM movement was that it did not bring a new method of thinking. Rather, it focused on incremental improvements of the

existing assumptions or the status quo. In other words, it attempted to reformulate existing management thinking, instead of building a new philosophy of managing people, work and organizations. This led many organizations to rethink and reengineer the quality goals of their organizations from a strategic vision of their mission, business, and customers, stakeholders combined with their overall long-term objectives of where they want to be in the future. That is, an alignment between organization strategy and process innovation was necessary as a precondition to bring fundamental performance changes (i.e. a quantum leap) in the ways in which organizations operate and conduct their businesses.

5. It has been known that reengineering calls for a shake-up in existing power, leader and follower relationships. It "entails a shift from the traditional leadership model of command and control to one of commitment and trust" (Spadaford, 1992/93: 71). A radical program of cultural change requires a reduction of management hierarchy, which encourages team work and empowers employees (Frigo & Robert, 1993). These changes can be accomplished through the participatory style of management where management clearly sets the strategic vision, encourages staff involvement in all phases of the decision-making process, and utilizes several forms of formal and informal communication channels. Management can set high personal and ethical standards of behavior in conducting the business activities of the organization, create a cooperative working climate, and experiment with new cultural values and methods that would contribute to new ways of performing the job and attaining a higher level of performance.

6. For example, Ray and Gupta (1992) argued that the motivational devices of conventional accounting systems such as feedback from variance reports, profit and loss, and other aggregated financial statements do not fit the current manufacturing environment needs of JIT and quality requirements. Most of the time, reports are either too late or too aggregated on a monthly basis to be relevant for decision-making purposes (pp. 47–49). They recommended that internal auditing departments could provide non-financial performance evaluation measures that are consistent with the current manufacturing environment. This includes ". . . manufacturing cycle time, order backlog, throughput time, delivery cycle time, customer satisfaction, and productivity" (p. 49).

# 10. TOTAL QUALITY MANAGEMENT AND REENGINEERING: A COMPARISON OF INCREMENTAL VS. RADICAL INNOVATION STRATEGIES

## INTRODUCTION

The adaptive systems view suggested that recent developments in information technology, advances in scientific knowledge, and changes in business institutional environments required organizations to be innovative. Chapter 9 discussed the paradigm shift from total quality management (TQM) to process reengineering, also referred to as business process reengineering (BPR). The process reengineering approach holds that organizations must adopt new structures, policies and strategies if they are to remain competitive.

Chapter 10 applied the adaptation theory of structural intervention – incremental and radical to outline the theoretical and organizational management perspectives of TQM and reengineering. In this chapter, the differences in organizational and cultural change management approaches between TQM and reengineering are described. Chapter 10 explores the implications these two approaches have on the design of internal auditing and accounting control systems.

## MANAGEMENT RATIONALE FOR PROCESS INNOVATIONS IN ORGANIZATIONS

Prominent management scholars and practitioners (Clancy, 1994a; Davenport, 1993a; Hammer & Champy, 1993) have advocated for new methods and paradigms of managing people and organizations. These management paradigms have necessitated process innovative changes in accounting control and internal auditing systems.

Process innovation changes become critical in improving the functions of internal control systems, and are required for internal auditing systems to support business-reengineering projects. Process innovation approaches enable internal auditing systems to develop new control techniques to measure important business performance indicators such as cost, quality, service, speed, customers' satisfaction of products and services, and production innovations. They can assist in aligning accounting performance indicators across all operating units and functional management areas in innovative organizations (Sisaye, 1996).

The organizational innovation processes changes of the 1990s followed either institutional-incremental or transformational-radical strategies. TQM followed the incremental and process reengineering the radical change strategies. Internal auditing and control systems have been affected by these two contrasting adaptive approaches to organizational changes: incremental and radical changes. If the innovation approach is institutional-incremental, the organizational learning approach is single-loop, first order and convergence and follows a reactive-gradual change strategy. On the other hand, if the intervention strategy is radical-transformational, organizational learning is double-loop, second order and reorientation, and utilizes a proactive-revolutionary strategy. The next section discusses incremental-institutional and radical-transformational innovation strategies, to provide the context for TQM and reengineering approaches to internal auditing and accounting control systems.

# RADICAL AND INCREMENTAL INNOVATION STRATEGIES

One of the main functions of organizations is to be able to integrate specialized and technical innovations and knowledge into business processes, including accounting and internal auditing. Innovation is a broad concept that ranges from a minor change in a business function, to a complete transformation of the organization. Innovation involves:

- a change management process that is planned, organized, systematic and purposeful (Drucker, 1992: 95–104);
- institutionalized as a formal organizational activity (Robert, 1993: 24–39);
- more likely to occur in organizations that are change oriented;

- provides the greatest opportunity for growth and competitive advantage to organizations (Woodman, Sawyer & Griffin, 1993: 293–321); and
- requires a commitment from organizations to invest more resources and take risks accordingly.

Organizations have selectively adopted either an institutional or a radical/revolutionary approach to innovation. An institutional approach is a gradual piece-meal strategy that embraces TQM. This strategy focuses on incremental changes that involve process modification and/or experimentation to continuously improve existing systems, technologies, products and services (Robert, 1993; Skeleton & Miller, 1993: 15–16).

On the other hand, a radical/revolutionary approach to innovation, such as reengineering, requires an organization to utilize visionary and exploratory methods to radically change existing paradigms and current work practices (Skeleton & Miller, 1993: 15–16; Mezias & Glynn, 1993: 77–101). Thus, engineering requires organizations to change existing paradigms to overcome individual, group and institutional bottlenecks to innovations. Organizations question existing assumptions and norms and replace them with new paradigms. They apply reengineering innovation programs to bring new cultures, internal control practices, technologies and problem-solving techniques that enable them to perform better than in the past (Davenport, 1993a; Hammer & Champy, 1993).

# THE ROLE OF ACCOUNTING AND INTERNAL AUDITING SYSTEMS IN INNOVATIVE ORGANIZATIONS

The 1990s brought the importance of innovative organizational change to the forefront. Organizations are continually attempting to introduce changes, which affect their major operating functions including accounting and control systems. Innovative organizations have adopted new emerging technological developments to compete effectively in the world marketplace.

Accounting and internal control systems have played integral and central roles in innovative organizations. They have enabled organizations to compete effectively and successfully in today's volatile and changing global marketplace. The role and importance of internal control and auditing systems have increased significantly in an information society. Nowadays, control systems perform the multiple functions of custodial oversight, management advisory and consulting services, and information gathering and reporting among others. The suggested agendas are for proactive and comprehensive approaches to internal auditing systems, which included among others: sharing audits, expert systems, innovative audit targets, audit report effectiveness, and audit identity (Newton, 1990: 33–39).

Business process innovations are more likely to improve business performance if strategy, process, compensation and control systems are in alignment. Higher levels of performance can be realized if organizations integrate their internal control and auditing systems with their business innovation process practices. The preferred strategy is to first institute corporate-wide cultural and management systems and processes, before fundamental changes in accounting and internal auditing systems are implemented. Accordingly, Chapter 10 provides an overview of the cultural and organizational management literature approaches to business process innovations. This review provides a framework for comparing TQM and reengineering approaches to internal auditing and control systems.

## CULTURAL AND MANAGEMENT APPROACHES TO ORGANIZATIONAL PROCESS INNOVATIONS

Cultural and organizational changes involve job and organizational design, production and manufacturing processes, work restructuring, and accounting and reporting systems. A corporate-wide cultural change approach is needed for innovation change programs to bring "radical shifts in business strategy, and revolutionary changes throughout the whole organization" (Dunphy & Stace, 1993: 918). Structural changes are unlikely to succeed, if not introduced with or followed by cultural and behavioral changes.

Organizations develop their own widely shared, accepted and learned culture over time. Culture defines the values, norms, roles, behaviors and customs expected from employees, customers and suppliers (Buchowicz 1990: 45–55). A cultural change program requires a long-term time frame. The change process addresses the entire range of work structuring in the organization, including its mission, vision, values, goals, strategies, customers and labor force (Porter & Parker, 1992: 45–67). It defines the general framework for initiating innovative change processes. Such changes could arise from a 'felt need' for change to address existing problems.

The support and commitment of top management is critical for the success of the change process. Management provides shared vision, direction and a planned approach to managing change. Management can implement the innovation change process by:

- sponsoring or managing the change process;
- recruiting agents to facilitate the implementation process;

- ensuring full participation and involvement of employees in the process; and
- providing training programs through seminars and conferences for disseminating the new corporate cultural changes to employees (Porter & Parker, 1992: 45–67).

If the goal of an organization is to radically change employee behavior and business practices, the cultural change program requires a long-term process to bring about these desired changes. According to Beatty and Ulrich (1991), "for organizations seeking to increase the probability of renewal, new mindsets must be created that will be shared by employees, customers and suppliers" (p. 23). A fundamental cultural change requires that employees' work mindsets can be changed over time to accept the impact of new technology on work restructuring and employee relationships.

## TOTAL QUALITY MANAGEMENT AS AN INSTITUTIONAL INNOVATION STRATEGY

Table 10.1 compares the organization and management approaches of TQM and reengineering on several cultural, behavioral and organizational dimensions. These dimensions are adapted from Davenport (1993a); Davidson (1993: 65–79); Gulden and Reck (1992: 10–16); Lawler III (1994: 68–76); Mezias and Glynn (1993: 77–101); Olian and Rynes (1991: 303–333); and Skeleton and Miller (1993: 15–16). They present the major elements and characteristics that distinguish TQM and reengineering approaches to managing organizational and cultural changes.

Table 10.1 shows that TQM emphasizes an institutional approach to change that focuses on a reactive, more of a short-term rather than a long-term solution to the problem. A reactive approach overlooks the cultural constraints that are involved when organizations attempt to introduce innovative changes.

The drawback with TQM can be traced to its roots and origins in the scientific management school of the 20th century, where the focus has been exclusively on productivity improvements with little or no supportive cultural change program. Organizations that implemented TQM programs without management commitment, employee support and cultural change activities discovered that the impact of TQM programs was short-lived.[1]

TQM exclusively focused on quality improvement programs without cultural change. It adopted quality control techniques to measure quality improvements and minimize unexplained variation in production processes. Statistical processes and control charts provided good indicators of the performance of individual employees, machines and products without regard to process

***Table 10.1.*** A Comparison of Total Quality Management and Reengineering
Approaches to Managing Organizational and Cultural Changes.

| Dimensions | Total Quality Management | Reengineering |
|---|---|---|
| Organizational structure | Pyramid structure Command and control system with decentralized decision making approaches at the departmental or divisional levels | Flat/matrix structure Cross-functional teams and network support systems to maximize individual and group involvement |
| | Less autonomous functional area work groups | Highly autonomous self-management teams with decisions made at the lowest level |
| Decision making approaches | Employee empowerment, not necessarily involved in decision-making processes | Employee involvement in all decisions |
| Location of decisions | Decisions made by supervisory management | Decisions located at the lowest level of the organization |
| Organizational types | Learning organizations | Innovative leading organizations |
| Cultural change approaches | Focus on individual attitudinal changes and work orientation followed by structural job design changes | Systematic identification of processes requiring cultural change, when to start the process, who will be involved, what level of the organization will implement the process |
| Paradigm approach | Modify existing paradigm to keep the status quo | Create a new paradigm to change the status quo |
| Time frame | Short-term oriented | Long-term oriented |
| Degree/type of change | Incremental approach | Radical/leap forward approach |
| | Gradual-institutional change Continuous improvement | Revolutionary change Discontinuous transformation process |
| Scope and focus of change process | Detailed attention to single functions, tasks and processes Small scale improvements of existing systems and technologies to correct short-term problems | Selective, but broad focus on business enterprise processes Major breakthroughs or discoveries of new systems and technologies to achieve long- term massive improvements |

***Table 10.1.*** Continued.

| Dimensions | Total Quality Management | Reengineering |
|---|---|---|
| Strategic change management | Reactive and adaptive change strategic approach to threats, signals and crisis | Proactive, imaginative and creative change strategic approach to anticipate and respond to environmental changes even in times of uncertainty |
| Reasons for change | Necessary to improve existing chronic and bottleneck conditions | A compelling case is required to initiate a radically new way of operating the organization |
| Diffusion of innovation techniques | Initial stage requires massive education and training programs for workers and senior management at all organizational levels which later becomes a bottom-up effort to improve work activities | Heavier participation by senior management to bring the desired fundamental changes in jobs and structures |
| Leadership orientation and involvement | Technocratic/expertise directive role at the beginning of the process | Inspirational/generalist consultant providing intensive role throughout the entire process |
| Management innovation styles | Modification | Visionary/entirely new |
| | Emphasis on experimentation on a limited scale where there is no major breakdown in innovative changes | Explore new assumptions/ ideas and novel approaches that will bring a quantum quality change |
| Risk-taking behavior | Calculated minimal risks | Substantial risks with a higher payoff or failure |
| Basis for comparison performance | Inward-industry focus | Outward focus to be 'the best class' for that given area or function regardless of the industry the organization is operating |
| | Use of benchmarking to incorporate outside perspective including customers | Prospector and leader in developing new products, services, and methods in the industry |

**Table 10.1.**  Continued.

| Dimensions | Total Quality Management | Reengineering |
|---|---|---|
| Quality management techniques | Scientific management quality improvement techniques such as statistical control techniques and process charts, among others | Human resources management approaches that simultaneously address organizational culture, strategy, workforce and technology |
| Change objectives | Optimization – maximization and minimization techniques | Transformation |
| Type of projects | Multiple, diverse and several projects at the same time | Integrated, cross-functional and single business process focused projects |
| Job design and restructuring | Consultants, quality groups/ circles work on job design process Intrinsic job satisfaction is limited if there is no full involvement in the process Restructuring gives importance to line positions by realigning staff positions Importance given to supervisory management | Individuals or teams are involved in the job design process Intrinsic job satisfaction is high since individuals have full autonomy in the process Restructuring gives importance to line positions by realigning staff positions Self-managing teams do not need supervisory management |
| Role of information technology | Crucial to collect data and measure process performance of quality improvements, e.g. computerized statistical processes | A central role as enabler of entirely new, cross-functional business processes by providing information to several people simultaneously |

*Sources*: Adapted from Davenport 1993; Davidson 1993; Gulden and Reck 1992; Lawler III 1994; Mezias and Glynn 1994; Olian and Rynes 1991; Skeleton and Miller 1993.

innovation and cultural change (Cupello, 1994: 80). Internal control systems are implemented to support quality control techniques. However, they did not incorporate systems to assess whether the quality improvement programs had improved customer satisfaction and increased market share. Marketing and product management specialists perform these tasks independently. The shortcomings of TQM and the quality movement could be attributed to the relative emphasis on the use of accounting systems to control, rather than direct employee behaviors towards creating business process innovations.

# THE CONVENTIONAL PARADIGM OF INTERNAL AUDITING AND ACCOUNTING CONTROL

The conventional paradigm of internal auditing and accounting control has its roots in the scientific management movement. Under this paradigm, the role of accounting is to set budgets and standards to control management behavior and business operations. The goal is to set short-term reward systems and performance measures using accounting numbers, manufacturing process controls, compensation and related performance measurement systems (Johnson, 1992a; Kaplan, 1991: 201–218; Ross, 1990: 23–27). Accounting systems generate variance reports, profit and loss statements, and other financial information to be used for motivational purposes. However, most of the time the reports are either too late or too aggregated to be relevant for decision-making purposes (Johnson, 1992a).

Internal auditing and control systems have subscribed to the conventional accounting paradigm. They have established a "direct relationship between the level of internal control and the existence of formal control mechanisms. [Accordingly] audits confirm the existence of formal controls and the degree of compliance with them. Audit recommendations tend to promote the use of formal mechanisms . . . which tend to be authoritarian and rely on a hierarchy of enforcement" (Maskosz & McCuaig, 1990: 44–45).

# TOTAL QUALITY MANAGEMENT APPROACHES TO INTERNAL AUDITING AND ACCOUNTING CONTROL SYSTEMS: THE CASE OF ACTIVITY-BASED COSTING

Reengineering and TQM show significant differences in their approaches to internal auditing and control systems. Table 10.2 uses several dimensions adapted from Fortuin (1988: 1–9); Gulden and Reck (1992: 10–16); Maskosz and McCuaig (1990: 44–45); and Vondra and Schueler (1993: 34–39) to present these two views.

As Table 10.2 indicates, TQM programs have brought quality improvements in products and services. TQM has focused exclusively on detailed attention to selected tasks and single functions, at the expense of broadly integrated business enterprise processes. Such a view has reinforced the conventional paradigm of accounting and control, which has focused exclusively on improving existing operations through incremental changes in accounting techniques. TQM did not formulate a new philosophy of managing people, work and organizations. Instead, it reformulated the scientific management

***Table 10.2.*** A Comparison of Total Quality Management and Reengineering
Approaches to Internal Control Systems.

| Dimensions | Total Quality Management | Reengineering |
|---|---|---|
| Organizational structure | A divisional or a departmental structure of internal control/auditing functions | A matrix-flat organizational structure where internal auditors work in cross-functional teams |
| Definitions of internal control | Narrow – functional focus | Broad – comprehensive, integrative and organizational wide focus |
| Approaches to internal control/auditing functions | Safeguarding and custody of the organizational resources | Institutionalization of internal control processes at all levels of the organization that management uses to achieve organizational objectives |
| | Internal control viewed as a series of discrete separate functions | Internal conflict viewed as a process from beginning to end, similar to case team or case worker approach, of getting the service to customer |
| Control systems typologies | Formal, administrative, and bureaucratic control systems | Less formal, clan-type systems based on professional norms, group/peer standards or company philosophy |
| | Control systems adhere to management hierarchy of enforcement | Control systems develop employees' competence as well as create a cooperative team work environment |
| Control systems characteristics | Internal control rules and procedures support formal control systems that support the use of accounting measurements for achieving goal congruence | Internal control philosophy encompasses organization control, development change controls, reporting and safeguarding controls, supervisory/peer based controls among others |
| Role of internal auditors | Staff function – providing expert advice and management advisory support services | Line function – becoming part of the decision-making management team like production and marketing personnel |
| Rationale for change | Continuous improvement of existing internal control and auditing processes | Design new internal control processes to manage both internal and external changes for long-term success |

### *Table 10.2.* Continued.

| Dimensions | Total Quality Management | Reengineering |
|---|---|---|
| Paradigm/philosophy | Conventional paradigm based on independence and isolation from other functional area managers | New paradigm shift based on control self-assessment process that emphasizes collaborative working relationships with other functional areas as members of cross-functional teams |
| Effect of control systems | Influence management behavior consistent with organization goal congruence through the use of budgets and standardized measures of performance | Management has the discretion to change or design a new flexible control system to align control policies with organization's long-term innovation strategy |
| Evaluation/assessment techniques | Captures the performance of individual employees, machines, products, services, and processes through the use of objective performance measures such as ABC, JIT, MBO, process or activity value analysis | Address the alignment of employees, products, services, and processes with organizational and functional area goals |
| Performance indicators of internal audit service quality | Efficiency measures focusing on input/output relationships, error recovery, system understanding, convenience of access, volume of output, and documentation | Effectiveness measures such as timeliness, currency (up-to-dateness), reliability, response/turnaround time, relevance, completeness, and flexibility |
| Performance focus | Financial/accounting goals | Multiple benefit goals including production, financial, and marketing services |
| Reward systems | A competitive merit system that focuses on individual performance incentive systems/ compensation packages | A cooperative merit system that emphasizes team/group performance based incentive systems |
| Role of information technology | Incidental and necessary | Cornerstone and enabler of the newly designed control systems that can provide business process systems perform multiple functions |

*Sources*: Adapted from Fortuin 1988; Gulden and Reck 1992; Makosz and McCuaig 1990; Vondra and Schueler 1993.

philosophy to bring a continuous improvement to the existing internal auditing and control processes.

Several accounting techniques for reporting and control are introduced as a result of TQM and the quality movement. These include process or activity value analysis, activity-based costing (ABC), activity-based management (ABM),[2] feature costing,[3] and just in time (JIT) inventory management. These developments represent technical innovations in accounting. "ABC has been adopted by companies as a means to reconcile management accounting information with advanced manufacturing practices" (Anderson, 1995: 47).

Argyris and Kaplan (1994) implied that competitive and technological environmental changes in the 1980s contributed to the development of new products and services. Accounting systems developed new techniques to account for changes in product costs, quality and customer requirements. The ABC approach developed techniques "for assigning the indirect and support expenses of production, marketing, and selling activities" (p. 86).

According to Drucker (1995), the underlying assumption in ABC "is that manufacturing is an integrated process that starts when supplies, materials, and parts arrive at the plant's loading dock and continues even after the finished product reaches the end user. Service is still a cost of the product, and as is installation, even if the customer pays." ABC takes these costs into consideration to assist managers with 'better cost control' and gives them 'results control', (p. 55. italics in original). By doing so, "activity-based costing integrates what were once several activities-value analysis, process analysis, quality management, and costing – into one analysis" (p. 55). When calculating product cost,[4] the objective of ABC is to help eliminate those activities i.e. non-value added activities, which do not contribute to improved performance (Beaujon & Singhal, 1990; McGowan, 1998).

ABC is designed to provide accounting information on the cost of activities associated in producing products and delivering them to customers. Activity drivers that generate costs are assigned to products and customers, while cost drivers are assigned to all activities that generate those costs. Product costs are determined by adding costs of each activity incurred in making the product (Kaplan 1989). Overhead is identified with those activities that generate the costs, instead of being allocated to products or operating departments based on selected already existing allocation bases, such as direct labor hours, units of volume produced, or processing/machine hours spent on the product. ABC attempts to provide cost information on each activity and other quality costs associated with each activity (Kaplan, 1989). Cost drivers associated with each activity, determine the workload required to perform an activity and thereby measure the work force productivity for the work done in the activity.

ABC assists to identify the major activities needed to make the product and provide the associated quality costs,[5] to assist production managers to control quality costs through continuous improvement of the major product activities. The ABC system thus allows for: (a) identifying the costs associated with the activities of the product, (b) accurately determining the total and unit costs for each product, and (c) facilitating a more profitable product pricing system.[6] Overall, "ABC addresses inadequacies of traditional labor-based cost systems by using a two-stage method that attributes costs first to production and business activities, and then to products on the basis of resource usage" (Anderson, 1995: 2).

Accordingly, the focus of ABC's cost objectives has been directed at those activities that affect production decisions. As an accounting method, ABC "refers only to the actual technique for determining the costs of activities and the outputs that those activities produce ... the aim of ABC is to generate improved cost data for use in managing a company's activities" (Roberts & Silvester, 1996: 24). In other words, "ABC avoids arbitrary allocations by assigning the cost of resources to the activities being performed and then assigning activity costs to the products, services, and customers that create the demand for the activities. ABC systems encompass costs beyond the factory floor including administrative distribution, and marketing activities" (Brimson, 1998: 7). It gathers information on operational activities that support continuous improvements (Cooper & Kaplan, 1998: 110).[7]

Drake, Haka and Ravenscroft (1999) also viewed ABC as being useful for cost control and management that is not related to volume. For them, "ABC systems differ from more traditional volume-based costing (VBC) systems by highlighting the consumption of process resources that are under the control of multiple individuals. These resources are typically related to batch-level, product-sustaining or facility-sustaining costs. To reduce such costs typically requires the coordinated effort of multiple workers rather than isolated efforts by individuals" (p. 324). They suggested that team effort is needed in ABC systems. "By fostering or inhibiting cooperative efforts among workers, incentives can play a key role in the type of decisions that occur" (p. 324).[8]

Overall, the objective of ABC is to avoid the mismatch between traditional cost accounting systems and the current business environment, by providing improved accounting information on product costing. ABC improves a company's competitive advantage through cost control,[9] improved decision-making, performance evaluation and reward allocation systems (McGowan, 1998: 31–34). As ABC is becoming increasingly associated with improving organizational performance, process innovations are more likely to be accepted if they are perceived to be instrumental in improving performance.

More recently, the importance of ABC in strategic planning and resource allocation decisions has been recognized. Cooper and Kaplan (1998) noted "ABC provides strategic cost information about the underlying economies of the business" (p. 110). It enables managers

> to understand the economics, which sustain the making products and serving customers. ABC systems trace costs from resources (people, machines and facilities), to activities and processes, and then to specific products, services, and customers. The cost of all resources used to make a product and serve a customer (including resources at a great distance from the factory floor) is included in the strategic costs of products and customers. Strategic costing can be done for products, services, customers, or organizational units, allowing managers to understand profitability at various levels of disaggregation and organizational hierarchy (p. 110).

Lukka (1998) believed that these technical changes in accounting have altered the traditional record-keeping staff function of accounting. As a result, "the accounting function is connected to other parts of the organization in a more business and future oriented matter, pointing to new possibilities for accounting to intervene in such previously 'taboo' areas such as product development and marketing; for instance" (p. 334). Accounting has been increasingly integrated in organization processes at both strategic and operational levels.

For accounting to play a role in promoting change in organizations, the contribution of accounting for improvement should be directed on the 'real activities' of the organization, but "not on objectives or general principles." Improving the activities of the organization is interactive work handled through dialogue, negotiation and communication among divisions/units. Results that are obtained are based on concrete experiments with defined time periods. The learning process in organizations requires identifying problems, collecting data and solving problems in a step-by-step format incrementally with the objective of satisfying people, improving employees' competence and organizational performance (Lukka, 1998: 338).

However, these technical changes in accounting have been targeted to incremental improvements of specific/discrete tasks. As a result, the internal auditing function has a narrow orientation and focus. It has been limited to the implementation of ABC and other costing systems to specifically address product costing systems and overhead allocations (Turney & Anderson, 1989: 37–47). As Table 10.2 indicates, these accounting techniques do not have broader applications for the institutionalization of internal control systems at all organizational levels. Nevertheless, they have been successful in establishing performance links between the costs of total quality products/improvement programs and the price customers are willing to pay for these products/ services.

These accounting changes, even though incremental, have been able to extend accounting information systems to business and information technology strategies. For example, Brecht and Martin (1996) proposed that it is necessary for accounting systems to go beyond financial performance and transaction costs, to include information "on the economics of business operations, strategic management, and information systems development" (p. 17). At present, the need for change necessitated by the computer and information technology has required accountants to make themselves visible in the organization's planning and decision-making process.

Brecht and Martin (1996) outlined five information system design areas that have promising prospects and opportunities for involvement by accountants. These include involvement to decide: "(1) What information is distributed or reported, (2) system delivery methods and timing, (3) the impact of technology on decisions and the decision-making process, (4) database designs, and (5) system analysis capabilities" (p. 17). In database design, accounting information can thus become central in planning for short and long-term periods. Short-term planning may be related to operational task problems associated with purchasing, pricing and delivery schedules. Long-term planning, on the other hand, addresses market and competitive forces information for the coming years (p. 19).

Thus in the 1990s, many organizations have started rethinking their quality goals in terms of the relationship between the cost and return on quality. The link between cost and return on quality brought a paradigm shift from TQM to reengineering:[10] quality is now seen as a selective business process that is multi-faceted, involving both technical-manufacturing and administrative-accounting and internal control changes.

# THE NEW MANAGEMENT PARADIGM: REENGINEERING AND ORGANIZATIONAL PROCESS INNOVATION

The shift from the conventional to new management paradigm occurred in the early 1990s, with the publication of reengineering (Hammer, 1990: 104–112; Hammer & Champy, 1993), and business process innovations (Davenport, 1993a). These works advocated for major cultural and paradigm shifts involving organizational cultures and values, management's strategic vision, management and employee relationships, customer and stockholder relationships, product innovations, quality management and global competitiveness (Table 10.1).[11]

Reengineering is based on the principle that the support of senior management and their sponsorship for individual reengineering projects is present. It also assumes that there is commitment and willingness of top management, to bear the costs and consequences associated with the success or failure of reengineering projects.

In the past, business process reengineering has been targeted at individual manufacturing and production processes at the departmental/divisional level. It did not involve the entire organization, nor solicited corporate-wide commitment of resources to launch full-scale organizational reengineering programs. These reengineering efforts have been successful in radically changing production and on-time delivery schedules, inventory management and development of new or improvement of existing products and services.

However, the selective focus on technical innovations has contributed to minimal investment in administrative process innovations such as accounting and internal control systems (Davenport, 1993a). The potential benefits of administrative control innovations, including accounting and internal auditing, are generally less observable, less quantifiable, and require a longer time horizon for the benefits to be realized. Accordingly, advances in internal control innovations have lagged behind technical innovations in manufacturing processes (Dunk, 1989: 149–155; Sisaye, 1998b).

*Reengineering Approaches to Internal Auditing and Control Systems*

At the present time, there is still a lag in reengineering approaches to internal control and auditing systems. The lag can be attributed to the predominant assumption that internal control and auditing projects are short-term in scope. They are primarily designed to initiate incremental changes in audit operation tasks and services. They do not result in radical transformation in audit organizations and functions. In spite of these drawbacks, reengineering can be applied to examine the total environment that affects technical and administrative aspects of the internal audit processes (Adamec, 1994: 3–13; Bodnar, 1994: 59–63; Sisaye & Bodnar, 1996; Sisaye, 1999).

Recently, there has been an attempt to minimize those constraints involved with administrative innovation lag. Reengineering projects have been designed and implemented with a company-wide objective of bringing multi-faceted, radical (not incremental) changes in critical business indicators of performance: cost, quality, service and speed (Hammer & Champy, 1993). They are targeted to "achieve major reductions in processes cost or time, or major improvements in quality, flexibility, service levels, or other business objectives" (Davenport, 1993a: 1). They focus on process-activities that transform inputs into outputs to satisfy customers, but not on specific tasks, structures and people (Hammer & Champy, 1993).

Reengineering projects can be directed towards specific business design processes such as internal auditing and control systems. The process innovation framework allows the examination of interrelationships and interdependencies of internal control systems with other organizational functional areas. Reengineering as a process innovation view, examines the cross-links and interdependencies of the internal control function to various organization activities/functions. In other words, the internal auditing system addresses all internal control processes that management uses to intervene to achieve organizational objectives. This requires the use of both formal and informal controls based on team/group norms (accepted behavior), and the development of a decentralized flexible control system that can be adapted to work process requirements.

Reengineering requires that internal control systems have to be both comprehensive and broad. Internal control systems encompass all organizational control issues, including administrative control rules and procedures, accounting system controls and management supervisory controls. In other words, internal controllers cannot work independently to accomplish these objectives, without collaborating with functional managers affected by these changes. This relationship is itself new: when auditors work jointly with other managers to reengineer internal control systems, they are changing the conventional paradigm and philosophy of auditors' 'independence-isolation' with a new paradigm that emphasizes, "control self-assessment-collaborative relationships" (Maskosz & McCuaig, 1990: 44–45).

In a collaborative cross-functional setting, internal controllers are taking 'case teams' or 'case workers' approaches. They share responsibility with other team members in determining the exact steps to be taken and perform the entire internal audit process to get the final output. Radical internal control system changes are more likely to support an organization's objective to build employee competence, cooperative teamwork, and design of jobs that intrinsically enrich workers, thereby creating a spiritually enriching organization.

## *Effects of Reengineering on Accounting Control Systems*

Chapter 10 compared the institutional-incremental (TQM) and radical-transformation (reengineering) innovative approaches to organizational and cultural management (Table 10.1). Table 10.2 compares TQM and reengineering approaches to internal control and auditing systems. Managers' uses of accounting control information to evaluate organizational performance and profitability goals were also examined.

Chapter 10 documents that application of reengineering principles to internal control functions can make internal auditing and accounting control systems more responsive to the requirements of the new competitive manufacturing environment. Internal auditing and control systems play important adaptive roles by providing feedback on organizational performance by measuring its profitability, efficiency of operations, and customer satisfaction. More importantly, a reengineering approach to internal control systems can help establish functional links between accounting and internal auditing systems and other organizational operating units.

Chapter 11 elaborates on administrative and technical innovation changes in accounting control and internal auditing systems. It discusses the concept of administrative lag and applies it to explain the innovation lag in accounting. Chapter 11 also outlines process innovation strategies that support changes in accounting information systems.

## NOTES

1. For example, Laza and Wheaton (1990: 17–21) documented the cultural limitations of TQM programs at Florida Power and Light Company (FPL). To become a cost-effective performer, FPL relied on technical improvements to reduce customer complaints. Nevertheless, the company did not realize successful implementation of TQM required a long-term cultural change program supported by management. They recommended a thorough study of functional areas to assess needed change, as a prerequisite before beginning a TQM program (Laza & Wheaton, 1990: 19; and Sisaye & Bodnar, 1995: 19–31).

2. While the focus of ABC is on tracing costs directly to activities, the emphasis on activity-based management (ABM) "is a much broader concept. It refers to the fundamental management philosophy that focuses on the planning, execution, and measurement of activities as the key to competitive advantage. Viewed from this perspective, ABC implementation failure could be defined as the inability of a company to move from simply generating ABC information toward actually using the information to improve profits" (Roberts & Silvester, 1996: 24).

In designing a new ABM system, the concern is on the design approach that "starts with bill of activities" (Wiersema, 1996: 17). ABM has shifted the accounting issue from 'emphasizing data' to "correct assignment of costs among products." The end product leads to an ABM system that can forecast and prepare 'activity driver budgets' for products (p. 17).

However, McGowan's (1998) study on the usefulness of activity-based cost management (ABCM) system showed significant differences in attitudes between preparers and users. "The evidence suggests that preparers generally respond more favorably to ABCM implementation than do users. However, although both groups generally agree that the implementation of ABCM system has resulted in significantly more accurate, reliable, timely and understandable information than that produced by predecessor systems, they do not find ABCM information to be more accessible. Further, respondents' report that they find ABCM useful in their jobs and that the implementation of ABCM has had a significant positive impact on the organization. However, perceptions concerning changes in waste reduction, relationships and communication vary from site to site" (p. 46).

3. Brimson (1998) introduced feature costing to overcome the difficulties and skepticism associated with ABC. He noted that activity costs are used to calculate product costs. While ABC has improved cost control and product cost data "by assigning the cost of resources to activities and then assigning activity costs to the cost object," it is "a very complex system to create and maintain." ABC "still remains primarily a historical financial tool" (p. 6).

Instead Brimson advocates the use of feature costing. "Feature costing uses a process approach to define activities and relate those activities to products or customers using the product's features" (p. 6). The process is simple and provides detailed cost information. While ABC has allowed assigning activity costs to the products that caused these costs, it has become costly to maintain. Sometimes, the cost information becomes historical and "less useful at the operational level that requires feedback about the efficiency of activities performed to aid workers in controlling and improving operations" (p. 7).

Product features are important in production, sales and marketing, and research and development. Accounting and finance provides cost information "used to compute a product cost based on features" (p. 8). The cost information can be used for planning and control purposes. Over time, when product mix varies; businesses can improve product features or modify existing products. "Feature costing uses product character-istics to assign cost to activities and processes to differentiate cost by products. Attributing cost and value based on how product characteristics impact a process is the most proficient tool available for accurately assigning cost" (p. 8).

Brimson outlined seven steps for computing a product feature cost. "Step 1: determine the product features. Step 2: determine the activity routing associated with each product feature. Step 3: determine the cost of each activity. Step 4: determine product characteristics that will cause the process to vary. Step 5: determine how much the product characteristics cause the process to vary. Step 6: associate features and characteristics to products. Step 7: adjust the activity cost based on the product's features and characteristics" (pp. 8–12).

4. Beaujon and Singhal (1990) stated as follows the relationship between ABC and product costing. "The basic concept behind product costing in an ABC system is that the cost of a product equals the cost of the raw materials, plus the sum of the cost of all the activities required to produce the product. Thus, ABC systems trace costs to activities and then to products. Product management benefits from having costs assigned more accurately to products. Activity management benefits from having costs associated with specific manageable activities" (pp. 51–52).

5. Accounting is in the process of developing reliable indicators to measure quality costs, the intangible asset attributes associated with quality, and the relationship of quality to improved financial performance. It has been estimated that poor product quality costs in terms of design, manufacturing, inspection, shipping and customer service account for 20% of manufacturing sales and 30% of service companies' sales. The present emphasis on activity-based costing is to provide information to production

managers on those activities that generate quality costs. Production managers can use these reports to identify quality costs and correct them at the production stage (prevention costs) and avoid those costs associated with recall and external failure costs.

6. Traditional accounting techniques are primarily designed to measure short-term financial performance indicators – that is, operating expenses and net income. ABC has included the less tangible non-financial measures – such as product quality, customer satisfaction, order lead time, factory flexibility, and time it takes to launch a new product, that are related to the main activities that generate actual production costs.

7. According to Cooper and Kaplan (1998) "Operational learning and control systems provide data to support continuous improvement efforts. The information, therefore, must be timely, accurate, and specific to the work group involved. The systems generally include non-financial measures such as cycle time, defects, and scrap; these are reported daily, even batch-by-batch, to give employees immediate feedback on the quality and efficiency of the processes they are responsible for. These control systems also collect relevant financial information about the cost of resources – people, materials, machines, and energy – used in the operating processes.

Operational control systems, in addition to reporting on departmental and responsibility-center performance, can have an activity-based subsystem that collects information about the actual cost of activities in order to give short-term feedback on local process efficiencies." The information, which is disaggregated "provide[s] valuable feedback to improve local sub-processes." The data, which is accurate at the local levels "support cost reduction efforts and also evaluate employee and departmental performance against specific cost targets" (p. 110).

8. Drake, Haka and Ravenscroft (1999) recognized the need for team effort in ABC systems. "By fostering or inhibiting cooperative efforts among workers, incentives can play a key role in the type of decisions that occur" (p. 324). The results of their experimental study "shows that innovative activity can produce a higher *or lower* level of firm profit when workers have ABC information . . . (p. 325. Italics in original). In ABC-type settings, where significant cost reductions can be gained primarily from coordinated efforts of multiple workers, incentives that motivate cooperative innovations result in higher profits. Providing ABC information to workers with individually oriented incentives results in fewer multi-person process innovations and lower profits" (pp. 324–325).

They stressed the role of team incentives as being important in the successful implementation of ABC. Since individual incentives work against team effort, it is only cooperative work that can contribute to higher profit (p. 326).

9. Mak and Roush (1994) discussed the relevance of ABC in flexible budgeting and variance analysis in manufacturing organizations, for cost control and its use for performance evaluation purposes. In this context of ABC application, the distinction between variable and fixed costs can be formulated for each activity. "Costs which vary relative to the cost driver for the period under consideration are 'flexed' for changes in the quantity of the cost driver. For variable activity costs, price and efficiency variances can be computed, whereas for fixed activity costs, budget and capacity variances are calculated" (p. 102). The relevance in capacity variances is in the elimination of excess capacity for cost savings. If capacity variances are favorable, indicating production beyond capacity, it shows the existence of "potential future increases in spending on particular activities" (p. 102).

10. Coburn, Grove and Ortega (1998) described the relationship between business process reengineering (BPR) and activity-based management (ABM) and their impact on redesign work processes, cost control and sales management. "To redesign business processes, managers must fully understand what activities are done within a process and what resources are consumed when performing these activities" (p. 41).

ABM manages cost control activities to increase profit and maximize customer satisfaction. "By focusing on activities, ABM addresses the issue of cost, quality, service, and speed that underlie BPR. Therefore, ABM plays an integral role in BPR efforts by allowing managers to understand the activities that make up a business process. Once these activities are understood, the manager is in a position to redesign the process" (pp. 41–42).

To implement BPR, it is critical to obtain the support of top management, and select BPR project teams and a leader to manage these projects. In business process redesign, they advocated the use of a value added activity approach "to identify essential and non-essential activities" (p. 45). The activities then specify the works to be performed that add value to a product.

11. Rigby has outlined four major components of business process reengineering. They are: (1) A fundamental rethinking of the way work gets done (process design), leading to improvements in productivity and cycle times. (2) A structural reorganization, typically breaking functional hierarchies into cross-functional (horizontal) teams. (3) A new information measurement system using higher technology to drive improved data dissemination and decision making. (4) A new value system, typically placing greater emphasis on the company's customers (1993: 24).

# 11. THE DIFFUSION OF ADMINISTRATIVE INNOVATION CHANGES: IMPLICATIONS FOR ACCOUNTING CONTROL AND INTERNAL AUDITING SYSTEMS

## INTRODUCTION

The two most important process innovation changes in the 1980s and 1990s were total quality management (TQM) and business process reengineering (BPR). As mentioned in the introduction, the terms BPR, process reengineering, and reengineering are used interchangeably. Complex organizations have adopted either TQM or BPR to change their structural operations to improve performance. In Chapter 10, the incremental-gradual and radical-revolutionary approaches of organizational change and development were applied to compare and contrast TQM and process reengineering's approaches to internal auditing and management accounting control systems. A comparison of the technical and administrative innovations indicates that administrative innovations in internal auditing and control systems have lagged behind technical innovations in manufacturing and production systems.

Chapter 11 discusses the process innovation impact of TQM and reengineering on the design and implementation of management control systems. Two types of process innovation strategies, technical and administrative, are utilized to describe innovative changes currently occurring in internal auditing and accounting control systems.

The sociological approach to diffusion of innovations is used as the underlying framework to study accounting control and internal auditing systems as administrative innovation strategies to improve organizational productivity and performance. However, the administrative innovation lags in accounting has slowed the pace change in management control systems, and has minimized the effectiveness of accounting systems in recording and reporting organizational output and productivity.

## RECENT DEVELOPMENTS IN DIFFUSION RESEARCH

In general, the diffusion of process innovation has been broadly applied in organizational behavior literature to study the transfer of information technology, adoption of new innovative practices, and use of change agents to communicate innovative methods to organization members (Rogers, 1971; Rogers & Shoemaker, 1971). The diffusion approach focuses on the relationship between technological innovations and their successful implementation in the organization. The "analysis of the diffusion of innovation usually begins with the design, and continues through implementation of the innovation" (Davenport, 1993a: 317). While the diffusion of innovation has concentrated on how technological process changes can be successfully adopted, the approach has not been extended in the study of business process innovation strategies. In Chapter 11, the diffusion of innovation approach has been applied to study the implication of reengineering as an administrative process innovation approach for the internal auditing and accounting control functions of business organizations.

Davenport (1993a) pointed out that the diffusion of innovation approach as a behavioral process change has been limited to the study of how new information technology can be successfully adopted, rather than "how innovation can improve organizational performance." Chapter 11 attempts to respond to Davenport's challenge and bridge this research gap, by applying the diffusion of innovation approach to study accounting and control systems as administrative process innovation strategies for improving business performance. Internal control and auditing constitute an important aspect of administrative process innovation programs that are critical for improving business performance.

To provide the context for the diffusion of administrative innovation approaches in organizations, sociological approaches to process innovations have been utilized to discuss corporate renewal, business process reengineering and benchmarking. Chapter 11 draws from organizational sociology literature to study the relationship between innovation and changes in the overall operation of the organization. In this approach, process innovation changes are viewed as part of corporate renewal strategies, that are designed and implemented to bring both incremental and radical changes in accounting and internal control systems.

# CORPORATE RENEWAL AND THE NEED FOR
# PROCESS INNOVATION

When process innovation strategies, such as reengineering are targeted to bring forward changes in the internal auditing and control systems of large organizations, it is referred to as corporate renewal. According to Mezias and Glynn, corporate renewal focuses "on strategies that enhance the ability of large, bureaucratic organizations to make radical change to existing practices, routines, and structures" (1993: 78). When corporations renew, they adopt innovation as a process of bringing new problem solving ideas and methods to an organization (p. 79).

Process innovation can be associated with strategies that involve incremental change of new ideas which affect a specific scope of business, such as internal auditing in an organization. Or, it may involve radical (revolutionary) innovations that produce fundamental changes in the operation of the organization. Organizations adopt either radical or incremental changes consistent with their strategic orientations. Innovation strategies can be best understood if they are studied within the context of existing organizational structures.

Table 11.1 outlines two types of process innovation approaches: radical and incremental. The radical approach is referred to as reengineering, while the incremental approach is labeled as TQM. Table 11.2 uses several dimensions based on management researchers (Beatty & Ulrich, 1991; Davenport, 1993a; Davidson, 1993; Davis, 1993; Dixon et al., 1994; Mezias & Glynn, 1993; Parker, 1993; Sisaye, 1996) who have done extensive work in process innovation literature. The dimensions compare differences in the two approaches. While incremental changes are compared to radical approaches, the focus in Chapter 11 is on transformational process innovation approaches in accounting and internal auditing systems.

Organizational renewal can be accomplished through continuous or transformational changes. While incremental innovation supports continuous change, radical change entails organizational transformation. Innovation thus entails several changes, ranging from incremental changes in products and technological processes, to organizational creativity in new structures, strategies and systems. Organizational change requires a time transition that links the past, present and the future; and creates direction and continuity of change[1] as organizations adapt to the environment.

According to Brown and Eisenhardt (1997), "continuously changing organizations are likely to be complex adaptive systems with semi-structures

***Table 11.1.***  Approaches to Innovations.

| Dimensions | Radical | Incremental |
|---|---|---|
| Approach | Revolutionary change – occurs within a short period of time | Piece-meal/gradual change – occurs over a long period of time, characterized by organized, purposeful and systematic process |
| | Discontinuous change – characterized by a leap | Focus on refinement of exchange systems and technologies |
| | Attempt to bring new approaches to problems | Focus on the best preferred alternative among available programs |
| Aspects of Change | Fundamental change – characterized by breakthroughs in business, transformation, discontinuity, and quantum leap | Continuous improvement resulting in gradual change |
| Response Type | Proactive step toward the future | Reactive response to handle immediate crisis |
| Effect of New Ideas | The whole operation of the organization | A specific scope of the business |
| | Focus on the entire systems of operation and the inter-functional relationships to enable to system to function well | Focus on a single function or area of activity such as service, customers, external relations, or product development |
| Approaches to Cultural Change | Organizational-wide teams working at several levels of the organization | Employee involvement, shared mindset |
| | | Focused training on new initiatives and behaviors: reward systems, new roles |
| Degree of Employee Involvement | Top-down approach to introduce new designs or work improvements. Little or no involvement at the lower level | A bottom-up participative approach |
| | Direct involvement by top management accompanied by commitment, communication and trust | Minimal involvement by top management |
| Systems Approach | Organic | Mechanic |
| Production Systems | New innovations to change existing production technologies and relations | Efficiency of production by structuring work groups |

### *Table 11.1.*   Continued.

| Dimensions | Radical | Incremental |
|---|---|---|
| Relations with the Status Quo | Change the status quo Accept new paradigm to discover new operating changes in the organization Break the dominant organizational culture through ad hoc teams, autonomous work groups | Improve the status quo Introduce change within the existing paradigm Relax existing culture by modifying existing rules, and ensuring that rational approaches prevail in the organization |
| Duration of Time Period | Long-term | Short-term |
| Level of Resource Commitment | Major resources are committed to support the needed expenditures for innovation | Resource commitment varies, and pooled only when needed |
| Effects on control systems | Replace traditional control measures with empowered work force Develop new strategy that institutes new control systems. Include organizational software such as people and information and information systems in addition to the management hardware | Revise existing control systems with performance based evaluation system Focus on improving management hardware such as strategy, structure and control systems |
| Mapping process | A complete mapping of the process of change from initiation to implementation | The mapping process is limited to a specific aspect of the change process |
| Resistance to change | Highly resisted since existing organizational structures and work operations are changed Higher degree of uncertainty concerning innovation process | Lower level of resistance since changes cause minimal disruptions to existing work patterns and relationships Lower level of uncertainty |
| Scope of change | Attempts to change the entire direction of the organization by calling for new directions and plans Focus on major new and different innovations | Change supports existing system, plans, policies, work structure and technology Institutional approach to refine existing systems and technologies by focusing on the best preferred alternative among available programs |

***Table 11.2.***   Approaches to Diffusion of Innovation

| Dimensions | Technical | Administrative |
|---|---|---|
| Objectives | Affects organization products or services including production schedules, inventory management, delivery techniques and quality improvement programs | Social and control systems related to organization control, reward and management operations, including structuring of the organization, design of accounting and internal auditing and control systems |
| Role of management in the diffusion process | Minimal or no influence | Strong influence as a champion and facilitator of the process |
| Degree of freedom in choosing innovation | Less freedom when choosing technical innovation | Management has more freedom and latitude in choosing administrative innovation |
| People involved in the innovation process | Engineers, production managers and other technically oriented managers | Advisors are less technical, but experts in information technology software |
| Degree of innovation acceptance in the organization | More likely to be accepted since perceived as effective, easy to measure results | Less likely to be accepted, since innovation results are difficult to measure |
| Perceptions of innovation | Accepted as rational – observable and quantifiable approaches to changes: formalization and uniformity practices in the innovation process can be implemented, production quality circles and teams do not affect existing bureaucratic system | Perceived as less rational and observable due to barriers with political interference in the innovation, ignoring the social context of the organization, lack of compatibility with existing bureaucratic structures, personality interests due to uncertainty of innovation outcome |
| Potential benefits of innovation | Known, and benefits are realizable in a short time; enormous advantage/benefits | Uncertain, takes a long time to realize the benefits; lower relative advantage |
| Impact of benefits on the organization | Limited only to the production and manufacturing systems | Substantial, affecting the entire organization internal control systems including the control of technical innovation; acceptance of technical innovations are dependent on and influenced by changes in administrative innovation |

that poise the organization on the edge of order and chaos and links in time that force simultaneous attention and linkage among past, present and future. These organizations seem to grow over time through a series of sequenced steps, and they are associated with success in highly competitive, high-velocity environments" (p. 32).

Organizational structures and contextual factors affect innovations. Innovations entail several changes, including organizational creativity as well as accounting changes. "Innovations in managerial accounting systems are influenced by the propensity of organizations to innovate and their capability to implement innovations. Strategy affects organizations' needs for management accounting innovations . . . organizational structure encourages or discourages the implementation of innovations" (Gosselin 1997: 105). In other words, while strategy sets the framework whether there is a need to adopt, structure provides the capability for implementation.

Gosselin (1997) related the type of strategy and the need for innovative changes. Organizations that have prospectors' strategies seek market opportunities and the need to develop new products and services to meet customer demands. For them, the environment is unpredictable and changing. There is a need to respond continuously to those changes. Prospectors have flexibility that enables them to adapt to the environment (p. 108). In general, "prospectors are organizations that continually experiment with innovations . . . Prospectors have structures that enable them to facilitate and coordinate numerous and diverse operations" (p. 108). Their desire for more information creates the need for innovation in both accounting and operations management, such as activity management and activity analysis.

## THE ADAPTIVE SYSTEMS VIEW OF INNOVATION

Innovations when viewed within the context of strategy, structures, and systems become subsets of the broader organizational transformation systems changes (Woodman, Sawyer & Griffin, 1993: 293). That is, organizational change and development affect strategy, systems and structures, and occur at many levels including the individual, group, organizational or at a larger level, groups or communities of organizations.

According to Van Den Ven and Poole (1995), "this nesting of entities into larger organizational entities creates a hierarchical system of levels. The question of change may focus on . . . a single organizational entity or the interactions between two or more entities" (p. 521). This dialectic approach allows one to study process innovation as both "the internal development of a single organizational entity" as well as "the relationships between numerous entities" of change in organizations. While several entities can be studied in organizations, the "dialectical theories require at least two entities to fill the role of thesis and antithesis" (p. 521). The dialectical approach enables one to examine the thesis and antithesis issues involved in radical process innovation changes of internal auditing systems.

## Strategy and Innovation Change

For corporations to adopt innovation, a need for felt change must be expressed in their strategies. Organizations make a calculated, not spontaneous, decision to innovate. Such changes follow a purposeful and systematic process. Even though external factors create the precondition for change, the predominant factors that bring about the need for change are internal requirements and organizational characteristics. Organizations with supporting infrastructure, including information technology, realize improved long-term benefits from the adoption of new innovation practices. Organizational culture provides the environment, in which the need for technological and administrative changes can emerge. Since organizations need to survive, expand and be profitable, employees have a stake in the change process and in the ability of the organization to survive. They will support any technological change that makes the organization profitable and places the rival at a competitive disadvantage (Howells, 1995: 883–894).

To accomplish these objectives, the need for change has to be articulated in the strategic planning process, and then communicated to organization members. Rigby (1993) stresses the importance of strategic planning in process innovation. He argues that innovations such as reengineering cannot be used as a substitute for strategic planning. "It won't help to perfect a process that is fundamentally doing the wrong thing. Successfully reengineered companies have first created compelling strategic visions for their businesses, and then employed reengineering as a means to help the organization achieve those ends.

Organizations that lack a strategic vision, or that don't have effective measures and feedback processes to highlight elements of the systems that are either in short supply or over-extended, are especially vulnerable to toxic side effects" (p. 27). In this context, it is easy to understand the seven award criteria used by the Department of Commerce, U.S. Government (1997) for the Malcolm Baldrige National Quality Award. The award stresses the importance of leadership, strategic planning, customer and market focus, information and analysis, human resource development and management, process management and business results in measuring organizational performance excellence (pp. 5–19).

### Culture and Innovation Change

In addition to strategic planning, successful organizations have developed a system of cultural change that defines the nature of work to be done; the type of strategies, structures, workforce and technologies to be changed; the people who will be involved; and the champions or agents of change. Successful organizations have cultures and behaviors that are unique and identifiable (for example; logo, foundation, history, evolution, innovation, people, events, resources, products and services). These organizations share some common characteristics (control systems, work design, human resources management, technology), with others, particularly their competitors (Kimberly & Bouchikhi, 1995: 10).[2] Field work has been employed as the primary research methodology to collect data and information on the organization's culture and behavior.[3]

Management commitment, particularly at the executive level, is critical to accept and initiate cultural and innovation changes as long-term processes. Senior management provides a visionary and charismatic leadership in managing the change process (Gulden & Reck, 1992:11; Premkumar & Ramamurthy, 1995: 308). Management's vision and concern for the future, commitment, trust, communication and shared cultural ideology are instrumental for organizations to engage in opportunities to develop new products or enter into new markets (Dixon et al., 1994: 98).

According to Vasilash, the success of BPR rests on "the commitment of the most senior management," because it requires "a comprehensive revamping of what exists, a massive change and reorganization of the status quo" (1993: 13). "This direct involvement of top management differentiates reengineering from the continuous improvement process" (Dixon et al., 1994: 104). The role of the leader is critical to champion the change; to be a visible supporter, to recognize the need for change, and to set up the process to design and implement change (Davenport, 1993a; Shane, 1994).

Porter and Parker (1992) have outlined some of the cultural factors that facilitate innovative change in organizations. These include: the change process needs to be led by the general manager of the organization; the change agent has to work closely with the general manager of the organization; organizational members develop a climate of shared learning; a system of continuous change is developed; change is systematic not fragmented; and employees are actively involved in the change process. They also suggest the importance of dissatisfaction among employees: "the change process must be based on a level of dissatisfaction with the status quo of the business, somehow, people must believe that things can and must be better" (p. 66).

## Leadership, Teams and Innovation

In process innovation, managers can play a critical role in technological development and administrative changes, if they champion the change and take personal risks in overcoming organizational resistance to change. Managers as champions can provide alternatives to existing organization rules and procedures, by allowing employees to be autonomous in formulating their own implementation guidelines for innovation changes. They can facilitate organiz-ational support for intra-functional coordination, joint use of resources, consensus decision-making processes and loose monitoring mechanisms that encourage risk-taking behavior (Shane, 1994: 397–421). Managers can use their strategic influence behavior to create a socio-political process of contested change within the organization (Maute & Locander, 1994: 161–174).

One of the main problems facing innovation change programs, for example quality circles, is the lack of cooperation from middle managers. Without their support, quality circles cannot overcome obstacles from existing organizational power structures, which require changes to systems of reward, communication and decision-making, as well as the availability of resources, such as time, information, people and finance (Brenan, 1992: 35–45). The commitment of management to change-oriented programs such as TQM or reengineering, make these programs company-wide policies that are continuous and never-ending (Dale & Cooper, 1991: 20–26).

In successful radical change programs such as BPR, top managers "were involved in both the *direction* of re-engineering projects and in the *details* of their design and implementation. Teams were empowered to do the work, but top management was clearly at the helm" (Dixon et al., 1994: 96–97. italics in original).

Dixon et al. (1994) suggested that successful teams "included a flexible mix of line managers and internal experts. Team leadership was often drawn from staff level management with close involvement from line managers. Teams were almost all cross-functional in composition, though the extent of cross-functionality varied" (p. 103). Those teams responsible for the project design were also involved in project implementation. Empowering teams to make decisions in both the development and implementation phases insured the success of BPR projects (Vasilash, 1993: 10).

A team-based approach to innovation systems, transforms organizational structure from a hierarchical control to "a flat confederation of concertively controlled self-managing teams" (Barker, 1993: 412). Team groups eliminate unneeded supervisory and other bureaucratic staff management hierarchical structures. Self-managed teams follow corporate vision and directives to guide their actions in the change process.[4]

Ripley and Ripley (1992) argued that in the 1990s, business organizations shifted their competitive strategies from cost volume-based to customer value-based, on improved production processes and maximum utilization of workforce talents. New organizational structures have emerged that support self-managing teams. Teams respond better to customer needs, effectively manage resource allocation decisions, and implement policies and strategies developed by top management into specific programs and projects.

Team members not only direct their efforts to achieve the corporate mission, but they also coordinate with other company program areas. Teams are responsible for making collective decisions, completing tasks on time, eliminating unnecessary middle-level managerial positions to save costs, as well as increasing employee motivation, productivity and commitment to the organization (Barker 1993: 413–414).

For teams to be effective work groups, Campion, Medsker and Higgs (1993) considered process characteristics to identify the group interactions. Campion et al. (1993) identified several themes that included potency, social support, workload sharing, and communication and cooperation within the group. They defined potency in terms of team spirit and a high expectation/belief that the group would get the work done. Potency induces task commitment and hard work among members. Social support facilitates groups to "have positive social interactions" to sustain group effectiveness. Workload sharing prevents "social-loafing or free-riding. To enhance sharing, group members should believe their individual performance can be distinguished from the group's, and that there is a link between their performance and outcomes." Communication and cooperation within the group enhances group effectiveness (p. 830). Their study supported the conclusion that process characteristics were related to group productivity and can be affected by management through positive feedback, encouragement, modeling and reinforcement (p. 842).

Top management can solicit commitment from teams and work group members by providing positive reinforcement that their contributions make a critical difference in the successful adoption and implementation of the innovation process. When trust and cooperation develop between senior

management and team members, there are higher quality exchange relationships (Deluga & Perry, 1994). Under such an environment, innovations can be
successfully implemented and institutionalized throughout the organization.
Mezias and Glynn suggest "successful innovation is seen as the outcome of an
organized, purposeful and systematic process" (1993: 80). Reengineering is
viewed as a planned process innovation approach to bring changes in business
organizations.

## REENGINEERING APPROACHES TO BUSINESS PROCESS INNOVATION

Hammer and Champy (1993) view innovation in terms of organizational
transformation, where a collection of business activities with several inputs is
transformed into outputs that the user/customer values. According to Harrison
and Pratt, "a business process is a sequence of activities that fulfills the needs
of an internal or external customer . . . the best organizations are assigning clear
accountability for process performance and realigning functional objectives
and performance measures to support process performance goals" (1993: 7–8).
The focus of process innovation centers on the entire inter-related process,
rather than individual isolated tasks that may result in consolidation of
functions, jobs or areas of specialization.

Both Hammer and Champy (1993), and Harrison and Pratt (1993) suggest
reengineering is a strategy to restructure organizations, overhaul the labor
force, and produce products and/or services that are valued by customers. They
target BPR to restructure large organizations into smaller, flatter and less
hierarchical units. Davenport (1993b) views the process as an "attempt to
identify the technological or organizational process factors that will maximize
variation and create fruitful changes" (p. 8). These fruitful changes may include
cost-cutting techniques, improve manufacturing process lead-time, or the
application of new methods to change existing work techniques (Hammer &
Champy, 1993). In internal auditing, process improvements may include quick
response logistic systems, invoiceless accounts payable systems and purchasing orders (Harrison & Pratt, 1993: 7).

BPR has been accepted as a strategy consisting of several methodologies that
involve a series of discrete functions. The approach is rooted in the hard
systems approach, where the machine metaphor dominates the underlying
principles and assumptions of BPR (Burgess, 1995). Using the machine
metaphor, BPR involves "the radical redesign of work processes, organizational structure, information technology, job content and flow, to achieve
quantum improvements in customer-value productivity" (Richman & Koontz,

1993: 26). BPR addresses issues such as personnel skills, resources and signals that affect overall organizational performance. BPR focuses on product quality, quality costs, activity-based management /costing and value added (Housel & Kanevsky, 1995). Primarily, BPR is concerned with "the radical redesign of the business processes, organizational structures, management systems, and values of an organization to achieve breakthrough in business performance" (Gulden & Reck, 1992: 10).

BPR is not a completely new approach to performance improvement having its roots in the scientific management school of the 1950s. What makes BPR more appealing nowadays is a combination of technological changes, market demands and industry competition. Reengineering projects have called for changes in organizations directions and goals. As a result, some goals have been replaced by other goals, e.g. flexibility replaced by cost reduction, and the organizations' priorities have changed. Employees are working differently than in the past, since customary rules have become obsolete (Dixon et al., 1994: 94–99). The competitive environment has affected the status quo of some firms, where some firms have positioned themselves to compete against others by developing benchmarks.

### Benchmarking

According to Drucker (1995), benchmarking is "used to obtain productivity information [by] comparing one's performance with the best performance in the industry, or better yet, with the best anywhere in the business. Benchmarking assumes correctly that what one organization does, any other organization can do as well. And it assumes, also correctly, that being at least as good as the leader is a prerequisite to being competitive" (p. 59).

When organizations experience persistent resistance to innovative change, benchmarking can be used to overcome organizational resistance. Davidson suggests that, "benchmarking is often useful as a means to focus attention on performance shortfalls and to support a case for significant change in operations. The identification of substantial performance gaps can catalyze action." Defining new performance measures and standards, and linking them to compensation "was used by companies to overcome resistance to change" (1993: 76).

Benchmarking provides valuable information to BPR, if the objective is to use breakthrough innovation in business performance. Benchmarking supports BPR by providing examples of best business practices that have been implemented. It serves as a reference point to identify bottleneck areas that require improvement (Ruchala, 1995). Information on implementation of good practices allows teams and work groups to work harder, to formulate workable plans based on industry best practices and aspire to establish operating targets that exceed current best practices (Richman & Koontz, 1993: 26–27).

When auditing is introduced to assess performance, either self or external practices, comparisons with best-known practices become key to evaluating innovation processes. When benchmarking is used to evaluate performance after the implementation of reengineering projects, both financial and non-financial indicators focus on operational results of the process being changed (Dixon et al., 1994: 102).[5]

When reengineering projects are done in conjunction with benchmarking, they will have an impact on the entire organization. Unlike incremental changes that focus on a single area of business activity, "BPR addresses corporate issues through aligning processes, people and the technology to delivering [in line with] the corporate goals and objectives. BPR can be used either within core processes and/or in redesigning the whole business process" (Parker 1993: 52).

## Organizational Transformation and Information Systems

Davidson (1993) has suggested that quality and reengineering programs focus on business transformation, followed by organizational change. Accordingly "transformation focuses first on business processes and infrastructure, and second on organizational structures and systems." In other words, business activities can be structured to improve performance "and to then drive organizational change to align with the new business model" (p. 77).

Business transformation thus encompasses more than improvement in operating performance. Davidson outlined three phases of business transformation that include: stage one, the pursuit of operating excellence; stage two, build on existing capabilities and infrastructure to achieve operating excellence; and stage three "where new business units can appear, as new product and service offerings become independent ventures" and where capabilities developed in stage one materialize in core business competencies (1993: 65).

Davidson emphasizes that the focus of transformation should be on the development of core competencies and infrastructure to support core business. Eventually, organizations can build their "capabilities to introduce enhanced services and value-added processes that in turn can grow into new stand-alone businesses. A philosophy that focuses on the latent business growth potential of the core business represents a fundamental shift in management focus" (1993: 77).

For process innovation change to materialize, the role of information technology is critical. Information occupies "a central role as the enabler of entirely new, cross-functional business processes. Computer and communications technology enable organizations to break the old rules and conventions that dictated the design of business processes" (Gulden & Reck, 1992: 16). Information technology can serve "to increase flexibility, to improve communication, and to integrate different functions and organizations" (Dixon et al., 1994: 105). Accounting as an economic information system, becomes a cornerstone in business process innovation.

Accounting provides financial information that supports process innovation and quality improvement programs. As information managers, accountants/ internal auditors monitor information on organizational performance, which will require improvement, assess the need for functional integration of the organization, and appraise the capability of the human, financial and technological resources that will carry out BPR programs.

## ORGANIZATIONAL STRUCTURES AND ADMINISTRATIVE INNOVATION CHANGES: ACTIVITY-BASED COSTING AS AN ADMINISTRATIVE INNOVATION

Organizational structures such as decentralization, centralization, formalization and differentiation affect innovation. Organizations with organic structures tend to have structures that are decentralized, less formalized and undifferentiated, while those with mechanistic structures are centralized, formalized and differentiated. Organic structures are more appropriate for technical innovations. On the other hand, mechanistic structures are associated with the adoption and implementation of administrative innovation (Daft, 1978; Damanpour, 1987).[6] "ABC is an administrative innovation because its implementation may lead to new administrative procedures, policies and organizational structures" (Gosselin, 1997: 109).

When organizations decide to adopt activity-based costing (ABC) first time, need to spell out first, bureaucratic structures including centralization, play an important role in the adoption decision. According to Gosselin (1997), "centralized and formal organizations that adopt ABC are more likely to implement ABC than decentralized and informal organizations . . . Decentralized and less formal organizations may have greater flexibility to stop the ABC implementation process . . . if they feel it would be relevant to do so . . . Vertical differentiation may have more impact on the adoption decision than on

Mechanistic organizations prefer to adopt ABC, because it is a formal accounting system. Since bureaucratic organizations are centralized and have higher levels of vertical differentiation that encourage ABC adoption, they are able to carry the administrative innovation all the way through implementation. Centralization and formalization become the appropriate organizational structures to commit the resources needed for ABC implementation (Gosselin 1997: 117). Organizational contextual factors affect the diffusion innovation process and either "encourages or discourages the implementation of innovation" (p. 105).

## THE DIFFUSION OF ADMINISTRATIVE INNOVATION: ACTIVITY-BASED COSTING AND ACCOUNTING CHANGE IMPLEMENTATION ISSUES

The diffusion of innovation literature differentiates between technical innovations in manufacturing and administrative innovation in accounting and control systems. Table 11.2 provides a comparison of technical and administrative innovation along several dimensions. The table incorporates concepts used by several management scholars (Daft, 1978; Damanpour, 1987; Dunk, 1989; Ibarra, 1993; Johns, 1993) in their study of administrative innovative approaches, which illustrate that administrative innovations in organizations encounter less acceptance and receive minimal support by senior level management. As a result, administrative innovations have lagged behind technical innovations in manufacturing systems. These lags have been attributed to the slow pace in innovation, due to constraints in organizational, personnel and hierarchical structures.

ABC is a formal accounting system that is more likely to be adopted by mechanistic organizations. It benefits organizations that are hierarchical, interdependent with cross-functional arrangements[7] and incur a great deal of transaction costs.[8] The key to ABC is the understanding and analysis of transaction costs, activities and intra-organizational relationships (Roberts & Silvester, 1996: 32). The economies of scale advantage that centralized organizations enjoyed as low cost producers, created barriers for ABC implementation. They include "too many or too few identified activities and cost drivers; overly complex system design; reciprocal cost allocation; and lack of technical expertise on the identification and analysis of activities" (p. 26).

Implementation problems are largely organizational issues associated with the socio-technical settings of ABC.[9] ABC requires the commitment of materials and resources for the project. If senior managers mandate ABC without commitment from lower level personnel,[10] it will have minimal impact.

ABC systems met the least resistance in situations "where senior operating executives had sponsored the project and were actively involved in its early phase" (Argyris & Kaplan, 1994: 89).

Senior management involvement provides legitimacy to ABC that it is a serious and important undertaking, and promotes coordination and interaction among functional and divisional managers. If senior managers can provide job security to employees and possible reassignment for employees affected by ABC, they can receive ABC support at lower personnel levels. By minimizing barriers through incentive structures and performance reward systems aligned to ABC, implementing ABC at a critical time when information is available,[11] and knowing the potential savings and costs ensure the success of ABC (Roberts & Silvester, 1996: 33–35).

Argyris and Kaplan (1994) stressed that ABC would promote changes in organizations when ABC has incentives aligned with organizational support programs. Organizations develop "systems or structure that facilitate, reward, and reinforce collective change. Examples of such organizational enablers include employees empowered to act at the local level, reduced managerial layering, financial and non-financial rewards for successful implementation, and information systems that produce relevant information in a timely and user friendly manner" (pp. 89–90).

Managers can include both long-term and medium-term performance measures[12] to stress the success of ABC innovation and reward allocation purposes. These changes should be accompanied by reports that are understandable and useful (Young, 1997).

The adaptive systems view of organizations suggests that external environmental factors influence the adoption and diffusion of innovation. Competition is an important institutional environment that has bearing on innovation. Anderson's (1995) study of ABC implementation at General Motors Corporation (GM) revealed that competition brought with it the importance of cost and the need to design new cost systems. GM adopted ABC, because GM's competitors had adopted ABC. It corroborated the assertion that "the identity of voluntary adopters of ABC is consistent with the claim that competition and environmental uncertainty promote ABC adoption" (p. 42). Anderson's (1995) GM study supported the idea that external communication through publicity and competition from outsiders provided internal support and external validity to ABC implementation. It helped to "overcome internal resistance by management" and "reinforced management's commitment to ABC" (p. 42).

ABC, as an administrative innovation change program requires a series of process stages for the successful completion of the initiation process. The initiation process includes data gathering, resource funding availability, cultural program of attitudinal change, education and training, and management support/sponsorship.[13] The implementation process requires structural support of formalization, centralization and decision-making in the organization's bureaucratic structure. While organic structures support initiation, it is the mechanistic structures that implement them. The implementation of ABC and other accounting and internal auditing changes as administrative innovations, will thus be influenced by the prevalence of mechanistic structures in organizations.

## ADMINISTRATIVE INNOVATION APPROACHES FOR INTERNAL AUDITING AND CONTROL SYSTEMS

In the previous sections, potential problems and barriers – organizational structures, management support, competition and external environmental factors and resources – to administrative innovations were discussed. These bottlenecks have slowed the progress of administrative innovation, where it has lagged behind technical innovation. It has contributed to administrative innovation lag. Nevertheless, recent technological advances in computer information systems, on-line networking and telecommunication, and the Internet have minimized the gap between technical and internal auditing and control systems. These developments have highlighted the increased importance of accounting and internal auditing in the post-industrial information society of advanced capitalist economic systems.

Administrative innovations address the structure and management processes of organizations and the internal control systems. Reengineering projects have addressed the need for radical administrative innovations. In most organizations, higher levels of management are associated with mechanistic structures, which are highly formal, specialized and centralized. If top management does not support administrative innovations, they are unlikely to succeed.

Internal auditing and accounting systems are part of administrative structures, and changing them requires a phased innovation approach. Dixon et al. (1994) suggest a two-stage radical approach that involves "initiation and implementation. A decentralized organization best supports generation and innovation ideas, while a centralized organization is best able to implement the innovations, implying that leadership roles and project structure might need to vary significantly in the two phases" (p. 101). Internal auditing systems operate in centralized structures, tend to be micro-oriented, and can be implemented more easily, than innovations that are large-scale and involve macro-radical improvements. Process analysis, when used within the context of internal auditing, stresses continuous improvement programs that focus on optimization of resource mix and allocation strategies, designed to minimize waste and reduce non-value added organization activities.

In a centralized organization, administrative innovation is a top-down approach coming from senior management. Internal auditing as an administrative innovation process is less technical, allowing higher management levels to be actively involved in the planning process (Daft, 1978; Damanpour, 1987; Ibarra, 1993). When information specialists are only involved in carrying out innovation implementation, it may not succeed. Senior managers are less likely to be committed to administrative innovations, since they are not easily identifiable and cannot be championed like technical innovations.

Process innovation in administrative processes commonly addresses routine practices, strategies or reporting systems less subject to objective measures of evaluation than technical innovation. Mezias and Glynn (1993) refer to this subjectivity of administrative process innovation as experiential learning systems (p. 78). Organizations employ a low scale, gradually phased intervention strategy for incremental changes to materialize in the experiential learning process.

In spite of problems associated with administrative innovation, the diffusion of process innovation has contributed to an organized continuous process strategy, designed to bring structural changes in accounting, ABC and auditing systems. Roberts and Silvester (1996) suggested "the preexistence of an ongoing process-oriented improvement program supports ABC" (p. 33). These process change programs may include "computer integrated manufacturing, just-in-time manufacturing, or statistical process control." ABC is likely to succeed if there exists a "tested and proven interdependent infrastructure, along with a climate that supported continuous improvement and change . . . The use of cross-functional teams in activity analysis recognizes the need to dissolve structural barriers. However, actually implementing the changes often requires strong leadership from both inside and outside the team to overcome any remaining structural barriers to change" (p. 33).

Since the 1990s, the quality movement has changed the role of accounting in performance measurement. Information technology has changed the accounting function from that of producing financial reports, to that of providing service (Dixon et al., 1994: 100). In the past, accounting has played a staff function as a producer of financial reports. Traditional management practices and control systems were built on centralization, hierarchy, and the separation of duties into staff and line functions.

Information technology has transformed accounting's role from a staff function/group into a line function management group, such as manufacturing or marketing, where accountants now serve as an expert in information management, rather than as a custodian of company resources. These changes in reporting relationships have enabled accountants to be technical experts and participate in decision outcomes like cost, quality, downtime, maintenance, inspection, delivery, and related factors that indicate improved performance. Accounting and internal auditing systems are being transformed to meet information requirements of global competitive economic systems, and meet the requirements of increased management accountability.

Process innovation has now become the tool used by internal auditors to adapt to current information needs of the competitive business environment. Moore (1997) suggests that internal auditors can manage process change, if they use process skills like TQM and BPR to change traditional audit skills of flow charting and internal control assessment skills. The trend is to use technical innovation[14] process skills to introduce organizational transformation into auditing systems and functions.

Process based approach innovation has contributed to an organic view of the firm's auditing function. It can contribute to technical innovation in auditing, allowing firms to audit their innovation capability and performance. Technical innovation audits are developed and applied "to identify the processes relevant to innovation, to develop performance measures for each process of innovation and to assess the overall impact of innovation on competitiveness" (Vittorio, Coughlan & Voss, 1996: 126). A process audit selects processes and practices that support innovation programs and defines corrective actions to improve organizational performance.

Internal auditing is key to process innovation in organizations. Organizations can use process audits to assess their performance, technological capability, human and financial resources, and competitive strategies. Auditing not only identifies quality processes in organizations; it identifies gaps between current and desired performance. It locates problems, needs, and delivers information to develop action plans for better results.[15]

Process innovation attempts in internal auditing are considered micro-reengineering projects. Davidson suggested that "micro re-engineering efforts typically involve discrete, stand-alone solutions, technologies, and systems executed by local management. Such projects usually require relatively small investments and short implementation and payback periods. But this approach increases the enterprise's portfolio of technologies, software, systems, and data formats. Without alignment of these projects, a series of problems may appear" (1993: 71). In internal auditing, micro-reengineering projects may focus on improved reporting systems for quality improvement, cost-reduction techniques, better response time, quick delivery cycle time, faster variance reporting time and customer service and satisfaction.

# ADAPTIVE CHANGE AND ADMINISTRATIVE INNOVATION

The current competitive environment requires organizations to adapt, change, and renew their business conditions (Beatty & Ulrich, 1991; Duck, 1993). The population ecology approach suggests that crisis, whether real or perceived, creates the conditions for innovative technological and organizational change, requiring in some instances, an immediate solution to the current crisis. A crisis may be necessary to create the conditions for innovative change. Managers can use crisis to stimulate innovative organizational responses (Beatty & Ulrich, 1991). Organizations are more likely to stimulate process innovation, only when management believes that it will enable them to solve the current crisis or provide better techniques than are currently available. To survive and remain competitive, organizations have to be adaptive to change. In order to compete, organizations have to make changes faster.

Market conditions/demands and "emerging technological capabilities . . . encourages organizations to take the risks associated with radical customer-oriented change" (Dixon et al., 1994: 94). However, the degree and level of innovation varies, whether it is incremental and/or radical change. The previous chapters in the book have addressed these two types of change strategies and their impact on technological and administrative changes. Accounting and internal control systems are approached within the context of administrative process changes. It is argued that these two types of innovative changes have to occur simultaneously if accounting and control systems are to play major roles in supporting improved organizational performance. If administrative control systems are loosened to introduce several changes into the organization, they increase the likelihood of innovation process success.

However, there are potential barriers to the diffusion of administrative innovation programs in an organization, particularly the design of internal control and auditing systems, where these barriers tend to be exacerbated (Johns, 1993: 576–583). Some of these barriers arise due to political interests which block the adoption process, lack of compatibility between the social context of the organization and change process, relative absence of a new paradigm that articulates change and external threat from government regulation and competitors.

Chapter 11 discussed administrative innovation and development in accounting and control systems. However, the pace of change and progress in accounting has been affected by several organizational factors. Organizational impediments arising from mechanistic structures, management hierarchy, and lack of functional coordination have slowed down progress in the design and implementation of ABC and other accounting innovation changes. While accounting still experiences innovation lags, recent technological advancements in computerized information systems have quickened the pace of innovation in accounting and internal auditing systems. Nevertheless, there still remains substantial disparity among organizations in the adoption and diffusion of innovation.

Organizational size is a critical factor in the diffusion of innovation changes. Large complex organizations, in comparison to smaller organizations, have slack resources and economies of scale. Since complex organizations can afford to take calculated risks associated with administrative innovation, they have adopted innovations to improve and/or change accounting and internal auditing operational functions. The sociological adaptation approach for management control systems suggests that process innovation in internal auditing and management accounting and control systems be implemented as part of overall organizational change and development strategy.

# CONCLUSION

In conclusion, this book documented that management and accounting researchers need to pay particular attention to an organization's approach to change and development strategy, when designing and implementing process innovation programs such as TQM and reengineering. It is imperative for managers and researchers to examine relationships among organizational change strategies: gradual-incremental and revolutionary-radical; learning strategies: single loop-convergence (first-order) and double loop-reorientation (second-order); planned change and intervention strategies: organizational development (OD) and organizational transformation (OT); and diffusion of innovation: administrative and technical.

This book describes the influence that organizational change, learning, planned change and intervention, and diffusion of innovations have on the successful design and implementation of management control systems.

Accounting and organization management researchers and policy makers can benefit from the sociology of organizational change and development approaches, in the adoption of process innovation strategies in accounting control and internal auditing systems. Throughout the book, it has been shown that these contrasting approaches in organizational change and development strategies account for differences in the type, nature, and degree of innovation in internal auditing and accounting control systems.

## NOTES

1. Brown and Eisenhardt (1997) linked continuous change to organizations with successful multi-product portfolios. These organizations are innovative and exhibit well defined project priorities and schedules, managerial responsibilities, clearly defined goals and easy communication channels among divisions and throughout the organization. When extensive communication is combined with clearly defined responsibilities and priorities, it contributed to a high degree of motivation and performance. "Extensive communication with colleagues and the external environments is likely to create feedback on performance, while clear responsibilities and priorities provide autonomy and accountability for significant aspects of the task" (p. 15). These organizations are 'aggressive', 'opportunistic', "know where they are going in the future," and have "explicit organizational practices that address past, present, and future time horizons and the transitions between them" (p. 29).

2. Kimberly and Bouchikhi (1995) advocated for research in organizational biography, which record those characteristics that are unique to the organization, as well as those that it shares with others. They suggest that in most historical research, "biography is a vehicle for illuminating the lives of individual people. The astute biographer places the subject in a historical context and traces how the subject both shaped and was shaped by external and internal events and forces . . . Analogously [Kimberly and Bouchikhi] argue [that] biography should become a vehicle for illuminating the developmental trajectories or organizations" (p. 10).

A case study of an organization can be used to demonstrate the utility of the approach and to show "how the past shapes the present and constrains the future and how organizational 'passages' are shaped by combination of internal and external forces." They "argue[d] that without an appreciation for past experience, present behavior and future action cannot be fully understood, either for people or for organization" (p. 10). In depth interviews with senior managers reveal important information about the foundation, history and founding leaders of the organization. By "varying the seniority of those interviewed, [the authors] hoped to explore how differences in time of entry into the company might be related to perceptions of company culture and priorities" (p. 11).

Kimberly and Bouchikhi (1995) viewed organizations in terms of "both the contexts for and the result of human behavior. Over time, people's perceptions of the past shape the conditions of their participation in the present and influence how they think about participation in the future" (p. 12). They advanced that "a central task in the creation of organizational biographies is capturing the evolution of the subjective side of the organization. While the 'facts', objective indicators of structure and performance, may speak for themselves, the engines of development and change are frequently less obvious." The challenge "is to get beneath surface descriptions and uncover deeper patterns" (p. 12).

Accordingly, a study of the history of organizations allows researchers to understand the founder's values; role of the leader/founder in shaping the organization's development, strategy and policy; and ability to adapt and respond to internal and external environmental forces (p. 17). They recommended the importance of comparative research in learning the foundation of competitive organizations in organizational biography studies (p. 18).

3. Schensul (1980) described fieldwork in anthropology as "involving 'face-to-face interactions', 'participant observation', and 'cultural immersion' describe situations in which the anthropologist comes to know what it means to be a member of the group under study" (p. 309). In general, "field work deals with primary rather than secondary data, emphasizes inductive rather than deductive reasoning, and focuses in immediate personal experience rather than armchair theorizing. Central to its practice is suspension of judgement: the anthropologist must adopt the attitude of the novice or learner, rather than critic. The anthropologist is the 'learner', being taught both by the formal 'scientific' process of data collection and by informal involvement in human interaction" (p. 309).

According to Schensul (1980), the field work for anthropologists is a "residentially/geographically defined community" with a "distinct ethnically and culturally" group from the national system that they are part of. "These have also been communities which lacked political and economic power and access to resources within the wider society" (p. 309). The field worker develops personal ties, friendly relationships, acquire key informants, and share the local activities – dances, games, rituals, among others to be part of the group that they study. "Such *participant* observation is as much a part of the ethnographic method as field notes, interview schedules and kinship genealogy" (p. 309. italics in original). These are scientific endeavors in fieldwork, in that the questions asked and results obtained are in response to theoretical concerns in the discipline. Schensul argued that fieldwork could be limited to the sociopolitical process of the studied communities. "The interaction of scientific objectives and community needs could be established as a basic part of the overall fieldwork enterprise" (p. 310).

The strength in field research is that it has relevance for research in social change and applied work in policy making. Schensul (1980) reaffirmed the role of field research in social and cultural changes, by suggesting that "anthropological field work must contribute to that change despite the fact that the intent may be to do 'basic' research in response to theoretical concerns" (p. 311). The contributions of field research to society may include: "reporting of interim results; designing and implementing short-term research based on the needs of change activities; writing reports and proposals to assist groups in advocating for needs; as well as conducting the participant observation, interviewing and survey research that may be a part of the overall research design" (p. 312). The implications for future fieldwork is that there is a need for the establishment of social science 'rules of conduct' guidelines, "which would permit the scientific enterprise to serve the needs of community residents" (p. 317). In other words, there has to be a link between the field study of culture and sociopolitical changes in organizations.

However, it needs to be noted that the relevance of social research may be affected by the way in which sites are selected, measurements are made (e.g. choice of observations, wording of questionnaires in public opinion polls), interview techniques and choice of subjects/participants. Measurement and methodological issues affect the findings of empirical research and their use for policy-making purposes (Presser, 1990).

4. Ezzamel and Wilmott (1998) challenged Barker (1993) and other management scholars, who suggested that teamwork is prominent in work and organizational re-structuring, as well as in decentralized flexible work settings. They applied a critical perspective and argued that the self-management democratic approach of teamwork may contribute to less autonomy and disempowerment, through concentration of managerial control and coercive features of team culture and ideology. In other words, teamwork reveals political aspects in work reorganization that may include coercion and control of teamwork (pp. 358–359).

In their study, Ezzamel and Wilmott (1998) studied machinists at Stitch Company and found that the pressure for teams to become self-managing was inconsistent with the notion of self-identity. "In practice, machinists restricted their boundaries of responsibility, to the distribution or work according to available skills and personal preferences within the teams. [They reported] that many of the machinists experienced team work as 'more like line work', 'except that to earn a (team-based) bonus it was necessary to 'help' others 'to get the work through' " (p. 390). There was the perception that team work was a "more oppressive and divisive system of managerial control that threatened to disrupt a sense of self identity vested in social relationships with fellow machinists." Their empirical study showed "how team work reforms and elaborates, rather than replaces or eliminates, a traditional, hierarchical system of management control" (p. 391).

Ezzamel and Wilmott (1998) noted that "the shift to teamwork was generally experienced as posing a threat to the narrative of self, not as an empowering relaxation of managerial control" (p. 392). To counter the negative effects of teamwork coercion and control, accounting numbers were used as rituals to justify the team approach. Accounting has played an important role in justifying; supporting and rationalizing the team based approach to management control at Stitch Company. They stated that "at Stitch Co., accounting provided a rhetoric of value added and an associated set of calculations with which to pose and address the strategic question of whether to withdraw from manufacturing or to reorganize its capability around a team work system. Within the reorganized manufacturing operations, accounting measures were applied in the day-to-day operation of team work by quantifying performance targets, measuring results, and through the team-based bonus scheme, aligning the activity of machinists with the demand from the retail outlets" (p. 391).

5. Benchmarking can support reengineering in several ways. Rigby (1993) has identified four major components of reengineering projects as follows: (1). A fundamental rethinking of the way work gets done (process design), leading to improvements in productivity and cycle times. (2). A structural reorganization, typically breaking functional hierarchies into cross-functional (horizontal) teams. (3). A new information and measurement system, using higher technology to drive improved data dissemination and decision making. (4). A new value system [culture] typically placing greater emphasis on the company's customers (p. 25).

6. Gosselin (1997) in a study of Canadian manufacturing firms, found that not all features of mechanistic structures facilitate the adoption of ABC, which is an administrative innovation. "Only one organizational determinant, vertical differentiation, proved to have a significant impact on the decision to adopt ABC. Vertical differentiation is a critical determinant in the mechanistic/organic model since it captures how bureaucratic the decision process is in the organization. The selection of an administrative innovation like ABC is facilitated in SBU's [strategic business units] that have a higher level of vertical differentiation because this type of innovation is much more formal . . . When a mechanistic organization decides to innovate in the cost management area, it prefers to select an administrative innovation like ABC" (p. 115).

7. Roberts and Silvester (1996) noted that cross-functional arrangements create barriers for the implementation of ABC. In organizations where there are cross-functional and organizational interdependencies, correct identification of activities and the assignment of associated costs might create potential problems for ABC. These problems include the identification of transaction costs, where there are interdependencies and process oriented functions. To manage these activities, organizations have developed hierarchical structures that are complex and less capable of reducing transaction costs. The lack of experts with technical background and training to identify and trace all activities that drive costs in organizations, minimize the success of ABC (pp. 23–25, 31–32).

8. Argyris and Kaplan (1994) noted that there would be a resistance to ABC, if the information gathered becomes a threat to certain managers "by revealing that past and continuing organizational decisions are either contradictory or erroneous. For example, the analysis could reveal that certain favored product lines or customers are highly unprofitable. The product managers responsible for introducing and maintaining these product lines, or the account managers responsible for the highly unprofitable customers, become threatened by the quantitative and defensible evidence of their value-destroying activities. As another example, the revelation of large expenditures on non-value added and wasteful activities will threaten the reputation and self-image of, say, manufacturing managers who are responsible for improving quality and productivity, or the ABC analysis could reveal the existence of substantial excess capacity in many organizational activities and processes" (p. 93). They concluded that these revelations affect the credibility of marketing managers' sales plans, production managers' ability to reduce excess capacity and costs, and financial managers reporting of distorted numbers that lead to bad decisions on products, prices, customers and were unable to control production wastes and cost overruns.

9. Anderson (1995) noted that "in the early 1990s, it was assumed that the challenges of implementing ABC were believed to be primarily technical: defining the scope of the model; identifying activities; selecting cost drivers; and analyzing ABC costs. Management support was to be obtained through training. Implementation was seen as a rational process of educating managers about ABC and developing an ABC model . . . Like the early IT [information technology] literature, the ABC literature did not recognize that ABC systems exist in social settings in which technical rationality may diverge from individual rationality . . ." (p. 8).

10. Arygris and Kaplan (1994) indicated that "if subordinates are implementing the concepts only because of the mandate from the senior manager, there will be less vigilance, learning, and continuous improvement in implementing the approach. As a consequence, the impact and persistence of the implementation will be lower than

hoped for and expected. When managers implement a new approach because of externally-generated incentives and authoritative mandates, they will hold the senior manager responsible for monitoring and maintaining the effectiveness of the change process" (p. 103).

While it is not related to innovation, managers make discretionary accounting changes for "opportunistic or earnings management purposes" (Pincus & Wasley, 1994: 22).

11. Argyris and Kaplan (1994) recommend the use of mini-experiments to gather information for ABC. Managers can use these experiments to test their assumptions, uncertainties and doubts on ABC, concerning costs, profits and performance. "The underlying logic for building internal commitment to ABC is to create change situations where data exists or can be created so that statements can be tested" (p. 101). They also recommended that an alternative strategy for ABC systems is to find ways in which defensive behaviors of resistance to change can be used to generate questions and answers that can be used to support the new system (p. 104).

12. Young (1997) recognized that bottom-line (profit) results from management accounting changes usually take at least five or more years to happen. Instead, he recommends the use of "some medium-term measures that will assess whether employee attitudes, behaviors, and performance are changing. Such measures involve using behavioral science methods, such as psychometrically sound attitude surveys, focus groups, and direct and indirect observation of the work environment" (p. 19).

13. According to Argyris and Kaplan (1994), after education and training, the next process step is to "persuade key individuals/managers to serve as sponsors to lead the change processes" (p. 87). Sponsors can be assigned in each functional area to specific roles for the ABC technical innovation. Usually individuals from the finance organization or line function, provide the insight and analysis for ABC. They then move to the action phase where "management acts on the insights revealed from the ABC model to produce improved organizational performance" (p. 87). Then those who are aware of ABC, serve as the project's advocate and seek budgetary approval from the organizational authority. The finance person serves as the project sponsor.

Then a project leader is assigned as the change agent, who launches a specific target project. The project that is "intended to produce organizational change should also have a project *Target*, the person or groups whose behavior and actions are expected to change based on the newly revealed information" (p. 88. Italics in original).

14. Technical innovations are easier to implement if organizations follow a series of processes. Argyris and Kaplan (1994) described the steps as follows: "First, the technical theory must be demonstrably valid. Its internal consistency and external validity should be established." This should be followed by an "Education and Sponsorship process [that] enables change advocates to explore and articulate the technical merits of the new proposal, and gain senior management support for acting in accordance with the articulated ideas." This should be followed by "a second process, which they referred to as 'Create Internal Commitment', . . . to overcome the barriers to change" from employees and managers threatened by these programs (p. 83).

15. Vittorio, Coughlan and Voss (1996) have developed a process model of technical innovation that utilizes process auditing to evaluate a firm's innovation capability. "This model has four core processes: the identification of new product concepts – concept generation; taking the innovation from concept to launch – product development; the development of innovation in production – process innovation; and the development of

management of technology per se – technology acquisition. The model links the core to enabling processes and outcomes that together constitute the innovation process in the firm. It facilitates two ways of assessing an organization: a process audit and a performance audit. The process audit focuses on the individual processes necessary for innovation and the extent to which best practice is applied. The performance audit focuses on the effectiveness of the individual processes and the overall process of innovation, in terms of their impact on competitiveness" (p. 106).

They also suggested that "innovation scorecards can be used to describe the characteristics of good practice and poor practice" of process innovation. This information in turn can be used to compare their practices with other companies to provide "an overview of their strengths and weaknesses with regard to technical innovation management" (pp. 109, 112).

# PART IV

# APPENDICES

# OVERVIEW

Part IV contains five appendices which elaborate on several issues central to organizational change and development and process innovation. These appendices apply organizational sociological perspectives: contingency theory, systems analysis, and ecological theory, to illustrate process innovation changes in accounting control and internal auditing systems. The topics discussed include systems approach to organizational growth and development, divisional collaboration, total quality management (TQM), and reengineering. A brief introduction on each of the appendices is provided below.

Appendix 1 presents two externally oriented acquisitive growth strategies, diversification and absorption, as alternatives to internal growth through process innovation. Organizations pursue acquisition because it is less risky and costly compared to growth through process innovation. Diversification is sometimes preferred because it allows organizations easy entry into new markets and geographical areas. Appendix 1 proposes that while some successful organizations prefer acquisition and diversification as organizational change and development strategies, many organizations have pursued both internal growth through innovation and external growth through acquisition.

In addition to corporate growth and development, organizations are concerned with performance issues, particularly with efficiency and the effectiveness of their service and program delivery to customers/clients. Cost and quality have become important objectives of many organizations, including not-for-profit and governmental organizations. Collaboration among divisions, departments and agencies has been commonly used to minimize costs and improve efficiency in delivery of public goods and services.

The systems approach suggests that collaboration, voluntary cooperation among organizational units to deliver programs and services, is becoming a more common organizational practice. Appendix 2 examines the relevance of collaboration in today's organizations. It argues that voluntary inter-organizational collaboration and long-standing relationships among units may provide a flexible solution to resolving complex organizational process innovation issues when several units share responsibility for implementing a policy directive or delivering a program. Inter-departmental collaboration is a systems approach based on incremental change management strategy. This view corroborates TQM's approach to gradual process innovation in the management of organization activities. Thus, Appendix 2 extends the systems approach to inter-organizational collaboration examining the importance of collaborative efforts in process innovation and organization management.

Organizations which pursue collaboration, process innovation, and growth through acquisition and diversification are concerned with structural and cultural barriers that affect the quality of their services and cost of their programs. Educational and cultural intervention programs are commonly used as organizational development (OD) strategies to bring about attitudinal and cultural changes to support process innovation. Nowadays, ethics and quality education are integrated in higher educational curriculum to raise environmental and social awareness, as well as shaping the attitudes and intellectual thinking of college graduates who will be involved in process innovation changes in business and public organizations.

Appendix 3 presents two types of educational programs: accounting ethics and quality management that have currently received prominence in higher educational institutions. Both accounting ethics and quality management education have been shaped by institutional and consequential/adaptive approaches to organizational change and development. The institutional approach, which follows the OD intervention strategy, advocates incremental-convergence teaching methodologies, such as lectures and case studies which have been effective in presenting factual and theoretical information in a logical manner. The radical framework, which is adaptive and organic, tracks the organizational transformation (OT) strategy and utilizes the consequential teaching instruction methodology of reorientation through internships and critical inquiry. The consequential approach incorporates discovery and exploratory techniques to communicate real life organizational experiences to students.

Appendix 3 documents that these two approaches have important implications for TQM process innovation and teaching quality management issues in higher education. Appendix 4 provides several cases where improved cost accounting innovations have improved management accounting and reporting control systems.

Appendix 4 further elaborates on the adaptive-organic approach to incremental changes in management accounting systems. It provides several cases, which demonstrate that the incremental change approach in TQM for cost accounting has positively changed the method for accounting production and quality costs. The cases indicate that innovative changes like TQM require a phased-in OD planned intervention strategy, initiated and supported by management before successful implementation can take place. As a planned intervention strategy, the TQM cost management program becomes part of overall corporate strategy. These cases demonstrate that accounting has become an integral part of TQM.

Process reengineering, which advocates a radical intervention strategy, views TQM as appropriate for initiating operating administrative procedural changes in internal auditing and accounting control systems. When innovation focuses on reorganization and restructuring of internal auditing and management accounting functions, process innovation strategies advocate reengineering as the preferred strategy for changing internal auditing and management accounting operating structures. Accordingly, Appendix 5 outlines a five step radical framework for the adaptation and application of business process reengineering (BPR) in the design and implementation of internal auditing and accounting control systems. Appendices 4 and 5 provide a comparison between incremental and radical strategies of process innovation. While Appendix 4 details an incremental gradual change strategy – TQM, Appendix 5 provides a five step strategy that utilizes a radical innovation approach – BPR or process reengineering.

APPENDIX 1

# CONTINGENCY FACTORS AFFECTING EXTERNALLY ORIENTED ORGANIZATIONAL CHANGE AND GROWTH STRATEGIES

## INTRODUCTION

Organizations may adopt externally oriented instead of internally induced growth strategies. Externally oriented growth strategies involve growth through acquisition. Appendix 1 presents two externally oriented acquisitive growth strategies, diversification and absorption. They are discussed as alternatives to internal growth through innovations of products and services. The choice of either diversification and/or absorption depends upon two factors:

(1) The degree of environmental uncertainty (or the degree of the firm's interdependent relationships with the environment).
(2) The degree of business/product market interrelationships.

Based on these factors, the following two propositions are formulated.

*Proposition 1:* When the degree of environmental interdependency and the business/product market relationships is low, acquisition decisions involve diversification strategies.

*Proposition 2:* When the degree of environmental interdependency and the business/product market relationships is high, acquisition decisions involve absorption strategies.

The contingency theory of mergers and acquisitions proposes that choosing absorption or diversification acquisition as an organizational growth and development strategy depends on the decision-making strategy and rational/ political choice models adopted by management. Managers choose the acquisition decision-making model that best matches organizational resources with opportunities offered by their external environment. They tend to adopt the rational/economic decision-making model when a growth through acquisition decision involves absorption, and the political/behavioral model when organizational growth calls for diversification.

However, it needs to be noted that the choice of either a rational or political decision-making model, does not preclude use of the other model in an acquisition decision. The decision to diversify or absorb involves consideration of both economic and political factors. It is argued that the primary motive leading managers to choose absorption or diversification can be found in either economic or political factors. A managerial decision for absorption reflects rational/economic choices, while a diversification decision involves political choices. An organization may choose to adopt absorption and/or diversification growth strategies. The preferred choice for acquisition decision-making models: rational vs. political, are contingent upon several factors including stability of the external environment, complexity of business/product market interrelationships and the human, financial and technical capabilities of the organization (Sisaye, 1998a).

## CONTINGENCY THEORY AND ACQUISITIONS RESEARCH

Contingency theory has contributed significantly to empirical research through its case studies of complex organizations. These case studies have enabled researchers to examine the unique characteristics of each organization, including relevant environmental industry structure, organizational variables, characteristics and resource factors (Steiner, 1979: 406–408). Contingency models have allowed researchers to develop system-based approaches to organizational studies using empirically derived case studies of particular organizations.

Other studies have applied more than one model to study environmental decision-making. For example, Allison (1971) employed a contingency approach using three models – rational, organizational process and governmental politics – to analyze the Cuban missile crisis. His study demonstrates that it may not be necessary to choose one framework over another in organizational decision-making situations, but rather the use of multiple models can help researchers better understand the processes of complex decision-making.

A contingency model has been developed to examine the acquisition strategies of complex business organizations. Appendix Fig. 1.1 presents two contingency approaches, 'diversification' and 'absorption', based on the complexity of product/market interrelationships and the degree of dependency on the external environment, which are used to study the organizational growth strategies of complex organizations.

Organizational theory offers several decision-making models, including bureaucratic, normative decision theory and behavioral decision theory (Nutt, 1976). While existing conceptual frameworks have studied merger and acquisition decisions involving either rational or political decision-making strategies, these approaches have provided a limited view of the complex process involved in acquisition decisions. It is suggested that a contingency framework, which can incorporate economic and political variables can provide an integrated approach to the formulation and implementation of acquisitive growth strategies. Appendix 1 Fig. 1.1 presents a contingency approach of mergers and acquisitions that incorporates economic factors, strategic fit and synergy considerations from the rational decision-making model in conjunction with the study of financial risk reduction strategies, organizational fit and management philosophy/cultural fit from the political decision-making model. This contingency framework can help eliminate many of the contemporary conceptual difficulties in acquisition research, since the approach recognizes contingencies which link particular acquisition objectives with the strategic means chosen to implement/pursue them.

The rational and behavioral/political decision-making models are applied to identify those organizational characteristics associated with absorption and diversified acquisitive growth strategies. Since the choice of particular decision-making models to guide organizational growth strategies largely depends on the leadership style of top management (Hambrick, 1987), acquisition growth strategy has been approached within the context of leadership style.

The contingency approach identifies several types of decision-making models applicable to particular decision-making situations (Nutt, 1976). Of these models, the rational/economic and political/behavioral (Dean & Sharfman, 1993) are selected as the most appropriate approaches to evaluate acquisition growth strategies of complex business organizations.

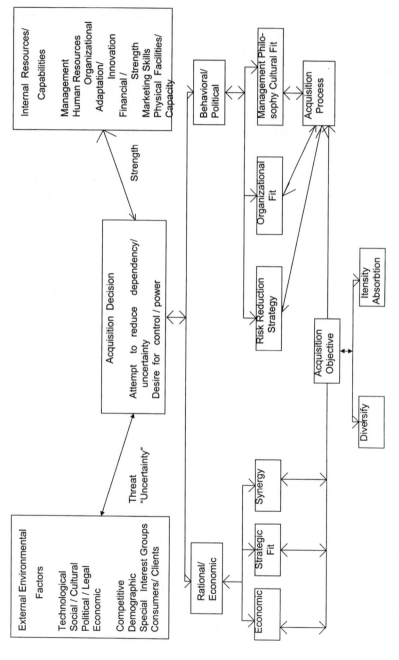

*Appendix. 1 Fig. 1.1.* A Contingency Model of Mergers and Acquisitions.

# DISTINGUISHING RATIONAL VS. POLITICAL CHOICE MODELS

## *Rational-Economic Choice Model*

The rational choice model begins with the assumption that there exists a consistent set of organizational goals. The model assumes that individuals make choices to maximize their values of interest, subject to specified constraints or a given set of information. The decision criterion is based on 'subjective expected utility', where the decision maker selects the alternative with the highest expected monetary value (Nutt, 1976: 85–88). The choice indicates, 'the action [that is] chosen is a calculated solution to a strategic problem' (Allison, 1971:13).

Given a set of decision-making alternatives, the rational choice model assumes that decision makers can differentiate among the alternatives, by applying a set of principles within limited constraints to select the optimal alternative for achieving organizational goals and objectives. The course of action selected "maximizes the social actor's likelihood of attaining the highest value for achievement of the preferences or goals in the objective function" (Pfeffer, 1981: 20. see also Pfeffer, 1992; and Dean & Sharfman, 1993). It is suggested that the action selected is indifferent with respect to particular interest group members or dominant coalitions within the organization, since it provides the best alternative for achieving organizational goals.

In examining mergers and acquisitions, the rational choice attempts to explain management motivation, in terms of maximizing firm value or shareholder wealth (Halpren 1983; Michel & Shaked 1985). The rational choice model in general assumes that acquisition decisions are based on economic, strategic fit and synergy criteria.

*Economic Profit.* Acquisitions are expected to provide economic profit if the acquisition decision meets the discounted cash flow (DCF) criterion, a technique commonly applied to evaluate capital investment decisions. Economic theory assumes that an acquisition is made when real positive gain occurs, or only when the DCF is positive (Rappaport, 1979). Acquisitions are profitable if the rate of return from the acquired firm is positive, and if the acquisition increases the market value of the firm. Mergers and consolidation of firms are based on economic aspects of corporate growth and influence economic performance at the corporate level (Pickering & Holl, 1991). Economic motivations of mergers and acquisitions include improved marketability, economics of scale, geographical expansion, and competitive advantage in global economic developments (Hermanson, Plunkett & Turner, 1990: 12–15).

*Strategic Fit.* A rational acquisition decision involves consideration of the strategic fit between the two merging companies (Barney, 1988). Strategic fit exists "if the target firm augments or complements the parent's strategy and thus makes identifiable contributions to the financial and non-financial goals of the parent" (Jemison & Sitkin, 1986: 146. see also Shelton, 1988). A successful acquisition candidate has a well-developed corporate strategic plan that defines its purpose, markets, customers, products, and resources. Rational decision makers can evaluate those plans, identify the distinctive competence of the target firm and decide to acquire if a strategic fit exists between the companies (Singh & Montgomery, 1987).

*Synergy.* It is assumed that there is synergy when a corporation is more efficient as a total operating entity than as the sum of its individual operating business components. Acquisition provides a synergetic effect, for example, when a firm acquires another firm to take advantage of its existing marketing and distribution facilities. Marketing-related factors play a major role in acquisition decisions. According to Hise (1991), some of the marketing factors behind mergers and acquisitions include sales and asset growth, increase in market share or penetration, avoiding risk associated with new products or markets by adding already developed new products and/or services, and reducing dependence on existing products (pp. 46–51). Acquisition can enhance a firm's competitive position by improving product quality and pricing decisions, expanding production capabilities through greater economics of scale, or utilizing managerial skills in marketing or production gained through acquisition to expand existing markets or open new market opportunities (Baker, Miller & Ramsperger, 1981; Lubatkin, 1983).

### Political-Behavioral Choice Model

Strategy formulation is effective when it incorporates political and behavioral variables within the context of the broader environment. Maintaining an adequate balance among various competing political interest groups enhances the probability of strategic success. The political choice model assumes that choices or decisions reflect the interests of certain groups and individuals within the organization. Accordingly, strategy formulation and decision-making in an organization becomes a political process shaped by the ideological/personal values of dominant coalitions (Litschert & Bonham, 1978: 224–225). Since decisions are influenced by individual and group interests rather than organizational objectives, "the political model presumes that parochial interests and preferences control choice" (Pfeffer, 1981: 22 and 1992).

According to the political choice model, intra-organizational power is derived from the ability of an individual or a group to reduce organizational uncertainty (Jemison 1981). Power is explained in terms of management's ability to control and influence the allocation of organizational resources (Bower 1970). Organizational politics arise from competing interest groups attempting to exercise power to modify, protect and dominate an organization's resource distribution system (Boeker, 1989a; Cobb & Margulies, 1981; Farrell & Peterson, 1982).

Power[1] plays an important role in the interactions among employees in organizations. It mediates structural and control communication[2] in organizations. Power affects the basis of leadership and influence processes in the organization decision-making process.[3] Leadership in organizations has usually been derived from legitimate power. Leadership provides sources of formal influence and the ability to affect organizational decision outcomes. Such formal influence is usually a downward process, whereby management or supervisors provide instructions to their subordinates. In this context, people who have high interests in decision outcomes are more likely to exert influence than those who are less interested. On the other hand, informal influence is an upward process and "occurs without formal authority and usually at the follower's initiative" (Hollander & Offerman, 1990: 185).[4] Both formal and informal influences provide the capability to change the behavior of individuals or groups or to affect decision outcomes (Sisaye, 1997b, 1998d).

As power seekers, managers attempt to expand their power bases[5] and organizational resources by going outside organizational boundaries (Jauch & Osborn, 1981: 494). They adopt a non-economic value based organizational growth maximization policy through active acquisition programs to build a corporate conglomerate within a shorter period of time. Managers attempt to manage and reduce environmental uncertainty through diversification. Diversified acquisition growth is politically preferable, because it minimizes the losses that may result from environmental changes. Acquisition of a firm unaffected by those changes can reduce uncertainty for the acquiring firm.

Using the political choice model, three reasons for diversification are identified. They include financial risk reduction strategies, organizational fit and management philosophy/cultural fit. Financial risk reduction strategies are used by organizations that try to maintain favorable balance in their relationships with the external environment. They attempt to gain legitimacy to survive or dominate the environment by modifying their dependency relationships (Jemison 1981; Summer 1980).

*Appendix 1 Table 1.1.*  Acquisition Types Based on Aquisition Motives and
                         Resource Mix Factors

|  | Motives (Rationales) for Acquisition | |
|---|---|---|
| Resource Mix | Economic | Political |
| Absorption | Concentration | Collusion |
| Diversification | Portfolio | Power Dependency |

*Financial Risk Reduction Strategies.* One of the best alternative strategies to break an organization's dependence on the environment is through the use of risk reduction strategies. Organizations can manage risk by selecting acquisition-absorption and/or diversification growth strategies that match their resource mix and acquisition motive. As noted in Appendix 1 Table 1.1, an organization can choose from among at least four general types of acquisition strategies, which are labeled as concentration, collusion, and portfolio and power dependency relations.

Organizations acquiring firms for economic reasons and utilizing an absorption resource mix strategy tend to prefer the *concentration* strategy. Absorption becomes an economically motivated acquisition strategy, whereby a firm expands in the same or selected markets to pool its resources so that it becomes a more competitive industry participant.

Firms undertaking absorption as a politically motivated acquisition strategy are pursuing a *collusion* strategy. Companies acquire other firms in the same or closely related industry in an attempt to control the industry through an active acquisition program. This process leads to an oligopolistic market situation where few firms dominate the industry. In an oligopolistic market situation, it is possible for the dominant firms to enhance their control of an industry sector by market signaling and other cartel-like behavior.

An economically motivated diversification strategy results in a mix of acquisitions in related and/or unrelated markets. This approach utilizes a *portfolio* acquisition mix from various unrelated industries to accomplish the dual objectives of risk reduction and return (profit) maximization. A well-balanced portfolio acquisition enables a firm to minimize the impact of seasonal market fluctuations, industry downturns and business cycles on profitability. Planned diversification is intended to safeguard against sudden environmental changes that could adversely affect firm performance. Diversification buffers environmental impact on one aspect of the firm, whereby a change in one can be buffered and balanced by diversity of unrelated markets.

An effective portfolio acquisition mix is based on an economically sound diversification strategy. Research has found that the relationships between corporate-level distinctive competencies and performance vary by type of diversification strategy (Hitt & Ireland, 1986). Hence, it can be inferred that firms with distinctive corporate-level competencies that utilize a portfolio acquisition mix based on absorption growth strategy in related industries will be associated with a high level of economic performance compared to firms using a portfolio acquisition mix based on unrelated diversification growth strategy.

Firms following a politically based diversification strategy utilize the *power dependency* approach to acquisition. The political motives of diversification involve entering related and unrelated markets to increase organizational size. Firms acquiring other companies for non-financial reasons can be described by the growth-maximization theory, an approach that holds that management maintains an active acquisition program to build corporate size, visibility, and consolidate power. Management incentives to control a large corporation and to maximize their power bases within the organization become the primary motives for initiating an acquisition. Diversified acquisition is also used to hedge against political risks and minimizes the dependency/vulnerability of the organization to external environmental factors.

Depending on the predominant acquisition motives of managers, there will be shifts from one acquisition type to another. Since a risk reduction strategy focuses on a diversified acquisition strategy, managers can choose the acquisition type that best fits their economic or political acquisition motives. Whether the motives for acquisition strategy are primarily economic (portfolio) or political (power-dependency), diversification as a risk reduction strategy is employed to balance cyclical patterns in the business economic environment and/or minimize the firm's political/power dependency relationship with its external environment.

Diversification as an acquisition strategy is preferred when the degree of business/product market relationships and degree of environmental inter-dependency is low. Its objective is to "reduce [product market] interdependence by diversifying into other activities so that the organization's reliance on a particular set of organizations in its environment is reduced" (Pfeffer, 1972: 391). Conglomerate mergers are used to reduce the risk associated with a single business (Jauch & Osborn, 1981: 496. See also Rumelt, 1974).

In making a diversified acquisition, an organization with little or no experience in the new markets it plans to enter is likely to acquire profitable firms with established markets. While the rational choice model provides an economic rationale for selecting acquisition candidate firms, it is plausible to assume that executives employ unrelated diversification growth strategies to minimize financial and political risks.

For multinational corporations (MNCs), planned geographical diversification can sustain political risks arising from expropriation or government instability, whereas unrelated product diversification can minimize effects of seasonal/cyclical business patterns. MNC's can use diversified acquisition strategies to expand their markets either domestically or internationally.

*Organizational Fit.* Successful acquisitions depend on a pre-acquisition analysis of organizational fit. "Organizational fit is defined as the match between administrative practices, cultural practices, and personnel characteristics of the target and parent firms" (Jemison & Sitkin, 1986: 147). Organizational fit involves an analysis of the organization's structure, including examination of its hierarchy, reward systems, task structures, decision-making patterns and the degree of organizational centralization. A change in organizational contingency variables, such as size, degree of product specialization or diversification, requires "structural adjustment to regain fit." This adjustment maintains functional behaviors in the organizational system and achieves the desired level of economic performance and firm profitability objectives (Donaldson, 1987). Organizational contingency variables can thus facilitate the effective integration of the acquired company with the parent company (Datta, 1986; Nahavandi & Malekzadeh, 1988).

*Cultural Fit.* An organizational variable with significant impact on the acquisition process is the existence of cultural fit. Organizational culture refers to the system of values, beliefs, ideologies and norms commonly shared by the members of the organization (Beer, 1980; Kilmann, 1984). A corporate culture shared by organizational employees provides support for organizational goals and objectives and facilitates implementation of corporate plans (Feldman, 1986).

Successful integration of an acquired firm into the parent firm depends upon the structural match between the two organizations in terms of leadership, personnel, resources, business and management systems (Schweiger, Ivancevich & Power, 1987). Some of the factors that affect personal and interpersonal attributes of the leader and follower include: the quality of exchange relationships influence on commitment (Yukl & Tracey, 1992); performance and satisfaction (Deluga & Perry, 1994); locus of control (Phillips & Bedeian, 1994); and subordinates/followers growth need in the organization (Phillips & Bedeian, 1994). The success of the leader-follower exchange relationships depends on the type of influence techniques (Lamude & Scudder, 1993) and on how well subordinate growth needs are met and satisfied. These factors are likely to moderate the effective integration of acquired firms into the parent company. An acquisition outcome also depends on the friendliness of the acquisition strategy, social networks shared by executives, and on how well the organization addresses individual and cultural concerns of organizational employees (Daveni & Kesner, 1993).

*Organizational and Cultural Fit.* It is important for firms to develop organizational and cultural fit when pursuing diversified acquisition growth strategies. Managers who respond to individual employee concerns by providing job security, offering out-placement assistance to executives when necessary, and maintaining the autonomy of acquired firms are recognizing the importance of behavioral factors in the acquisition process. Since diversified acquisition is often pursued as an external risk reduction strategy, the politics of such acquisitions involve the use of organizational and cultural fit variables to accomplish acquisition objectives. Political variables and social relational factors (Eckstein & Delaney, 1993) are particularly critical in acquisition and investment decisions, when an organization faces uncertainty due to a high degree of environmental uncertainty and numerous product/market inter-relationships.

# ENVIRONMENTAL INFLUENCES ON ACQUISITION DECISION PROCESSES

It is proposed that strong relationships exist between external economic environmental factors, internal sociopolitical risks and firms' acquisition decisions. When the degree of environmental interdependency/uncertainty and the business/ product market inter-relationships are low, firms enjoy a relatively stable market for their products. The tendency of the external economic environment to generate internal sociopolitical risks is low. Firms attempt to maintain existing markets by gradually improving their services or products.

Acquisition provides an attractive alternative to internal expansion, since existing firms will not bring additional capacity into the market (Goolrick, 1978: 20–22). Since acquisition is less likely to affect existing price and profitability levels, it has an additional advantage in enhancing managers' political power. However, in the short-run, a major political effect of an acquisition may be low economic performance. Acquisition may not help managers achieve their short-term profitability goals, since costs associated with acquiring a successful company with an established product or brand name are higher than costs incurred in developing a new product internally (Duberman, 1990). Because the acquiring firm has a political interest in the acquired company, management tends to be preoccupied with consolidating political power, a preoccupation that can have a negative impact on the firm's economic performance. An acquisition strategy geared to maximize short-term political power, which induces managers to attempt to maintain an adequate (average) level of economic performance to sustain the firm's reported profitability.

While acquisition enables big firms to enter into new markets easily, the acquisition process may not be the best route to organizational growth and development. As Davidson (1991) indicated, the acquisition of smaller firms by larger corporations might not be the best strategy for bigger firms to acquire, develop and market innovations that were originated by smaller companies. While bigger corporations provide organizational infrastructure, they are less capable of adapting to change and providing information and technological capability to support innovation processes.

Once managers have established political power, their objectives focus on long-term improvement of economic performance and the maximization of firm profitability. An acquisition strategy concentrated on long-term, stable political power emphasizes an economic performance above the industry average.

Appendix 1 Table 1.2 presents a contingency model, that shows whether a firm utilizes the rational or political model in a given acquisition decision depends upon the degree of market stability and type of growth strategy (external or internal). For example, when the degree of environmental interdependency/uncertainty and business/product market interrelationships are low, firms can expect to have relatively stable markets for their products. Under such circumstances, they tend to employ the rational/economic model in their acquisition decision-making processes. Decisions can be based on facts and figures according to portfolio criteria or general organizational guidelines. The organization's environment is largely predictable and routine, so the appearance of rational choice is rather easy. Nevertheless, the motivations

***Appendix 1 Table 1.2.***   Organizational Growth Strategies in Competitive Markets Environment

| | Markets | |
|---|---|---|
| Growth Strategies | Stable | Unstable |
| External | Diversification | ? |
| Internal | ? | Absorption |

underlying many seemingly rational decisions may be non-economic and rooted in political and behavioral factors. In such instances, economic factors may simultaneously be used to provide justification/rationale for the leader's political motives or ambitions. In other words, to promote their political interests, managers may seek to ensure that the firm maintains a satisfactory level of economic performance.

## DIVERSIFIED ACQUISITIONS AS EXTERNALLY INDUCED ORGANIZATIONAL GROWTH STRATEGY

Appendix 1 Table 1.2 suggests that when firms face a relatively stable market environment exhibiting a low degree of business/product market interrelationships, acquisitive organizational growth strategies center primarily on diversification strategy. In such a stable market environment, organizational growth strategies tend to be externally oriented and entail the acquisition of unrelated companies. The strategy of diversifying acquisitions may provide the necessary technological and managerial resources to enter new markets, with minimum delays and outlays. This offers acceptable earnings within a relatively short period of time. Acquisition is less likely to affect existing market price and profitability of firms, since existing firms are less likely to bring additional capacity in the form of new products and/or services.

On the other hand, internal growth and development is risky and costly, since it requires investment in additional plants and equipment, as well as research and development that requires long-term commitment to realize the returns on investment. Additional internal growth costs include licenses and fees for new product innovations. Accordingly, regulatory costs for new product developments through internal innovations are higher than costs associated with mergers and acquisitions.

However, diversification if uncontrolled, can become a purely political growth strategy solely based on financial risk reduction, organizational fit and management philosophy/cultural fit (Appendix 1 Fig. 1.1). Politically oriented growth strategies are closely related to a leader's sources of power within the organization, and are strongly influenced by the leader's desire to satisfy personal ambitions and meet the needs of intra-organization coalitions.

*Implications of Contingency Theory for External Growth Through Acquisitions*

Contingency theory focuses on the study of organizations in relation to their environment. The theory provides a situational or an 'if-then strategic decision model' that can be used to understand organizational change and development over time. Two contingency-based strategic decision models have been developed and applied. They are referred to as the rational and political choice models, which both study acquisition growth strategies in complex business organizations. The political choice model emphasizes a strategy of financial risk reduction, organizational and management philosophy/cultural fit, and is applicable to the study of diversified acquisition strategies. On the other hand, the rational choice model assumes that acquisition decisions should be based on economic factors, strategic fit, and synergy criteria, all of which are relevant to study absorption acquisition growth strategies.

The acquisition process model itself is potentially an important determinant of acquisition success, as is the pre-acquisition economic and strategic fit analysis (Jemison & Sitkin, 1986). As discussed above, the behavioral and political variables affecting the acquisition process outcome include organizational and cultural fit. The process by which the acquired company's management is integrated into the parent company (the strategy of co-optation), management systems are introduced to administer acquired divisions, and the reward systems designed to monitor employees are all important factors that affect acquisition outcomes. Long-term profitability depends on the importance leadership gives to organizational human resource management. In conclusion, the application of the contingency model of acquisition in organizational growth and development strategies enables one to examine those situational variables relevant for that organizational growth period under consideration.

## NOTES

1. Kemper and Collins (1990) defined power within the context of social interactions within the organization. For them, power relationships are based on 'enforced compliance', where sanctions can be imposed to secure compliance and strict adherence to organizational rules and regulations. They suggest, "*power* in a social relationship entails conduct by which actors have (or try to gain) the ability to compel other actors to do what they do not wish to do. Compliance, if obtained, is coerced. Force, threat, withdrawal of benefits, manipulation, deception, and other negative sanctions are tools of power relations" (p. 34. italics in original).

For Dietz and Burns (1992), power involves "the ability to influence the rules upon which others act . . . Over time, the use of power in interaction can influence the distribution of rules in the culture, making some rules uncommon, other more common . . . Power resides in cultural structure, since that structure can influence adoption and implementation" (p. 190).

2. Arno's (1985) view of power and control in society suggests that in both structural and control communication, power will contribute to the regularization of behavior. "Power theories, cast in terms of rules backed by sanctions, imply a vision of society as an intricate network of power relationships operating in overlapping spheres, from

the interpersonal dyad to the family, group, and nation. . . or even a world system . . . A communication theory, by contrast, must portray social organization as well as regularization processes in terms of meaning and message exchange. In describing social ordering from this perspective, [Arno] propose [s] using the terms 'control communication' and 'structural communication'" (p. 87). Control communication addresses the question about the appropriateness of a given behavior in the relationship categories or social structures of the group. On the other hand, structural communication deals with references of behavior expected with position or social ordering. It has significance in terms of the actors' relative structural positions during communication (Arno, 1985).

3. Eisenhardt and Bourgeois III (1988) recognized the importance of power and politics in the organizational decision-making process. They declared that "politics are observable, but often covert, actions by which executives enhance their power to influence a decision" (p. 736). The political process includes coalition formation, co-optation of key executives to influence policies and decision outcomes, lobbying, being secretive, withholding access to information as well as controlling agendas (for details, see Pfeffer, 1981, 1992). In their research, Eisenhardt and Bourgeois III (1988) found that "politics arise from power centralization. Domination by powerful chief executive officers (CEOs), combined with the desire for control by top management teams, leads to politics. Conflict, although necessary, is not a sufficient condition for the emergence of politics. [They] also found that politics are not fluid. Rather, they become entrenched into stable patterns that are often based on characteristics such as age and office location. Finally, politics, because they restrict information flow and are time consuming, are associated with poor firm performance" (p. 739). They noted that power centralization leads to competition among executives. When there is centralization, "dominant CEOs transformed a collaborative situation into a competitive one, and politics emerged as people competed for the time and attention of the CEO" (p. 753).

4. In some cases, informal influence as a source of power may be derived from one's social status position within the organization. Kemper and Collins (1990) have examined status as an informal influence. For them, "status (or status conferred) in a social relationship is conduct by which actors give voluntary compliance to other actors and is marked by willing deference, acceptance, and liking. It involves the voluntary provision of rewards, benefits, and gratifications without threat or coercion" (p. 34). Membership within a group is based on equality and egalitarian relationships unlike power relationships that are based on unequal relationships. Kemper and Collins (1990) noted also "status group power derives from life-style communities with cultural identities that emphasize the criterion of membership . . . in some cases status groups might be crystallizations of classes into communities, but they can also be based on such autonomous cultural and ecological factors as religion and ethnicity. Thus, status groups, both in nomenclature and in reality, are sources of mutual conferral of enhanced benefits and compliance" (pp. 51–52). In general, "the dimension of status consists of voluntary, unforced relationships, typically called solidarity, sociability, congeniality, or friendship" (p. 59). While there is stratification in status relationships, it is socially accepted and not imposed like power relationships.

5. Managers form coalitions to solidify their power bases. Eisenhardt and Bourgeois III (1988) have noted that demographic factors such as "age, office location, similarity of titles, and prior experience together" contributed to coalition formation (p. 756). While status differences affected coalition formation, coalitions were formed among

managers with the same status (titles). Other factors relevant for coalition formation included interpersonal attraction such as friendship formation. When it comes to issues, managers selectively make alliances on issues with other managers they personally like (pp. 756–758). Managers cultivate these relationships over time to develop "stable patterns of political behavior." Once these alliances are formed, they "are slow to change" (p. 759). There is a tendency to resist change that alters existing patterns of stable relationships.

APPENDIX 2

# COLLABORATION AND ORGANIZATIONAL MANAGEMENT: SYSTEMS APPROACH TO INTER-DIVISIONAL COLLABORATION

Eileen S. Stommes*

## INTRODUCTION

Collaboration, voluntary cooperation among organizational units to deliver programs and services, is becoming a more common organizational practice. Appendix 2 examines the relevance of collaboration for organizations today. First, a literature review describes the theoretical underpinnings of collaboration among organizations in the management of process innovation. Second, a template to guide research on the collaborative process and its components is outlined. Last, a suggested set of operational guidelines to conduct collaboration across organizational systems is compiled from the literature.

The systems approach underlies this review of collaboration, and suggests that voluntary inter-organizational collaboration and long-standing relationships among units may provide a flexible solution to resolving complex, fast moving issues when several units share responsibility for implementing a policy directive or delivering a program. The inter-departmental collaboration approach is based on incremental change management strategy. It corroborates

* Eileen S. Stommes works for The Economic Research Service, United States Department of Agriculture. The opinions expressed are those of the author and do not represent official views of her employing organization.

total quality management's (TQM) approach to gradual process innovation change in the management of organization activities (Basadur & Robinson, 1993). This Appendix extends the systems approach to inter-organizational collaboration to examine the importance of collaborative efforts in process innovation and organization management.

The literature and anecdotal information both suggest that collaboration has increased over the last decade in complex organizations. Organizations have aligned their resources to meet changing customer needs and demands, shifts in stakeholder characteristics, and increases in competitive forces. Organizational accounting systems have been shaped to support the efforts of collaborative realignments. Organizations have responded to these systems changes by broadening their missions, seeking new organizational partners and developing new cooperative relationships with stakeholders. Collaboration tends to take place around critical issues that an organization alone cannot address, with managers identifying organizations sharing a common concern or problem. The collaborative relationship is generally informal, with memoranda of understanding serving as a resource exchange document that sets broad parameters for cooperation.

Collaboration is changing organizational systems, structures and culture. Accounting systems in particular are adapting to these changes. In a hierarchical organizational structure that follows strict chain-of-command communications channels, collaboration has encouraged lateral communications across programs and agencies. Effective collaboration appears to change the organizational climate by fostering and requiring extensive communication as well as sharing of accounting data and cost information both up the chain-of-command and laterally across programs. By definition, collaboration requires staff to work in inter-divisional teams to resolve issues and deliver cost-effective services.

Application of systems theory suggests several proposed guidelines for effective collaboration. First, it is critical that employees know and understand their organization's missions. Second, employees should collaborate only when it furthers their organization's missions, extends resources, highlights a critical agency issue, and can be effectively implemented. Third, managers should realize the importance of creating an accounting control system that balances individual performance with reward and recognition systems for teamwork. Fourth, managers ought to encourage broad communication and information sharing both up the chain-of-command and across program levels. Fifth, organizations should train staff on effective collaboration techniques. Lastly, it is imperative that organizations remain patient and persistent until objectives are accomplished.

# ORGANIZATIONAL ISSUES THAT CALL FOR COLLABORATION

Today, organizations face increasingly complex issues that cut across traditional organizational and program boundaries. Large-scale organizations in particular face an increasingly dynamic environment to which their functional structures may no longer correspond, structures that in fact create barriers to resolving complex issues. In response to these changes, organizations are in the process of restructuring their functions. Reorganization may resolve many of the functional barriers to effective resolution of complex issues. Yet reorganization alone will not address continually evolving issues that stubbornly evade organizational boundaries. A more flexible, dynamic response is called for.

Inter-organizational collaboration is one mechanism that can offer continued structural flexibility to resolve complex, crosscutting issues. Collaboration can provide an ongoing solution to resolving complex, fast moving issues when several divisions share responsibility for a common policy or program.

Collaboration can offer several advantages in resolving complex issues without requiring extensive structural reorganization:

• No additional space or office reconfiguration is required.

• No reallocation of personnel is necessary.

• No additional funding is needed.

Collaboration can also offer organizations a flexible way to re-deploy scarce financial and personnel resources as new issues emerge and demand immediate response.

## *Effects of Environmental Factors on Collaboration: A Look at the Literature*

Systems approach addresses the relationship of an organization to its environment to examine the change dynamic (Van de Ven & Poole, 1995). Lawrence and Lorsch (1969) explored "the relationships between the structural characteristics of complex organizations and the environmental conditions these organizations face" (Foreword). Their findings suggest that viable organizations will need to develop and "integrate the work of organizational units that can cope with even more varied sub-environments" (p. 238).

Pfeffer and Salancik (1978) examined how "organizational environments affect and constrain organizations and how organizations respond to external constraints" (p. xi). They suggested organizational systems be shaped by the demands of the organizations and groups making up their environment. To gain greater control over those demands and reduce environmental uncertainty, organizations typically increase coordination. Participating organizations thus increase mutual control over each other's activities (p. 43). By shaping the organizational environment, stakeholders affect the development, financing, and implementation of products and services (Wilson 1989). Organizations that bring stakeholder perspectives into the management process can thrive as they become more responsive to their organizational environment (Beckett-Camarata, Camarata & Barker, 1998; Haveman, 1992).

## Inter-Organizational Relations

Inter-organizational relations can provide a mechanism to resolve complex, crosscutting issues. Systems approach examines the emergence, process, and outcomes of inter-organizational relationships. The next section briefly defines inter-organizational relationships, explores the context for those relations, examines conditions that lead to collaboration, describes phases of the collaborative process, and outlines the barriers to collaboration within the context of systems analysis.

Van de Ven (1976) states that an inter-organizational relationship [IR] "exhibits the basic elements of any organized form of collective behavior. (1) Behavior among members is aimed at attaining collective and self-interest goals. (2) Interdependent processes emerge through division of tasks and functions among members. (3) An IR can act as a unit and has a unique identity separate from its members" (p. 25). Oliver (1990) describes inter-organizational relations as "the relatively enduring transactions, flows, and linkages that occur among or between an organization and one or more organizations in its environment" (p. 241).

Organizations enter into inter-organizational relations for a variety of internal and external considerations. Oliver (1990) summarizes the literature by listing six contingencies leading to the formation of inter-organizational relations. The first is necessity, including mandates from higher authority and legislation. Oliver draws a distinction between mandated collaboration and voluntary activities, stating that explanations and consequences for organizational behavior differ when the organization controls its interaction and when it complies with mandates.

The second condition is described as asymmetry, and takes place when an organization sees the potential to exercise power or control over another organization and/or its resources. Reciprocity, a third condition, takes place when organizations pursue common goals. Fourth, efficiency is an internally motivated reason that seeks to improve organizational efficiency, such as joint performance of administrative functions and the delivery of timely information and accounting data for improved decision-making. Fifth, a search for some measure of environmental stability leads organizations to initiate and manage inter-organizational relations, particularly with potential competitors. A sixth condition is the enhancement of organizational legitimacy, when collaboration with another, more prestigious organization lends greater credibility to one's own organization.

Systems approach further examines the process through which inter-organizational relationships develop, and explores necessary conditions for successful collaboration. O'Toole and O'Toole (1981), in their study of a complex of eleven rehabilitation agencies over a 25-year period, indicated that the context for beginning discussion of a collaborative relationship is an "over-lapping societal, communal, inter-organizational, organizational, and interpersonal" setting (p. 29). As a first step, organizations must share ownership of some aspects of a common issue, and be able to contribute to its resolution.

Cigler, Jansen, Ryan and Stabler (1994) provided descriptive case studies of collaboration among Midwestern rural communities to promote rural economic development. The study suggests that collaboration among rural communities arises in response to a set of pre-conditions, including changes in the external environment (pp. 44–45). Murray and Dunn (1996) examined the emergence of organizational collaboration within rural communities, describing the effort as a necessary prelude to successful community development. Sisaye and Stommes (1985) analyzed the green revolution strategy from an organizational development perspective, focusing on the adaptive changes taking place within agricultural institutions. Sisaye (1999) suggested that the success of this form of collaboration depends on the development of innovative accounting and reporting systems that track changes in market forces and the competitive environment.

Gray (1985) looked closely at the conditions that facilitate collaboration, suggesting the process moves through three sequential phases: problem setting, direction setting, and structuring (p. 916). Certain factors ensure the successful completion of each phase. Completion of one phase does not necessarily predict progress through the succeeding phase. During problem setting, "stakeholders are identified and legitimized, interdependence is recognized, preliminary expectations are established, and the boundaries of the domain are defined" (p. 924). Direction setting involves the development of a common way of defining the problem and a satisfactory distribution of power among stakeholders. Structuring involves negotiating the rules of collaboration and designating the actor(s) responsible for carrying it out. Radin, Agranoff, Bowman, Buntz, Ott, Romzek, Sykes and Wilson (1995) described the emergence of the National Rural Development Partnership, a collaborative mechanism adopted at the Federal level in 1990 to leverage delivery of rural programs from multiple departments. The study describes the process of defining the issues, setting the agenda and structuring the partnership for a wide-flung set of Federal, State, local and non-government organizations.

Although systems approach focuses on facilitating inter-organizational relations, it is useful to explore if any barriers to collaboration exist. O'Toole and Montjoy (1984) pointed out that organizations' "goals, world views and routines" bind them so that their ability to collaborate with another unit may be limited (p. 492). Wilson (1989) stated that "Government agencies . . . view any interagency agreement as a threat to their autonomy," (p. 192) making it difficult to coordinate the work of several agencies. Alter (1990) examined conflict patterns in human service interagency coordination, concluding that highly complex, multi-layered systems serving "client populations for which there are multiple goals" (p. 497) exhibit greater levels of conflict. She suggested that such systems coordinate not only at managerial levels, but also at staff levels. While a more complex system requires still additional coordination, accounting rules and bureaucratic procedures should not replace personal contact between managers and workers.

Weiss (1987) summarized the barriers to collaboration by stating that they are costly to organizations that implement inter-divisional collaboration (p. 94). Obstacles to collaboration are inherent in organizational structures and are exhibited in organizational behavior. Each agency seeks to preserve its autonomy; "organizational routines are difficult to synchronize" (p. 95), goals may overlap, but are not identical; constituents expect different things from each agency; managers wish to minimize uncertainty for their own organization, but are not particularly concerned about other organizations. Coordination often requires scarce resources that could be better spent meeting client needs.

Collaboration goes beyond mere cooperation, implying that a relatively long-standing relationship to meet mutually agreed upon goals is needed. Mattessich and Monsey (1992) defined collaboration as "a mutually beneficial and well-defined relationship entered into by two or more organizations to achieve common goals. The relationship includes a commitment to mutual relationships and goals; a jointly developed structure and shared responsibility; mutual authority and accountability for success; and sharing of resources and rewards" (p. 39). To provide organizational benefits, the collaborative relationship should be long-standing in nature and involve the commitment of management (Baker, Faulkner & Fisher, 1998).

Two additional factors affect a division's ability to initiate collaborative partnerships with other divisions. Organizational culture provides the work environment that shapes all organizational activities, including collaborative relationships. An integral component of that culture is boundary spanning, or those activities that link an organization with its external environment. Each is briefly reviewed below for their impact on inter-divisional collaboration.

### *Organizational Culture*

Inter-organizational relations are shaped not only by the external environment, but also internally by the organizational culture itself. Schein (1990) defined organizational culture as: "(a) a pattern of basic assumptions, (b) invented, discovered, or developed by a given group, (c) as it learns to cope with its problems of external adaptation and internal integration, (d) that has worked well enough to be considered valid and, therefore (e) is to be taught to new members as the (f) correct way to perceive, think, and feel in relation to those problems" (p. 111). Hatch (1993) extended Schein's definition by arguing that organizational culture is a dynamic process in which relationships among values, assumptions, symbols, and artifacts change as organizational members adapt the culture to changing external and internal contingencies. Accordingly, organizational culture shapes not only the way in which work is done, but also what is perceived as eligible for policies and programs.

Culture does not characterize any collection of individuals, but rather requires a "set of people with enough stability and common history (for) a culture to form" (Schein, 1990: 111). Schein outlines the external and internal tasks facing all groups, tasks that require consensus before an organization can be described as having a culture. External adaptation requires consensus on core missions, functions and primary tasks, specific organizational goals and how they are to be met, how results are to be measured, and remedies if goals are not met. Internal integration tasks involve development of a common language and conceptual system and definition of group boundaries. Organizational culture also includes criteria for allocation of status, power, and authority; the definition of friendship in different work and family settings; the allocation of rewards and punishment; and concepts for managing the unmanageable, or ideology/religion (p. 113).

Large organizations may have an umbrella organizational culture, but exhibit sub-cultures common to a specific unit or cluster of responsibilities (Kerr & Slocum, 1987: 99; Keeton & Mengistu, 1992). The dominant organizational culture and its sub-cultures shape the ability of organizations to initiate inter-organizational collaboration, and to implement that collaboration successfully.

The ability of an agency to collaborate across organizational boundaries may be affected by its organizational culture. This culture shapes both the organizational ability to adapt to external changes and the ability to integrate these changes internally. The organizational mission itself may delimit opportunities to collaborate. Internal organizational rules and cultural tradition may further influence ability to reach across organizational boundaries, including adherence to chain-of-command procedures, reward and recognition systems, and emphasis on individual accomplishments. An additional cultural dimension, the ability of an organization to create a learning environment open to adaptive change, is gaining recognition as important to collaborative efforts (Lawson & Ventiss, 1992; Porra & Silvers, 1991). Management can shape the culture to encourage collaboration by fostering gradual, incremental change through employee training (Porter & Parker, 1992).

*Boundary Spanning Activities*

Boundary spanning refers to activities that link an organization with its environment. The boundary spanner brings outside information into the organization, processes it and distributes it throughout the organization. In most cases, the boundary spanner gathers information specific to program costs and service delivery. The accounting system in turn supports boundary spanning by providing information that can be used for cost-benefit analysis. The boundary spanner also represents the organization to outside organizations, stakeholders or clients. It can be assumed that collaborative activities emerge from boundary spanning activities. Second, boundary spanners are more or less active in encouraging collaboration based on agency culture and administrative procedures, including training, responsibilities and reward systems.

Boundary spanning links an organization with its environment. Aldrich (1979) indicated that boundary spanning activities fill two types of functions: "information processing and external representation" (p. 249). Information about the external environment enters the organization through boundary roles, and these roles in turn link organizational structures to environmental conditions by "buffering, moderating, and influencing external events" (p. 249). Rosenthal (1984) further describes this function as filtering inputs and outputs, such as technical assistance; searching for and collecting information on program costs and benefits; and protecting the organization from external threats or pressures (p. 472).

The information processing function protects organizations against information overload, since boundary spanners select and process relevant information before passing it along to the organization. Boundary spanners can assist in the design and implementation of accounting and internal auditing systems capable of providing customized cost and budget information on specific collaborative projects. Boundary spanners can facilitate organizational adaptation to its external environment. They ensure that inaccurate information that hinders organizational ability to respond to environmental demands is not utilized or transferred. Ulrich and Lake (1991) emphasized the importance of encouraging employees to adopt innovative behavior that coincides with customer values, and focuses on the significance of boundary spanning in organizational adaptation to environmental change.

The external representation function involves "resource acquisition and disposal, political legitimacy and hegemony, and social legitimacy and organizational image management" (Aldrich, 1979: 252). Rosenthal (1984) described this function as including budgeting, reporting, community relations, and developing program/policy plans (p. 472).

While information processing and external representation are carried out through individual roles, organizations engage in boundary spanning to better adapt to environmental pressures. In a boundary spanning study on hospital environments, Fennell and Alexander (1987) listed three types of organizational boundary spanning. The first type is boundary redefinition, or joining an association of similar organizations to centralize administrative and repetitive accounting information functions. Second is buffering, which is protecting an organization against harmful/disruptive environmental influences. The third type is bridging, or creating innovative linkages to other organizations rather than developing internal, structural buffers (pp. 458–9).

In this appendix, boundary spanning has been approached as a necessary prelude to inter-departmental collaboration, and focuses on ways boundary spanning roles create organizational linkages and promote organizational innovations. Boundary spanner functions are examined, along with incentives and barriers to boundary spanning found within the organizational culture.

## THE COLLABORATIVE SYSTEMS PROCESS IN ORGANIZATIONS – A RESEARCH TEMPLATE

Collaboration is a multi-step organizational process. The following section outlines a suggested research template to approach the study of the collaborative process. As derived from the literature, the process involves five systems components: emergence of a collaborative effort, collaboration, outcome evaluation, collaboration and organization culture, and boundary spanning.

*Emergence of a Collaborative Effort*

Collaborative efforts within organizations generally emerge from issues. While lack of financial and personnel resources are primary considerations in collaborative efforts, issue-based collaboration has a greater chance of success than collaboration founded solely on lack of resources. The use of collaboration as a strategy is not likely to come from any department level within an organization; rather the need arises from all levels, as very few issues today are confined to a single program (Baker, Faulkner & Fisher, 1998).

Systems analysis corroborates that organizations make initial contacts for collaboration with potential partners on the basis of complementary missions and philosophical alignment. In most instances, organizations voluntarily make direct contact with a potential partner without utilizing the service of an intermediary organization, such as consulting firms. When initial contacts are made, most early contacts involve exploration of the issue, including evaluation for successful collaboration. The initial contacts allow units to lay out program objectives, including their contributions to the effort. These contacts serve to further define the issue, to bring it into the realm of the feasible project – or one that can be captured within existing departmental authorities and funding capabilities. The success of collaboration depends upon organizational capability to jointly coordinate their programs by sharing costs and resources for delivering cost-effective quality products. However, if an organization is perceived as delivering a less viable product, further collaborative activities with that organization are less likely to happen in the future.

Early phases of a collaborative effort can be described as a courtship process in which a decision is made to walk away or collaborate. The systems rule of collaboration requires that enough time should be spent courting, so that a "new direction that we all own" can be developed. During collaboration, even though organizations have their own objectives, they need to share those with the larger group in an iterative process to reach a shared mission – and shared recognition for all participating units. Successful collaboration depends on the development – and recognition – of a win-win situation for all participating organizations in early stages of the partnership.

Initial agreement to collaborate could range from informal working relationships to interdepartmental compacts to formal charters, complete with working principles. Formalized agreements and accounting rules develop when significant resources are exchanged, when multiple partners are involved, or when a contentious issue is being addressed. Formalized procedures for information sharing and reporting could emerge if organizations collaborate on highly sensitive issues that are considered confidential and/or trade secrets. Or,

Congressional mandates could shape the direction of collaboration: a good example is the passage of the Intermodal Surface Transportation Efficiency Act of 1991 (ISTEA), which required public involvement in state transportation planning. While ISTEA mandated that state transportation officials work with local officials, it did not prescribe procedures to do so, allowing for a variety of collaborative processes to evolve (Braum, Dittmar, Hoover, Murray, Siwek, Stanley & Younger, 1994; North Central Regional Center for Rural Development, 1996). Formalized agreements and mandates can legitimize the effort within respective organizations, giving program staff the license to work openly on collaborative programs.

## Collaboration

As collaboration moves towards implementation, responsibility for carrying out agreed-upon activities varies both across and within departments. Communications within a collaborative activity are shaped by information requirements of the task itself, cost accounting information needs of the collaborative project, its importance to organization mission, its stand on competitiveness, level of resource commitment, and level of political or policy sensitivity surrounding collaboration issues. In most cases, less formal verbal communications when accompanied by up-to-date reports are effective forms of communication for program implementation. Lateral or program-to-program communication chains are functionally suitable for informal, working level exchange of information.

During collaboration, formal chain-of-command communications are used on 'sticky' issues that required higher level intervention. When formal agreements are in place, formal, written, chain-of-command communications are more common as a means of tracking progress and maintaining an audit trail. Nowadays, strict formal adherence to the chain-of-command structure and reporting requirements as the principal means of communication in a collaborative activity is considered less effective. The recent development in communications technology and activity-based costing systems facilitate lateral communication across programs and divisions/departments (Johnson, 1992(a)).

Avenues of communication involve all mediums, including formal written memos, telephone calls, e-mail, meetings, and conferences. The level of communication varies with each collaborative activity. Some involve infrequent face-to-face meetings, relying on e-mail and telephone contacts. Others involve frequent site visits. Still others require quarterly written reports, with some involving quarterly meetings of policy-level representatives. These avenues of correspondence indicate that collaborative efforts require a relatively frequent high level of communication to maintain program implementation.

Effective collaboration requires financial and personnel resources, and well developed accounting systems. While funding is critical for collaboration, personnel commitments are central to accomplishing collaborative goals. In many cases, staff time represents a significant resource, while funding is a relatively minor component. Personnel availability will affect performance accomplishments and outcome evaluations (Premkumar & Ramamurthy, 1995).

## Outcome Evaluation

Organizations conduct evaluations to determine cost-benefits and whether or not it is viable to continue programs or activities. At the conclusion of a project, evaluation is used to assess both outcomes and processes. Outcomes can be defined as direct results from project intervention, while processes can be described as project delivery mechanisms. The formality of an evaluation depends partially on the sophistication of the accounting system, the amount of slack in organizational resources, and the demands placed on the organization. Since collaboration as a voluntary activity is discretionary, it is less likely for a formal project evaluation to be built into the collaborative activity. In most organizations, formal evaluation of collaborative outcomes is conducted by an outside organization under contract.

Process evaluation examines the efficiency and effectiveness of collaborative activities. The major criterion for continuing a collaborative activity is the organization sense that the project had produced results, each partner had conducted responsibilities as agreed, and working relationships had been amicable. An unintended consequence of collaboration can be innovative changes within the collaborating agencies. Adaptive changes can occur in policies, programs, mission, organizational flexibility, customer base, staff empowerment, evaluation systems, and reporting procedures, all of which can enhance organizational culture (Sisaye, 1999).

## Collaboration and Organizational Culture

Collaboration takes place within the context of organizational culture. Organizational culture shapes not only the way in which work is done, but also what is perceived as eligible for policy and program. The culture of an organization is a combination of formal and informal structures and behaviors as well as accounting rules and regulations, which influence how an individual functions and performs in the workplace. Organizational culture in congruence with the organizational mission is a prerequisite for collaboration and shapes the ways in which collaboration takes place (Kimberly & Bouchikhi, 1995).

As organizations revise their mission and organizational strategies to include collaboration, staffs are encouraged to initiate and carry out collaborative activities. In the context of broad organizational strategies and flexible program delivery, collaboration can be interpreted as a new behavior that facilitates program delivery. As such, management can encourage collaboration as key to the organizational culture. But collaboration with external partners or other agencies is not an isolated exercise that takes place outside of accepted cultural practices. Rather, collaborative activities can be seen as culturally acceptable ways to meet program goals, funding requirements and organization innovation changes. Internal collaboration can take place through teamwork, a method of bringing together diverse disciplines and different functions to deliver program services. If internal collaboration or teamwork is not seen as a culturally acceptable way to do organizational business, then it is unlikely that organization personnel will embrace external collaboration.

Many organizations now encourage collaborative activities with outside organizations. Increasingly, teamwork is an internal practice fostered by management to deliver high quality services. Ezzamel and Wilmott (1998) suggest that management can turn to teams as a way to encourage both collaboration and organizational accountability, with management instituting self-imposed accounting control procedures of team work. However, traditional organizational practices and accounting systems continue to favor individual over group performance. Bottom-line performance indicators and cost saving mechanisms are largely designed for individual instead of group performance. As a result, star performers are rewarded and professionally recognized, whereas teams are more likely to be neglected. Nevertheless, there is still recognition that teamwork is becoming an increasingly important cultural practice, as issues growing in complexity and programs expand in scope.

The amount of information generated by collaborative activities can be much greater than in routine program functions, and greater organizational flexibility is necessary to tailor program delivery to meet customer needs. As a result, collaboration contributes towards decentralization, a process that allows greater decision-making at lower levels in the organization. The shift is not taking place without some confusion about how much information should be communicated up the chain-of-command, and how much decision-making can take place at lower organizational levels.

*Boundary Spanning*

Boundary spanners promote collaboration in one or both of the following ways: First, collaboration is likely to emerge from boundary spanning activities. Second, boundary spanners themselves encourage collaboration based on agency culture and administrative procedures.

Boundary spanning can be highly centralized, as in public relations or accounting systems. Many organizations have centralized their accounting systems to improve the dissemination and reporting functions to meet the information needs of managers. It is cost-effective to distribute and process information from a central location to divisions, sales territories and geographical locations. On the other hand, some functions like sales and marketing and investment functions, require decentralization to provide decision-making autonomy and power to program managers when they work outside their organizations.

Boundary spanning can be defined and evaluated as a process that links organizations, or it can be evaluated on the basis of results. While boundary spanning can be evaluated on both aspects, it is a heavily process-oriented activity. While the objective of boundary spanning is to produce results, it requires significant investment in both time and resources before results can occur. Relationships, commitment, and trust are built over time, so that when a collaborative opportunity arises, it can be acted upon quickly. If no boundary spanning has taken place, collaborative relationships will take longer to establish before joint program action can be initiated. In a sense, boundary spanning can be considered a strategic investment for future collaboration (Radin et al., 1995).

Within a collaborative activity, boundary spanners can operate with a high degree of autonomy. While policy level decisions are elevated to the appropriate management level, boundary spanners are given an operating framework and function within broad program parameters. Variations are found according to the nature of the activity, partner, and the capabilities of the individual to carry out the activity. Relatively senior level staffs who are grounded in agency mission, operating procedures, and internal auditing and reporting systems thus carry out boundary spanning and collaboration. This senior level staff can be relied upon to accurately represent the organization mission and program to its stakeholders.

# COLLABORATION – A SUMMARY OF KEY FACTORS

Collaboration, the voluntary cooperation among units to deliver programs and services, is becoming more common in organizations as organizations attempt to deliver quality programs at lower cost. Several external and internal factors have heightened the need for more cooperation among organizations.

Externally, consumer differentiation, market segmentation, and competitive environments have increased the need for collaboration. Internally, organizations are actively involved in continually revising their mission to broaden their focus and address increasingly complex issues. Changes in mission have been accompanied by innovative changes in organizational culture, operating policies and structures, and accounting control and reporting systems such as activity-based costing. The traditional chain-of-command of organizational structure is adapting to collaboration, as lateral flows of information take place simultaneously with vertical transmission of information. Individuals involved in collaborative activities are given broad licences to carry out their responsibilities, with reporting requirements and accounting systems tailored to the particular activity's sensitivity.

Along with mission changes, organizations are also facing limited or reduced resource levels. Collaboration can maximize the impact of limited resources by working with organizations that have complementary products/services and similar sets of stakeholders. However, collaboration does not come without an opportunity cost. Developing relationships with other organizations takes time, resources and personnel. This does not minimize the need for collaboration, due to the complexity of issues and changing consumer needs. In most cases, process innovations in new products/services, as well as accounting information systems, could not take place without collaboration.

Collaboration is changing the culture of many organizations. First, the hierarchical, chain-of-command structure adheres to strict vertical communications requirements. These requirements are now complemented by lateral communications taking place across programs and agencies. Collaboration both fosters and requires a higher level of communication, so that the number, depth, variety, and diversity of communications increase. Second, collaboration by definition involves teamwork across program and agency boundaries. Yet the accounting evaluation and reward and recognition system is oriented toward individual performance, not team accomplishment. Today, most organizations acknowledge the need to include team recognition as part of the performance evaluation system and cultural change accompanying collaboration. However, individual performance is still preferred over team activities. Training and group performance systems are among several options that may begin to change the cultural preference for individual recognition.

Lastly, collaboration is offering organizations a flexible response mechanism. Existing administrative and personnel structures can be modified and utilized. Collaboration can take place on an as-needed basis, with a particular collaborative activity terminating at the project conclusion. While reorganization is an option to restructure programs and services, collaboration offers the least costly approach to mediate changes in the external environment and accommodate internal operating changes while effectively delivering program services in a dynamic, complex situation. Collaboration can offer a flexible, incremental approach to implement process innovation that takes advantage of existing accounting, financial, and human resources.

## PROPOSED GUIDELINES FOR COLLABORATION WITHIN ORGANIZATIONS

The literature review and the research template derived from this review suggest that organizational collaboration requires incremental yet innovative system changes. These changes, which call for a gradual step-by-step innovative change, apply to both organizations and their employees. The organizational guidelines outline what organizations can do to encourage collaboration to carry out programs and policies. Employee or professional conduct guidelines describe how to collaborate effectively across organizational boundaries.

### *Organizational Guidelines*

1. Clearly articulate and publicize organizational mission.
2. Identify stakeholders.
3. Encourage flexible program delivery.
4. Reward and recognize successful collaboration.
5. Provide training on effective collaboration.
6. Encourage open communication channels throughout the organization, both through the chain-of-command and across programs.
7. Encourage innovation in carrying out organizational mission.
8. Evaluate the collaborative process to improve process effectiveness and efficiency.
9. Evaluate program results of collaboration.
10. Strike a balance between process and outcome in collaboration: recognize when collaboration is not furthering organization's mission.

11. Align internal auditing and accounting reporting systems with organizational collaborative objectives.

*Employee or Professional Conduct Guidelines*

1. Know your organization's mission.
2. Familiarize yourself with your organization authorities, programs, procedures, operating guidelines, and accounting systems.
3. Commit your organization to collaborate only when it furthers agency mission, extends resources, institutes cost-effective processes, highlights a critical departmental issue, and can be effectively implemented.
4. Establish a good track record for your organization by honoring your commitments.
5. Be dynamic and flexible to accommodate changes required to meet the objectives of collaboration.
6. Keep communication lines open both up the chain-of-command and across organizational and program boundaries. Minimize the need for excessive communication, information sharing and reporting.
7. Be honest and report when collaboration is being used to build personal political power.
8. Prepare for sudden aggravation, slow progress, logjams and red tape. Be patient and persistent.
9. Work closely with top level managers and policy makers.
10. Seek the advice of experienced collaborators; work with a mentor.
11. Approach your collaborator as a stakeholder and ask what do you want me to do.
12. Cultivate your contacts and develop credibility.
13. Know when to walk away if collaboration is failing.
14. Focus on your mission – time and resources are scarce.

## CONCLUSION

This appendix has reviewed the use of collaboration to bring about organizational change. Collaboration, voluntary cooperation among organizational units to deliver programs and services, is an increasingly common organizational practice. A literature review indicates that the theoretical underpinnings of collaboration can best be described as falling within the systems approach to organizational development. Collaboration embodies the TQM approach to gradual process innovation change and organizational management.

Collaboration has increased over the past decade since it can provide organizations with a flexible response to rapidly changing environmental conditions. Collaboration can allow organizations to broaden their missions, seek new organizational partners and develop new relationships with stakeholders – all without reorganizing or increasing overall resource requirements. Collaboration generally takes place when an organization shares a critical issue with another organization, and can best address that shared issue in cooperation with a partner. Accounting systems in turn adapt to changes brought about by collaboration – hierarchical, strict chain-of-command organizations adapt to increased lateral, informal communication and reporting procedures. Collaboration involves staff taking on boundary spanning activities that require greater communication both within and across organizational boundaries.

The collaborative process itself provides a template for research on organizational collaboration. The emergence of a collaborative effort takes place as an organization faces an increasingly complex environment that requires meeting new demands. Research unveils the conditions that give rise to collaboration, and then describes the ways in which collaboration unfolds within complex organizations. Outcome evaluation is a critical component of collaboration, an activity that helps an organization maintain focus on its mission throughout its collaborative efforts. Organizational culture in turn adapts to collaboration, with hierarchical organizations incorporating more lateral and informal communication channels. To carry out effective collaboration, staff engages in boundary spanning activities within the organization itself and across organizational boundaries.

The appendix concludes by suggesting a set of guidelines for collaboration within organizations. Organizational guidelines focus on clear definition of mission and purpose of collaboration, along with operational procedures, training and guidance for staff involvement in collaboration. A good understanding of why collaboration is important to the organization and how best to collaborate are key components of the organizational guidelines. Employee guidelines emphasize the centrality of organization mission to all collaboration and focus on open, honest communication as key to successful collaboration.

APPENDIX 3

# CONTINGENCIES INFLUENCING THE EFFECTIVENESS OF ACCOUNTING ETHICS EDUCATION: COMPARISON OF INSTITUTIONAL AND CONSEQUENTIAL APPROACHES AND THEIR IMPLICATIONS IN HIGHER EDUCATION QUALITY INSTRUCTIONS

## INTRODUCTION

Accounting ethics education has been shaped by institutional and consequential adaptive instructional methods of lectures and case studies to develop the moral and ethical reasoning abilities of students. The incremental institutional teaching methodologies focused on single loop, first-order convergence learning strategies. Incremental approaches have been effective in presenting factual and theoretical information in a logical manner. However, most cases presented in classrooms were hypothetical and devoid of actual organizational conditions and societal realities.

On the other hand, the consequential teaching instruction methodology has a radical orientation, which advocated double loop, second-order and reorientation organizational learning strategy. The consequential method incorporated discovery and exploratory approaches to communicate real life organizational experiences to students. Experiential learning through internships, project assignments or short-term visits to organizations enabled students to learn interactively and cooperatively from real organizational settings.

It is suggested that accounting ethics education can be effective in developing moral and ethical reasoning only when the teaching methodologies utilized both institutional and consequential organizational learning strategies. Such an approach has important implications for process innovation changes of total quality management (TQM) and the teaching of quality issues in higher education.

## EFFECTS OF ENVIRONMENTAL FACTORS ON ACCOUNTING ETHICS EDUCATION: A CONTINGENCY APPROACH

The accounting education environment has significantly changed since the mid-1980s. The stock market crash, collapse of the savings and loans institutions, increases in business bankruptcies, and liability suits against public accounting firms have all impacted accounting education. The most significant change has been increased emphasis in accounting ethics and quality instruction in higher education. Accounting educators have stressed the importance of ethics and quality issues (to be discussed later) in the accounting curriculum. The question of ethics education has been addressed by either developing a separate accounting ethics course or integrating ethics into upper level accounting courses.

The underlying rationale in formal accounting ethics education in the classroom is "based on the premise that moral development can be enhanced through the educational process" (Huss & Patterson, 1993: 235). In other words, ethics education increases the moral depth, cognitive development, and analytical and ethical reasoning development of students (Ponemon & Glazer, 1990). It allows higher order thinking, objective reasoning and questioning of ethical issues and dilemmas (Shenkir, 1990). Since accounting is a public profession, any policy decisions made by public accountants may have broader ethical and societal implications. Thus, accounting choices and decisions are contingent upon environmental factors and involve moral choices, which affect organizations and society. Formal education provides both the framework and skills to address questions of moral obligations and societal responsibilities.

A contingency framework has enabled researchers to apply an open systems decision-making approach that takes into consideration external environmental factors. Environmental factors include social, economic, political/governmental, socio-cultural, markets and technological development (Steiner et al., 1982). The approach has focused on the development of contingency guidelines that are appropriate and adaptable to specific decision-making situations/contexts of interest to researchers (Tushman et al., 1986). Within the contingency framework, a strategic decision is assumed to mediate the process by which an organization utilizes its resources or competencies to maximize environmental opportunities, while minimizing potential threats raised by the environment (Porter 1987). The approach thus provides a situational and 'if-then' strategic decision-making guideline, tailored by specific organizational decisions including accounting ethics education.

A contingency framework examines those situational factors, which impact faculty, department/school and university decisions on the integration of ethics in the accounting curriculum. An 'if-then' perspective considers the extent to which business schools restructure and revise their accounting curriculum to respond to changes called for by external environmental factors, which include among others, accreditation agencies, public accounting firms, governmental organizations and professional associations. Schools/colleges have adopted adaptive strategies to ensure a fit exists between the requirements of external environmental forces and internal resources and capabilities of faculty, to revise and develop accounting ethics and business curriculums. Accordingly, the contingency framework presents both the institutional and consequential teaching approaches and evaluates the effectiveness of accounting ethics education.

The institutional framework has been applied to examine the current status of accounting ethics education by exploring the normative and functional assumptions inherent in single loop, first-order and convergence learning. The consequential approach is presented to minimize the shortcomings of the institutional accounting ethics teaching approach. It advocates a double loop, second-order, reorientation learning approach. A comparative analysis of the institutional and consequential approaches of accounting ethics teaching instruction and methodologies: lectures, cases and experiential learning have been provided. It is argued that a balanced approach between the institutional and consequential approaches is instrumental to achieving the objectives of accounting ethics education.

# THE INSTITUTIONAL APPROACH TO ACCOUNTING ETHICS EDUCATION

*The Institutional Approach as an Adaptive Change Strategy*

The institutional approach focuses on incremental change involving modification and/or experimentation to continuously improve existing systems, technologies, products and services (Mezias & Glynn, 1993). An institutional approach follows a reactive/adaptive approach to change focusing on a quick fix, rather than a long-term solution. It utilizes a gradual, step-by-step change strategy to respond to environmental threats, signals and crises. The emphasis is on maintaining the status quo by introducing incremental change. The teaching methodology relies on a single loop, first order and convergence learning.

In the short-term, organizations that adopt the institutional approach can institute modifications and small-scale improvements to correct problems. Gradual improvements enable the system to respond to external threats without major commitment in technical, financial and human resources (Mezias & Glynn 1993).

### The Adaptive Incremental Strategy of Accounting Ethics Education

The institutional approach offers a valuable framework to examine accounting ethics education in relation to the external environment. The approach suggests that current college educational systems need to be responsive to the concerns of the environment through gradual and incremental changes. That is, environmental changes in business and government regulatory climates will have an effect on ethics education and accounting practices.

External environmental factors including government regulations, professional association requirements and accrediting agency standards impact accounting education. The American Assembly of Collegiate Schools of Business (AACSB) is a prominent external regulatory agency that oversees the curriculum of accredited business schools. The AACSB standards for a separate accounting accreditation require an accounting ethics course that addresses the accounting profession, government-business relationships and their effect on emerging accounting issues (Mintz, 1990: 53). The recommendation of the Treadway Commission [National Commission on Fraudulent Financial Reporting] to increase ethics coverage in accounting is an example of an external environmental agency influencing accounting education.

Accordingly, ethics education at the college level has narrowed the scope of accounting ethics education to those ethical issues that accountants face at work. Accounting educators have followed the single loop, first order and convergence learning in bringing incremental changes that support the existing status quo, cultural and educational systems. Convergence learning is utilized to address professional codes of conduct that adhere to the standards of professional accounting organizations such as the American Institute of

Certified Public Accountants (AICPA), Institute of Management Accountants (IMA) and the Institute of Internal Auditors (IAA).

Loeb (1989) discussed the professional codes of conduct of AICPA and other professional organizations and the ethical dilemmas that accountants face within the context of accounting ethics education (see also Loeb, 1988). Some of these ethical dilemmas include "independence; scope of services; confidentiality; practice development; and differences on accounting issues" (p. 2). He suggested the role of professional accounting ethics committees might involve the review of the "formal ethical philosophy of the firm" and "coordinating ethics education for the firm" (p. 7). Loeb advocated teaching accounting ethics on issues that directly affect the public accounting profession.

Following the Treadway Commission's recommendation, accounting education and training programs instituted an incremental change strategy, to bring a stage-by-stage convergence learning approach to ethics education that largely supports the existing status quo. Ethics education concentrated on teaching students accounting professional values derived from auditing standards, codes of professional conduct and other AICPA and IMA professional standards (Huss & Patterson, 1993: 238). The education process followed the principle that conformity/adherence to professional standards depends upon familiarity with and internalization of the profession's ethics code. Adherence to professional codes of conduct may be used as one criterion to assess the outcome of accounting ethics education (Loeb, 1991).

The institutional approach, links the educational process to organizational and societal goals, and stresses ethical dimensions of accounting decisions in organizations and society. The accounting ethics education bases its philosophy within the context of the public accounting profession. The accounting questions usually address those ethical dilemmas that the profession encounters as it interfaces with organizations and society (Sisaye, 1997a).

## *The Functional and Normative Assumptions in Ethics Education*

Several studies have reinforced the functional view where ethics education can become functional and incremental by increasing members' adherence to professional standards of conduct. An incremental-convergence learning becomes functional in accounting ethics education if it addresses codes of professional conduct and related issues. Beets and Killough (1990) reported that college graduates who had ethics education showed a higher degree of compliance to AICPAs code of professional conduct of competence, independence, objectivity and integrity (pp. 118–120). Claypool, Fetyko and Pearson (1990) have argued that formal ethics education is critical in a public profession like accounting where enforcement depends on peer reviews and self-regulation, since the AICPA does not have the power to suspend licences to practice accounting. If a profession has structured rules where conformity depends on self-policing and peer review rather than external enforcement, formal ethics education can increase public accounting practitioner adherence to a professional code of ethics learned at school.

Generally in the accounting profession, there is a tendency for Certified Public Accountant (CPA)s to show greater adherence to their professional code of ethics, rather than to more general ethics principles such as integrity and objectivity used by theologians and philosophers (Claypool, Fetyko & Pearson, 1990: 704–705). It is assumed that conformity/adherence represented maturity, higher order thinking and stages of moral development. However, an educational system that legitimizes existing systems through adherence to existing codes of professional conduct, does not necessarily promote moral inquiry and critical thinking. While conformity shows internalization of codes of conduct, it does not necessarily reflect higher order thinking and the application of moral reasoning to solve ethical dilemmas and issues.

The educational process has thus a tendency to make relatively minor adjustments that will not change existing curriculums. The goal is to commit limited resources to achieve short-term results. The curriculum changes are considered as purposeful, goal-oriented actions designed to contribute to better educational system performance. The ethical education system tends to stress the teaching of goals, norms, beliefs and values that affect decision-making. Accordingly "the ethical principles of analysis are derived from normative philosophy. Philosophy is the study of thought and conduct, and normative philosophy is the study of the proper thought and conduct; that is, how we should behave" (Hosmer, 1988: 13).

In accounting, the normative philosophy approach is used to teach students ethical systems of analysis through cases that involve business ethics decisions. It provides a framework to evaluate moral development and analytical reasoning ability. Students can apply different levels of moral reasoning to handle critical situations that involve ethical dilemmas. The normative approach provides a benchmark to evaluate the relationship between ethical education and moral cognitive development.

Hiltebeitel and Jones (1992) reported a positive relationship between the integration of ethics modules in accounting courses and student moral development and reasoning ability. Their study showed that ethics integration in accounting courses affected the moral principles that students applied when making ethical decisions. They recommended the goals of ethics education should go beyond improving ethical awareness and moral reasoning, to integration of ethics throughout accounting and business curriculums (pp. 38–45). Their study supported the functional role of ethics education in organizations and society, through its contribution to the awareness of ethical issues and dilemmas in business and society.

The strength in the normative approach to business ethics research is that it allows individuals to apply moral reasoning principles to evaluate subjective situations. While ethical reasoning does not lend itself to mathematical proof or logical consistency, it enables researchers to apply sets of ethical principles to measure individuals' moral development stages as they function within an organizational setting (Dobson, 1992). As such, the normative approach employs a functional-rational view of ethics with theoretical assumptions amenable to hypothesis generation, testing, verification, criticism and analysis. Researchers have applied empirical research methods from psychology, sociology, economics and applied social science disciplines to study economic, social and political issues that affect business ethics (Donaldson & Dunfee, 1994).

On the other hand, a great deal of the normative accounting theory, particularly in financial accounting, has been influenced by financial economics. Financial theory has ignored the ethical and social responsibility of firms and has avoided the discussion of unethical behavior in financial practice. According to Hawley, "society has failed to establish rules that reward socially responsible actions on a level commensurate with the rewards for economic efficiency" (1991: 714). The economic rationale of market forces and impersonal decisions underscore the importance of ethical behavior and social responsibility.

Today, the development of the functional ethical theory in business has not deviated from the normative theory of accounting. Business ethics attempt to bridge the gap between socially responsible firms and economics performance. In other words, while ethical issues impact performance, firms can use a normative approach to social responsibility to support economic objectives.

In ethics education, the normative approach employs a functional view of business ethical behavior. The teaching of ethics promotes congruency among business profitability objectives, organizational cultures and societal values. Accordingly, the goal of accounting education is to ensure that accounting ethics instruction considers both business performance objectives and social responsibility issues.

*Institutional Approach Inherent Weaknesses*

The major limitation of the institutional approach to accounting ethics education is that it focuses on professional and organizational values and codes of conduct as the major referent for accounting ethics education. It does not address accounting ethics within the context of broader multi-disciplinary and philosophical approaches underlying college education. The noted exception is the Ponemon and Glazer (1990) study, which examined the impact of liberal arts and social sciences backgrounds in accounting ethics education. The study defined ethical values in accounting to include both professional codes of conduct as well as individual, organizational and societal values.

Even though the institutional approach has narrowly focused on normative and functional utilities of ethics education, it can be expanded to include the social and political multi-faceted aspects of ethics education. The consequential approach can be incorporated to add a proactive and pro-intervention strategy to ethics education.

# A CONSEQUENTIAL APPROACH TO ACCOUNTING ETHICS EDUCATION

The consequential approach takes a proactive, double loop learning approach to ethics education. A proactive strategy utilizes reorientation and exploratory methods that are inspirational, imaginative and creative in order to change existing organizational assumptions and norms. Planned innovation change programs, including education, are designed and implemented to bring fundamental changes in teaching instructions learning methodologies. The strategy is to explore with new assumptions, ideas, and novel approaches that will have a positive consequential effect on society. The objective is to bring about major breakthroughs in educational programs to achieve long-term improvements (Mezias & Glynn, 1993). The process focuses on an integrated, cross-functional and multi-disciplinary approach to ethics education.

The consequential approach views the educational process in relationship to organizations and society. Accordingly, any change in the educational process is directed towards significant impacts in society. However, such changes are not likely to materialize unless educational systems can affect functional and normative corporation practices. Similarly, ethics education attempts to bridge the gap between the educational system and corporation goals to create positive consequences in society.

Metzger and Phillips (1991) advocated a consequential approach to ethics education provided ethics instruction is targeted to change institutional assumptions of corporations. A consequential approach applies a utilitarian view to evaluate the contribution of ethics education by examining the educational system's ability to shape individual and corporate behavior into more socially responsible and accountable patterns. For example, one criterion to examine the consequences of ethics education is its ability to reduce certain practices, such as auditing errors in detecting firm failure. If ethics education does not minimize the incidence of audit failures, it would have an adverse effect on business, economy and society.

The consequential approach thus questions the present structure of ethics education, which focuses on organizational rules and professional codes of conduct. However, teaching the rules and appropriate codes of individual behavior without any attempt to understand institutional logic or operations and their consequences, would make ethics education less relevant to real world situations (Metzger & Phillips, 1991). Therefore, ethics educational methodology and instruction need to provide a framework by which instructors and students address the consequential impact of ethics education in organizations and society.

## INTEGRATING ETHICS IN THE ACCOUNTING CURRICULUM

Business schools/colleges, accounting programs and faculty members have adopted incremental approaches to accounting ethics education. They continuously revise their curriculums in response to accrediting agencies – the AACSB, industry, public accounting firms, and professional organizations such as the AICPA, IMA, IIA, and American Accounting Association (AAA). One recommendation made by these agencies addressed the integration of ethics and business societal issues in business course offerings. Accordingly, accounting faculty members have developed a separate accounting ethics course and/or incorporated ethical issues into existing courses. This effort has been aided by faculty involvement from the arts and social sciences, particularly the field of philosophy, to provide a multi-disciplinary approach for teaching and research in accounting ethics.

Instructional and research grants to support accounting ethics education have been extended by business organizations and public accounting firms. To strengthen their programs, several schools have recently created a Center for Accounting Ethics Education, and have established an endowed professorship for senior faculty members to teach and conduct research in business and professional ethics education. A substantial collaborative effort is taking place among colleges/schools, business and governmental organizations to sponsor contributed to increased emphasis on ethics education in the business curriculum.

Accounting educators and practitioners have stressed the contribution of formal ethics education in the classroom, to the analytical and moral/ethical reasoning development of students. However, there are varying opinions as to the rationale and goals of ethics education. Some of these include: the argument for teaching accounting ethics as a separate course or integrating it throughout the curriculum, the role of faculty in ethics instruction, teaching methodologies, and accounting ethics instruction.

## APPROACHES TO ACCOUNTING ETHICS EDUCATION

An important question that a contingency framework raises is the issue of the extent to which ethical subjects should be covered in accounting curriculums. The amount of ethical materials covered in a classroom depends on whether ethics is being taught as a separate accounting ethics course or is integrated throughout the accounting curriculum. If ethics is taught as a separate course, there is the question of course structure and format. In other words, if formal ethics education is to contribute to the moral reasoning development of students, what ethical subject matter should be covered, as well as what sources of materials and references should be incorporated in the classroom to accomplish this objective. Another related issue is whether or not ethics can be taught exclusively from published materials, or should it be presented in reference to societal values, laws, regulations, churches/religious institutions, and communities and professional associations' codes of values and conduct.

An important question that needs to be addressed in a separate accounting ethics course centers on the various methods of instruction used to teach students and the instructor's role in the classroom. If ethics is integrated throughout the accounting curriculum, there is a question of the interest, willingness and expertise of accounting instructors to incorporate ethics into their courses. Further, how often and regular are ethics materials covered and if covered, to what extent? These issues have not been effectively addressed in accounting ethics literature.

Teaching methodologies have received substantial attention in accounting education. There is now an emphasis on cooperative and interactive learning, as opposed to the conventional lecture and case methods of teaching. While these teaching methodologies are being addressed in several business disciplines, they have not yet been fully addressed in ethics instruction. The questions of what teaching methods should be employed to teach students and what role instructors play in the classroom are subjects addressed in this appendix. A contingency framework of accounting ethics education is used to address these issues in relation to whether ethics should be taught as a separate accounting ethics course or integrated throughout the accounting curriculum.

Most accounting faculty feel that it is important to integrate ethics into the accounting curriculum. However, there is no general consensus as to how ethics should be taught in accounting classes: whether it should be taught as a separate accounting ethics course or integrated throughout the accounting curriculum.

## Teaching Ethics: A Separate Accounting Ethics Course or Integrating Ethics throughout the Accounting Curriculum

The development of ethical behavior is a life-long process that is acquired from family, neighborhood, churches, peers, mentors, formal training at school, on the job training, and membership in professional associations. The socialization process shapes ethical and moral behavior over time. There is a debate among educators, that moral principle and convictions are established early in life before an individual enters college or professional school. That is, moral values are acquired and learned at a young age from families, local communities and churches, and cannot easily be taught in the classroom. Society expects colleges and universities to teach students about national values, goals and cultures that shape societal ethics and introduce them to the broad range of moral issues and problems facing society and the nation at large (Sims & Sims, 1991: 214–215). In addition, one of the main objectives of college education is to develop analytical, conceptual and problem solving skills in students.

Moral reasoning as an analytical and conceptual skill requires a learning process that can only be acquired through a formal educational process (Milan & McNair, 1992: 59). In other words, since moral and ethical values consist of individual, organizational, societal and professional values, formal education can teach students the principles of professional and ethical values. However, the greatest impact of ethics education will be on those students who are open-minded, willing to listen and capable of entertaining diverse and complicated ethical issues/dilemmas (Metzger & Phillips, 1991: 47). Accordingly, ethics instruction does not exclusively focus on normative behavior, but on social awareness and the encouragement of students to reach their own ethical decisions.

The educational process goal is to contribute to the ability of students to resolve and process complex ethical dilemmas and issues. Similarly, the rationale for "ethics education in accounting is based on the premise that moral development can be enhanced through the educational process" (Huss &

Patterson, 1993: 235). Since accounting is a public profession, any public choices/decisions made by public accountants are not made in a vacuum, but have broader ethical and societal implications. Thus, accounting choices and decisions involve moral choices that affect organizations and society. Formal education provides both the skills and framework to address questions of moral obligation and social responsibility. It enables students to rationalize, articulate, and take and defend positions when faced with dilemmas/issues surrounding accounting decisions.

Formal education increases the moral depth of students (Ponemon & Glazer, 1990). It allows higher order thinking, objective reasoning and questioning of ethical issues and dilemmas. The educational process can contribute significantly to the analytical ability of students, if it provides a learning climate of honor and trust (Shenkir, 1990). Ethics education, whether offered as a separate accounting course and/or integrated throughout the accounting curriculum, can increase awareness, develop moral reasoning ability, improve analytical skills and broaden the ethical knowledge of students.

## A Separate Accounting Ethics Course

Accounting educators and practitioners have expressed concern that a one-semester course in business and society, or business and social responsibility does not provide an adequate knowledge base to resolve ethical dilemmas. Some accounting professors have suggested that a separate course in accounting ethics is needed to supplement the required three-hour course in business and society. It has also been suggested that a separate accounting course is necessary to familiarize students with the professional ethical guidance of the public accounting profession, as well as ethical reasoning principles (Loeb, 1988).

The argument in favor of a separate course in accounting ethics has been based on the premise that even though accounting faculty members have shown interest in the integration of ethics in accounting courses, actual faculty commitment to include it in their introductory courses has been minimal. The importance of ethics coverage has been stressed, primarily at upper level auditing and taxation courses (Milan & McNair, 1992: 65).

In spite of the importance of accounting ethics education, less time is being spent on ethics coverage in accounting courses. This can be attributed to the fact that "in most business schools, the faculties do not have a knowledge of ethics or the writings of moral philosophies that would allow them to teach ethics" (Sims & Sims, 1991: 213). In addition, most faculty members do not feel comfortable discussing ethical issues in the classroom.

At a minimum, a separate accounting ethics course can overcome these constraints, since it addresses the question of in-depth coverage of ethical issues and problems affecting the accounting profession. However, such a course by itself may not be enough unless these issues are integrated throughout the accounting curriculum. Huss and Patterson (1993) discussed the Treadway Commission's recommendation for increased ethics coverage in accounting courses. The commission recommended "for the integration of moral and ethical issues of financial reporting into the accounting curricula." It stressed the need for "fraudulent and financial reporting ethics issues . . . to be integrated into accounting curriculum" (Donnelly & Miller, 1989: 90). This recommendation cannot be effectively met in a one-semester accounting ethics course. If students are to know how to detect, prevent and deter fraudulent financial reporting, they need a broader exposure to ethics education than what can be offered in one accounting course.

### Integration of Ethics in the Accounting Curriculum

The integration of ethics in all, if not most accounting courses, is based on the premise that if ethical education is to have a long-term impact on student moral reasoning and professional development, ethics needs to be integrated in all accounting and related business courses. Ethical maturity is a by-product of a continual learning process in all accounting and business courses. Formal training and incorporation of ethics in all courses, whether introductory or advanced courses, would enable students to appreciate the continuity, applicability and relevance of ethical issues in their education and organizational decision-making processes. A survey of business graduates from undergraduate business programs by David, Anderson and Laurimore (1990), revealed that most graduates indicated that "ethical issues should be emphasized in undergraduate business programs" (p. 29). Graduates indicated that business ethics training was important to enable them to address ethical dilemmas at work. They felt that ethics should be integrated, at a minimum, into core courses to familiarize students with ethical issues that they might face in their professional work settings.

Therefore, if ethics is integrated throughout the business curriculum, the curriculum demonstrates that ethical education is important in business and professional practices. Integration thus avoids the problem of mandating or requiring a separate ethics course in business management education (Murray

1987: 26). Integration further allows students to understand the importance of a multi-disciplinary approach to ethics education.

McNair and Milan (1993) reported that a majority of accounting faculty "believed the most appropriate place to expose ethics to undergraduate accounting students is in one or more of the accounting courses" (p. 799). If ethics is effectively integrated in all accounting and business management courses, students will benefit substantially from a multi-disciplinary approach to ethics education. Mintz (1990) stressed that if ethics is integrated in accounting courses, students will be aware of the importance of ethics and ethical dimensions of accounting in decision-making (p. 52).

Bassiry (1990) argued that a multi-disciplinary social science approach to teaching ethics and social issues is likely to produce socially aware and responsible graduates and leaders, compared to the specialized ethics curriculum generally offered in most business schools today. A multi-disciplinary approach emphasizes an ethics curriculum that addresses social and ethical values; major social, economic and political issues affecting society; and the applicability of business ethical issues in organizational decision-making processes. The approach broadens students' perspectives by leading them to understand the inter-relationship among disciplines. For example, the implications of auditing standards on business law, tax regulations or the accounting profession. More importantly, since business ethics occurs in an organizational setting, the approach will advance a practical and theoretical approach in ethics education. A multi-disciplinary approach to an ethics curriculum that combines philosophical knowledge, historical perspective, and social and cultural dimensions, can provide a broad-based theoretical framework from which to approach ethics education.

As a field of study, if ethics education is grounded in work-place issues, it can help students develop process skills, which will benefit them when they are challenged to think logically and critically when faced with ethical uncertainties and dilemmas. Ethical education can teach college students the value of self-discipline and respect, and the importance of "accepting responsibility for the educational choices and constraints they are faced with" (Castro, 1989: 582).

Even though ethics education requires practical training, it cannot be presented in a format comparable to public practice oriented disciplines such as accounting and law. In other words, there is no relationship between taking and passing a business ethics course and committing unethical behavior, for example, fraud or embezzlement. Ethical education alone will not deter someone from engaging in unethical activity (Henderson, 1988). In contrast, public professions such as accounting and law are governed by professional licensing requirements, which provide incentives for members and practitioners to refrain from unethical practices that would affect their professional careers and credibility.

Thus, the integration of ethics in accounting and business ethics courses reinforces the importance of ethical issues in decisions that affect business and governmental organizations and society. However, ethical behavior is situational, which is either intentional or inadvertence, an act of omission or commission (Henderson, 1988: 53). Therefore, one has to examine the consequences of the act, whether there is an intentional or unanticipated harm to life, property, environment and society. Taking the consequential approach to ethical decisions, ethics education requirements at college becomes critical, and sends an important message to business and governmental leaders to be aware of the ethical implications of their public policy decisions. Ethics education provides an intellectual framework for decision makers to analyze societal implications that arise from technological developments and the conflict between economic objectives and societal welfare that new product development and legislative mandates can create.

At the individual level, it is expected that ethical education reinforces the importance of responsibility, respect and dignity, and enhances self-gratification. Individuals who have received ethical training have a greater tendency to show concern for the social welfare and well being of others, and adhere to professional and societal moral codes of conduct. Ethical behavior is internalized based on the desire of individuals to avoid punishment and adversarial relationships, and to meet expected behavioral norms associated with their professional roles in organizations and society. Faculty can have a positive impact on students, when they demonstrate that ethics can be taught objectively without imposing their own personal values and beliefs. Faculty and student relations need to be strengthened and sustained to provide a learning environment that enhances ethics training in the classroom.

# ROLE OF FACULTY IN ETHICS INSTRUCTION

If professional ethical behavior can be taught in the classroom, it is important that a collegial relationship that fosters respect, honesty, trust and integrity develop between faculty and students (Shenkir 1990). In ethics education, faculty play an important role. They can create an environment that promotes inter-active learning. Ethics education raises philosophical, moral, religious and professional issues that are intertwined and implicated in our actions and behaviors on a daily basis. As such, students' perceptions are critical factors in ethics education. Students expect faculty members to show honesty, integrity, fairness and objectivity both inside and outside the classroom.

Faculty serve as role models and mentors for students. They can serve as an example of a reference group that has a positive impact on ethics education. As sources of referent power, they can advance the learning of good ethics, only when their personal and professional actions are consistent with their words in the classroom. Accordingly, schools and universities need to ensure that faculty members, who teach ethics, demonstrate maturity, confidence, responsibility and knowledge. They must be able to interact with students. Faculty also needs to be able to argue, question and reason with students in a trusting and respectful manner in the classroom (Henderson, 1988: 53).

In other words, ethics is best learned from actual observation and through the experiences of people who teach ethics. Dobson (1992) used the Aristotelian moral philosophy analogy to emphasize that "ethical behavior is learned from observation of the actions of ethical individuals" (p. 114). Those individuals include business and government leaders, as well as ethics instructors. Similarly, David et al. (1990) stressed that the role of faculty is to lead by good example and personal actions. They advanced the view that "professors' personal actions are as important as their words in developing students' ethical values" (p. 30). That is, "management or faculty must lead by example to implement good ethics into students and young people in the work place" (p. 31). Faculty members can have a significant impact on student ethical development, by nurturing collegial relationship with students when they invite students to attend seminars, conferences and meetings on ethics and related subjects (Huss & Patterson, 1993: 241). They should follow up by encouraging students to bring ideas back and discuss them in the classroom.

On the other hand, there are those who argue that teaching ethics can be separated from a person's ethical behavior: that there is no relationship between the teaching of ethics and the practice of ethical behavior. Castro (1989) has expressed the danger presented in this line of argument and its negative effect on ethics education as follows: "in separating business ethics from the ethics of business education, as we commonly do, we have not only failed to apply the course to the students immediate situation, but have also failed to take advantage of the opportunity to open up a faculty dialogue about the business school's own curriculum and procedures" (p. 481).

In other words, ethics education needs to encourage dialogue among faculty, students and administrators to restructure the program, as well as to show exemplary behavior links between ethical education and behavior. Unless links between ethics education and personal conduct are established, the likelihood that ethical education will be reinforced and have a long lasting influence on professional conduct is minimal. Thus, the choice of ethics instructional methods is essential to accomplish ethics education goals in business and public policy decisions.

# ACCOUNTING ETHICS INSTRUCTION

Teaching methodologies have recently received substantial attention in accounting education. There is a growing concern among educators that the impact of ethics instruction on students is short-lived and has limited impact outside the classroom. The lack of external relevance in ethics education can be partly attributed to teaching instruction and methodology.

The most commonly used instructional methods in accounting courses combine lecture and case studies. To some extent, some programs have incorporated experiential and clinical approaches, in addition to the conventional lecture and case study combination. Both lecture and case methods are classified under the institutional framework, and the experiential under the consequential approach to accounting ethics education.

## *The Institutional Approach of Ethics Instruction*

Lecture and case methods of instruction follow an institutional-adaptive strategy to ethics instruction. Both methods support incremental, gradual approaches to institute changes in ethics instruction. As incremental approaches, both case and lecture methods are highly receptive and adaptive to institute short-term changes in response to environmental crises or threats, such as the savings and loans banks crisis. Lecture and case methods employ a phased step-by-step approach to develop and improve analytical and conceptual abilities, and to strengthen students' moral reasoning capabilities. The objective is to shape students' moral reasoning skills consistent with existing professional norms, business practices, and social responsibilities. However, there are several constraints associated with both the lecture and case methods of instruction.

### *Lecture*

Lecture is widely used in accounting classrooms to teach ethics. This method allows incorporating ethical issues into several topics. It is very effective in conveying factual and theoretical knowledge. Instructors can deliver lectures to the classroom with less preparation. In most cases, instructors can incorporate ethical materials available in textbooks and articles into lesson plans. The objective and subjective-essay exam methods can be used to evaluate student performance.

However, the lecture format has been considered ineffective in increasing student communication skills and critical thinking abilities. McNair and Milan (1993) discovered the lecture teaching format as the least effective accounting ethics instruction method. They reported that there are fewer interactions between faculty and students. Students are passive, least involved in the learning process, and are expected to absorb and learn the material to pass classroom exams.

In general, the lecture format relies on student ability to recite and assemble theoretical and factual information, with limited application to organizational settings. It can be effective to inform students about organizational rules, appropriate conduct, compliance to professional code of ethics and the institutional environment of organizations. However, it is the least effective method to integrate critical ethical inquiry into the decision-making process.

## Case Method

The case study method of instruction is widely used in accounting ethics instruction. It has been used to address practical issues and problems. Instructors have integrated short and detailed hypothetical and real cases, presented in textbooks or provided by professional organizations such as the AICPA, AMA, IIA and public accounting firms. Video presentations and supplementary materials accompany some of the cases from sponsoring organizations (Sisaye & Lackman, 1994). Cases provide students with "an external referent" (Castro, 1989: 481) to apply business situations to actual and/ or hypothetical organizational settings. Cases allow students to evaluate, criticize and discuss with fellow classmates the decision-making process in organizations. The case method encourages students to present competing arguments, compare costs and benefits of alternative choices and reach informed decisions (Sims & Sims, 1991: 213). Cases increase student awareness and sensitivity to ethical issues and dilemmas (Mintz, 1990: 51–52). They allow instructors an opportunity to present their views on the role of ethics in business and society.

McNair and Milan (1993) have reported that the case method has not been commonly used in accounting instruction. They reported a lack of available ethics cases outside of those provided by professional organizations – AICPA, IMA or the Big Five CPA firms. Instructors do not have to devote class time to discuss cases, since they have a great deal of factual information to cover in their classes (pp. 804–805).

In spite of the fact that the case method is the most commonly used teaching method, it has certain potential drawbacks. Armstrong (1990) found several inherent weaknesses in the eight-step case method approach to ethics instruction in accounting. She argued that the eight-step format of case analysis is geared towards a problem-solving approach to improve analytical skills. She further argued that a strict application and analysis of the step method might inhibit student ability to tie cases to actual practices in the accounting profession. The method might be less suited to promote higher order or moral reasoning and analysis.

The functional and normative assumptions of accounting ethics dominate the case method of teaching. Case studies in general train students to accept the status quo, without further inquiry into actual business and government practices. Cases are presented with several constraints and scenarios; the analysis accepts certain conditions as given; the alternatives/choices presented are purposeful and conform to the functional-rational view of organizations; and student behavior and ethical reasoning are influenced by the stated objectives of the organization. In most cases, the ethical inquiry exists in a vacuum devoid of business, organizational and social realities.

Even in situations where case scenarios are non-fictional, they may not facilitate ethical inquiry. Cases are written so that students can learn about their operations – past, present and future, but they are less likely to reveal unusual business practices or situations that would change the company's operations. According to Castro (1989), cases that do not reflect organizational and social realities do not advance ethics education. Ethical reasoning and inquiry in these cases will be less realistic and "is not intended to interfere with business as usual, either in the school or in the real world" (p. 481). Students are less likely to appreciate the relevance of ethics case instruction, unless these cases reflect actual business and public policy ethical dilemmas. Social awareness is gained from the application of ethical reasoning in actual (not simulated) situations and experiential learning.

*Constraints on Institutional Approaches to Ethics Instruction Methods*

Accounting faculty members and scholars have discussed the relevance of ethics education outside the classroom, particularly after students graduate from college and enter business and public environments. A study by Arlow and Ulrich (1988) revealed that "after graduation, business school graduates feel that school and university training becomes less important in influencing ethical conduct" (p. 299). These graduates indicated that religious and family training and organizational culture played important roles in their decisions.

They noted that industry practices played an important role in shaping their behavior and institutional ethical values and practices. They gave formal ethical education at schools and universities as having the least impact on their business decisions. Arlow and Ulrich (1988) suggested that formal education declined in importance, when it dealt with personal values and business decisions, but received high marks in increasing student awareness and sensitivity to ethical issues and dilemmas.

Such issues raise fundamental questions about the importance and effectiveness of business ethics education after graduation. Why does ethical education have so little impact outside the classroom? It is suggested that the lack of external relevance of classroom ethics training and short-lived nature of ethics education can be attributed partially to weaknesses in teaching methods.

The lecture and case study methods utilize an adaptive approach to ethics instruction. Both methods support incremental, gradual, phased step-by-step approaches to develop and improve the analytical and conceptual ability of students. They are based on single loop, first-order and convergence learning strategies, which attempt to shape students' moral reasoning skills consistent with existing professional norms, business practices, and social responsibilities. However, there are several constraints associated with both the lecture and case study methods of ethics instruction.

The lecture method is generally passive, encourages students to observe, and does not attempt to involve them actively in the learning process. The lecture format relies on the student's ability to recite and assemble theoretical and factual information with limited application to actual organizational settings.

On the other hand, the case study method requires students to apply a step-by-step approach to resolving ethical dilemmas and issues. Its objective is to develop ethical reasoning through analysis of the alternatives required to make morally informed decisions (Murray, 1987: 26). While it attempts to make connections between ethical theories and organizational reality, in most instances case studies are devoid of business and social realities. As Henderson (1988) pointed out, "too many of the ethical dilemmas posed in case studies are hypothetical dilemmas" (p. 53). Castro (1989) expressed his reservation that the case method of teaching does not necessarily facilitate ethical inquiry, since most cases exist in a vacuum. He stated that "the underlying message is likely to be that ethical inquiry is not intended to interfere with business as usual either in the school or in the 'real world'" (p. 481). Case studies train students to accept the status quo, without further inquiry into actual business and government practices. In most instances, it attempts to influence student ethical reasoning, without attempting to establish linkages between ethical dilemmas presented in the cases and those currently operating in organizations and the broader society.

Current teaching methods do not encourage students to apply their ethical training, since there is minimal relationships between classroom experience and actual organizational settings. Students will not appreciate the relevance of ethics case instructions unless those cases reflect actual business and public policy ethical dilemmas. Application of ethical reasoning emerges from actual observation and experience, rather than from hypothetical case studies.

*The Consequential Approach of Ethics Instruction – Experiential Learning*

The consequential approach of ethics instruction is a radical, proactive and interactive teaching methodology. It focuses on double loop, second-order and a well-planned imaginative and creative change approach. A consequential approach is based on reorientation learning, which is capable of anticipating and responding to environmental changes, even in times of uncertainty. It is an action-oriented approach to the development of ethical and moral reasoning.

Experiential learning is conducted in actual organizational settings. It might involve short-term visits, internships or specific project assignments. Experiential learning has been commonly conducted in classroom settings. Videos of actual cases might be presented in class. If it involves video-satellite conferences, it is followed by question and answer sessions from attendees. Guest speakers can be used to bring their business, professional and personal experiences to the classroom to share with students. Students can participate actively in the learning process through questions and answers, role playing or peer group settings where they can review, discuss and evaluate alternative choices.

In the experiential learning setting, students are given scenario cases or problems to address. The objective is to discover from dialogue, open-ended questions, and assessments of unforeseen and unanticipated consequences. Exploratory learning of moral issues that arise from home, work, school and society take place. Students work cooperatively to identify and analyze ethical dilemmas/situations that have affected organizational practices.

Ethics education has a dual purpose of developing ethical reasoning and internalizing ethical issues. The criticism of lecture and case methods of instruction is that ethics education has minimal impact outside the classroom, little external relevance, and is short sighted. A proactive experiential teaching strategy can facilitate the internalization of moral and ethical issues that students can use in their work settings. If internalized, it is less likely that students will be tempted to commit unethical behavior (Sims & Sims, 1991: 217–218; Metzger & Phillips, 1991: 148–149).

Experiential learning has a life-long impact on ethics education. Topics or issues addressed in actual organizational settings, help to enlighten students intellectually and morally. Students can explore several topics that are highly sensitive and pose ethical dilemmas. These topics might include confidentiality, conflict between personal and organizational interests, relationships between ethical awareness/behavior and prospects for promotion in organizations. These issues are controversial and will solicit active participation in the learning process. More importantly, experiential teaching methods personalize the learning process. Students will appreciate and learn more when they can relate ethical dilemmas to their professional obligations and future career goals.

# FUTURE DIRECTIONS OF ACCOUNTING ETHICS EDUCATION

A contingency framework considers the impact of environmental factors, including industrial organizational structures, technological development, government regulatory agencies, and cultural/social forces that shape and generate conflicting goals for ethics education. The utility of the contingency approach has been in documenting that ethics education has taken an adaptive approach to gradually and incrementally influence student behavior. However, it has not yet established an adequate linkage between ethical behaviors/ dilemmas presented in the classroom, with those currently operating in organizations and society. Accordingly, dilemmas and constraints associated with teaching ethics as a separate accounting ethics course or integrated throughout the accounting curriculum are discussed. A multi-disciplinary approach to ethics education is recommended to provide students with moral reasoning skills. These moral reasoning skills help students understand and evaluate the impact of ethical decisions in public and business organizations.

It is recommended that faculty members who have academic experience and professional backgrounds in social sciences, as well as business and professional ethics teach ethics. Students expect higher moral standards from their ethics instructors. Ethics instructors can facilitate the learning process by using examples from personal and professional experience, creating an open learning environment by showing respect for student opinions and by encouraging a diversity of views in the classroom and developing collegial student-faculty relationships. Faculty members can introduce innovative methods of teaching ethics, which encourage students to internalize ethical and moral issues in their future professional careers.

It has been noted that institutional approaches of learning based on lecture and case study methods of ethics instruction are not sufficient to teach students the skills needed to behave ethically in actual situations. Seminars and guest lectures from business, government and industry, communicating real life experience and observations to students should supplement them. Guest lecturers who have worked on ethical cases can bring experiential learning into the classroom. Seminars by faculty members from the fields of social sciences, arts and philosophy bring different perspectives to bear on the theory and application of ethics. More importantly, these seminars add to the intellectual and theoretical relevance of ethical issues in a personal, professional and organizational decision-making context.

Presently in business education, there is an emphasis on consequential approaches of cooperative and interactive learning, particularly in accounting/ business ethics. The underlying premise is that effective education is both cooperative and interactive, focusing on reorientation by providing both theoretical and practical education. Ethical education requires both students and faculty to be active participants in evaluating organizational ethical situations through field studies, on-site visits, internships, and participant observation. Exploratory and discovery teaching methods encourage students to be active participants in the learning process. They allow students and faculty to experience hands-on learning of ethical issues, which may include risk-taking exploration in a classroom setting. The cumulative effect of interactive learning is to overcome shortcomings of current ethics education and contribute to the life-long learning process of ethics education.

An analysis of the institutional and consequential approaches to accounting ethics education reveal, that current accounting ethics education has generally followed the institutional approach, teaching students how ethics relate to organizational norms and operations. Ethics instructions, both lecture and case studies, contributed to the moral development of students. Formal accounting ethics education increased the ability of students to apply moral reasoning principles to resolve ethical dilemmas. However, accounting ethics instruction followed the normative approach in teaching students the positive relationship between increased responsibility and business economics performance.

On the other hand, the consequential approach, utilized a proactive strategy of accounting ethics education. Teaching instruction applied experiential learning to involve students actively in the learning process. Students participate in internships, specific project assignments or short-term organization visits. Whether the session is conducted in classroom or organizational settings, the objective is to provide students an opportunity to learn interactively and cooperatively from real organizational experiences.

Ethics as a theoretical and practical policy-oriented discipline needs to be taught from both institutional and consequential approaches. The lecture and case study methods alone are not sufficient to teach students the skills needed to behave ethically in actual situations. They need to be supplemented by consequential-experiential instructions to communicate real life organizational experiences. Exploration and discovery teaching methods through field studies, internships and participant observation enable students and faculty to experience hands-on learning of ethical issues through evaluation of actual organizational ethical dilemmas and situations. Accounting ethics education can be effective when it is institutional and consequential, as well as cooperative and interactive, thus providing students with both theoretical and practical education. When process innovative changes disrupt existing organizational order, ethics education can be used as building bridges to restore order and maintain/improve organizational performance. In this context, the contingency approach has important implications in the teaching of quality issues and concepts in higher education.

## IMPLICATIONS OF ETHICS EDUCATION: MANAGING QUALITY INSTRUCTIONS IN HIGHER EDUCATION

The external environment of business has required changes in the ways business organizations plan and operate performance activities. In order to meet these demands, business expectations from higher education, college graduates and their employee performance in the work place have increased over time. Today, colleges require graduates to acquire skills that will enable them to work in self-managed teams. Corporations, in addition to college education, have stressed the importance of non-academic skills, "but social – a good worth ethic, a pleasant demeanor, reliability" (Stone 1991: 52).

While social skills are important, the diversity of skills acquired through education affect the success of college graduates in the work place. Ethics, quality and productivity issues have now become the focus of education among business schools. It has been expressed that analytical and quantitative skills are not enough by themselves, unless they are combined with ethics, social and environmental skills, and quality. In order to allow students to take more elective courses in quality, partnership and entrepreneurship; there is a suggestion to reduce the number of required courses in the major and minor fields of studies. This has necessitated the need for a phased-gradual approach to curriculum change and development.

Business schools are professional programs whose sole objective is to train students to assume leadership positions in industry and government. In addition, business schools provide education that will improve business processes for quality products to satisfy customers, thereby increasing corporate owners' wealth. They play critical roles in reshaping and changing society for future growth and development. These trends require that educational systems remain increasingly adaptive and responsive to continual changes in institutional environments. Only through continuous improvement programs of quality education can such concerns be addresses and accomplished, through cooperative team efforts among faculty, students and employing organizations. Accordingly, consultants should not dominate quality education. But rather, it has to be team taught by faculty, visiting scholars and practitioners through cases, cross-functional courses and modules.

Publications and interdisciplinary research can contribute to the advancement of quality education and training. To promote scholarship in teaching as evidenced in ethics education, there has to be a coordinated effort of balancing research through effective teaching – course design and curriculum development. New guidelines for incorporating quality improvement in business programs include curriculum development, teaching, research and services, and developing criteria to evaluate outcomes.

In order to make the evaluation system more responsive to teaching, faculty are encouraged to develop portfolios to guide their teaching, research and service activities. According to AACSB, "the portfolios bring together evidence of a faculty member's teaching strengths and accomplishments. They might include copies of course syllabi, video-tapes of classes taught, student's evaluations, letters, and records of their success in graduate school, articles published about teaching, development workshops attended, and so on" (1991: 17). Portfolios are thus viewed not as a remedial to teaching deficiencies, but rather teaching development process aspects. It makes the evaluation system responsive to teaching. As a result, teaching is viewed as complementing research, but not taking time away from research. There is scholarship for teaching that directs research to instructional and curriculum development.

Collaborative, non-competitive team learning, interaction with customers, frequent contact, and involvement of workers in the educational process have been advocated when designing new courses or revising existing courses. These approaches are advocated to make educational programs functional and purposeful for business organizations.

At present, business schools are divided/grouped by functional disciplines including accounting, finance, marketing and production. The departmentalization and compartmentalization of disciplines by functional areas does not support quality education, since quality involves multi-disciplinary approaches. Quality education draws from several disciplines including statistics, operations/production management, and organizational behavior and human resources management. Emphasis on ethics, culture, technology, leadership, small business management, environment, international relations, and crisis management have contributed to developing new quality education seminars and workshops.

There is an emphasis that education has to be broad and comprehensive. Continuous learning and education support human relation skills, motivation, and networking so as to develop contact and professional visibility (McMillan, 1992: 23–24). Today, the competition among developed countries is not primarily focused on economic power and control of world natural resources, but rather on education, trained manpower, and productive labor force. Education has now become the main factor that accounts for differences in income and earning power (Wooldrige, 1992). The best companies compete for a trained labor force and provide continuing education for their employees. Foreign investment and the location and entry of industries/corporations are largely influenced by the availability of a trained labor force.

As companies compete nationally and internationally, globalization of education has increased awareness on the importance of internal issues, as markets become open and accessible. Advances in computer and telecommunication technologies have increased corporations' adaptation and flexibility to local and international competition, as global markets became intertwined with regional/continental regions. It is now possible "through benchmarking, conferences, training and consultants, TQM knowledge diffuses rapidly, so competitor quality improves and prices fall (though with a lag)" (Sterman, Repenning & Kofman, 1997: 513). Since TQM lowered unit costs, improved productivity and cycle time, global competition has changed from low pricing strategies to quality products and customer satisfaction.

Globalization and internationalization have contributed to reengineering and overhauling the educational process. Consistent with the consequential approach, the focus of education has shifted from short-term career orientation to life-long/continuous learning, which serve students/customers and employers on a continuous basis to ensure satisfaction with services rendered. This has brought the need for continuous assessment of programs, incorporation of vision and creativity, and teamwork in quality education to the forefront (Marchese 1991). There is now an emphasis on proactive, rather than reactive changes where new programs are initiated to change old assumptions of management accounting and control, inspection and employee motivation. Reactive changes have increased the gap between managers and workers. The prevalence of these attitudes does not promote teamwork and cooperation, creating barriers to quality education. Changing these old assumptions through reward and incentive systems for team performance and productivity, are key factors for quality education success.

In total quality education, the student becomes the focus of continuous learning processes and improvement programs. If the student is the product, the student gets actively involved in the learning process. The question centers on promoting those instructional methodologies that allow the student to solve problems and learn by oneself with minimal instructor guidance. Alumna, graduates, and employers can contribute substantially to curriculum development, advisement and short-term course offerings – seminars and workshops that expose students to both technical and cultural aspects of business organizations.

It is true that most business graduates, due to an over-emphasis on theory, methods, and applications lack the practical skills needed to manage businesses in competitive environments. The curriculum is weak on topics of quality management in manufacturing organizations, globalization and leadership. Cooperative research, course offerings, and training programs with industry and government are developed to overcome the shortcomings associated with real world experience. Internships, on the job training, and summer placement programs are offered in factories and shops, so students learn actual organization operations and functions.

Many business schools are offering short seminars and mini-courses on change management, globalization strategy, diversity management, communications, and corporate culture. These changes are made to counter-attack recent proliferation on in-house corporate management training and development programs. In addition, Japanese comparative management educational programs have brought changes in the education paradigm. They have relied on less formal graduate management education, and more on short course offerings on quality and productivity, just-in-time technology (JIT), and manufacturing management (McMillan, 1992: 21–32).

Comparative educational systems not only brought changes in curriculums, but also required changes in professors' teaching styles and methodologies. Education is key to developing corporate culture that guide employee behavior to common long-term goals of high economic performance and delivery of quality products and services to customers. Corporations that develop such culture focus on serving their constituents: customers, stockholders and employees. Customers benefit from these corporations by receiving better economic performance than those who do not show improved performance. In this respect, quality and ethics education can serve as guiding philosophies to inculcate these values and socialize students to become good corporate citizens. These values support existing structures and systems, and support incremental changes that contribute to organizational performance, as well as maintenance and functioning of social systems.

# TOTAL QUALITY MANAGEMENT AND ITS EFFECT ON QUALITY COSTS MANAGEMENT IN MANUFACTURING ORGANIZATIONS: LESSONS FROM SOME CASE STUDIES

## INTRODUCTION

There are several attributes of total quality management (TQM) that are applicable to accounting for quality costs. Some of these examples include:

1. Continuous quality improvement of management accounting reports and their usefulness for internal control purposes.
2. Understanding customer needs, thereby meeting and satisfying requirements of accounting reports, particularly those of internal users (managers) within the organization by providing timely and relevant quality cost information for organizational decision-making processes.
3. Employee involvement in planning and implementing cost accounting systems.
4. Development of a management by objective/results cost accounting data approach for organization activities.
5. Institution of strategic planning and implementation techniques to achieve organization's long-term total quality goals.
6. Incorporation of TQM philosophy in carrying out day-to-day organizational activities.

# IMPLICATIONS OF TOTAL QUALITY MANAGEMENT ON MANAGEMENT ACCOUNTING AND CONTROL SYSTEMS

The management accounting systems of most manufacturing organizations have gone through several changes in the ways cost accounting data are collected and reported over time. New developments in statistical quality control (SQC) and Just-in-time (JIT) have emphasized changes in the overall approach of accounting, from that of reporting to a management device. This management device assists in the decision-making process at the lowest level of organization hierarchy including the factory floor (Drucker, 1990). This has brought a reconsideration of the current practices for allocating overhead costs to production departments. There were questions as to the appropriate selection and use of allocation bases to allocate service and other overhead costs. The expensing of research and development activities that benefit the future period as expenses for the period – primarily for purely accounting purposes was re-examined. The emphasis on short-term profitability performance was considered financially sound, since it discouraged long-term investment.

There is now a realization that accounting techniques are primarily designed to measure tangible financial performance measures – such as operating expenses and net income. They "downplay or ignore less tangible non-financial measures – such as product quality, customer satisfaction, order lead time, factory flexibility, the time it takes to launch a new product, and the accumulation of skills by labor over time" (Peters, 1988: 488). Accounting has not yet developed indicators to measure the attributes of quality and its relationship to better financial performance (Johnson & Kaplan, 1987). It has been estimated that poor quality costs in terms of design, manufacturing, inspection, shipping and customer service account for 20% of manufacturing sales and 30% of service company sales (Eisner 1990). Since improving poor quality costs is considered one of the ingredients for improving financial performance, today's concept of cost accounting has been broadened to cost management, to include TQM as one of the main components of the accounting data base.

An organization's success depends on the quality of internal reports generated by the cost management system. In other words, successful organizations are managed by fact and are data driven. The scope of data they need – the majority from their cost accounting system is on their customers, markets, employees, operations and benchmarks (Reiman 1991). Therefore, the question is can the accounting system respond fast enough to process and analyze these informations? The TQM approach to cost accounting suggests that a quality cost accounting system can facilitate fast response in production and service areas that "focus on design of products and processes; measure and improve cycle time, lead time, and response time; and evaluate all work paths" (Reiman, 1991). The system can provide data in cost savings, as well as productivity gains in all organization operations.

It should be noted that cost savings that arise due to economies of scale in production, might conflict with the concept of JIT and quality, since large scale production might not be economically sound due to costs associated with storage, spoilage and damage from excessive inventories. "The TQM management philosophy supports production of only what is needed" and under-scores the "economies of scale production philosophy [that is] strongly reflected in many cost accounting systems" (Reeve 1989: 27).

This means that standardized measures of cost performance based on variance analysis (comparison of actual and budgeted costs) and unit costs are not in compliance with the TQM concept. "Standards used in performance evaluation are antithetical to a continuous improvement philosophy [of TQM]. Standards tend to place an upper limit on improvement, or hide improvement possibilities" (Reeve, 1989: 28). Since standards in many organizations are negotiated and employees/managers build slack into the standards to attain them, the use of standards to measure and evaluate performance inhibits system improvement. If the cost management system has the objective of supporting TQM, the emphasis must be centered on the identification and removal of waste or slack from standards that inhibit organization productivity. Instead, the accounting system should focus on the quality of products as measured by inventory lead time, flexibility of scheduling and delivery, and the response time to meet customer requests and specification.

## TOTAL QUALITY MANAGEMENT AND QUALITY COSTS MANAGEMENT

The principle of TQM is based on the assumption that products or services are designed, produced, and delivered to satisfy customer needs. The applications of TQM to service and support functions – like accounting, require similar approaches focusing on meeting customer informational needs. The customers or users of accounting information can be broadly classified in the following two categories: (a) external users, i.e. investors, government regulatory agencies; and (b) internal users, such as managers. This appendix focuses on the provision of accounting reports on quality costs to assist internal users in management decision-making processes.

Accounting reports, as internal products should be of high quality to assist management in making decisions that affect organizational performance. Quality implies that the accounting methods and procedures used for collecting, recording, analyzing and disseminating information are timely and capable of producing up-to-date relevant quality production costs on material, labor and other inputs used in the production process. That is, indirect and support costs will be traced to the activities/transactions incurred in the production process.

An organization can develop a cost model that will enable managers to predict future costs when decisions on production capabilities and schedules, marketing and distribution facilities and/or new product designs or changes are enacted. The cost model will identify the costs of support staff and other indirect activities that would be incurred on the product. A cost model based on activity-based costing (ABC) systems helps reduce production defects, improves production scheduling activities, minimizes excess production of raw materials and inventories, and allows managers to change product mixes between high volume and specialty products. The system allows managers to study the cost structure and thereby adjust production systems accordingly to meet customer needs/requirements (Christofi & Sisaye, 1992).

Cost management information systems have the capability to provide timely data to managers. This data assists managers in evaluating quality costs associated with the implementation of TQM systems and their effect on cost improvements, customer satisfaction, profitability, and the overall financial well-being of the company. The cost management system can assist in the identification of quality cost factors related to product costs, marketing/ administrative expenses, operating results, and product segment performance.

Management accounting systems can be designed to generate quality cost reports that highlight cost differences due to quality improvements and identify potential areas for improvement associated with control of quality errors and defects. While initial TQM costs are expected to be high, a cost-benefit analysis of TQM suggests that such initial costs, in the long run, will contribute to lowering quality costs. Past experiences support that benefits outweigh the initial costs incurred in TQM system implementation.

## TOTAL QUALITY MANAGEMENT APPLICATIONS: SOME EMPIRICAL CASES

This section illustrates TQM integration in cost management systems with empirical evidence. Among manufacturing companies, Westinghouse Electric

Corporation (Fooks, 1991) has benefited substantially from TQM implementation. The cost-time profile of TQM at Westinghouse reveals a decline in quality costs over time, i.e.; the new quality production costs have decreased by more than 50 percent when compared to old costs within the same time period. The resultant cost-time process management benefits include cycle time reduction; cost and quality improvement; innovation; fewer people; simpler information system; less inventory, facility, and profile 'cash' employee participation; and customer satisfaction which can be leveraged for revenue growth (p. 31).

The following cases from the early 1990s when TQM and activity-based costing were very popular illustrate their contributions in controlling production costs. The cases and examples from General Electric (GE), Ling Temco Vought (LTV), and National Semiconductor Corporation (NSC) support the argument that early adopters of new innovations, in this case ABC systems and TQM, have experienced positive effects on their management accounting reporting systems, customer satisfaction, and company profitability.

Johnson (1992b) discussed the development of ABC systems at GE. ABC has enabled GE to trace indirect costs to sources of origin, rather than being allocated to the output of a particular manufacturing department. In other words, engineering decisions such as parts ordering, parts stocking or machine changeovers can contribute to indirect costs in improving internal and external failure costs. The ABC system allows someone to trace such costs to the engineering decisions that produced these costs, rather than focusing attention on the incurred costs. Thus, the reporting system enables managers to control the activities that caused indirect costs. Since changes in activities in one department, cause other departments to adjust or change their activities to meet the new activity demands, ABC helps identify linkages among the concerned departments of engineering, marketing and manufacturing.

GE has been able to calculate the percentage of time spent on each activity, estimate related costs incurred for each activity, and calculate estimated cost per unit for each activity driver. This information can be used by the engineering department to determine the additional indirect costs that will be incurred in the future, particularly when planned changes in product designs cause such increased costs. GE's ABC systems contributed to better allocation of overhead costs, resulting in improved product cost information for inventory pricing. This information also helps marketing managers evaluate product costs and determine product mix profitability. They can use the information to aid the production department to integrate customers' product needs and preferences into the manufacturing process, thereby contributing to a continuous process improvement and total customer satisfaction.

According to Reid (1992), LTV has developed and implemented a customized approach to TQM, called Teamwork for Excellence (TEX). TEX is a comprehensive strategy of process management for continuous improvement, which serves as the main avenue to advance excellence in everything done within the organization. The ABC information system has been incorporated into the Integrated Process Management Methodology (IPMM). The accounting department supports the manufacturing and other departments, by providing information on product costing and operating activities to evaluate performance, identify deficiencies and quality costs arising from internal and external failure of products, and customer product requirements. The reports provide performance indicators that enable the process management approach to integrate customer requirements with product improvement strategies, ultimately leading to total customer satisfaction.

Turney and Stratton (1992) discussed how NSC had been implementing ABC to support continuous product improvement by providing up-to-date product cost information. The ABC system provided both macro (aggregated) and micro (detailed)-cost activities that contained individual units of work incurred for product improvement. While macro-costs are used for product costing, micro-activity costs are provided to concerned managers for evaluation and control purposes.

Thus NSC has a two-dimensional ABC system serving two customers, where the micro-activities provide detailed cost information, including cost drivers and performance measures to support improvement efforts. The micro-activities are summarized and aggregated into macro-activities to facilitate product-costing reporting and assist in the improvement of individual micro-activities. The two-dimensional micro and macro-ABC model facilitated a dual reporting system. The micro-ABC aspect generated cost information on detailed activities, and comprised the responsibility model and organization structure that supported process improvement. The macro-ABC model constituted the economic model, where aggregate costs are established for assigning product costs.

The two-stage activity-based cost model facilitated the assigning of detailed cost activities from any number of departments to a single cost pool, where the cost of each pool was then eventually assigned to products. While the two-stage system is more complex, it has the advantage of reporting reliable and accurate product cost information compared to traditional cost accounting volume-based approaches.

The three cases of ABC systems at GE, LTV and NSC show the importance of integrating TQM in the accounting system, a manifestation in improving the accumulation and reporting of accounting systems for quality costs. Particularly, the NSC case shows a two-dimensional ABC system, contributing to an advanced cost management reporting system for internal control and responsibility accounting (micro-ABC) and product costing (macro-ABC).

If there are any lessons to be learned from such empirical cases, it is that quality should be considered the ultimate goal of accounting reports. Cost management systems should strive for continuous improvement in reporting quality information through innovation and development of new accounting techniques for TQM. To accomplish this objective, a planned phased strategy is needed to institute TQM in cost accounting systems.

Smith (1990) suggested six stages of TQM intervention strategies: problem identification, ranking, analysis, innovation, solution, and evaluation to implement quality improvements. He recommended total employee involvement in all aspects of the design and implementation process of the accounting information system, if the reporting system has the ultimate objective of providing quality reports that are timely, relevant, and used for management decision-making.

Woods (1989), based on his experience with TQM at six Naval Aviation Depots, suggested setting up executive steering committees composed of top management personnel, to institute total quality concepts in all functional areas of management including accounting. The objective is to have top level management's full support for TQM implementation in the organization. In addition, all personnel within the accounting department will be involved in all phases of the implementation process to ensure organizational wide support for the TQM system. As such, an inter-disciplinary team consisting of personnel with expertise in cost behavior, production improvement, and management costs (fixed or variable), and the redefinition of cost centers and allocation bases to bring the cost accounting system in line with TQM principles.

Woods (1989) listed those specific changes introduced by the TQM system. The system contributed to the automation of manual cost procedures that reduced labor costs. It resulted in improved allocation bases using several criteria including number of employees (personnel services), floor space, and capital equipment used (maintenance) for the allocation of general and administrative expenses to the production departments. It allowed the generation of timely and simplified reports for production cost centers and operational managers.

These cases (examples) suggest that the TQM approach to cost accounting has positively changed the method for accounting production and quality costs. The cases indicate that for TQM to be successfully implemented in functional areas of management – including accounting, it requires a phased planned intervention strategy supported and initiated by management. As a planned intervention strategy, the TQM cost management program becomes part of the overall corporate strategy. Since cost management systems provide information services that assist decision-making processes, design and implementation of cost management systems must be directed by the quality cost information needs of organizational strategic planning systems (Kaplan, 1991). That is, the decision to institute cost management systems involves strategic decisions that require a long range time frame and futuristic orientation, if TQM goals for quality accounting products and services are to be accomplished.

These cases demonstrate that accounting has thus become an integral part of TQM. Quality costs such as internal and external appraisal including tangible and intangible costs of quality, as well as product liability, recall and modification costs are reported for internal use for pricing and production decisions. Reporting these quality costs has become one of the main reporting objectives of cost management systems.

## TOTAL QUALITY MANAGEMENT AND COST MANAGEMENT

Appendix 4 included several cases/examples which demonstrated that the TQM approach to cost management has positively changed accounting production and quality costs methods. Based on the experiences of GE, LTV and NSC, for TQM to be successfully implemented in all functional areas of management – including accounting – it requires a planned intervention strategy, supported and initiated by top management. A process management system has been the key factor for using ABC as the underlying basis to support continuous product improvement and total customer satisfaction.

Since cost management systems provide information services that support decision-making processes, the quality cost information need of the organizational strategic planning and process management systems must direct the design and implementation of cost management systems. That is, the decision to institute improved cost management systems such as JIT and ABC, involve strategic decisions that are oriented toward long-term performance. A TQM approach to cost management systems, thus involves an integrated approach that combines a cost accounting perspective of providing quality costs for product costing and pricing purposes, and a process view that focuses on using cost information for continuous product improvement and total customer satisfaction.

# A FIVE STEP APPROACH FOR THE IMPLEMENTATION OF REENGINEERING IN INTERNAL AUDITING AND CONTROL SYSTEMS

## INTRODUCTION

A contingency framework of organizations examines how business process reengineering approaches can be adapted and applied to study internal auditing and control systems. As an example, Tomasko (1993) applied reengineering to evaluate organizational restructuring as a form of intelligent resizing. This appendix presents the incorporation of Tomasko's (1993); Davenport's (1993a, b, 1994); Clancy's (1994a, b); and other management scholars and practitioners' approaches to discuss how reengineering and process innovation approaches can be applied to initiate innovative methods of internal auditing and control work processes.

Tomasko (1993: 20–22) suggested that for process reengineering to be successfully implemented in the design of new organizational structures and work processes, it requires five steps: These are:

1. Seize control of the process by giving it to those individuals who have the authority and expertise to make work process changes.
2. Map out the process by defining the necessary required steps needed to achieve the final result.
3. Eliminate sources of friction by forming cross-functional teams that will coordinate the change program.
4. Close the loop by being selective on the number of feasibility studies and plans that have to be conducted to facilitate new technique adoption.

5. Don't drop the ball after changes have been realized, but adopt a continuous reengineering approach to retool and avoid slow-down of the changes that have already been accomplished.

Similarly, Davenport (1993a: 25) has listed a five-step approach to process innovation. These include:

1. Identifying processes for innovation.
2. Identifying change levels.
3. Developing process visions.
4. Understanding existing processes.
5. Designing and prototyping new processes.

The process reengineering and innovation steps outlined by both Tomasko (1993) and Davenport (1993a) are combined into the following five steps to reorganize accounting control and internal auditing systems. They are:

1. Identifying processes for innovation and seizing control of the process.
2. Mapping the processes.
3. Formation of cross-functional area teams.
4. Closing the loop.
5. Adopting a continuous process reengineering approach.

The following sections apply these steps to study internal auditing and control processes.

## IDENTIFYING PROCESSES FOR INNOVATION AND SEIZING CONTROL OF THE PROCESSES

The first step in reengineering is to identify and list the major processes that require innovation changes and assign authoritative expert individuals to these processes. Since top management initiates process innovative changes, they reflect management's priority and strategic vision for future changes. It is necessary that management seizes control of the processes to filter them down through the organizational hierarchy.

In internal auditing, identification and enumeration of innovative processes deal with operating audit services that support a company's overall internal control environment. The first priority is to identify those areas that require improvement of the reporting process to various customers of the internal audit department. The use of state of the art computerized information systems (CIS) is required to develop and continually monitor organizational control systems. Conducting a quality assurance review program ensures the information received by customer groups is timely and relevant for decision-making purposes. The internal auditing processes are broadly defined to include reporting requirements, information systems management, customer relationships and feedback, and evaluating the service outcome of the internal auditing and control function services.

While these processes specifically deal with operational audits, they have implications on the staffing and management of audit services. On the management side, enumeration of these processes needs to address changes in hierarchy levels of auditing personnel, impact of CIS on personnel cuts and downsizing, and the positioning of the internal auditing function in the organizational structure.

However, the question arises whether or not the present structure would enable the internal auditing staff to seize control of the change process. Traditionally, accountants and internal auditors occupy staff instead of line positions, and their roles have been limited to the provision of expert advice to organizational line managers. Reengineering requires rethinking the importance of accountants' role as organizational change agents, by improving their status from staff to active participants in line decision-making processes, similar to that of marketing and production managers. According to Ross, the revolution in management control necessitated by information technology, has required changes in accountants' positions in organizations, i.e. "positions management accountants to be senior participants on the management team rather than staff accountants" (1990: 27). Vondra and Schueler suggest there is a need to give organizational visibility to the internal audit function by having internal auditors "report to the CEO [Chief Executive Officer] or president instead of to the CFO [Chief Financial Officer]." This will "make internal audit[ing] a part of ... corporate management structure" [and] "encourage proactive participation in the process of improving productivity and delivering a high-quality product" (1993: 36).

## MAPPING THE PROCESSES

Mapping internal audit operating processes involves defining the necessary steps with a schedule of timetables needed to achieve the final result. Operating audits are easily amenable to a step-by-step definition of required processes. Appendix 5 does not attempt to provide a cookbook recipe for defining the steps involved in operating audit process implementation. Rather, it identifies those factors that have to be considered as part of operating audit process mapping. This refers to the determination of process boundaries as well as an assessment of their strategic relevance for the organization (Davenport, 1993a: 30–34).

A process perspective examines the inter-relationships and linkages of the internal auditing function with various organizational activities across all functional areas of management. Any planned change in the audit process is likely to affect the workflow of various organizational activities. Under these circumstances, it is necessary to define the process boundaries in terms of where they start and end. While the definition of a process boundary is artificial and arbitrary, it enables internal auditors to better manage the process from beginning to end. It allows auditors to visualize if the completion of one process gives rise to another process, or whether there is a need to reinvent new or modify existing processes.

Adamec (1994) described the interactive role of process audit changes as follows: "hence, one method change in internal auditing practice can improve operational auditing results is to focus on processes, rather than departments, tasks, or functions. Full scope business process reviews can allow systematic coverage of entire business organizations and can move the internal auditing department from a reactive mode for a small portion of an organization to a proactive one which considers all relevant activities during an audit" (p. 11). A business process perspective considers audit process changes as they affect the organization's internal control environment. A map of the audit process beginning and ending with a clear definition of boundaries, if supplemented with an assessment of its strategic relevance, will help accomplish targeted process results.

The strategic relevance "suggests that the scope of the innovation effort should be based on an organization's capabilities and resources" (Davenport 1993a: 31). An internal auditing inventory of resources includes people, technology (computers), funds, as well as time to start and complete audit process changes. Moreover, it requires an analysis of whether the organization's top management supports the process innovation changes and which of the processes they are willing to get involved with sponsoring, coordinating and communicating the processes. According to Davenport, "the most obvious approach to process selection is to select the processes most central to accomplishing the organization's strategy" (1993a: 32). Process selection by definition implies that some processes that do not add incremental value to the auditing process will be eliminated.

Issac (1993), in his study of mortgage loans, emphasized the importance of process selection as follows:

> By analyzing existing process flows, companies are able to identify redundant or costly steps that could be eliminated or improved. Once the process is streamlined, the cost reductions can be passed on to the customer in the form of reduced mortgage rates. As a result, these companies are able to lower pricing without reducing profit margins. At the

same time, the improved process flow creates an environment with fewer mistakes and better customer response. This translates into a better corporate image (p. 75).

Once the process is selected, the goal is to ensure a committed sponsor will carry the chosen process from beginning to end through the cultural, social, economic and political climate of the organization. It is suggested that top management, such as the CEO or president, sponsor internal auditing process changes to ensure changes can be accepted and implemented throughout the organization.

# FORMATION OF CROSS-FUNCTIONAL AREA TEAMS

Process changes affect all organization operations. The process view assumes a broad view of internal auditing and control, which affects all organizational processes that managers use/influence to achieve organizational objectives. In spite of the internal auditing and control functions importance, the internal audit department or staff in most organizations is relatively small when compared to staff members in other functional areas of management such as production, marketing and finance. The question involves whether or not the internal auditing department has the required staff to successfully design and implement process audit changes in an organization. Such changes are not likely to be accomplished, unless there is close collaboration with other functional area managers. In other words, the conventional paradigm of internal control, based on independence has to be replaced with a process paradigm, which calls for collaborative work relationships and committee/team work on audit process changes.

According to Davenport (1993a), teams serve as one of many kinds of structural enablers of process innovation. He listed several benefits for team approaches to innovation. First, teams combine several functional areas of expertise, information, skills and behavior into one group. Second, teams can improve the quality of work life by providing opportunities for social interactions and the development of friendships. Socialization of organization work norms and professional requirements can be facilitated through teams (pp. 96–99).

The formation and composition of team members is very critical for the success of process changes. Particularly, care has to be taken in the formation of cross-functional teams. The selection and composition mixes of team members have to be followed by a clear definition of their locations and boundaries within the organization's structure. It is essential to establish clear lines of communication and define the nature of dual reporting responsibilities between functional managers and teams. Since an internal auditing staff is normally small, staff members are less likely to have the required expertise to form cross-functional teams, and depend on the skills and knowledge of experts from other functional area managers. Under such circumstances, it is important that team members are carefully selected for their expertise and functional knowledge

This has to be supported by a well developed mission of the process that clearly defines the composition of functional team members, establishes process boundaries, and defines team roles and their decision-making authorities (Davenport, 1993a: 102–103). Process teams are more likely to be successful as change agents or interventionists, if they have clearly defined goals and purposes for their formation and enjoy the support and commitment of top management and executives.

Process teams are usually made up of experts that span traditional boundaries, defined in terms of divisions and/or departments with the purpose of planning and implementing process innovation changes throughout the organization's functional areas (Tomasko, 1993: 19–20). Thus, the formation of cross-functional internal auditing teams enables the impact assessment of process audit changes in other organizational work areas. The internal audit team can gather information, do all detailed plan work, define benchmarks, makes changes when necessary to the plan at the design stage and avoid potential implementation problems. The team can help elicit support for internal audit change programs through seminars, workshops, training, retreats, and other group facilitation activities such as brainstorming.

Brainstorming allows people to get involved in the process by providing them with the opportunity to ask questions about the process and understand the need for process changes. It encourages innovative and creative thinking, where team members can generate alternative ideas/plans and can suggest ways of improving or changing existing internal audit work activities to reduce costs, personnel and time. Such dialogue and interaction among team members will improve communication, understanding and create a cooperative organization work climate. Teams assist in evaluating the viability of internal audit process changes and control systems and suggest innovative methods for future improvement.

## CLOSE THE LOOP

Close the loop refers to the logo that "becoming a fast cycle company involves mind-set-change as well as technique adoption. In reengineered businesses, the most common phrase you hear as an explanation for taking a certain course of action is 'Life is short'" (Tomasko, 1993: 21). In other words, an unnecessary period of time should not be wasted in implementing process engineering. In process changes, there is a tendency for teams, management and consultants to spend a great deal of time on feasibility studies that produce unnecessary volumes of studies and documents supported by appendices, graphs, charts and diagrams.

The extent of this problem has been noted by *Business Week*, August 8, 1994. "But at too many companies, it turns out, the push for quality can be as badly misguided as it is well-intended. It can be popular with managers and their consultants, but as at variant, it can evolve into a mechanistic exercise that proves meaningless to customers. And quality that means little to customers usually doesn't produce a payoff in improved sales, profits, or market share. It's wasted effort and expense" (pp. 54–55). As this quote implies, many companies have realized that management techniques have become very expensive. There has to be a limit as to the number of studies, consultants, seminars and retreats that a company can devote to institute a change process program. Unless management consultative studies are minimized, they are likely to cost more than they are worth, and might not pay off if measured in terms of the desired level of return on quality.

Thus, when an organization closes the loop, it becomes very selective by minimizing the number of feasibility studies, committee assignments, and group meetings in order to focus on those planned actions and programs that immediately put process changes into effect. This has significant implications on internal audit process studies where the emphasis is not on the number of studies, but rather on the significance of those studies and their effect on making planned process changes occur faster, while allowing the organization to save time, money and personnel costs. Audit processes that enable organization changes to happen faster are more likely to have a long lasting tenure.

If an organization wants to realize from a process innovative change program improved market position and profitability performance, speed and simplicity become verty critical. This requires a shorter time frame, which can be quantitatively and qualitatively measured through performance indicators (PI's). According to Fortuin, "a performance indicator is a variable indicating the effectiveness and/or efficiency, of a part or whole of the process or system against a given norm/target or plan" (1988: 3). He listed several performance indicators of effectiveness and efficiency, which describe the quality of information systems and services that are applicable to evaluate the quality of internal auditing services. Some of the performance indicators of effectiveness that are relevant to internal auditing include timeliness, currency (up-to-date), reliability, response/turnaround time, relevance, accuracy, completeness and flexibility. On the other hand, the PI's for efficiency comprise means of input/output, error recovery, understanding of the system, convenience of access, volume of output, documentation, flexibility and integration (Fortuin, 1988: 8).

Therefore, the ability of PI's to quantify organizational objectives allow managers to monitor the internal audit process change in such a manner that the required timetable to achieve target objectives becomes shorter and simpler. In other words, PI's ability to quantify organizational objectives and target internal audit innovation programs to achieve specific objectives, will allow managers to shorten the time frame and close the loop as fast as possible.

## ADOPT A CONTINUOUS PROCESS REENGINEERING APPROACH

Any process innovation including audit process changes is not likely to last indefinitely. Customer tastes, preferences and values change as technology improves and produces improved and/or new products and services. New developments in technology affect organizational structures, job configurations and work processes. Internal auditing has been continually changing over time, due to changes in information technology, computers and data processing.

Once implemented, audit process changes have to be followed up so that they are permanently in place. They need to be revised and continuously updated to keep pace with recent developments in technological innovations. However, there has been a realization that administrative innovations such as internal auditing and control are not constantly changing at the same pace and speed as technical process innovations in production and manufacturing technologies. That is, there are administrative innovation lags that hinder continual process innovation improvements in organizations. Many times, the potential benefits of administrative innovations are less observable to others and more complex to understand. They are perceived to bring relative advantage in terms of quantifiable measures of performance such as profitability indicators. They are less amenable to experiments on limited trial bases, which test the degree of innovation program risks (Dunk 1989).

Dunk (1989) argued that the theory of administrative innovation lag applies to explain the lag in accounting and control. Accounting and control systems are one of several types of formal control systems. Similarly, internal auditing control procedures confirm and support accounting and formal administrative/ management control systems. Internal auditing innovations are more likely to be "perceived as having lower relative advantage, since [they] would be difficult to quantify, particularly in the short term economic benefits that are likely to accrue from such innovations. Accounting innovations are also likely to be more complex, less trial-able and less observable than technical innovations" (Dunk, 1989: 152).

Dunk (1989) suggested that the problem in accounting lag might have created administrative and structural problems that have constrained the adoption of technical innovations. That is, without changes in administrative systems, the degree of adoption for new technical innovations in accounting and internal auditing control systems will be slower. It is possible that the formation of cross-functional internal audit process teams, that work cooperatively with other functional managers, including production/operations, could help minimize the administrative innovative lag of internal audit and control process changes.

At present, the focus of reengineering and process innovations is to minimize the administrative process innovation lag. There is a realization that an organization is more likely to adopt technical innovations faster, if supported by administrative innovations. Internal auditing process innovations, as an administrative process innovation strategy can trigger and accelerate adoption rates of technical organizational innovations. Therefore, a continuous reengineering and retooling of audit process changes that have already been implemented and occur in an organization is consistent with Tomasko's (1993) philosophy of "Don't Drop the Ball." Tomasko argued that once process-reengineering change happened, it didn't stop there, but rather continued to 'retool' or 'reengineer' the ball in order to invent a better new ball.

## REENGINEERING AND ORGANIZATIONAL DESIGN ISSUES

It was noted in Chapter 8 that total quality management (TQM) and continuous improvement programs have limited successes in improving organizational performance. The debate over TQM pitfalls brought a paradigm shift, which called for a radical surgery in the existing form of organizational structures, whether functional, product, or divisionalized structures. Radical surgery approaches have focused on new innovative methods of work processes involving reengineering and process innovative changes. Process innovative changes comprise technical innovations focusing on reengineering manufacturing and production processes, and administrative innovations dealing with internal control and auditing systems. The success of reengineering is thus contingent upon its ability and feasibility to be adapted and modified to meet internal auditing and control process change requirements.

Several writers have outlined a planned intervention strategy for designing and implementing process reengineering projects. Appendix 5 utilized a contingency approach to apply and adapt Davenport's (1993a) and Tomasko's (1993) five steps approach for the successful planning and implementing of internal audit process innovative changes. However, it needs to be noted that the theory of administrative innovations lags, suggests that internal auditing process reengineering changes are more likely to fall behind, compared to those technical innovation changes happening in manufacturing and production processes.

In spite of these limitations, the effect of reengineering is to dramatically alter the structure and work configuration processes of internal auditing and accounting control systems. The recent technological changes in computers, information technology and data processing have radically changed organizational structures, processes, administrative systems, and management control and internal auditing systems. Administrative innovation and reengineering the rate of adoption and diffusion are slower in internal auditing and control systems than that of technical innovations in manufacturing systems. Recently, there has been significant progress in business process reengineering projects in internal auditing and control functions.

The five steps required for process innovation and reengineering suggested by Davenport (1993a) and Tomasko (1993) are consistent with radical innovation change strategies. It is recommended that these five planned steps need to be followed sequentially and simultaneously, if the objective is for successful planning and implementation of internal audit process projects consistent with management's strategic vision, corporate mission, current business competitive needs and performance requirements.

# REFERENCES

AACSB (1991). *Critics nudge pendulum*. St. Louis, Missouri: American Assembly of Collegiate School of Business, Mimeo: Fall: 12–17.

Abernethy, M. A., & Chua, W. F. (1996). A field study of control system "redesign": The impact of institutional processes on strategic choice. *Contemporary Accounting Research, 13*(2), 596–606.

Ackoff, R. L., & Emery, F. E. (1972). *On Purposeful Systems*. Chicago: Aldine.

Adamec, B. A. (1994). Using process engineering in operational auditing. *Internal Auditing, 10*(1), 3–13.

Aldrich, H. E. (1979). *Organizations and Environment*. Englewood Cliffs, N.J.: Prentice-Hall.

Allen, T. H. (1978). *New Methods in Social Science Research*. New York: Prager.

Allison, G. T. (1971). *Essence of Decision: Explaining the Cuban Missile Crisis*. Boston: Little, Brown & Co.

Alter, C. (1990). An exploratory study of conflict and coordination in inter-organizational service delivery systems. *Academy of Management Journal, 33*(3), 478–502.

Alvesson, M. (1990). On the popularity of organizational culture. *Acta Sociologica, 33*(1), 31–49.

Amburgey, T. L., Kelly, D., & Barnett, W. P. (1993). Resetting the clock: The dynamics of organizational change and failure. *Administrative Science Quarterly, 38*(1), 51–73.

Anderson, S. W. (1995). A framework for assessing cost management system changes. The case of activity based costing implementation at General Motors, 1986–1993. *Journal of Management Accounting Research, 7* (Fall), 1–51.

Anderson, U. L. (1991). Quality assurance, total quality management, & the evaluation of the internal audit function. *Internal Auditing, 7*(2), 66–71.

Anthony, R. N., & Herzlinger, R. F. (1980). *Management Control in Nonprofit Organizations*. Homewood, Ill.: Irwin.

Argyris, C., & Schon, D. A. (1978). *Organizational Learning: A Theory of Action Perspective*. Reading, MA: Addison-Wesley.

Argyris, C., & Kaplan, R. S. (1994). Commentary- implementing new knowledge: The case of activity-based costing. *Accounting Horizons, 8*(3), 83–105.

Arlow, P., & Ulrich, T. A. (1988). A longitudinal survey of business school graduates' assessments of business ethics. *Journal of Business Ethics, 7*(4), 295–302.

Armstrong, M. B. (1990). Professional ethics and accounting education: A critique of the 8-step method. *Business and Professional Ethics Journal, 9*(1&2), 181–190.

Arno, A. (1985). Structural communication and control communication: An interactionist perspective on legal and customary procedures for conflict management. *American Anthropologist, 87*(1), 40–55.

Attewell, P. (1992). Technology diffusion and organizational learning: The case of business computing. *Organization Science, 3*(1), 1–19.

Baba, M. L., & Falkenburg, D. R. (1996). Technology management and American culture: Implications for business process redesign. *Research Technology Management, 39*(6), 44–54.

Bacharach, S. B., Bamberger, P., & Sonnenstuhl, W. J. (1996). The organizational transformation process: The micro-politics of dissonance reduction and the alignment of logic's of action. *Administrative Science Quarterly, 41*(3), 477–506.

Bailey, K. D. (1982). Post-functional social system analysis. *The Sociological Quarterly, 23*(4), 509–526.

Baiman, S. (1990). Agency research in managerial accounting: A second look. *Accounting, organizations and Society, 15*(4), 341–371.

Baiman, S. (1982). Agency research in managerial accounting: A survey. *Journal of Accounting Literature, 1*, 154–210.

Baker, H. K., Miller, T. O., & Ramsperger, B. J. (1981). An inside look at corporate mergers and acquisitions. *MSU Business Topics, 29*(1), 49–57.

Baker, W. E., Faulkner, R. R., & Fisher, G. A. (1998). Hazards of the market: The continuity and dissolution of inter-organizational market relationships. *American Sociological Review, 63*(2), 147–177.

Baligh, H. J. (1994). Components of culture: Nature, interconnections, & relevance in the decisions on the organization structure. *Management Science, 40*(1), 14–27.

Barfield, R. M., & Young, S. M. (1988). *Internal Auditing in a Just-in-Time Environment*. Altamonte Springs, Florida: The Institute of Internal Auditors, 1988.

Barker, J. (1993). Tightening the iron cage: Concertive control in self-managing teams. *Administrative Science Quarterly, 38*(3), 408–437.

Barnett, W. P., & Carroll, G. R. (1995). Modeling internal organizational change. *Annual Review of Sociology, 21*, 217–236.

Barney, J. B. (1988). Returns to bidding firms in mergers and acquisitions: Reconsidering the relatedness hypothesis. *Strategic Management Journal, 9* (Special), 71–78.

Barron, D. (1999). The structuring of organizational populations. *American Sociological Review, 64*(3), 421–445.

Basadur, M., & Robinson, S. (1993). The new creative thinking skills needed for total quality management to become fact, not just philosophy. *American Behavioral Scientist, 37*(1), 121–138.

Bass, B. M. (1983). Issues involved in relations between methodological rigor and reported outcomes in evaluations of organizational development. *Journal of Applied Psychology, 68*(1), 197–199.

Bassiry, G. S. (1990). Ethics, education, and corporate leadership. *Journal of Business Ethics, 9*(10), 799–805.

Bate, P. (1990). Using the culture concept in an organization development setting. *The Journal of Applied Behavioral Science, 26*(1), 83–106.

Beatty, R., & Ulrich, D. (1991). Reengineering the mature organization. *Organizational Dynamics, 20*(1), 16–30.

Beaujon, G. J., & Singhal, V. R. (1990). Understanding the activity costs in an activity-based cost system. *Journal of Cost Management, 4*(1), 51–72.

Beckett-Camarata, E. J., Camarata, M. R., & Barker, R. T. (1998). Integrating internal and external customer relationships through relationship management: A strategic response to a changing global environment. *Journal of Business Research, 41*(1), 71–81.

Beer, M. (1980). *Organization Change and Development: A Systems View*. Glenview, Ill.: Scott, Foresman & Company.

Beets, S. D., & Killough, L. N. (1990). The effectiveness of a complaint-based ethics enforcement system: Evidence from the accounting profession. *Journal of Business Ethics, 9*(2), 115–126.

Bhimani, A., & Bromwich, M. (1991). Accounting for just-in-time manufacturing systems. *CMA Magazine, 65*(1), 31–34.

Bing, G. (1980). *Corporate Acquisitions*. Houston: Gulf Publishing Company.

Birnberg, J. G. (1998). Some reflections on the evolution of organizational control. *Behavioral Research in Accounting*, Supplement 10, 27–46.

Blau, P. M., & Scott, W. R. (1962). *Formal Organizations*. San Francisco: Chandler.

Bodnar, G. H. (1994). Business reengineering projects. *Internal Auditing, 9*(4), 59–63.

Boeker, W. (1989a). The development and institutionalization of sub-unit power in organizations. *Administrative Science Quarterly, 34*(3), 388–410.

Boeker, W. (1989b). Strategic change: The effects of founding and history. *Academy of Management Journal, 32*(3), 489–515.

Boulding, K. L. (1968). General systems theory: The skeleton of science. In: W. Buckley (Ed.), *In Modern Systems Research for the Behavioral Scientist* (pp. 1–10). Chicago: Aldine.

Bower, J. L. (1970). *Managing the Resource Allocation Process*. Boston: Harvard University, Graduate School of Business Administration.

Bradshaw-Camball, P. (1989). The implications of multiple perspectives on power for organization development. *The Journal of Applied Behavioral Science, 25*(1), 31–44.

Brass, D. J., & Burkhadt, M. E. (1993). Potential power and power use: An investigation of structure and behavior. *Academy of Management Journal, 36*(3), 441–470.

Braum, P., Dittmar, H., Hoover, J., Murray, D., Siwek, S., Stanley, R., & Younger, K. (1994). *ISTEA Planner's Workbook.* Washington, D.C.: Prepared for surface Transportation Policy Project, Mimeo, October.

Brecht, H. D., & Martin, M. P. (1996). Accounting information systems. The challenge of extending their scope to business and information strategy. *Accounting Horizons, 10*(4), 16–22.

Brenan, M. (1992). Mismanagement and quality circles: How middle managers inflect direct participation. *Management Decision, 30*(6), 35–45.

Brimson, J. A. (1998). Feature costing: Beyond ABC. *Journal of Cost Management, 12*(1), 6–12.

Brown, S. L., & Eisenhardt, K. M. (1997). The art of continuous change: Linking complexity theory and time-paced evolution in relentlessly shifting organizations. *Administrative Science Quarterly, 42*(1), 1–34.

Brynjolfsson, E., Renshaw, A. A., & Alstyne, M. V. (1997). The matrix of change. *Sloan Management Review, 38*(2), 37–54.

Buckley, W. (1967). *Sociology and Modern Systems Theory.* Englewood Cliffs, N.J.: Prentice-Hall.

Buchowicz, B. (1990). Cultural transition and attitude change. *Journal of General Management, 15*(4), 45–55.

Buller, P. F., & McEvoy, G. M. (1989). Determinants of the institutionalization of planned organizational change. *Group and Organization Studies, 14*(1), 33–50.

Burgess, T. F. (1995). Systems and reengineering: relating the reengineering paradigm to systems methodologies. *Systems Practice, 8*(6), 591–603.

Burke, W. W., & Litwin, G. H. (1992). A casual model of organizational performance and change. *Journal of Management, 18*(3), 525–545.

Burns, T., & Stalker, G. M. (1961). *The Management of Innovation.* London: Tavistock.

Burns, W. J., & DeCoster, D. T. (1969). *Accounting and Its Behavioral Implications.* New York: McGraw Hill.

Burt, S. (1987). Social contagion and innovation: Cohesion versus structural equivalence. *American Journal of Sociology, 92*(6), 1287–1335.

*Business Week* (1994). *Quality: How to make it pay.* August 8: 54–59.

Butler, J. E. (1988). Theories of technological innovation as useful tools for corporate strategy. *Strategic Management Journal, 9*(1), 15–29.

Campion, M. A., Medsker, G. J., & Higgs, A. C. (1993). Relations between work group characteristics and effectiveness: Implications for designing effective work groups. *Personnel Psychology, 46*(4), 823–850.

Caplan, E. H. (1966). Behavioral assumptions of management accounting. *The Accounting Review, 41*(3), 496–509.

Carroll, G. R. (1984). Organizational ecology. *Annual Review of Sociology, 10*, 71–93.

Cashell, J. D., & Presutti, A. H. (1992). Using activity-based costing to search for operational inefficiencies. *Internal Auditing, 8*(1), 18–30.

Castro, B. (1989). Business ethics and business education, A report from a regional state university. *Journal of Business Ethics*, 8(6), 479–488.

Cavallo, R. (1982). *Methodology in Social Science Research, Recent Developments*. Boston: Klwver-Nijhoff Publishing.

Chapman, C. S. (1997). Reflections on a contingent view of accounting. *Accounting Organizations and Society*, 22(2), 189–205.

Chatterjee, R., & Eliashberg, J. (1990). The innovation diffusion process in a heterogeneous population, A micro-modeling approach. *Management Science*, 36(9), 1057–1079.

Checkland, P. B. (1981). *Systems Thinking, Systems Practice*. Chichester: Wiley.

Child, J. (1970). Organizational structure, environment and performance, The role of strategic choice. *Sociology*, 6 (January), 1–22.

Child, J., & Smith, C. (1987). The context and process of organizational transformation-cadbury limited in its sector. *Journal of Management Studies*, 24(6), 565–593.

Christensen, C. R., Andrews, K. R., & Bower, J. L. (1982). *Business Policy, Text and Cases*. Homewood, Ill.: Richard D. Irwin, Inc., 5th ed.

Christofi, P., & Sisaye, S. (1992). *Total Quality Management (TQM), Implications for Management Accounting Systems*. Paper presented at the 1992 Annual Meeting of the American Accounting Association Mid-Atlantic Region. Pittsburgh, PA. April.

Churchman, C. W. (1979). *The Systems Approach and Its Enemies*. New York: Basic Books.

Churchman, C. W. (1968). *The Systems Approach*. New York: Delacorte Press.

Cigler, B. A., Jansen, A. C., Ryan, V. D. & Stabler, J. C. (1994). *Toward an Understanding of Multi-community Collaboration*. Washington, D.C.: U.S. Department of Agriculture, Economic Research Service, Agriculture and Rural Economy Division, Mimeo., February.

Clancy, T. (1994a). Radical surgery, A view from the operating theater. *Academy of Management Executive*, 8(2), 73–78.

Clancy, T. (1994b). Executive voice, The latest word from thoughtful executives. *Academy of Management Executive*, 8(2), 8–10.

Claypool, G. A., Fetyko, D. F., & Pearson, M. A. (1990). Reactions to ethical dilemmas. A study pertaining to certified public accountants. *Journal of Business Ethics*, 9(9), 699–706.

Cobb, A. T., & Margulies, N. (1981). Organization development, A political perspective. *Academy of Management Review*, 6(1), 49–59.

Coburn, S., Grove, H., & Ortega, W. (1998). Business Process Reengineering using activity-based management. *Journal of Cost Management*, 12(5), 41–47.

Conner, R. C. Jr. (1992). A success formula, IA (Internal Audit) + TQM (Total Quality Management) = AS (Audit Services). *Internal Auditor*, 49(2), 33–36.

Cool, K. O., Dierickz, I., & Szulanski, G. (1997). Diffusion of innovations within organizations, Electronic switching in the bell system, 1971–1982. *Organization Science*, 8(5), 543–559.

Cooper, R., & Kaplan, R. S. (1998). The promise-and peril- of integrated cost systems. *Harvard Business Review, 76*(4), 109–119.

Cronin, J. J., & Taylor, S. A. (1992). Measuring service quality, A re-examination and extension. *Journal of Marketing, 56*(3), 55–68.

Crosby, P. Associates, Inc. (1988). *Quality education system for the individual.* Winter Park, Florida: P. Crosby Associates Inc. Mimeo.

Cunningham, G. M. (1992). Management control and accounting systems under a competitive strategy. *Accounting, Auditing & Accountability Journal, 5*(2), 85–102.

Cupello, J. M. (1994). A new paradigm for measuring TQM progress. *Quality Progress, 27*(5), 79–82.

Daft, R. L. (1978). A dual-core model of organizational innovation. *Academy of Management Journal, 21*(2), 193–210.

Daghfous, A., & White, G. R. (1994). Information and innovation, A comprehensive representation. *Research Policy, 23*(3), 267–280.

Dale, B. G., & Cooper, C. L. (1991). Introducing TQM, The role of senior management. *Management Decision, 30*(6), 20–26.

Damanpour, F. (1987). The adoption of technological, administrative, and ancillary innovations, Impact of organizational factors. *Journal of Management, 13*(4), 675–688.

Damanpour, F., & Evan, W. M. (1984). Organizational innovation and performance, The problem of 'organizational lag'. *Administrative Science Quarterly, 29*(3), 392–409.

Datta, D. K. (1986). *Assimilation of acquired organizations.* Unpublished Ph.D. dissertation, University of Pittsburgh.

Davelaar, E. J., & Nijkamp, P. (1990). Technological innovation and spatial transformation. *Technological Forecasting and Social Change, 37*(2), 181–202.

Daveni, R., & Kesner, I. (1993). Top managerial prestige, power and tender offer response, A study of elite social networks and target firm cooperation during takeovers. *Organization Science, 4*(2), 123–151.

Davenport, T. H. (1994). On tomorrow's organizations, Moving forward, or a step backwards. *Academy of Management Executive, 8*(3), 93–95.

Davenport, T. H. (1993a). *Process Innovation, Reengineering Work Through Information Technology.* Boston: Harvard Business School Press.

Davenport, T. H. (1993b). Need radical innovation and continuous improvement? Integrate process reengineering and TQM. *Planning Review, 21*(3), 6–12.

David, F. R., Anderson, L. M., & Laurimore, K. (1990). Perspectives on business ethics in management education. *SAM Advanced Management Journal, 55*(4), 26–32.

Davidson, K. (1991). Why acquisitions may not be the best route to innovation. *Journal of Business Strategy, 12*(3), 50–73.

Davidson, W. H. (1993). Beyond re-engineering, The three phases of business transformation. *IBM Systems Journal, 32*(1), 65–79.

Davis, T. R. (1993). Reengineering in action. *Planning Review, 21*(6), 49–54.

Dean, J. W., & Sharfman, M. P. (1993). The relationship between procedural rational and political-behavior in strategic decision-making. *Decision Sciences, 24*(6), 1069–1083.

Delano, J. E. K. (1994). On tomorrow's organizations, Moving forward, or a step backwards. *Academy of Management Executive, 8*(3), 95–98.

Deluga, R. J., & Perry, J. T. (1994). The role of subordinate performance and ingratiation in leader-member exchanges. *Group & Organization Management, 19*(1), 67–86.

Deming, W. E. (1986). *Out of the Crisis.* Cambridge, MA: MIT Center for Advanced Engineering Study.

Department of Commerce, U.S. (1997). *Malcolm Baldrige National Quality Award, 1997 Criteria for Performance.* Washington, D.C.: National Institute of Standards Technology. Mimeo.

Department of Commerce, U.S. (1993). *The Malcolm Baldrige National Quality Award.* Washington, D.C., mimeo.

Department of Commerce, U.S. (1987). *The Malcolm Baldrige National Quality Improvement Act of 1987 – Public Law 100–107.* Washington, D.C., mimeo.

Dewar, R. D., & Dutton, J. E. (1986). The adoption of radical and incremental innovations, An empirical analysis. *Management Science, 32*(1), 1422–1433.

Dietz, T., & Burns, T. R. (1992). Human agency and the evolutionary dynamics of culture. *Acta Sociologica, 35*(3), 187–200.

Dirsmith, M. W. (1998). Accounting and control as solutions to technical problems, political exchanges and forms of social disclosure, The importance of substantive domain. *Behavioral Research in Accounting*, Supplement 10, 65–77.

Dirsmith, W. M., & McAllister, J. P. (1982). The organic vs. the mechanistic audit. *Journal of Accounting, Auditing and Finance, 5*(3), 214–228.

Dixon, J. R., Arnold, P., Heineke, J. L., Kinn, J. S., & Mulligan, P. (1994). Business process reengineering, improving in new strategic directions. *California Management Review, 36*(4), 93–108.

Dobson, J. (1992). Ethics in financial contracting. *Business and Professional Ethics Journal, 11* (Fall–Winter), 93–127.

Donaldson, L. (1987). Strategy and structural adjustment to regain fit and performance, In defense of contingency theory. *Journal of Management Studies, 24*(1), 1–24.

Donaldson, T., & Dunfee, T. W. (1994). Toward a unified conception of business ethics, Integrative social contracts theory. *Academy of Management Review, 19*(2), 252–284.

Donnelly, W. J., & Miller, G. A. (1989). The Treadway Commission for Education, Professors' opinions. *Business and Professional Ethics Journal, 8*(4), 83–92.

Drake, A. R., Haka, S. F., & Ravenscroft, S. P. (1999). Cost system and incentive structure effects on innovation, efficiency and profitability in teams. *The Accounting Review, 74*(3), 323–345.

Drucker, P. E. (1995). Redesigning the corporation requires a new set of tools and concepts, The information executives need. *Harvard Business Review, 73*(1), 54–63.

Drucker, P. E. (1992). The new society of organizations. *Harvard Business Review, 70*(5), 95–104.

Drucker, P. E. (1990). The emerging theory of manufacturing. *Harvard Business Review, 68*(3), 94–102.

Duberman, L. (1990). When internal growth is the goal. *Financial Executive, 6*(2), 24–27.

Duck, J. D. (1993). Managing change-the art of balancing. *Harvard Business Review, 71*(6), 109–118.

Dugger, W. M. (1988). An institutional analysis of corporate power. *Journal of Economic Issues, 22*(1), 79–111.

Duncan, O. D. (1961). From social system to ecosystem. *Sociological Quarterly, 21*(1), 140–149.

Dunk, A. S. (1989). Management accounting lag. *ABACUS, 25*(2), 149–154.

Dunphy, D. C. (1988). Transformational and coercive strategies for planned organizational change, Beyond the O. D. Model. *Organization Studies, 9*(3), 317–334.

Dunphy, D., & Stace, D. (1993). The strategic management of corporate change. *Human Relations, 46*(8), 905–919.

Dutta, S., & Manzoni, J. (1999). *Process Reengineering, Organizational Change and Performance Improvement*. London: McGraw-Hill Publishing Company.

Eckstein, R., & Delaney, K. (1993). Institutional investment patterns in troubled corporations, A sociological analysis. *American Journal of Economics and Sociology, 52*(3), 291–306.

Eisenhardt, K. M., & Bourgeois III, L. J. (1988). Politics of strategic decision making in high-velocity environments, Toward a midrange theory. *Academy of Management Journal, 31*(4), 737–770.

Eisner, R. A. (1990). Managing for quality, A self-assessment. *Trends and Development*. R. A. Eisner and Company. Mimeo, July.

Erickson, R. A. (1994). Technology, industrial restructuring, and regional development. *Growth and Change, 25*(3), 353–379.

Evans, J. H. (1998). Cost management and management control in health care organizations, Recent opportunities. *Behavioral Research in Accounting*, Supplement 10, 78–93; *Excellence*, 15–19.

Ezzamel, M., & Wilmott, H. (1998). Accounting for teamwork: A critical study of group-based systems of organizational control. *Administrative Science Quarterly, 43*(2), 358–396.

Farrell, D., & Peterson, J. C. (1982). Patterns of political behavior in organizations. *Academy of Management Review, 7*(3), 403–412.

Fayol, H. (1949). *General and Industrial Management*. London: Pitman & Sons.

Feldman, S. (1988). How organizational culture can affect innovation. *Organizational Dynamics, 17*(1), 57–68.

Feldman, S. (1986). Management in context: An essay on the relevance of culture to the understanding of organizational change. *Journal of Management Studies, 23*(6), 587–607.

Fennell, M. L., & Alexander, J. A. (1987). Organizational boundary spanning in institutionalized environments. *Academy of Management Journal, 30*(3), 456–476.

Fisher, J. (1998). Contingency theory, management control systems, & firm outcomes: Past results and future directions. *Behavioral Research in Accounting,* Supplement 10, 47–64.

Fisher, J. (1995). Contingency-based research on management control systems. Categorization by level of complexity. *Journal of Accounting Literature, 9,* 24–53.

Fligstein, N. (1987). The intra-organizational power struggle: Rise of finance personnel to top leadership in large corporations, 1919–1979. *American Sociological Review, 52*(1), 44–58.

Flynn, B. B., Sakakibara, S., & Schroeder, R. G. (1995). Relationship between JIT and TQM: Practices and Performance. *Academy of Management Journal, 38*(5), 1325–1360.

Fooks, H. (1991). *Total quality management at Westinghouse Corporation.* Paper presented at the World Class Quality Winning in Western Pennsylvania Conference. Pittsburgh: Duquesne University, May.

Fortuin, L. (1988). Performance indicators-why, where and how. *European Journal of Operational Research, 34,* 1–9.

Foucault, M. (1983). The subject and power. In: C. Gordon (Ed.), *Power/Knowledge: Selected Interviews and Other Writings* (pp. 78–108). New York: Pantheon.

Fray, L. L., Gaylin, D. H., & Down, J. W. (1984). Successful acquisition planning. *Journal of Business Strategy, 5*(1), 46–55.

French, J. R. P. Jr., & Raven, B. (1962). The bases of social power. In: D. Cartwright (Ed.), *Group Dynamics: Research and Theory* (pp. 607–613). Evanston, Ill.: Row, Peterson.

French, W. L., & Bell, C. H. Jr. (1984). *Organization Development: Behavioral Science Intervention For Organizational Improvement* (3rd ed.). Englewood Cliffs, NJ: Prentice-Hall.

French, W. L., & Bell, C. H. Jr. (1978). *Organization Development: Behavioral Science Interventions for Organization Improvement* (2nd ed.). Englewood Cliffs, N.J.: Prentice-Hall.

Frigo, R., & Robert, J. (1993). GE's financial services operation achieves quality results through workout process. *National Productivity Review, 13*(1), 53–56.

Frisbie, W. B., Krivo, L. J., Kaufman, R. L., Clarke, C. J., & Myers, D. E. (1984). A measurement of technological change: An ecological perspective. *Social Forces, 62*(3), 750–765.

Fruytier, B. (1996). The redesign dialogue: Organizational change and the theory of autopoietic systems. *Economic and Industrial Democracy, 17*(3), 327–357.

Galbraith, J. K. (1967). *The New Industrial State*. Boston, MA: Houghton Mifflin.

Garvin, D. A. (1991). How the Baldrige Award really works. *Harvard Business Review*, 69(6), 80–93.

Garvin, D. A. (1986). Quality problems, policies, and attitudes in the United States and Japan: An exploratory Study. *Academy of Management Journal*, 29(4), 653–673.

Garvin, D. A. (1984). What does 'Product Quality' really mean? *Sloan Management Review*, 26(1), 25–43.

Giddens, A. (1987). *Social Theory and Modern Sociology*. Cambridge: Polity Press.

Ginter, P. M., & White, D. M. (1982). A social learning approach to strategic management: Toward a theoretical foundation. *Academy of Management Review*, 7(2), 253–261.

Goldstein, F. (1987). Auditing: Facets of quality control. *CPA Journal*, (May), 98–101.

Goolrick, R. M. (1978). *Public Policy toward Corporate Growth: The ITT Merger Cases*. London: Kennikat Press Corp.

Gort, M., & Konakayama, A. (1982). A model of diffusion in the production of an innovation. *The American Economic Review*, 72(5), 1111–1120.

Gort, M., & Will, R. A. (1986). The evolution of technologies and investment in innovation. *The Economic Journal*, 96 (September), 741–757.

Gosselin, M. (1997). The effect of strategy and organizational structure on the adoption and implementation of activity-based costing. *Accounting, Organizations and Society*, 22(2), 105–122.

Grant, J. H. (Ed) (1988). *Strategic Management Frontiers*. Greenwich, CT: JAI Press Inc.

Grant, J. H., & King, W. R. (1982). *The Logic of Strategic Planning*. Boston: Little, Brown & Company.

Grattet, R., Jenness, V. & Curry, T. R. (1998). The homogenization and differentiation of hate crime law in the United States, 1978 to 1995: Innovation and diffusion in the criminalization of bigotry. *American Sociological Review*, 63(2), 286–307.

Gray, B. (1985). Conditions facilitating inter-organizational collaboration. *Human Relations*, 38(10), 911–936.

Green, S. G., Gavin, M. B., & Aiman-Smith, L. (1995). Assessing a multidimensional measure of radical technological innovation. *IEEE Transactions on Engineering Management*, 42(3), 203–214.

Gulden, G. K., & Reck, R. H. (1992). Combining quality and reengineering efforts for process excellence. *Information Strategy: The Executive Journal*, 8(3), 10–17.

Halpren, R. (1983). Corporate acquisitions: A theory of special cases? A Review of Event Studies Applied to Acquisitions. *Journal of Finance*, 38(2), 297–317.

Hambrick, D. C. (1987). The top management team: Key to strategic success. *California Management Review*, 30(1), 88–108.

Hamilton, E. E. (1988). The facilitation of organizational change: An empirical study of factors predicting change agents' effectiveness. *The Journal of Applied Behavioral Science*, 24(1), 37–59.

Hammer, M. (1990). Reengineering work: Don't automate, obliterate. *Harvard Business Review, 68*(4), 104–112.

Hammer, M., & Champy, J. (1993). *Reengineering the Corporation: A Manifesto for Business Revolution.* New York: Harper Business Publications.

Hannan, M. T., & Freeman, J. (1984). Structural inertia and organizational change. *American Sociological Review, 49*(1), 149–164.

Hannan, M. T., & Freeman, J. (1977). The population ecology of organizations. *American Journal of Sociology, 82*(3), 929–964.

Harrington, H. J., with Harrington, J. S. (1995). *Total Improvement Management: The Next Generation.* New York: McGraw-Hill.

Harrison, D. B., & Pratt, M. D. (1993). A methodology for reengineering businesses. *Planning Review, 21*(2), 7–8.

Hatch, M. J. (1993). The dynamics of organizational culture. *Academy of Management Review, 18*(4), 657–693.

Haveman, H. A. (1992). Between a rock and a hard place: Organizational change and performance under conditions of fundamental environmental transformation. *Administrative Science Quarterly, 37*(1), 48–75.

Hawley, D. D. (1991). Business ethics and social responsibility in financial instruction: An abdication of responsibility. *Journal of Business Ethics, 10*(9), 711–721.

Henderson, V. E. (1988). Can business ethics be taught? *Management Review, 77*(8), 52–54.

Hermanson, R., Plunkett, L., & Turner, D. (1990). Mergers among the big eight accounting firms: Some antitrust policy considerations. *Corporate Growth Report, 8*(3), 12–15.

Hiltebeitel, K. M., & Jones, S. K. (1992). An assessment of ethics instruction in accounting education. *Journal of Business Ethics, 11*(1), 37–46.

Hise, R. (1991). Evaluating marketing assets in mergers and acquisitions. *Journal of Business Strategy, 12*(4), 46–51.

Hitt, M. A., & Ireland, R. D. (1986). Relationships among corporate level distinctive competencies, diversification strategy, corporate structure and performance. *Journal of Management Studies, 23*(4), 401–416.

Hollander, P. E., & Offerman, L. R. (1990). Power and leadership in organizations: Relationships in transition. *American Psychologist, 45*(2), 175–189.

Horngren, C. T., & Foster, G. (1991). *Cost Accounting: A Managerial Emphasis* (7th ed.). Englewood Cliffs, New Jersey: Prentice-Hall.

Hosmer, L. T. (1988). Adding ethics to the business curriculum. *Business Horizons, 6* (July–August), 9–15.

Housel, T., & Kanevsky, V. (1995). Reengineering business processes: A complexity theory approach to value added. *Infor, 33*(4), 248–262.

Howe, M. A. (1989). Using imagery to facilitate organizational development and change. *Group and Organization Studies, 14*(1), 70–82.

Howell, J. M., & Higgins, C. A. (1990). Champions of technological innovation. *Administrative Science Quantity, 35*(2), 317–341.

Howells, J. (1995). A socio-cognitive approach to innovation. *Research Policy, 24*(6), 883–894.

Hrebiniak, L. G., & Joyce, W. F. (1985). Organizational adaptation: strategic choice and environmental determinism. *Administrative Science Quarterly, 30*(3), 336–349.

Hull, F., & Hage, J. (1982). Organizing for innovation: Beyond Burns and Stalker's organic type. *Sociology, 16*(4), 564–577.

Huss, H. F., & Patterson, D. M. (1993). Ethics in accounting: Values education without indoctrination. *Journal of Business Ethics, 12*(3), 235–243.

Ibarra, H. (1993). Network centrality, power and innovation involvement: Determinants of technical and administrative roles. *Academy of Management Journal, 38*(3), 471–501.

Inkeles, A., & Smith, D. H. (1974). *Becoming Modern.* Cambridge, MA: Harvard University Press.

Issac, S. (1993). A profitable management tool. *Mortgage Banking, 54*(2), 75.

Jauch, L. R., & Osborn, R. N. (1981). Toward an integrated theory of strategy. *Academy of Management Review, 6*(3), 491–498.

Jemison, D. B. (1981). The contributions of administrative behavior to strategic management. *Academy of Management Review, 6*(4): 633–642.

Jemison, D. B., & Sitkin, S. B. (1986). Corporate acquisitions: A process perspective. *Academy of Management Review, 11*(1), 145–163.

Jensen, R. (1983). Innovation adoption and diffusion when there are competing innovations. *Journal of Economic Theory, 29*(1), 161–171.

Johns, G. (1993). Constraints on the adoption of psychology based personnel practices: Lessons from organizational innovation. *Personnel Psychology, 46*(3), 569–592.

Johnson, H. T. (1993). To achieve quality, you must think quality. *Financial Executive, 9*(3), 9–12.

Johnson, H. T. (1992a). *Relevance Regained: From Top-Down Control to Bottom-up Empowerment.* New York: The Free Press.

Johnson, H. T. (1992b). It is time to stop overselling activity-based concepts: Start focusing on total customer satisfaction instead. *Management Accounting, 74*(3), 26–35.

Johnson, H. T., & Kaplan, R. S. (1987). *Relevance Lost: The Rise and Fall of Management Accounting.* Boston: Harvard Business School Press.

Kabanoff, B. (1991). Equity, equality, power, & conflict. *Academy of Management Review, 16*(2), 416–441.

Kanter, R. M. (1989). Management accounting for advanced technological environments. *Science, 245* (August 25). 19–23.

Kanter, R. M. (1983). *The Change Masters.* New York: Simon and Schuster.

Kanter, R. M. (1977). *Men and Women of the Corporation.* New York: Basic Books.

Kaplan, R. S. (1991). New systems for measurement and control. *The Engineering Economist, 36*(3), 201–218.

Kaplan, R. S. (1989). Management accounting for advanced technological environments. *Science,* (August 25), 19–23.

Katz, D., & Khan, R. L. (1978). *The Social Psychology of Organizations*. New York: Wiley.

Katz, D., & Khan, R. L. (1969). Common characteristics of open systems. In: F. E. Emery (Ed.), *Systems Thinking: Selected Readings*. Baltimore, MD: Penguin Books.

Keeton, K. B., & Mengistu, B. (1992). The perception of organizational culture by management level: Implications for training and development. *Public Productivity and Management Review, 16*(2), 205–213.

Kemper, T. D., & Collins, R. (1990). Dimensions of micro-interaction. *American Journal of Sociology, 96*(1), 32–68.

Kerr, J., & Slocum, J. W. Jr. (1987). Managing corporate culture through reward systems. *Academy of Management Executive, 1*(2), 99–108.

Kierulff, H. E. (1981). Finding the best acquisition candidates. *Harvard Business Review, 59*(1), 66–68.

Kilmann, R. H. (1984). *Beyond the Quick Fix*. San Francisco: Jossey-Bass Pub.

Kimberly, J. R., & Bouchikhi, H. (1995). The dynamics of organizational development and change: How the past shapes the present and constrains the future. *Organization Science, 6*(1), 9–18.

Kiser, E., & Hechter, M. (1991). The role of general theory in comparative sociology. *American Journal of Sociology, 97*(1), 1–30.

Krajewski, L. J., & Ritzman, L. P. (1990). *Operations Management: Strategy and Analysis* (2nd ed.). Reading, Massachusetts: Addison-Wesley Publishing Co.

Krone, R. M. (1980). *Systems Analysis and Policy Sciences: Theory and Practice*. New York: Wiley.

Krovi, R. (1993). Identifying the causes of resistance to IS implementation: A change theory perspective. *Information & Management, 25*(6), 327–335.

Kuhn, T. S. (1970). *The Structure of Scientific Revolutions*. Chicago: University of Chicago Press.

Lampe, L. C., &. Sutton, S. G. (1992). An application of quality circles to measuring bank audit quality. *Internal Auditing, 7*(4), 24–38.

Lampe, L. C., &. Sutton, S. G. (1991). Integrated productivity and quality measures for internal audit departments. *Internal Auditing, 7*(2), 51–65.

Lamude, K. G., & Scudder, J. (1993). Compliance gaining techniques of type a managers. *The Journal of Business Communication, 30*(1), 63–79.

Langfield-Smith, K. (1997). Management control-systems and strategy: A critical review. *Accounting, Organizations and Society, 22*(2), 207–232.

Lant, T. K., & Mezias, S. J. (1992). An organizational learning model of convergence and reorientation. *Organization Science, 3*(1), 47–71.

Laszlo, E. (1992). Information Technology and social change: An evolutionary analysis. *Behavioral Science, 37*(4), 237–249.

Lawler III, E. E. (1994). Total quality management and employee involvement: Are they compatible?. *Academy of Management Executive, 8*(1), 68–76.

Lawrence, P. R., & Lorsch, J. W. (1969). *Organization and Environment*. Homewood, Ill.: Richard D. Irwin, Inc.

Lawson, R. B., & Ventriss, C. L. (1992). Organizational change: The role of organizational culture and organizational learning. *The Psychology Record*, *42*(2), 205–219.

Laza, R. W., & Wheaton, P. L. (1990). Recognizing the pitfalls of total quality management. *Public Utilities Quarterly*, *125*(8), 17–21.

Lerner, D. (1958). *The Passing of Traditional Society*. New York: The Free Press.

Lewis, L. K., & Seibold, D. R. (1996). Communication during intra-organizational innovation adoption: Predicting users' behavioral coping responses to innovations in organizations. *Communication Monographs*, *63*(6), 131–157.

Litschert, R. J., & Bonham, T. W. (1978). A conceptual model of strategy formation. *Academy of Management Review*, *3*(2), 211–219.

Loeb, S. E. (1991). The evaluation of 'outcomes' of accounting ethics education. *Journal of Business Ethics*, *10*(2), 77–84.

Loeb, S. E. (1989). Ethics committees and consultants in public accounting firms? *Accounting Horizons*, *3*(4), 316–329.

Loeb, S. E. (1988). Teaching students accounting ethics: Some critical issues. *Issues in Accounting Education*, *3*(2), 316–329.

Loscalzo, M. (1988). Preparing for quality review. *CPA Journal*, *58*(12), 24–30.

Lubatkin, M. (1983). Mergers and the performance of the acquiring firm. *Academy of Management Review*, *8*(2), 218–225.

Lukka, K. (1998). Total accounting in action: Reflections on Sten Jonsson's accounting for improvement. *Accounting, Organizations and Society*, *25*(3), 333–342.

Mak, Y. T., & Roush, K. L. (1994). Commentary-flexible budgeting and variance analysis in the activity-based costing environment. *Accounting Horizons*, *8*(2), 93–103.

Manusco, A. J. (1990). Upgrading your quality control system. *CPA Review*, (December): 96–98.

March, J. G. (1996). Continuity and change in theories of organizational action. *Administrative Science Quarterly*, *41*(2), 278–287.

Marchese, T. (1991). TQM reaches the academy. *AAHE Bulletin*, *44*(3), 3–9.

Mark, N. (1998). Beyond individual differences: Social differentiation from first principles. *American Sociological Review*, *63*(3), 309–330.

Marple, D. (1982). Technological innovation and organizational survival: A population ecology study of nineteenth century American railroads. *The Sociological Quarterly*, *23*(1), 107–116.

Marshall, J. N. (1994). Business reorganization and the development of corporate services in metropolitan areas. *The Geographical Journal*, *160*(1), 41–49.

Maskosz, P. G., & McCuaig, B. W. (1990). Ripe for a renaissance. *Internal Auditor*, *47*(6), 43–49.

Maslow, A. H. (1954). *Motivation and Personality*. New York: Harper.

Mattessich, P. W., & Monsey, B. R. (1992). *Collaboration: What Makes It Work*. St. Paul, MN: Amherst H. Wilder Foundation.

Maute, M. F., & Locander, W. B. (1994). Innovation as a socio-political process. *Journal of Business Research, 30*(2), 161–174.

McClelland, D. (1961). *The Achieving Society*. New York: The Free Press.

McGowan, A. S. (1998). Perceived benefits of ABCM implementation. *Accounting Horizons, 12*(1), 31–50.

McKee, D. (1992). An organizational learning approach to product innovation. *Journal of Product Innovation Management, 9*(3), 232–245.

McMillan, C. (1992). Japan's contributions to management development. *Business and the Contemporary World*, (Winter), 21–32.

McNair, F., & Milan, E. E. (1993). Ethics in accounting education: What is really being done. *Journal of Business Ethics, 12*(10), 797–809.

Merchant, K. (1985). *Control in Business Organizations*. Boston, MA.: Pitman.

Merchant, K., & Simons, R. (1986). Research and control in complex organizations: An overview. *Journal of Accounting Literature, 5*, 183–201.

Merton, R. K. (1936). The unanticipated consequences of purposive social action. *American Sociological Review, 21*(6), 894–904.

Metzger, M. B., & Phillips, M. J. (1991). Corporate control, business ethics instruction and intra-organizational reality: A review essay. *American Business Law Journal, 29*(1), 127–154.

Meyerson, D., & Martin, J. (1987). Cultural change: An integration of three different views. *Journal of Management Studies, 24*(6), 623–647.

Mezias, S. J., & Glynn, M. A. (1993). The three faces of corporate renewal: Institution, revolution, and evolution. *Strategic Management Journal, 14*(2), 78–80.

Michaelson, A. G. (1993). The development of scientific specialty as diffusion through social relations: The case of role analysis. *Social Networks, 15*(3), 217–236.

Michel, A., & Shaked, I. (1985). Evaluating merger performance. *California Management Review, 27*(3), 109–118.

Midgley, D. F., Morrison, P. D., & Roberts, J. H. (1992). The effect of network structure in industrial diffusion processes. *Research Policy, 21*(6), 533–552.

Migdal, J. S. (1988). Individual change in the midst of social and political change. *The Social Science Journal, 25*(2), 125–139.

Milan, E., & McNair, F. (1992). An examination of accounting faculty perceptions of the importance of ethics coverage in accounting courses. *Business and Professional Ethics Journal, 11* (Summer), 57–71.

Miller, D. (1992). The Icarus Paradox: How exceptional companies bring about their own downfall. *Business Horizons, 35*(1), 24–35.

Mintz, S. M. (1990). Ethics in the management accounting curriculum. *Management Accounting, 71*(12), 51–54.

Mitroff, I. I., Mason, R., & Pearson, C. M. (1994). Radical surgery: What will tomorrow's organizations look like? *Academy of Management Executive, 8*(2), 11–21.

Moore, J. W. (1997). Auditing business process reengineering and TQM projects. *Internal Auditing, 12*(3), 47–52.

Morgan, G. (1986). *Images of Organization.* Beverly Hills, CA: Sage Publications.

Morrill, C. (1991a). Conflict management, honor, & organizational change. *American Journal of Sociology, 97*(3), 585–621.

Morrill, C. (1991b). Customs of conflict management among corporate executives. *American Anthropologists, 93*(4), 871–893.

Morse, W. J., Roth, H. P., & Rosten, K. M. (1987). *Measuring, Planning, & Controlling Quality Costs.* New York: National Association of Accountants.

Murray, M., & Dunn, L. (1996). *Revitalizing Rural America: A Perspective on Collaboration and Community.* Chichester, England: John Wiley & Sons. Ltd.

Murray, T. J. (1987). Can business schools teach ethics? *Business Month, 129*(4), 24–26.

Murrin, T. J. (1991). *Keynote address to the fourth annual conference on federal quality improvement.* Washington, D.C.: May 21, Mimeo.

Nadler, D. A. (1981). Managing organizational change: An integrative approach. *The Journal of Applied Behavioral Science, 17*(2), 191–210.

Nahavandi, A., & Malekzadeh, A. R. (1988). Acculturation in mergers and acquisitions. *Academy of Management Review, 13*(1), 79–90.

*News Week* (1992). *The cost of quality.* September 7, 48–49.

Newton, J. (1990). A 1990's agenda for auditors. *Internal Auditor, 47*(6), 33–39.

Nohra, N., & Berkley, J. D. (1994). An action perspective: The crux of the new management. *California Management Review, 36*(4), 70–92.

North Central Regional Center for Rural Development (NCRCRD) (1996). *Transportation Action: A Local Input Model to Engage Community Transportation Planning.* Ames, Iowa: NCRCRD, April.

Noves, R. (1980). The time horizon of planned social change. *American Journal of Economics and Sociology, 39*(1), 65–77.

Nutt, P. C. (1976). Models for decision making in organizations and some contextual variables which stipulate optimal use. *Academy of Management Review, 1*(2), 84–98.

Olian, J. D., & Rynes, S. L. (1991). Making total quality work: Aligning organizational processes, performance measures, & stakeholders. *Human Resources Management, 30*(3), 303–333.

Oliver, C. (1990). Determinants of inter-organizational relationships: Integration and future directions. *Academy of Management Review, 15*(2), 241–265.

Orlikowski, W. J. (1993). Case tools as organizational change: Investigating incremental and radical change in systems development. *MIS Quarterly, 17*(3), 309–340.

Ormrod, R. K. (1992). Adaptation and cultural diffusion. *Journal of Geography, 91*(6), 258–262.

Otley, D. (1980). The contingency theory of management accounting: Achievement and prognosis. *Accounting, Organizations and Society, 5*(4), 413–428.

O'Toole, L. J. Jr., & Montjoy, R. S. (1984). Inter-organizational policy implementation: A theoretical perspective. *Public Administration Review, 44*(6), 491–503.

O'Toole, L. J. Jr., & O'Toole, A. W. (1981). Negotiating inter-organizational orders. *The Sociological Quarterly, 22*(1), 29–41.

Parker, J. (1993). An ABC guide to business process reengineering. *Industrial Engineering, 25* (May), 52–53.

Parson, A. J. (1984). The hidden value: Key to successful acquisition. *Business Horizons, 2*(1), 30–47.

Parsons, T. (1951). *The Social Systems*. New York: The Free Press.

Perrow, C. (1986). *Complex Organizations* (3rd ed.). New York: Random House.

Peters, B. J. (1992). The quality revolution. *Internal Auditor, 49*(2), 20–24.

Peters, T. (1988). *Thriving on Chaos: Handbook for a Management Revolution*. New York: Harper & Row Publishers.

Pettigrew, A. M. (1987). Context and action in the transformation of the firm. *Journal of Management Studies, 24*(6), 649–670.

Pfeffer, J. (1993). Barriers to the advance of organizational science: Paradigm development as a dependent variable. *Academy of Management Review, 18*(4), 599–620.

Pfeffer, J. (1992). *Managing with Power: Politics and Influence in Organizations*. Boston, MA: Harvard Business School Press.

Pfeffer, J. (1981). *Power in Organizations*. Marshfield, MA.: Pitman Publishing Inc.

Pfeffer, J. (1972). Merger as a Response to Organizational Interdependence. *Administrative Science Quarterly, 17*(3), 382–394.

Pfeffer, J., & Salancik, G. R. (1978). *The External Control of Organizations*. New York: Harper & Row.

Phillips, A. S., & Bedeian, A. G. (1994). Leader-follower exchange quality: The role of personal and interpersonal attributes. *Academy of Management Journal, 37*(4), 990–1001.

Pickering, J., & Holl, P. (1991). Takeovers and other influences on economic performance: A plant level analysis. *Applied Economics, 23*(11), 1779–1789.

Pincus, M., & Wasley, C. (1994). The incidence of accounting changes and characteristics of firms making accounting changes. *Accounting Horizons, 8*(2), 1–24.

Plattner, S. (1983). Economic custom in a competitive marketplace. *American Anthropologist, 86*(4), 848–858.

Podolny, J. M., & Stuart, T. E. (1995). A role-based ecology of technological change. *American Journal of Sociology, 100*(5), 1224–1260.

Ponemon, L., & Glazer, A. (1990). Accounting education and ethical development: The influence of liberal learning on students and alumni accounting practice. Issues in *Accounting Education, 5*(2), 195–208.

Porras, J. I., Hargis, K., Patterson, K. J., Maxfield, D. G., Roberts, N., & Bies, R. J. (1982). Modeling-based organizational development: A longitudinal assessment. *The Journal of Applied Behavioral Science, 18*(4), 433–446.

Porras, J. I., & Silvers, R. C. (1991). Organization development and transformation. *Annual Review of Psychology, 42,* 51–78

Porras, J. I., & Hoffer, S. J. (1986). Common behavior changes in successful organization development efforts. *The Journal of Applied Behavioral Science, 22*(4), 477–494.

Porter, B. L., & Parker, W. S. Jr. (1992). Culture change. *Human Resources Management, 31*(1&2), 45–67.

Porter, M. E. (1992). Capital disadvantage: America's failing capital investment system. *Harvard Business Review, 70*(5), 65–82.

Porter, M. E. (1987). From competitive advantage to corporate strategy. *Harvard Business Review, 65*(3), 43–57.

Porter, M. E. (1985). *Competitive Advantage.* New York: The Free Press.

Porter, M. E. (1981). The contributions of industrial organization to strategic management. *Academy of Management Review, 6*(4), 609–620.

Porter, M. E. (1980). *Competitive Strategy.* New York: Macmillan Publishing Co.

Prasad, L., & Rubenstein, A. H. (1992). Conceptualizing organizational politics as a multidimensional phenomenon: empirical evidence from a study of technological innovations. *IEEE Transactions on Engineering Management, 39*(1), 4–12.

Premkumar, G., & Ramamurthy, K. (1995). The Role of inter-organizational and organizational factors on the decision mode for adoption of inter-organizational systems. *Decision Science, 26*(3), 303–307.

Presser, S. (1990). Measurement issues in the study of social change. *Social Forces, 68*(3), 856–858.

Radin, B. A., Agranoff, R. Bowman, A. O'M., Buntz, C. G., Ott, J. S., Romzek, B. S., Sykes, T. M., & Wilson, R. H. (1995). *Inter-governmental Partnerships and Rural Development: State Rural Development Councils in Sixteen States.* Washington, D.C.: National Rural Development Partnerships, Mimeo., May.

Ramakrishnan, R. T. S., & Thakor, A. V. (1991). Cooperation versus competition in agency. *The Journal of Law, Economics and Organization, 72*(2), 248–283.

Ramaprasad, A. (1982). Revolutionary change and strategic management. *Behavioral Science, 27*(4), 387–392.

Rappaport, A. (1979). Strategic analysis for more profitable acquisition. *Harvard Business Review, 57*(4), 99–110.

Ray, M. R., & Gupta, P. P. (1992). Activity-based costing. *Internal Auditor, 49*(6), 45–51.

Reeve, J. M. (1989). TQM and cost management: New definitions for cost accounting. *Survey of Business, 25*(1), 26–30.

Reid, L. (1992). Continuous improvement through process management. *Management Accounting, 74*(3), 37–44.

Reiman, C. (1991). *Quest for quality: A national overview. Paper presented at the World-Class Quality Winning in Western Pennsylvania Conference.* Pittsburgh, Duquesne University, May.

Reinganum, J. F. (1981). Market structure and the diffusion of new technology. *Bell Journal of Economics, 12*(2), 618–624.

Reisman, B. (1986). Management theory and agency management. *Social Casework, 67*(7), 387–393.

Richardson, P., & Denton, D. K. (1996). Communicating change. *Human Resource Management, 35*(2), 203–216.

Richman, T., & Koontz, C. (1993). How benchmarking can improve business reengineering. *Planning Review, 21*(6), 26–27.

Rigby, D. (1993). The secret history of process reengineering. *Planning Review, 21*(2), 24–27.

Ripley, R. E., & Ripley, M. J. (1992). The innovative organization and behavioral technology for the 1990's. *The SAM Advanced Management Journal, 57*(4), 30–36.

Robert, M. (1993). Opportunity search: What's that knocking at the door. *Journal of Business and Industrial Marketing, 8*(2), 24–39.

Roberts, M. W., & Silvester, K. J. (1996). Why ABC failed and how it may yet succeed. *Journal of Cost Management, 9*(4), 23–35.

Rogers, E. M. (1971). *Diffusion of Innovation.* New York: Free Press, 2nd ed.

Rogers, E. M., & Shoemaker, F. F. (1971). *Communication of Innovations: A Cross-Cultural Approach* (2nd ed.). New York: The Free Press.

Rosander, A. C. (1989). *The Quest for Quality in Services.* Milwaukee: ASQC Quality Press.

Rosenthal, S. R. (1984). New directions in evaluating intergovernmental programs. *Public Administration Review, 44*(6), 469–476.

Ross, G. H. (1990). Revolution in management control. *Management Accounting, 72*(5), 23–27.

Ruchala, L. (1995). New, improved, or reengineered? *Management Accounting, 77*(6), 37–41.

Rumelt, R. P. (1982). Diversification strategy and profitability. *Strategic Management Journal, 3*(4), 359–369.

Rumelt, R. P. (1974). *Strategy, Structure, and Economic Performance.* Boston, MA: Harvard Business School Press.

Schein, E. H. (1990). Organization culture. *American Psychologist, 45*(2), 109–119.

Schensul, S. L. (1980). Anthropological fieldwork and sociopolitical change. *Social Problems, 27*(3), 309–319.

Schroeder, D. M. (1990). A dynamic perspective on the impact of process innovation upon competitive strategies. *Strategic Management Journal, 11*(1), 25–41.

Schweiger, D. M., Ivancevich, J. M., & Power, F. R. (1987). Executive actions for managing human resources before and after acquisition. *Academy of Management Executive, 1*(2), 127–138.

Scott, W. R. (1987). *Organizations: Rational, Natural and Open Systems.* Englewood Cliffs, N.J.: Prentice-Hall.

Seal, W. B. (1990). De-industrialization and business organization: An institutionalist critique of the natural selection analogy. *Cambridge Journal of Economics, 14*(3), 267–275.

Selznick, P. (1957). *Leadership in Administration: A Sociological Interpretation.* Evanston, Ill.: Row, Peterson & Co.

Semich, J. W. (1989). Buying quality: Accounting for quality. *Purchasing, 106*(1), 74–79.

Sewell, W. H. Jr. (1992). A theory of structure: Duality, agency, and transformation. *American Journal of Sociology, 98*(1), 1–29.

Shane, S. A. (1994). Are champions different from non-champions. *Journal of Business Venturing, 9*(5), 397–421.

Shelton, L. M. (1988). Strategic business fits and corporate acquisitions: Empirical evidence. *Strategic Management Journal, 9*(3), 279–284.

Shenkir, W. G. (1990). A perspective from education: Business ethics. *Management Accounting, 71*(12), 30–33.

Siegel, P. A., & Hambrick, D. C. (1996). Business strategy and the social psychology of top management teams. *Advances in Strategic Management, 13*, 91–119.

Simon, H. A. (1957). *Models of Man.* New York: Wiley.

Simons, R. (1995). *Levers of Control.* Boston, MA: Harvard Business School Press.

Sims, R. R., & Sims, S. J. (1991). Increasing applied business ethics courses in business school curricula. *Journal of Business Ethics, 10*(3), 211–219.

Singh, H., & Montgomery, C. (1987). Corporate acquisition strategies and economic performance. *Strategic Management Journal, 8*(4), 377–386.

Sisaye, S. (1999). An organizational approach for the study of the diffusion of process innovation strategies in internal auditing and control systems. *International Journal of Applied Quality Management, 2*(2), 279–293.

Sisaye, S. (1998a). Contingencies influencing the effectiveness of acquisition- based corporate growth and development strategies. *Leadership & Organizational Development Journal, 19*(4&5), 231–255.

Sisaye, S. (1998b). Implications of reengineering to quality issues in accounting and internal control systems. *International Journal of Applied Quality Management, 1*(2), 117–127.

Sisaye, S. (1998c). An overview of the social and behavioral science approaches to management control research. *Behavioral Research in Accounting Supplement, 10*, 11–26.

Sisaye, S. (1998d). A power-control-exchange framework of accounting: Applications to divisionalized business organizations. *Advances in Management Accounting, 6*, 113–146.

Sisaye, S. (1997a). An overview of the institutional approach to accounting ethics education. *Research on Accounting Ethics, 3*, 233–244.

Sisaye, S. (1997b). *A Power Control Exchange Framework of Accounting: Applications to Management Control Systems.* Studies in Managerial and Financial Accounting, Vol. 5, Greenwich, CT.: JAI Press, Inc.

Sisaye, S. (1996. Two approaches to internal auditing: A comparison of TQM and reengineering. *Internal Auditing, 11*(4), 37–47.

Sisaye, S. (1995). Control as an exchange process: A power control framework of organizations. *Behavioral Research in Accounting, 7*, 122–161.

Sisaye, S., & Bodnar, G. (1996). Reengineering as a process innovation approach to internal auditing. *Internal Auditing, 11*(3), 16–25.

Sisaye, S., & Bodnar, G. (1995). TQM and internal auditing: A synthesis. *Internal Auditing, 10*(1), 19–31.

Sisaye, S., & Lackman, C. (1994). Ethics in accounting education: An empirical study. *Business and Professional Ethics Journal, 13*(1&2), 79–87.

Sisaye, S., & Stommes, E. (1985). Green revolution as a planned intervention strategy for agricultural development: A systems perspective. *Public Administration and Development, 5*(1), 39–55.

Skeleton, A., & Miller, W. C. (1993). Quality innovation. *Executive Excellence, 10*(9), 15–16.

Smirich, L. (1983). Concepts of culture and organizational analysis. *Administrative Science Quarterly, 28*(3), 339–358.

Smith, M. (1990). Management accounting for total quality management. *Management Accounting, 68*(6), 44–46.

Smith. M. E. (1982). The process of socio-cultural continuity. *Current Anthropology, 23*(2), 127–135.

Sniezek, J. A., May, D. R., & Sawyer, J. E. (1990). Social uncertainty and interdependence: A study of resource allocation decisions in groups. *Organizational Behavior and Human Decision Processes, 46* (August), 155–180.

Soete, L., & Turner, R. (1984). Technology diffusion and the rate of technological change. *The Economic Journal, 94* (September), 612–623.

Spadaford, J. F. (1992–1993). Reengineering commercial loan servicing at first Chicago. *National Productivity Review, 12*(1), 65–72.

Stata, R. (1989). Organizational learning- the key to management innovation. *Sloan Management Review, 30*(3), 63–74.

Stedry, A. C. (1960). *Budget Control and Cost Behavior.* Englewood Cliffs, NJ: Prentice-Hall.

Steiner, G. A. (1979). Contingency theories of strategy and strategic management. In: D. E. Schendel & C. W. Hofer (Eds), *Strategic Management* (pp. 405–416). Boston: Little, Brown & Company.

Steiner, G. A., Miner, J. B., & Gray, E. R. (1982). *Management Policy and Strategy.* New York: Macmillan Publishing Co., Inc.

Sterman, J. D., Repenning, N. P., & Kofman, F. (1997). Unanticipated side effects of successful quality programs: Exploring a paradox of organizational improvement. *Management Science, 43*(4), 503–521.

Stigler, G. J. (1968). *The Organization of Industry.* Homewood, Ill.: Irwin.

Stone, N. (1991). Does business have any business in education. *Harvard Business Review, 69*(2), 46–62.

Summer, C. E. (1980). *Strategic Behavior in Business and Government*. Boston: Little, Brown & Co.

Swanson, E. B. (1994). Information systems innovation among organizations. *Management Science, 40*(9), 1069–1092.

Tannenbaum, A. S. (1968). *Control in Organizations*. New York: McGraw Hill.

Taylor, F. W. (1947). *Scientific Management*. New York: Harper.

Teece, D. J. (1996). Firm organization, industrial structure, and technological innovation. *Journal of Economic Behavior and Organization, 31*(2), 193–224.

Tenner, A. R., & DeToro, I. J. (1992). *Total Quality Management: Three Steps to Continuous Improvement*. Reading, Mass.: Addison-Wesley Publishing Company, Inc.

Thompson, J. D. (1967). *Organizations in Action*. New York: McGraw-Hill Company.

Tomasko, R. M. (1993). Intelligent resizing: View from the bottom up. *Management Review, 82*(6), 18–23.

Tracy, L. (1993). Applications of living systems theory to the study of management and organizational behavior. *Behavioral Science, 38*(3), 218–230.

Turney, P. B. B. (1991). *Common Cents: The ABC Performance Breakthrough*. Hillsboro, Oregon: Cost Technology.

Turney, P. B. B., & Anderson, B. (1989). Accounting for continuous improvement. *Sloan Management Review, 30*(2), 37–47.

Turney, P. B. B., & Stratton, A. J. (1992). Using ABC to support continuous improvement: National semiconductor applies a two-pronged approach. *Management Accounting, 74*(3), 46–50.

Tushman, M. L., & O'Reilly III, C. A. (1997). *Winning Through Innovation: A Practical Guide to Leading Organizational Change*. Boston, MA: Harvard Business School Press.

Tushman, M. L., & O'Reilly III, C. A. (1996). Ambidextrous organizations: Managing evolutionary and revolutionary change. *California Management Review, 38*(4), 8–30.

Tushman, M. L., & Romanelli, C. A. (1985). Organizational evolution: A metamorphosis model of convergence and reorientation. In: L. L. Cummings & B. M. Staw (Eds), *Research in Organizational Behavior* (Vol. 7, pp. 171–222). Greenwich, CT: JA1 Press.

Tushman, M. L., & Nelson, R. R. (1990). Introduction: Technology, organizations, and innovation. *Administrative Science Quarterly, 35*(1), 1–8.

Tushman, M. L., Newman, W. H., & Romanelli, E. (1986). Convergence and upheaval: Managing the unsteady pace of organizational evolution. *California Management Review, 29*(1), 29–44.

Ulrich, D., & Lake, D. (1991). Organizational capability: Creating competitive advantage. *Academy of Management Executive, 5*(1), 77–92.

Van De Ven, A. H. (1986). Central problems in the management of innovation. *Management Science, 32*(5), 590–607.

Van De Ven, A. H. (1976). On the nature, formation, & maintenance of relations among organizations. *Academy of Management Review, 1*(4), 24–36.

Van De Ven, A. H., & Poole, M. S. (1995). Explaining development and change in organizations. *Academy of Management Review, 20*(3), 521.

Vasilash, G. S. (1993). Reengineering: Your job may depend on it. *Production, 15* (June), 10, 13.

Vittorio, C., Coughlan, P., & Voss, C. A. (1996). Development of a technical innovation audit. *Journal of Product Innovation Management, 13*(2), 106, 109, 112, 126.

Von Bertalanffy, L. (1975). In: E. Taschdjian (Ed.), *Perspectives on General System Theory: Scientific Philosophical Studies.* New York: George Brazuller.

Von Bertalanffy, L. (1969). The theory of open systems in physics and biology. In: F. E. Emery (Ed.), *Systems Thinking: Selected Readings* (pp. 70–85). Baltimore, Maryland: Penguin Books.

Von Bertalanffy, L. (1968). *General Systems Theory.* New York: George Braziller.

Vondra, A. A., & Schueler, D. R. (1993). Can you innovate your internal audit. *Financial Executive, 9*(2), 34–39.

Wacker, G. J. (1981). Toward a cognitive methodology of organizational assessment. *The Journal of Applied Behavioral Science, 17*(1), 114–129.

Walter, R. M., Higgins, M. M., & Roth, H. P. (1990). Application of control charts. *CPA Journal, 60*(4), 90–95.

Weber, M. (1947). *The Theory of Social and Economic Organization.* Glencoe, Ill.: The Free Press.

Weiss, J. A. (1987). Pathways to cooperation among public agencies. *Journal of Policy Analysis and Management, 7*(1), 94–117.

West, M. A., & Farr, J. L. (1989). Innovation at work: Psychological perspectives. *Social Behaviour, 4*(1), 15–30.

Wiersema, W. H. (1996). Implementing activity-based management: Overcoming the data barrier. *Journal of Cost Management, 10*(2), 17–20.

Williamson, O. E. (1987). The economics of organization: The transaction cost approach. *American Journal of Sociology, 87*(3), 548–577.

Williamson, O. E. (1975). *Markets and Hierarchies.* New York: The Free Press.

Willmott, H. (1993). Breaking the paradigm mentality. *Organization Studies, 14*(5), 681–719.

Wilson, J. Q. (1989). *Bureaucracy: What Government Agencies Do and Why They Do It.* New York: Basic Books.

Wilson, K. L. (1981). Methodological Observations on applied behavioural science. *The Journal of Applied Behavioral Science, 17*(1), 113–129.

Wilson, R. (1991). Quality: The pioneers survey the landscape. *Industry Week*, October 21, 73.

Witt, U. (1997). 'Lock-in' vs. 'critical masses' – industrial change under network externalities. *International Journal of Industrial Organization, 15*(6), 753–773.

Woodman, R. W., Sawyer, J. E., & Griffin, R. W. (1993). Toward a theory of organizational creativity. *Academy of Management Review, 18*(2), 293–321.

Woods, M. D. (1989). How we changed our accounting. *Management Accounting,* *70*(8), 43–45.

Woolridge, A. (1992). A survey of education-coming top. *The Economist, 21*(11), 3–18.

Yasaiardekani, M., & Nystrom, P. C. (1996). Designs for environmental scanning systems: Tests of a contingency theory. *Management Science, 42*(2), 187–204.

Young, R. L., Houghland, J. C. Jr., & Shepard, J. C. (1981). Innovation in open systems: A comparative study of banks. *Sociology and Social Research, 65*(2), 177–193.

Young, S. M. (1997). Implementing management innovations successfully: Principles for lasting change. *Journal of Cost Management, 11*(5), 16–20.

Young, S. M. (1992). A framework for successful adoption and performance of Japanese manufacturing practices in the United States. *Academy of Management Review, 17*(4), 677–700.

Yukl, G., & Tracey, B. (1992). Consequences of influence tactics used with subordinates, peers, and the boss. *Journal of Applied Psychology, 77*(4), 525–535.

Zamutto, R. F., & O'Connor, E. J. (1992). Gaining advanced manufacturing technologies' benefits: The roles of organizational design and culture. *Academy of Management Review, 17*(4), 701–728.

# AUTHOR INDEX

# SUBJECT INDEX